Economics and
Australian Health Policy

Economics and Australian Health Policy

Edited by
Gavin Mooney and Richard Scotton

Routledge
Taylor & Francis Group

LONDON AND NEW YORK

First published 1998 by Allen & Unwin

Published 2020 by Routledge
2 Park Square, Milton Park, Abingdon, Oxon OX14 4RN
605 Third Avenue, New York, NY 10017

Routledge is an imprint of the Taylor & Francis Group, an informa business

National Library of Australia
Cataloguing-in-Publication entry:

Economics and Australian health policy.

  Bibliography.
  Includes index.

  ISBN 1 86448 749 6.

  1. Medical economics–Australia. 2. Medical policy–Australia. I. Mooney, Gavin H. II. Scotton, R. B. (Richard Bailey).

338.433621

Set in 10 on 11.5pt Plantin by Midland Typesetters, Victoria

ISBN-13: 9781864487497 (pbk)

Contents

Figures

Tables

Contributors

Jim Butler is a Senior Fellow in Health Economics at the National Centre for Epidemiology and Population Health, Australian National University. He was recently Visiting Associate Professor in The Wharton School, University of Pennsylvania, for six months, and has a PhD in Economics from the University of Queensland.

Rob Carter is Associate Professor in Health Economics at the Centre for Health Program Evaluation at Monash University and Deputy Director of its Health Economic Unit.

Ron Donato is a lecturer at the University of South Australia's School of International Business. He has conducted intensive workshops in health economics to health professionals from developing countries as well as consulting in this area. His current research interests centre around the economics of health care reform.

Stephen Duckett is Professor of Health Policy and Dean of the Faculty of Health Sciences at La Trobe University. From 1994 to 1996 he was Secretary of the Commonwealth Department of Human Services and Health.

Anthony Harris is the Coordinator of Graduate Studies in Health Economics at Monash University. He has published in a number of areas in health economics, and most recently his work has focused on the economics of pharmaceuticals.

Suzanne Hill is currently appointed as a Research Academic in the Discipline of Clinical Pharmacology, Faculty of Medicine and Health Sciences, University of Newcastle. Her research interests are in the use of evidence in public policy and decision making, and in developing methods to apply the results of clinical trials to clinical practice.

Anna Howe has over 20 years experience in gerontological research and education. From 1989 to 1994 she was Director of the Commonwealth Office for the Aged and most recently has been Deputy Director of the National Ageing Research Institute in Melbourne. Internationally, she has contributed to projects of the OECD, WHO and the US National Centre for Health Statistics.

Stephen Jan is a health economist within the Department of Public Health and Community Medicine at the University of Sydney. His interests are in the areas of Aboriginal health, the use of community values in health care decision making and economic evaluation.

Andrew Mitchell works for the Australian government to help assess the cost-effectiveness of pharmaceutical drugs submitted for government subsidy and to develop and implement policy relating to these assessments.

Gavin Mooney is Professor of Health Economics in the Department of Public Health and Community Medicine, University of Sydney. He has published widely in health economics and has particular interests in the ethics of resource allocation and equity, especially in the area of Aboriginal health.

Helen Owens is a Commissioner at the Productivity Commission with responsibility for social policy issues relating to economic adjustment. She has undertaken a number of inquiries including private health insurance, the pharmaceutical industry and medical and scientific equipment industries. Until 1993 she was Associate Professor at the Centre for Health Program Evaluation, Monash University.

Jeff Richardson is the Director of the Health Economics Unit at the Centre for Health Program Evaluation and also a Professor of Economics at Monash University. He has worked for over 25 years in the area of health economics during which time he has written extensively on health systems and their reform, and the theory and practice of health economic evaluation.

Glenn Salkeld is a lecturer in Health Economics at the Department of Public Health and Community Medicine, University of Sydney. He has a particular interest in the application and development of economic evaluation in public health policy and is currently a member of the Economic Sub-Committee of the Pharmaceutical Benefits Advisory Committee.

Richard Scotton was involved in the 1960s in health economics research into the organisation and funding of Australian health services, which resulted in proposals adopted as the original Medibank program. In the following years, he served as adviser and consultant to various government departments and Commissions and is currently an Honorary Professorial Fellow in the Centre for Health Program Evaluation at Monash University.

Alan Shiell is an Honorary Research Associate in the Department of Public Health and Community Medicine, University of Sydney. His research interests include the economic evaluation of community development as a public health strategy and the political economy of health.

Virginia Wiseman is a health economist in the Department of Public Health and Community Medicine at the University of Sydney. Her research interests include equity, Aboriginal health, priority setting and the financing and delivery of health services in developing countries.

Preface

In many ways the links between economics and health policy are obvious. We have a sector of the economy that consumes a large proportion of the nation's resources—in the early 1990s 8.5 per cent of the Australian national income. There are major issues involved not only in deciding whether this amount is 'right' but also, whatever is spent, in determining how best to spend it, on which conditions and on whom. A plethora of issues surrounding cost-containment, funding, efficiency and equity arises.

These issues become more significant the more societies spend on health care and the greater the population's expectations of what health care can deliver. Thirty years ago Australia was spending just 5 per cent of its GNP on health care. As the technological frontiers of medicine have been pushed forward, there have been growing claims both for and on health care resources. The problems here are common to all industrialised countries, although the solutions attempted have often varied markedly across international boundaries. Yet there has been in recent years some convergence or 'resonance' in proposed solutions. In the 1990s, priority-setting, purchaser–provider splits, internal markets, managed competition, funding hospitals according to DRGs, have become part of the international currency of many health services.

There is little sign that the economic problems are easing. Health services seem destined to make ever-increasing demands on national economies. There are likely to be continuing expressions of concern about whether we can afford universal health care coverage, about whether the public sector is carrying too high a burden of the overall costs involved, whether the user ought not to be paying more at the point of consumption, whether the incentive structures for doctors can be improved to make them more efficient, whether the poor, in income terms and/or in health terms, are getting a fair deal.

It is thus surprising that there is no previous book-length presentation of current health policy in Australia from the perspective of economics. It is perhaps significant that such a book is commissioned now. There is today much closer scrutiny of the use of resources in health care than there was even a decade ago. The health sector now demands more of the discipline of economics—more examinations, more investigations, more techniques, more tools. A new breed has emerged of economists specialising in health care issues—health economists. This book draws heavily on that breed to provide economic insight into Australian health care policy.

The book should be seen as a series of essays on the economics of Australian health care policy. The editors have not attempted to encourage a standard view of the state of play. (We are not even convinced that such a standard exists or could exist.) We have certainly not requested that authors adopt particular stances in their chapters. We have asked them to adopt a lively debating style and not to hold back in expressing their own informed judgements and assessments.

The scope of the book is not confined to 'economic policy' in health care but extends to all aspects of health care policy on which economics has a bearing. The subject area covered is—with some exceptions—*health care* policy rather than *health* policy more broadly. Thus aspects of social policy in the spheres of income redistribution, housing, transport and the environment, which can have significant impact on health, are not included. Further, while some of the chapters draw on international work or make specific reference to developments in health care in other countries, the focus is overwhelmingly on the Australian system.

This is not a textbook in economics. The central objectives are to describe the various policy components of the system and to demonstrate the applicability of economic ways of thinking and economic analytical techniques to current issues in Australian health policy, thereby illustrating how economic tools have contributed or can contribute to the analysis and possible solution of problems. While a training in economics will inevitably be useful in understanding of the contents and arguments presented in this book, it is not solely for economists. To assist those less well informed about economics, some of the basic ideas of the discipline are presented and exemplified in the context of health care in Chapter 1.

What we hope is that the book will stimulate thought and not act solely to inform. The jest that economists are better at posing questions than answering them contains more than a grain of truth. There is no need to apologise for that, as getting the right questions asked is an important ingredient in the development of future health care policy in Australia. Writing about such policy, observing and appraising as the various contributors do, should help to stimulate new and creative ideas about where the Australian health service is heading, where it might lead and how best it might journey towards its goals, current or future. If the book contributes towards shaping that future, it will have been a truly worthwhile endeavour.

We are grateful to a number of people who have assisted in the production of this book. First we would like to acknowledge the contributions of our authors. It is their book, in that, within the terms of reference given them, their interpretations are along lines of their own choosing. Overall in their writing and timing they have been rather well behaved (at least for a bunch of economists!). We do not always agree with them in what has emerged, but believe that an edited book of readings should draw on the different views of the contributors rather than have the editors' will and views imposed on it. As it happens, nor are the two of us in total agreement about all the issues raised in the book—which is, we understand, partly why the publishers asked the two of us to team up to do it!

We thank Allen & Unwin for making this opportunity available, and especially Josh Dowse, our publisher, who has been most helpful throughout the whole process.

G.M. would like to acknowledge financial support from the NSW Department of Health.

Gavin Mooney, University of Sydney
Dick Scotton, Monash University
June 1998

Gavin Mooney

1   *Health economics and health policy*

The objectives of this book are to examine the main issues in Australian health policy from an economic perspective and to explain the relevance of economic thinking to decision-making in health care. Its general focus is on public policy choices at an aggregate level, about the allocation of scarce resources between a multitude of competing ends, inside and outside the health care sector. These decision-making processes, however, cannot realistically be divorced from the underlying value systems and ethical imperatives embedded in clinical decision-making at the grassroots level of health care. A paper presented by Raanan Gillon (1988), a general practitioner in London and editor of the *Journal of Medical Ethics*, at a conference on medical ethics and economics, epitomises some of these issues so neatly that I quote it at some length:

> I recall a patient who bled massively from his inoperable cancer of the stomach. I was the houseman and I had a strong sense that I must do my utmost for my patient and I ordered large quantities of blood to be cross-matched and set up an infusion to replace the blood the patient had lost. It was not that I believed the blood would cure him; but it would very probably save his life for a while longer, whereas without the blood transfusion he would probably have died there and then. A few days later the patient had another massive bleed and I again ordered more blood and set up a transfusion. Again the patient survived what would almost certainly have been a fatal blood loss. The patient himself, knowing his situation, was keen to 'fight it, as hard as possible'. After the second massive bleed and equally massive blood transfusion my chief gently pointed out that there was no point in pouring in the blood as I had been—the patient had widespread cancer secondaries, his stomach was riddled with cancer and likely to bleed whenever the cancer eroded a blood vessel; blood transfusions could do no more than prolong the patient's life by a very short time. If I went on ordering blood at the prodigious rate I had been I would literally break the bank—the blood bank—causing enormous expense while seriously jeopardising the chances of other patients for whom a blood transfusion could really be life-saving rather than merely prolonging. (What, it might be asked, is

the morally significant difference?) I wanted to discuss all this with the patient—but he died the same day from a further massive bleed—and that time I simply was not called. My superior had decided that there was nothing beneficial that could be done. More precisely, however, his analysis was surely based on a different assessment, notably that the benefit to the patient of repeated blood transfusions each time his stomach cancer bled, even if he himself wanted to fight to the last second, was insufficient to justify the enormous cost (to others) of providing the blood.

Of course it might be argued that cost to others did not come into the assessment and that it was only the patient's own best interests which decided the matter. However (a) I know that as a matter of fact it was cost which decided the matter—and the main point of this example is to show that in practice doctors do not always exclude third party cost considerations when these conflict with their therapeutic obligations to their individual patients. Further (b) those who would wish to argue that it was in the patient's best medical interests not to have been given blood and to have been allowed to die, despite his desire to fight to the last (thus evading the conclusion from this case that sometimes financial considerations do in practice override the therapeutic interests of the patient), might be more persuaded by a hypothetical variant of the case. Thus suppose I had a chance to discuss these economic considerations with the patient and suppose he had continued to say that he wanted to fight to the last possible moment, with blood transfusions each time he bled, until eventually he died despite the blood transfusion. Suppose he had said that his main concern was to fight death as long as he possibly could, and that even if he only gained a few days or even a few hours, let alone a few weeks, this would be worthwhile as far as he was concerned. Should his assessment have prevailed or should further transfusions have been withheld? If financial considerations were barred, presumably the patient should have been given blood transfusions for as long as he wanted such treatment. Indeed to generalise, presumably if the premise is accepted that third party financial considerations must never be allowed to override the doctor's therapeutic duty to his patients, then doctors should offer any potentially life prolonging treatment, no matter how expensive, whenever the patient definitely and autonomously desires it. In practice this is not the way doctors actually behave. If they did those providing the finance would rapidly stop them, on the grounds (a) that they would wish to have a say in how their money is spent and (b) that there was no obvious reason why expenditure on the sick should take priority, let alone absolute priority, over all sorts of other potential benefits which would otherwise have to be forgone.

Economics is the science of art of choice in the use of scarce resources. When reading about the contribution of economics to health policy, it is important to bear in mind that what health policy is often trying to influence is clinical decision-making. The sorts of ethical issues Gillon raises cannot be ignored either at the clinical level or in planning and priority-setting in health care more generally. Not to recognise the ethical problems that arise in trying to make decisions about the best use of available resources will lead to a less insightful read of this book than would otherwise be the case.

Once it is acknowledged that resources are scarce, choices about what to do with these resources are just as much about what to leave undone. For economists the central message of Gillon's quote is tied to the economic concept of opportunity cost—that every time resources are used in one way in health care, opportunities are forgone to use these resources in some other way. It is not enough 'to do good' with health care resources: we need to ensure that in choosing one particular way to use resources there is no better way to use them. It is this concept of opportunity cost that means that, while the discipline of medicine is about doing good, economics is about doing better.

A century ago and for several decades afterwards, the economic content of health policy was minimal. With respect to health, the primary considerations of governments were the control of communicable diseases and the protection of the public from quackery. Treatment services were largely ineffective and absorbed little of public and gross domestic expenditure.

The enormous increases in the effectiveness and cost of medical interventions in the intervening period have transformed this position. The growing relevance of economics to health policy is a result of the progressive growth in GDP devoted to health services over five decades, from about 3 per cent to typically 8 or 9 per cent in developed countries, the vast range of choices facing governments, providers and patients in modern health care, and the consequent uncertainty with which these parties have to cope. The fact that the real costs of health care have been rising faster than the rate of growth in the economy more generally means that the opportunity costs of health services (i.e. the benefits forgone in sacrificing the goods and services that could have been had from alternative uses of the resources) are becoming keenly felt in public and household budgets.

Health economics as a subdiscipline of economics is relatively young, its origins more or less coinciding with the growth in health care costs to a level at which they became burdensome. Indeed it is only 35 years since Kenneth Arrow, Nobel Laureate in Economics, published his seminal article (1963) on the special characteristics of the commodity, health care, that lead to the seeming inability of normal markets to bring about its efficient production. Health economics justifies its separate existence as a result of these special characteristics.

Economic theory and the economic way of thinking

Most economists tend to assume that human beings wish to maximise their 'utility'. This notion is sometimes translated as 'satisfaction' or even happiness (as in the underlying utilitarian basis of much 'neoclassical' economics, i.e. the economics that is seen to drive free markets—the greatest happiness of the greatest number). Sometimes utility is interpreted as simply whatever it is that individuals are attempting to maximise. Generally too economists tend to see human beings as acting as individuals, although through 'externalities' individuals can be interested in other people's welfare but only insofar as that affects their own utility.

There are two type of 'externalities' that are relevant in health care. I may suggest to a colleague that she take herself off home because of her nasty cold. If my motivation is a caring one (her unhappiness is my unhappiness), then this is the 'caring' externality. If I am concerned that I will be infected if she continues to spread diseases with coughs and sneezes, then this is the 'infectious' externality. In both instances, however, the caring is selfish—only more so in the latter than in the former case. In both instances I am concerned to maximise my utility. *Homo economicus* is essentially selfish man (and woman).

A potentially powerful body of economic theory has been erected on the axiomatic propositions of free exchange and, in its neoclassical ideal form, of perfect competition. Very few markets perform in a way that even approximates the conditions necessary for perfect competition to prevail, such as perfect information on the part of the consumer.

The discipline of economics divides into two parts. Macroeconomics is the study of economies, and covers such aspects as unemployment, inflation and the balance of trade. Microeconomics looks at the individual firm and consumer, and the interaction between the demand and supply sides of the market. Health economics is primarily a branch of the latter, although clearly in *health* economics as opposed to *health care* economics there are aspects of macroeconomics that are relevant to health. Questions of trade and tariff policy, for example, can affect the types of foodstuffs that can be imported and these in turn can have an impact on a population's health (such as in the Torres Strait, where trade policy restricts the importing of fresh foods from relatively close Papua New Guinea and means that such produce has to be brought at greater expense from further afield, albeit in Australia).

One of the key features of microeconomics, whether in health or elsewhere, is that of optimising (e.g. Varian 1984, especially for any reader seeking a good understanding of microeconomics more generally). What is important to the economist in this context is to determine (or to have determined for her) what is to be optimised: that is, what the 'objective function' is and what constraints there are on meeting that objective function. Often this optimising is simplified by economists into maximising. The question arises at various levels of health care both of what is to be optimised or maximised, and what constraints operate on doing this. The oncologist may have an objective of prolonging life as far as possible, giving relatively little weight to patients' quality of life or dignity. The patient may not be so desperate to live longer but want the days that remain to be of as high quality as possible, while the relatives may be more concerned that the patient be treated with dignity and given all the relevant information. There will inevitably be constraints on the resources available, and it is such constraints that are normally uppermost in economists' calculations in most microeconomic analyses. In health care these are indeed present but so too are ethical constraints that limit the freedom of doctors in their actions. Externalities are also stronger in health care than in most other sectors of the economy, as is the not-unrelated concern for fairness (or equity) in the distribution of health care (of which more later).

Very often, it is assumed that at the individual level it is utility that is to be maximised and there are then questions about what the arguments (i.e. components) are in the utility function. There is little consensus among economists about what constitutes the 'social welfare function', which is the utility function at the level of a society. Apart from the problem of deciding what it contains and how the various components might be aggregated, there is the vexed question of so-called 'interpersonal comparisions of utility' and how, if at all, these are to be made.

In health care this sort of question surfaces in the context of how health gains are to be measured and compared, whether one individual's health gain is to be valued equally with another's. There are two aspects to this. First, if I value health more highly than my neighbour, ought that to mean that I get better access to health care or better or more treatment if each of us has the same health problem? If my willingness to pay for health care is greater, then ought that to influence my consumption of health care vis-à-vis my neighbour's?

(It does with Tim Tams.) Does it matter whether my neighbour and I have different incomes, as, if I am richer than he is, my greater willingness to pay may be because of my greater ability to pay? Second, there is the question of whether the only utility-bearing argument is health (an issue returned to below in the section on health care economics).

The conventional demand side of the market deals with consumers' willingness to pay, with demand being greater the greater utility the consumer expects to derive from the consumption of a good or another unit of the good. It is assumed that as more and more of a good is consumed, less utility is derived from each extra unit consumed—what is referred to as 'diminishing marginal utility'. It follows that the higher the price of a good, the less consumers will normally be prepared to buy. The supply side of the market is in essence the mirror image, with suppliers willing to produce more the higher the price of the good. So the supply schedule is such that as price rises, producers will tend to produce more; it is more worthwhile to do so, as at least in many markets the assumption is that producers are trying to maximise their profits. (Other maximands are of course possible, such as revenue-maximising or maximising the share of the market.)

Demand and supply are assumed to be completely independent of each other, and it is through the price mechanism that the quantities demanded and supplied are made equal—that is, come into 'equilibrium'. In an ideal world (i.e. the economist's world of perfect competition) this will mean that markets will produce the right amounts of those goods and services that individuals want to purchase, and all at prices where markets 'clear' (i.e. where all that is produced of a good is bought at the ruling market price). Individuals both on the demand side of the market and on the supply side pursue their own interests through the market, and the price-mechanism results in all satisfying their desires or maximising their utility to the greatest possible extent with the resources available. This is economic efficiency (discussed below) brought about through Adam Smith's 'invisible hand'—the market price mechanism. This is not how health care markets tend to work (or in reality many other markets either), especially on the demand side. Demand and supply in health care are less independent, with the doctor for example often assisting patients in determining their demand. When it comes to looking at how best to allocate resources in health care, market prices often have a more limited role and some other mechanism is needed, such as government intervention. Here economists can offer the tools of economic evaluation, such as cost–benefit, cost–effectiveness and cost–utility analyses (discussed in detail in Chapter 8).

In most markets it is possible to alter the patterns of demand and supply by changing the incentive mechanisms that both consumers and suppliers face. Incentive mechanisms are important in economics and remain so in health care, although perhaps less pervasively. The most obvious incentive strategies in health care relate to patient payments at the point of consumption and the ways in which doctors alter their behaviour in terms of the use of their time and their treatment patterns in response to different systems of remuneration.

When various health interventions or treatments are analysed in terms of their benefits and costs we are into the assessment of efficiency, with the objective being to ensure that the benefits of any action are greater than the costs (where the costs are opportunity costs). This cost–benefit calculus may look like little more than structured common sense, which is fine. There is a considerable power at times in the simplicity of economic reasoning, and nowhere is this more true than in the use of the concepts of opportunity costs and the margin in determining priorities. The combining of marginal costs and marginal benefits provides a simple but powerful tool in economic evaluations—that of so-called 'marginal analysis'. This gives the decision rule that if it is possible to redeploy $1 million from program A (say maternity care) to program B (say mental health services) and thereby increase the total benefit, then this should be done. Efficiency is improved, as total benefits are increased for the same expenditure. This thinking comes through, for example, in the use of 'QALY league tables'. (QALYs, or quality-adjusted life-years, are a form of health status measurement, and are discussed in Chapter 8 in more detail.) Such tables list possible interventions in rank order of the extra or marginal cost per QALY gained, so that if any additional resources are made available for that health service it is possible to see where the cheapest marginal QALYs can be had.

It is at this level of evaluation both of individual services and in priority-setting across different services that there is a need to look at production functions (i.e. the ways in which inputs to any firm or any production process more generally relate to outputs). Different mixes of the factors of production—manpower, capital, land—can be used to produce different types of outputs. In health care these can be arranged in different settings (e.g. inpatients, outpatients, community clinics) and employing labour more or less intensively to produce them (e.g. with different mixes of nurses, doctors, therapists).

Health care economics

It is possible to debate at length just whether and to what extent health care is different from other commodities. Economists differ not only in their perceptions of health care as a commodity but in their perceptions of various other commodities. Some, such as Mark Pauly (e.g. Pauly 1986) are very neoclassicist in outlook and see most commodities, including health care, as sitting easily within a conventional market paradigm. Others (including myself) have problems with a neoclassical view of health care and many other commodities. Pauly and other neoclassicists generally argue that health care is not so different from other commodities, and that markets can and do manage to cope with health care as a commodity. Others might agree in part, but would approach this from the opposite perspective—that the market fails in health care just as it does (if to a lesser extent) with most other commodities. A third group of health economists will see health care as different, while accepting that most other commodities fit well within the neoclassical paradigm. (The classic work on the nature of the commodity health care is Arrow 1963.)

A key point of difference, from the perspective of conventional demand theory, is that there are information problems for the consumer which, if not unique to health care, are at one end of the spectrum and far removed from the perfect information of perfect competition. Information deficiencies arise at the level of the potential consumer (patient), who may not know whether there is a health problem, what the problem is, what services are available, or what the effectiveness of the different services might be in terms of the likely impact on health status. However, the patient is well- or at least better-informed than anyone else with respect to the impact of better or worse health status on his or her welfare or utility.

A number of other factors get mentioned on the demand side as making health care potentially different from most other marketable commodities. Markets work particularly well where there are regular, routine or repeat purchases. That is hardly a description of health care, where irregularity and unpredictability of consumption (arising largely because of the irregularity and unpredictability of ill-health) are more the norm. Not that health care is homogeneous in these respects: visiting a general practitioner is clearly closer to routine and regular than most episodes of acute care. Adam Smith's 'invisible hand'— essentially the market price mechanism—is meant to result in both consumers and producers being able to act in their own selfish interests but nonetheless serving the common good, in the sense of markets producing goods that people are prepared to pay for at the going market prices, which in turn results in social efficiency (i.e. society's resources get used to the greatest benefit). In health care, suppliers (doctors) act explicitly in the consumers' interests rather than wholly in their own (a partial explanation of the prevalance of ethical codes in medicine to prevent exploitation of the consumer). The concept of the rational, informed consumer lying behind the conventional market demand function seems far removed from the patient in health care who faces uncertainty and lack of information and who may be too ill or too scared to act rationally. The potential risks that are faced in health care generate a strong demand for insurance, with a resultant sharing of health care costs.

It is thus perhaps inevitable that in health care the concept of 'need' tends to take centre stage, ahead of the economists' conventional notion of demand. This latter requires an ability on the part of the 'consumer' to act rationally on an informed basis, whereas 'need' embraces the idea of some third party (most often a medical doctor) acting on behalf of the patient. The fact that the doctor is not indifferent to the outcomes to the consumer (much less indifferent at least than the butcher or baker) means that the notion of the doctor acting on behalf of the patient is acknowledged in the so-called 'agency relationship', in which it is explicitly recognised that it is the function of the doctor to try to maximise the patient's health (or welfare more generally). Patient and doctor—consumer and supplier—work together rather than independently as the conventional market analysis would have it. Finally, it is clear that assessing the outcomes of care is difficult, especially in judging what Weisbrod (1978) has called the 'counterfactual': that is, given the capacity of the human body for self-healing, it is often a problem for individual doctors and patients to judge precisely how successful a health care intervention has been. While parallels are sometimes drawn between health care and car repair, cars seldom—if ever—get better on their own!

At the level of the structure of the health care industry, Evans (1981) writes:

> In no society . . . are objectives and decision-making powers within the health care-industry assigned to the sets of elementary transactors (consumers, forms) on which conventional economic theory is built. The characteristic patterns of incomplete vertical integration, of 'leaky' transactor boundaries, has made the application of economic methodology to health-care research [and I would suggest to health care per se] particularly difficult and frequently misleading . . . Since decision-making powers are a form of property rights, their allocation is inherently political . . . If one starts from normative assumptions of consumer sovereignty and positive assumptions of complete information, zero transactions costs, and dynamic stability, one moves quickly to the position that whatever is, is right, and the market . . . yields the best of all possible worlds.

9

When we investigate health care *systems*, the nature of the commodity is central or, perhaps more accurately, the *perceived* nature of the commodity is central. In the consumption of health care the consumer sovereignty of the individual is threatened by the position occupied by the doctor. The patient has to trust that the doctor will act in his or her (the patient's) best interest. As part of a response to this market failure to cope with the characteristics of the commodity health care, the supply side of the market has been regulated in a manner that attempts to separate the doctor's medical behaviour from the resource implications of that behaviour. Along with a tendency to pool the risks associated with the uncertainty concerning the loss of health status, this attempt to insulate medical decision-making from economics has resulted, *inter alia*, in promoting financing by third parties.

Thus the conventional market, where the three functions—benefit-receiving, cost-bearing, and decision-making—of the individual consumer's 'cost–benefit calculus' are performed by the individual, may be contrasted with the health care sector. Here the decision-making may be delegated to the doctor, much of the cost-bearing function at the point of consumption may rest with the financing third party, and even the benefit-receiving aspect will in part be influenced by information from the doctor regarding the nature and size of the benefit.

The role of the doctor is then crucial because he/she is performing simultaneously on both sides of the market. While acting as an agent for the patient in shaping the demand for treatment, at the same time the doctor specifies the supply of treatment. In doing so the doctor is constrained, by his/her acceptance of medical ethics, to determine the treatment through his/her role as agent and not, as would be the case for suppliers in other sectors of the economy, for self-gain—pecuniary or otherwise. While it is normal to assume that this is true across all financing and remuneration systems, the extent to which it is true may well vary with the system. Unlike other sectors of the economy, there is little and indeed in most health care systems no analysis of the costs of production by the person specifying the level of production (treatments), that is, by the doctor.

To the extent that the doctor is concerned with opportunity costs, these will relate primarily to the individual treatment being specified at any particular point in time. In other words the view of opportunity cost to the clinician, if considered at all, will be constrained, *ceteris paribus*, to the short run and to a narrow frame of reference. The institutional framework within which the doctor operates supports these constraints, although how it operates in practice may vary depending on, for example, whether the immediate concern is with general practitioner or hospital clinician behaviour.

The prevalence of third party payment for health services makes it even less likely that doctors will perceive—let alone bear—their full opportunity costs, and this will result in an even greater loss in efficiency. Furthermore, in devoting some finite resources to an individual patient, the doctor is undertaking a distributional function. Maximisation of the benefits from health care would seem to require that the doctor act as an agent for society, as well as an agent for the individual patient involved in the particular short-run production process (treatment), although clearly the latter will dominate the doctor's concern at any specific point in time. It is impossible for the doctor to act as a perfect agent for both individual patients and society.

A key issue here (and one that in normal markets is not considered simply because it does not arise) is that, with the failure of the market in health care and the recognition that we are then not dealing with a simple consumer–supplier exchange, the frame of reference for opportunity cost becomes crucial. The individual clinician's frame is a narrow one (as currently perceived and often practised by clinicians, *too* narrow). The question then is how to ensure that decision-makers at different levels take adequate account of the appropriate opportunity cost for that level of decision-making.

At a conceptual level, it is on the 'demand' side of the market that most concerns seem to arise with regard to the nature of the commodity health care. The supply side, however, is also far removed from the standard view of neoclassical economics, with substantial government regulation, for example, of the medical manpower market (see Chapter 10); with the profession exercising considerable influence over market entry; and with a heavily regulated market, vis-à-vis entry and pricing policy, for pharmaceuticals (see Chapter 6).

It is difficult to see that health care as a commodity could possibly fulfil the requirements of the ideal market mechanism but, as Gaynor and Vogt (1997) point out, that is true of many other commodities. The question is then not whether but to what extent health care fits into the market paradigm. Certainly I have very great reservations about the extent to which it does or can. (For a useful debate on this issue of the relevance of the market, see the series of articles in the *Journal of Health Politics, Policy and the Law* 1997.) This does not mean that economics ceases to be relevant. The issue becomes how best to use the tools of economic analysis in the special circumstances applying to health care systems. That is the real challenge for economists with regard to health care policy.

Multiple objectives

Whatever health services are about they are about health. That is not a problem. Nor, to progress, is it necessary to define health with any great precision. But there is no agreement as to the extent to which health services are about maximising health (the most commonly cited efficiency goal of health care) or maximising social benefits more generally (with health still dominating but not monopolising), and to what extent they are about equity or fairness in the way resources are allocated. This 'tension' between efficiency and equity is one with which all health services have to grapple. It matters, and economists have made important contributions to the debate here. It is an issue that underlies much of the controversy surrounding funding arrangements in health care. Questions of competition, for example, through purchaser–provider splits, case-mix funding arrangements for the payment of hospitals, how to pay general practitioners and many other of the key issues of health policy cannot be moved forward without consideration of this efficiency versus equity trade-off.

Yet while efficiency can easily be defined, as can equity, getting agreement on them and giving the definitions content, in particular at a policy level, it is not so easy. Most commonly in economics there are seen to be two main types of efficiency: first, at a 'lower' level, there is the issue of producing given outputs at least opportunity cost; this is known as 'technical efficiency'; second, and at a higher level of concern with the allocation of scarce resources, there is 'allocative efficiency', which grapples with the fact that not all desirable objectives can be met and that, in choosing between these, resources are allocated in such a way as to try to maximise social benefit. Both forms of efficiency are relevant because of the fact that any society starts with scarce resources, which in turn means that there is likely to be some ethical imperative on decision-makers to ensure that resources are used to the greatest benefit of the society. There is no escaping the logic of scarcity and of opportunity cost—that there is always a benefit forgone when we use resources in one particular way.

There is fairly general agreement about the definition of efficiency but continuing debate in health care as to what constitutes the benefit we should be attempting to maximise. Is it just health or are there other arguments, such as information, reduced anxiety, respect for patient autonomy, that we would want to include as relevant when deciding on efficiency in health care resources allocation? At the level of the individual, this takes us back to the earlier discussion of the individual consumer's utility function and at the social level of a social welfare function and, in turn, what it is that a health service as a system is trying to maximise or optimise.

There is debate both in health economics and in health policy more generally as to what is meant by the term equity. The most common views are that it is about equal health, or equal access for equal need, or equal use for equal need. It is a debate that remains unresolved, although the consensus of opinion would suggest that equity in policy terms in Australia, and indeed elsewhere in the world, is best defined in terms of equal *access* for equal need (Donaldson & Gerard 1993).

Beyond that, what weight we as a society place on equity and what weight on efficiency—distribution versus maximisation—matters because they can often conflict. The issues of equity per se and of the relative weight to be attached to it vis-à-vis efficiency arise in various chapters in this book.

About the book

This chapter began by looking at issues of values and ethics. It is essential in any economic analysis in any sector of the economy to recognise the role of values. Once the concept of scarcity is accepted and with it the concepts of opportunity cost, of benefits obtained and benefits forgone, then value questions immediately arise. Decisions about how to pay hospitals cannot rationally be addressed without considering what the goals of hospitals are, and goals are value-laden concepts. Discussions about the relative priority to be attached to the treatment of cancer patients and cardiac patients cannot be assessed without value judgements being applied. Reviewing policies for trying to arrange a more geographically equitable distribution of primary health care doctors across Australia requires the application of values to the question of the weight to be attached to equity in health care. Beyond that recognition, there is the need to determine whose values are to count in which choices—those of doctors? politicians? patients? citizens? It is not for economists or economics to determine these values, but it is an important role of economics to try to make explicit whatever values are used or are to be used. Indeed, in health care policy this might be seen as one of its key roles.

There is much to debate in health care policy in the 1990s in Australia and much that economics can do to contribute to that debate. It is possible to observe various difficulties currently as policy-makers struggle to define objectives and in particular to recognise the competing nature of the different objectives of health care. Yet policy-makers—not least in the context of pharmaceuticals (see

Chapter 6)—are discovering and using economic evaluation. We have seen hospitals funded through case-mix mechanisms (as discussed in Chapter 5), and some wonder how it could ever have been otherwise, while others wish that it could be otherwise. That general practitioners are paid fee-for-service seems so ingrained in Australian health policy as to be now almost immutable. Debates continue almost unabated about waiting lists, with politicians still seeming to think that the optimal length of waiting lists is zero. Co-payment is a perennial topic for policy debate in health care as politicians try to control costs through trying to deter patients from using health care services. The public versus private funding debate still revolves around arbitrary targets for the percentage of the population covered by private health insurance.

'Prevention is better than cure.' This simplistic slogan of the 1970s and 80s has in the 90s been increasingly questioned and replaced by the less straightforward but nonetheless more apposite question: 'When and in what specific contexts is prevention better than cure?' Economists in their use of economic evaluation have been to the fore in bringing about this change. Debates in screening policy, for example, reveal that health service outcomes are complex and point to queries yet again about whether objectives and in turn effectiveness have been adequately defined.

Lying behind all of this is the question of the effectiveness of different interventions, all fighting for the health dollar. In recent years we have witnessed quite remarkable changes of thinking on this front. The basis of EBM (evidence-based medicine) is that both clinical medicine and health policy should draw on good evidence. It is difficult to dispute that! Yet it is new, and as with most innovations the watching throng is split into at least two camps—the worshippers, and the flavour-of-the-month brigade. Into this drive for effectiveness has been built the health outcomes movement, which emphasises that health policy must be geared explicitly to producing health rather than health services. The process of priority-setting has given added weight to the idea that priorities are about delivering health gains. Yet as soon as that has been realised, that belief has been abandoned by arguing, through the 'goals and targets' philosophy (Nutbeam et al. 1993), that health services are about addressing big problems whether health services are equipped to address them or not. Health policy has put epidemiology at the centre of this thinking when epidemiology itself faces something of a vacuum in terms of its philosophical underpinnings, beyond perhaps the idea that lots of ill-health is bad.

This is not to argue against epidemiology but simply against the role it is sometimes asked to play. Economics needs to combine with epidemiology in many of the key measurement questions facing health policy, especially the measurement of health. This focus on measurement of outcomes is important too for policy-makers. As Alan Shiell (1997) has written:

> Decision makers must demonstrate not only what they have achieved but must also show that what has been achieved is what is valued most highly by those who benefit and those who must pay. This requires us to move beyond the measurement and routine use of health outcomes data in clinical and health systems management to grapple with the more important and more interesting area of objectives and priorities.

There is a need for an examination of Australian health policy from many perspectives. This book does so from the perspective of economics.

In Chapter 2, Ron Donato and Dick Scotton provide a picture of the whole health care system. Many will be familiar with parts of this but few will have as good an overview as is provided here. Additionally, the chapter places the Australian system in an international setting and points to some of the issues facing health care policy-makers in Australia today. As the authors emphasise—and it is a theme that recurs through the other chapters—while we in Australia can learn from elsewhere, 'reforms to the Australian health system must ... reflect the historical, political and social characteristics peculiar to Australia'.

Jim Butler provides in Chapter 3 a description of current and past expenditure on health care. He also shows how expenditure, and how it is raised and used, can be a useful policy instrument. Trying to understand why the level of spending is as it is and why changes have occurred is important in looking to how levels might change in the future and to the possible ramifications. Examination of the current sources of funds—public, private, Commonwealth, state, local government, consumer out-of-pocket—can provide useful insights with respect to changing both the level of spending and the mix. For example, it is not surprising that governments often look to higher patient payments as a means of keeping public expenditure down. To appraise such a policy change, however, requires an understanding of the current sources of funds, which sources provide what proportion of spending in what areas of policy (e.g. general practice as compared with hospital inpatients), and what the behaviour change of potential patients (and health care professionals) might be. Butler also points to the fact that, while new products are likely to continue to flow onto the health care market, questions of their cost-effectiveness will loom ever large, as spending cannot rise at a rate to allow them to be adopted uncritically.

Doctors hold the key to health care policy, as is brought out by Dick Scotton in Chapter 4. How doctors are trained, how they are paid, how many there are of them, their access to pharmaceuticals and to technology more generally are all important policy variables on which it is possible to operate to influence health care policy. While in any sector of the economy the suppliers are well placed to affect the economic organisation of the sector, especially the production processes, factor mix etc., in health care, as a result of the agency relationship, there is a clear sense in which doctors also operate on the demand side of the market. The importance Scotton attaches to the doctor business and the many features of doctor behaviour that are capable of being influenced by economic incentives and other economic policy instruments that affect their behaviour cannot be overstated. How doctors get paid, for example, is one major variable that needs to be used more in health care policy. How and from what geographical areas medical students are recruited can influence where they then practise—an important policy consideration given the problems involved in getting doctors to practise in rural and remote Australia.

Given the stage Australian hospitals have reached by way of funding, it is not surprising that in Chapter 5 Stephen Duckett concentrates on case-mix funding. This system—essentially paying hospitals on the basis of the cases they perform rather than, say, on a per-diem basis—started in the USA and has now spread to many countries. It is one of many ways of funding hospitals. Given the importance of the hospital in the overall health care system, there have been many analyses conducted in many countries of the advantages and disadvantages of different bases for funding hospitals. To say that hospitals are complex is an understatement. This is recognised in economic analyses, although whether the economic models available represent sufficiently the complexities involved is something readers must judge for themselves. Perhaps this is an area where health economists need to mount yet more fundamental research to understand better how hospitals as 'firms' work.

In pharmaceutical policy, as Glenn Salkeld and colleagues note in Chapter 6, Australia leads the world in its use of economic evaluation. The Pharmaceutical Benefits Advisory Committee (the PBAC) requires that all new pharmaceutical products are subject to cost–effectiveness or cost–utility analysis to try to ensure that they represent good value for money before being listed on the Pharmaceutical Benefits Schedule (the PBS), thereby being eligible for public sector subsidy. As a case study in the use of economic evaluation in health care regulation, this is something of a classic, and is much quoted and admired in other countries keen to go down the same road. One hopes that the enthusiasm with which economic evaluation has been picked up in this aspect of health care might be infectious and spread to other areas of Australian health care policy where, although it has made a start, it is less pervasive.

Aged care has a chequered history in economic terms, as Anna Howe brings out in Chapter 7. It is particularly turbulent politically. There are major challenges for economists working in this sector in looking at questions of the nature and level of capital investment, the issue of user payments and finance more generally, and important issues of alternative, substitute forms of care which mean that the effects of different incentive structures are not always easy to predict. These are all important policy matters for which economics is well placed as a discipline to make a contribution. It is thus surprising that not more economic analysis has to date been conducted on aged care.

Chapter 8 is specifically on economic evaluation. Rob Carter and Tony Harris review the tools of cost–effectiveness, cost–utility and cost–benefit analysis. It is a particularly useful chapter for health care policy practitioners who need to use these techniques or at least to have more than a passing acquaintance with the ideas that lie behind them. The techniques are not perfect, as Carter and Harris bring out. They have improved in their application over the last decade. In particular, the advent of cost–utility analysis, which allows outcomes in terms of both morbidity and mortality to be set on a common measuring rod of 'quality-adjusted life-years', has been a major advance. These techniques can now form an important part of the armoury of policy-makers keen to ensure better value for money from health sector resources.

Helen Owens, in Chapter 9, addresses in detail one of the key features of the Australian health care system—health insurance. So many of the debates in Australian health policy relate to what to do about health insurance: it is in a sense the 'problem child' of Australian health care! One of the most important considerations in health insurance which Owens emphasises is the basis on which premiums are set. Equity considerations pull strongly in the direction of 'community rating', where all pay the same independently of the risk characteristics of the insured person. Other bases are likely to prove more efficient, and reflect the actual risk individuals face. Well-developed economic analysis on these issues can aid policy-makers in making informed judgements on the pros and cons of different bases for setting premiums.

The health care financing debate is a lively one in Australia, and in Chapter 10 Jeff Richardson provides a comprehensive and insightful overview of the key issues involved. Here the private versus public debate is not just economic but ideological, and the split between Commonwealth and the states' financing not just economic but political. In such a complex, highly emotionally and politically charged arena, with concerns for states' rights, two-tiered health care systems, equity etc., it is crucial that the basis of such considerations be as objective as possible. This is perhaps the most important role for economics to play in this area of policy. There are so many vested interests and it is too easy for them to muddy the waters in an attempt to ensure that their interests are looked after. Economic analysis can provide much of the necessary, objective information. Additionally, Richardson discusses policy options for reforming health care financing. In what is a most useful analysis, he sets out 14 different options for reform of financing health care: these include, *inter alia*, the privatisation of hospitals, a levy on the wealthy, and coordinated care. He then applies economic analysis to these options to indicate the possible implications of each.

Managed competition, as Dick Scotton highlights in Chapter 11, is seen by some at least as the way forward for the Australian health care system *qua* system. As he emphasises, while it is a complex concept, managed competition's defining feature is the establishment of 'competitive, at-risk budget-holders as the purchasers of health services on behalf of defined populations of consumers enrolled with them'. Beyond that there are many shapes and forms that managed competition can take. There are relevant experiences from Europe and the USA on which to draw if such major structural reform were to occur in Australia. It is necessary, however, to set any such change within the cultural and historical context of Australia, and the experiences elsewhere (the evaluation of which is still awaited) can act only as a partial guide to what might happen in Australia. What would seem highly desirable would be some further experimentation to establish what sorts of models of managed care might be adopted (Scotton sets out one in detail) and assess the likely impact in pilots before setting major system reforms in place. Certainly the idea of such an approach, providing distinct roles for the Commonwealth and the states and having the public and private sectors working in tandem, is attractive in principle. Whether it can be made to work in practice and whether the managed competition model is the best way to achieve improved efficiency and equity needs more detailed investigation.

In Chapter 12, Alan Shiell and Rob Carter examine policy-making in public health. These authors place emphasis on questions of values looked at, if from a different perspective, in this introductory chapter. Shiell and Carter discuss a number of important practical matters relating to policy, such as different approaches to priority-setting and the importance here again of the basic, simple concepts of opportunity cost and the margin. More fundamentally, however, the chapter is both stimulating and reflective, arguing for the importance of bringing issues of economic evaluation, priority-setting and financing together to allow the strengths of health economics to emerge in full, but adding the rider that economic methods cannot be expected to provide comprehensive answers to political and value-laden questions. Economic analysis can inform and assist policy in health care—it cannot make it.

In Chapter 13, with my colleagues Steve Jan and Virginia Wiseman, we have concentrated on concerns of equity in Aboriginal health funding; it is striking how little work has been done in examining alternative models of service delivery from an economic perspective. Using economic evaluation techniques in indigenous health is not easy, but it is unfortunate that in this crucial area of Australian health policy so little effort has been made to date to apply these techniques. This is an area in which it is necessary to step outside health care policy and look at health infrastructure more generally. We need to understand better than we do the relative efficiency of investing in health care, water, sewerage and housing.

2 *The Australian health care system*

Our primary aim in this chapter is to provide an overview of current arrangements of the Australian health care system, as a context for the discussion of selected policy issues by other contributors.[1] A secondary contextual objective is to indicate the extent to which the problems and reform issues engaging policy-makers in Australia are manifestations of factors common to advanced developed countries and how much they are the product of domestic characteristics.

Overview of health care arrangements

The Australian health care system is characterised by a blend of public and private sectors, in both the funding and provision of health care services. Total health care expenditure for 1995/96 was $41.7 billion (8.5 per cent of GDP), of which about 67 per cent was from public sources (AIHW 1997). In terms of service delivery, the balance is more even, with most medical services, pharmaceuticals, dental and other professional services being provided by private practitioners. Figure 2.1 shows that the principal categories of expenditure in 1994/95 were hospital services (34.8 per cent), medical services (18.9 per cent), pharmaceuticals (10.9 per cent) and nursing homes (7.1 per cent).

Australia operates a number of universal publicly financed programs, of which Medicare is the best known. Introduced in 1984, Medicare and related universal programs are financed out of general taxation and a 1.5 per cent levy on taxable income. Medicare benefits include access to public hospital care at no charge and cash benefits related to the cost of private medical services. Other major cash benefit programs provide subsidies for nursing home care and prescription medicines supplied by private pharmacists. Medicare and the Pharmaceutical Benefits Scheme (PBS) are administered through the Health Insurance Commission (HIC).

A dominant feature of the Australian system is the division of powers and responsibilities for health services between the Commonwealth and state governments. The Commonwealth government is directly responsible for financing medical services, pharmaceutical

Figure 2.1   The sources and uses of the health dollar in Australia, 1994/95

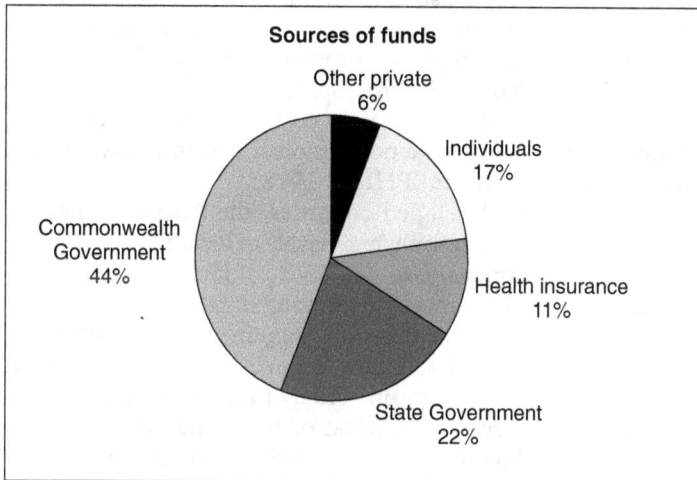

Sources of funds

Other private 6%

Individuals 17%

Commonwealth Government 44%

Health insurance 11%

State Government 22%

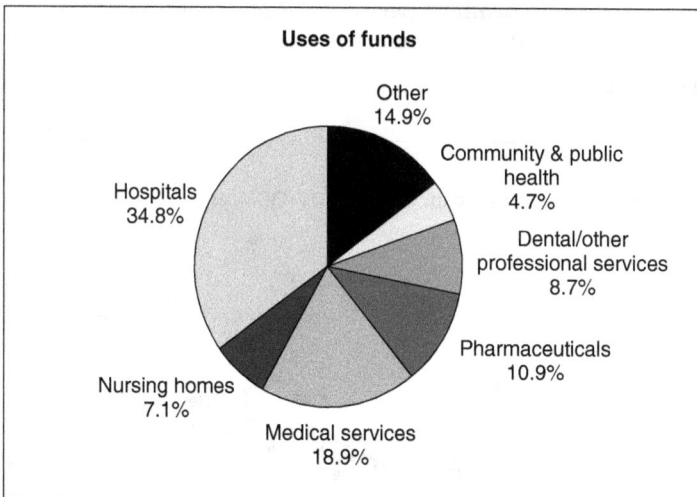

Uses of funds

Other 14.9%

Community & public health 4.7%

Hospitals 34.8%

Dental/other professional services 8.7%

Pharmaceuticals 10.9%

Nursing homes 7.1%

Medical services 18.9%

Source: AIHW (1997), derived from Table 17.

benefits and aged residential care services. State governments, with varying levels of Commonwealth financial assistance, are primarily responsible for the funding and operation of public hospital services, mental health programs, community support programs and women's and children's services.

Another feature of the Australian health system is the existence of a substantial private insurance sector operating alongside the universal system. Private insurance provides coverage for a range of services not included under Medicare, of which the largest component comprises accommodation costs in private hospitals. Approximately 32 per cent of the population is currently covered by some form of private insurance (PHIAC 1998).

In common with all developed countries, the Australian health system is characterised by relatively high levels of health, as measured by such indices as life-expectancies, low levels of mortality at all ages and low incidence of serious morbidity among non-aged members of the population. Achieving these outcomes requires the acquisition of advanced medical technologies, highly trained health professionals and sophisticated infrastructure in order to provide technically complex diagnosis and treatment. Most of these characteristics are largely a function of income: only developed countries have the resources to operate such health systems. Figure 2.2 shows the high correlation between per-capita health expenditure and income across

Figure 2.2   Per capita health expenditure as a percentage of per capita GDP, OECD member countries, 1992

Health expenditure per capita

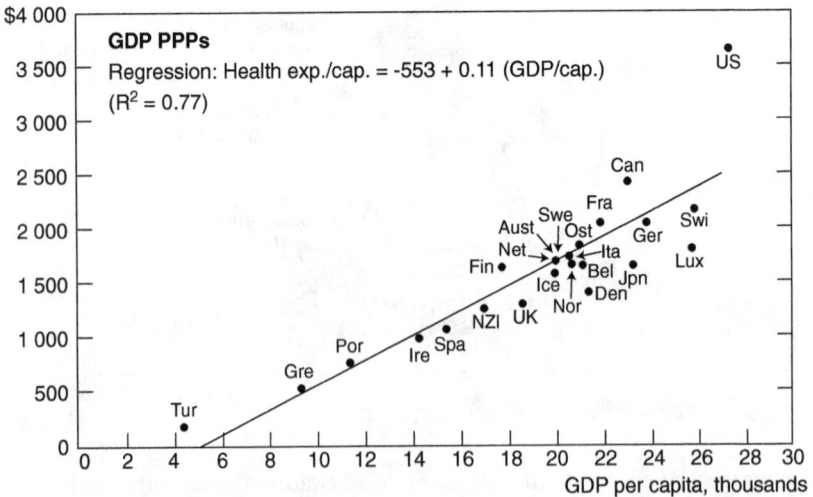

Note: PPP = Purchasing Power Parities
Source: OECD (1995) Figure 2, p. 25.

22

countries. Australia's per-capita expenditure is very much in line with the predicted level given its per-capita income.

With the exception of the USA, a feature common to all major developed countries, including Australia, is the adoption of some form of predominantly publicly financed compulsory health insurance system. The financing arrangements are usually via general taxation or social security, and governments have substantial control over aggregate health care expenditure, either through global budgets or through regulating and negotiating fee-scheduling and expenditure targets (OECD 1992).[2] Australia is consistent with other countries in this respect, although it tends to be at the lower end of the publicly financed spectrum (see Table 2.1). Table 2.2 shows that most countries were able to stabilise health expenditure during the 1980s and early 1990s at around the 7–9 per cent range. Australia's health

Table 2.1 **Public health expenditures as a percentage of total health expenditures for 24 OECD countries, 1980–95**

Country	1980	1985	1990	1991	1992	1993	1994	1995
Australia	62.9	71.7	68.1	67.8	67.8	67.9	68.5	66.7
Austria	68.8	77.6	75.0	74.9	75.1	75.7	76.0	75.6
Belgium	83.4	81.8	88.9	88.1	88.9	88.9	87.9	87.8
Canada	75.7	75.7	74.6	74.6	74.1	73.0	71.8	71.4
Denmark	85.2	84.4	82.3	83.3	83.6	83.1	83.4	82.7
Finland	79.0	78.6	80.9	81.1	79.6	76.3	74.8	74.7
France	78.8	76.9	74.5	74.7	74.6	74.2	78.4	80.6
Germany	79.2	77.9	76.8	78.6	78.9	78.5	78.4	78.4
Greece	82.2	81.0	82.3	80.2	76.1	76.2	76.2	75.8
Iceland	88.2	87.0	86.6	86.9	85.1	83.7	84.0	84.2
Ireland	82.2	77.4	74.7	77.2	7.8	88.2	80.7	80.8
Italy	80.5	77.2	78.1	78.4	76.3	72.9	70.6	69.6
Japan	71.3	70.7	77.6	78.3	78.1	79.3	76.8	78.4
Luxembourg	92.8	89.2	93.1	93.0	92.8	92.9	91.8	92.8
Netherlands	74.7	75.1	72.7	74.1	77.7	78.6	77.7	77.1
New Zealand	88.0	85.0	82.4	82.2	79.0	76.6	76.8	76.4
Norway	85.1	85.8	83.3	83.5	85.1	83.3	83.0	82.8
Portugal	64.3	54.6	65.5	62.8	59.6	63.0	63.4	60.5
Spain	79.9	81.1	78.7	78.9	78.8	78.6	78.6	78.2
Sweden	92.5	90.4	89.9	88.2	85.4	83.9	83.0	81.6
Switzerland	67.5	66.1	68.4	68.6	70.1	71.8	71.9	71.9
Turkey	27.3	50.2	40.0	50.0	33.3	60.0	50.0	–
UK	89.4	85.8	84.1	83.7	84.5	84.8	84.1	84.3
USA	42.4	40.7	40.8	42.0	42.6	42.3	44.8	46.2
OECD average (excluding Turkey)	78.0	77.0	77.4	77.4	74.0	77.1	76.6	76.5

Source: OECD (1997).

Table 2.2   **Total health expenditures in OECD countries as a percentage of gross domestic product, selected years, 1975–1995**

Country	1975	1980	1985	1990	1991	1992	1993	1994	1995
Australia	7.5	7.3	7.7	8.2	8.2	8.6	8.6	8.5	8.4
Austria	7.3	7.9	6.7	7.1	7.2	7.55	7.9	7.8	7.9
Belgium	5.9	6.6	7.4	7.6	8.0	8.16	8.2	8.1	8.0
Canada	7.2	7.3	8.4	9.2	9.9	10.2	10.2	9.9	9.7
Denmark	6.5	6.8	6.3	6.5	6.5	6.6	6.8	6.6	6.4
Finland	6.4	6.5	7.3	8.0	9.1	9.3	8.4	7.9	7.5
France	7.0	7.6	8.5	8.9	9.1	9.4	9.8	9.7	9.9
Germany	8.0	8.1	8.5	8.2	9.6	10.2	10.1	10.3	10.5
Greece	3.4	3.6	4.0	4.2	4.2	4.5	5.0	5.5	5.8
Iceland	5.8	6.2	7.3	8.0	8.1	8.2	8.3	8.1	8.2
Ireland	7.7	8.8	7.8	6.6	6.8	7.1	7.0	7.4	7.1
Italy	6.2	7.0	7.1	8.1	8.4	8.5	8.6	8.4	7.7
Japan	5.5	6.4	6.7	6.0	6.0	6.3	6.6	6.9	7.2
Luxembourg	5.1	6.2	6.1	6.6	6.5	6.6	6.7	6.5	7.0
Netherlands	7.5	7.9	7.9	8.3	8.6	8.8	8.9	8.8	8.8
New Zealand	6.7	6.0	5.3	7.0	7.5	7.6	7.3	7.1	7.1
Norway	6.1	7.0	6.6	7.8	8.1	8.2	8.1	8.0	8.0
Portugal	5.6	5.8	6.3	6.5	7.2	7.4	7.7	7.8	8.2
Spain	4.9	5.7	5.7	6.9	7.1	7.2	7.3	7.3	7.6
Sweden	7.9	9.4	9.0	8.8	8.7	7.8	7.9	7.6	7.2
Switzerland	7.0	7.3	8.1	8.4	9.0	9.4	9.5	9.5	9.8
Turkey	2.7	3.3	2.2	2.5	3.2	2.7	2.5	5.2	–
UK	5.5	5.6	5.9	6.0	6.5	6.9	6.9	6.9	6.9
USA	8.2	9.1	10.7	12.7	13.5	14.1	14.3	14.1	14.2
OECD average (excluding Turkey)	6.5	7.0	7.2	7.6	8.0	8.2	8.2	8.3	8.2

Source: OECD (1997).

expenditure trends appear to be consistent with most other major OECD countries, where it has remained around the 8–8.5 per cent range of GDP during this period. The USA is an outlier, with health care expenditure at over 14 per cent of GDP—far in excess of any other country. In addition, the reliance in the USA on voluntary private insurance as the principal financing mechanism saw 17 per cent of the population in 1992 without health insurance coverage, and millions more with inadequate coverage (Rowland et al. 1994). The strengths of publicly financed health systems in comparison with the USA are that they have been successful in achieving cost containment at the macro level, guaranteeing universal insurance coverage for medically necessary care and linking financing arrangements with ability to pay. The Australian health care system reflects the strengths of other publicly financed systems in this respect.

Health in Australia has improved considerably in recent decades, and compares favourably with most other major OECD countries. Table 2.3 shows that female life-expectancy at birth rose from 74.0 in 1960 to 80.9 in 1995, while male life-expectancy rose from 67.9 to 75.0 over the same period. Reductions in diseases of the circulatory system have been a major factor in improving life-expectancy in older adults. Australia has also experienced significant improvement in the reduction in perinatal and infant mortality rates along with other major OECD countries (see Table 2.4), with infant mortality declining from

Table 2.3 Life expectancy

Country	Male life-expectancy at birth		Female life-expectancy at birth	
	1960	1995	1960	1995
Australia	67.9	75	73.9	80.9
Austria	65.4	73.5	71.9	80.1
Belgium	67.7	73.3	73.5	80.0
Canada[a]	68.4	75.3	74.3	81.3
Denmark	72.3	72.5	74.1	77.8
Finland	64.9	72.8	71.6	80.2
France	67.0	73.9	73.6	81.9
Germany	66.9	73.0	72.4	79.5
Greece	67.5	75.1	70.7	80.3
Iceland	70.7	76.5	75.0	80.6
Ireland	68.5	72.9	71.8	78.5
Italy[a]	67.2	74.4	72.3	80.8
Japan	65.3	76.4	70.2	82.8
Luxembourg	66.1	72.5	71.9	79.5
Netherlands	71.6	74.6	75.5	80.4
New Zealand	68.7	73.8	73.9	79.2
Norway	71.3	74.8	75.8	80.8
Portugal	61.7	71.5	67.2	78.6
Spain	67.4	73.2	72.2	81.2
Sweden	71.2	76.2	74.9	81.5
Switzerland	68.7	75.3	74.1	81.7
Turkey[a]	46.5	65.4	49.7	70.0
UK	68.3	74.3	74.2	79.7
USA	66.6	72.5	73.1	79.2
OECD average (excluding Turkey)	67.9	74.1	73.0	80.3

Note: [a] Male and female life-expectancy data for Canada and Italy are for 1961. Male and female life-expectancy data for Turkey are for 1994.

Source: OECD (1997).

Table 2.4   Perinatal and infant mortality

Country	Perinatal mortality[a] (% all births)		Infant mortality (per 100 live births)	
	1960	1994	1960	1995
Australia	2.85	0.52	2.02	0.57
Austria	3.50	0.62	3.75	0.54
Belgium	3.19	0.83	3.12	0.70
Canada	2.84	0.72	2.73	0.60
Denmark	2.62	0.74	2.15	0.55
Finland	2.75	0.53	2.10	0.40
France	3.13	0.58	2.74	0.50
Germany	3.58	0.64	3.38	0.53
Greece	2.64	0.97	4.01	0.81
Iceland	1.97	0.45	1.30	0.61
Ireland	3.77	0.90	2.93	0.63
Italy	4.19	0.88	4.39	0.62
Japan	0.04	0.01	3.07	0.43
Luxembourg	3.23	0.62	3.15	0.50
Netherlands	2.66	0.86	1.79	0.55
New Zealand	2.70	0.6	2.26	0.70
Norway	2.40	0.75	1.89	0.40
Portugal	4.11	0.92	7.75	0.74
Spain	3.66	0.65	4.37	0.55
Sweden	2.62	0.54	1.66	0.41
Switzerland	2.56	0.61	2.11	0.50
Turkey	-	5.26	19.74	4.50
UK	3.36	0.89	2.25	0.60
USA	2.89	0.79	2.60	0.80
OECD average (excluding Turkey)	2.92	0.68	2.94	0.58

Note: [a] Perinatal data for Belgium are for 1991. For Denmark, Italy and Turkey perinatal data are for 1993. For the remaining countries the perinatal data are for 1994—the most recent year, at the time of writing, for which comprehensive figures were available for the majority of the OECD countries.

Source: OECD (1997).

2.02 per 100 live births in 1990 to 0.57 per 100 live births in 1995 (OECD 1997). Australia, along with other developed countries, has been able significantly to reduce morbidity and mortality rates associated with acute infectious diseases. The major causes of death in Australia today, however, are associated with 'diseases of affluence', such as heart disease and cancer, which are related to such factors as tobacco-smoking, poor diet, lack of exercise, stress and environmental issues (Palmer & Short 1994). Consequently all developed countries are devoting increasing resources to public health programs associated with disease prevention and health promotion.

Despite the high levels of publicly financed health expenditure as well as comparatively good health outcomes, a considerable degree of inequality in health status persists in Australia. Health inequalities tend to be associated with such factors as socioeconomic background, urban/rural location, gender and ethnicity. Recent studies show that groups from the most disadvantaged socioeconomic backgrounds in Australia have poorer health in terms of higher mortality rates, greater incidence of chronic illness, a greater prevalence of disability and handicap and higher self-reporting of fair and poor health (AIHW 1996; NHS 1992). Evidence suggests that good income, employment and level of education, in addition to behaviour and lifestyle, are important factors contributing to good health and longevity. The interdependence of various socioeconomic factors known to affect health status means that the task of attempting to alleviate health inequalities is likely to be particularly complex, as improving health status cannot be addressed satisfactorily by simply allocating more resources into health care services.

Nowhere is health inequality more evident than in the health of the indigenous population in Australia. Aboriginal and Torres Strait Islander people have the worst health status of any particular group in Australia, rivalling that of many Third World countries. The latest available data reveal that Aboriginal men and women have life-expectancies 15–20 years lower than other Australians and that perinatal and infant death rates are three times that of the rest of the population (AIHW 1996). Similarly, the rates of hospitalisation and burden of disease among Aboriginal people continue to be substantially higher than in non-Aboriginal Australians (AIHW 1996). Undoubtedly, the severe economic and social disadvantages experienced by Aborigines have contributed to these dismal health statistics (see Chapter 13).

Current health care arrangements

Medical services

Under Medicare, all Australians are automatically insured for medical services provided outside hospitals by private practitioners on a fee-for-service basis at 85 per cent of the fee set under the Medicare Benefits Schedule (MBS). The remaining out-of-pocket expense for medical services is subject to an indexed maximum gap for any individual service and to a safety-net limit per year for a family group or individual. Doctors are free to set their own fees above the MBS fee, in which case the excess must be borne by the patient. Doctors who send their patients' bills in bulk direct to the Health Insurance Commission accept the Medicare benefits (i.e. 85 per cent of the MBS fee) as payment in full. The advantages of 'bulk-billing' direct to the HIC for many medical practitioners are the avoidance of bad debts and lower administrative costs. Thus, patients visiting doctors who bulk-bill incur no out-of-pocket payments at the point of delivery. In 1995/96, 71 per cent of medical services were bulk-billed, up from 65 per cent in 1992/93, an upward trend that has continued since the inception of Medicare (CDHFS 1996a).

In-hospital medical services are provided free for public patients in public hospitals, and Medicare provides a rebate of 75 per cent of the MBS fees for medical services to private patients in public and private hospitals. Private hospital insurance covers the other 25 per cent of the MBS fee for private patients, but charges above the MBS fee are not insurable.

In 1995/96, approximately 40 000 medical practitioners provided 196 million medical services, a rise of 4.2 per cent over the previous year, when 188 million services were provided (HIC 1996). Unreferred attendances to general practitioners made up a substantial proportion (47.5 per cent) of medical services, while a further 24.8 per cent of services were pathology and 9.2 per cent were specialist attendances. Over the past decade, the average number of services per person processed rose from 7.5 per person in 1985/86 to 10.7 in 1995/96—an average annual increase of 4.3 per cent per year (HIC 1995, 1996). The number of medical practitioners has grown substantially over the past two decades, from 156 per 100 000 population in 1976 to 230 per 100 000 in 1991. Despite this increase, it is generally acknowledged that there is an imbalance of supply of doctors, with chronic shortages occurring in rural areas. In 1994 there were 120.4 general practitioners per 100 000 population, compared with 80.2 per 100 000 in rural and remote areas (AIHW 1996).

Between 1988/89 and 1994/95 expenditure on medical services grew at an average real rate of 5.4 per cent per annum, compared with 3.5 per cent for health care expenditure as a whole (AIHW 1997). This outcome of an *uncapped* fee-for-service medical benefits program has posed a growing policy dilemma for the Commonwealth government in recent years. To date most of the policy initiatives have been on the supply side, such as the reduction in medical school numbers and immigration quotas as well as limiting the number of new doctors who can apply for a Medicare provider number. Recently, the Coalition government has indicated its intention to make greater use of price signals, with the possibility of introducing consumer co-payments. So far it is unclear whether the demand- and supply-side strategies to control the expenditure growth of the MBS program will achieve the desired outcome.

A series of other reforms to general practice has also been underway since the early 1990s. The aims of the general practice reform strategies are to improve efficiency, effectiveness and consumer responsiveness, as well as to integrate and coordinate general practice better into the community setting. (Doctors' issues and medical services' markets are discussed in Chapter 4.)

Hospitals

The hospital sector in Australia is characterised by a mix of public and private provision as well as funding. In 1993/94 the total supply of hospital beds per 1000 population (bed ratio) was 4.4, of which the public sector accounted for 3.2. In the past decade, the supply of public hospital beds has fallen by about 25 per cent; the supply of private hospital beds has remained fairly constant over this period (AIHW 1996). Total patient admissions have risen steadily in recent years from 3.8 million in 1989/90 to 5.0 million in 1994/95, of which public hospital admissions made up about 70 per cent. Despite the rise in admissions, total hospital utilisation has remained fairly constant in recent years (21.2 million occupied bed days in 1994/95) because of a decline in the average length of stay, from 5.4 days in 1989/90 to 4.2 days in 1994/95, as a result of a growing use of day surgery and minimally invasive surgery (CDHFS 1996b).

The private hospital sector and the private health insurance industry are highly interdependent. In 1994/95 private health insurance funded about 70 per cent of private hospital expenditure, which represented nearly 48 per cent of total private insurance benefits (AIHW 1997). Private hospitals accounted for nearly 26 per cent of total hospital occupied bed days or about 8 per cent of total health care expenditure in 1994/95 (AIHW 1997).

The public hospital sector represents the largest single category of health expenditure (27.9 per cent of recurrent expenditure), and in 1994/95 totalled $10.2 billion, of which the Commonwealth contributed $5.1 billion and the state governments $4.2 billion (AIHW 1997). A feature of the public hospital sector is that expenditure grew by an average real rate of only 1 per cent per annum in the period 1988/89–1994/95, whereas total health care expenditure grew by 3.5 per cent. The private hospital sector, in contrast, grew by an average annual rate of 8.3 per cent over this period. The control of expenditure in public hospitals is due to the capped nature of budgets emanating from Commonwealth grants to the states and, in turn, from state government funding allocations to public hospitals. Tight capping of expenditures is a manifestation of the stringent fiscal conditions prevailing on all levels of governments in Australia (and on governments of most other developed countries) since the early 1990s.

Under the Medicare Agreement between the Commonwealth and state governments, all Australians are entitled to free access to public hospital accommodation and medical treatment. Five-year Medicare Agreements specify the formulae by which Commonwealth funds are channelled to state governments, which have the prime responsibility for the provision and regulation of public hospitals, as well as detailing the states' obligations in exchange for such funding. The current Medicare Agreement runs from 1993 to 1998.

The flow of funds from the Commonwealth to the states for public hospitals mainly occurs through specific-purpose grants. These are based primarily on a population formula, with supplementary components reflecting various performance measures. A complicating factor to these funding arrangements is that the basic components of the Medicare grants are subject to a process known as 'fiscal equalisation', which determines general Financial Assistance Grants (FAGs) given to the states. Administered by the Commonwealth Grants Commission (CGC), the aim of this equalisation process is to ensure that all states are able to provide an average level of services to all without recourse to levying higher taxes or surcharges on their citizens. As a result, the 'poorer' states are cross-subsidised by the 'richer' states. Since 1988 a growing proportion of Medicare hospital grants have been quarantined from this process, with a corresponding increase in the complexity of the funding arrangements. The adequacy and distribution of Medicare grants have resulted in considerable tension between the Commonwealth and the state governments. At the time of writing the Commonwealth government has signalled its intention to incorporate case-mix-based output measures into the formula for the 1998–2003 Agreements.

Funding constraints and rising costs are among the main contributors to the emergence of significant waiting lists for admission to public hospitals. State government expenditure on total health care grew by an average real annual rate of 1.6 per cent over the period 1989/90–1995/96, while Commonwealth outlays grew by an average of 5 per cent annually during the same period (AIHW 1997). The Commonwealth has tried to blame the states for withdrawing their own funds and shifting the costs onto Medicare programs (i.e. medical and pharmaceutical services), while the states have maintained that the failure of total Commonwealth funding to match the rising demand for hospital services resulting from the Medicare hospital arrangements and falls in private insurance membership has left them with no alternative. The issues of cost-shifting are part of a wider debate about the appropriate roles and responsibilities of the states and the Commonwealth in the funding and provision of health services.

Over the past decade a range of reforms has been introduced in the public hospital system by state governments in order to improve efficiency. A major initiative has been the development of sophisticated hospital output measures, known as Diagnostic-Related Groupings (DRGs). DRGs are now being used by various states either as a basis for *prospective* funding of their hospital system or as a management information tool. Other reforms have focused on introducing greater competition into the hospital sector, including contracting out of government 'non-core' services such as laundering, catering and cleaning (SAHC 1994). Similarly, benchmarking between hospitals, standardised for case-mix (using DRGs) and quality, is systematically being adopted by most states to assess relative performance. There have also been moves towards 'arms-length' *contractual* arrangements in the purchasing of public hospital services, with some states administratively separating the purchasing function of health services from the provision of those services (WADH 1995; Armitage 1994). A series of private sector initiatives is also underway, including the use of privately managed public hospitals and co-location and joint sharing of public and private hospital facilities. (A comprehensive account of the hospital sector, including the development of the DRG case-mix system and other reforms, is provided in Chapter 5.)

Pharmaceuticals

The Pharmaceutical Benefits Scheme (PBS) subsidises the cost of government-listed prescribed medicines dispensed by private retail pharmacies. Over 90 per cent of the drugs available for prescription by doctors are listed on the schedule. In 1995/96 the PBS subsidised over 132 million prescriptions and accounted for 80 per cent of the total cost of listed drugs of $2.84 billion (HIC 1997). In 1994/95 the PBS met about 49 per cent of the total cost of all pharmaceuticals consumed. Total pharmaceutical expenditure accounted for about 10.9 per cent of total health care expenditure in 1994/95 (AIHW 1997).

Originally substantially free, the PBS has progressively increased co-payments, subject to annual ceilings. Patients are categorised into two groups: concessional beneficiaries and general beneficiaries.

Concessional beneficiaries, comprising pensioners and persons in other designated low-income groups eligible for health care cards, are charged a relatively modest co-payment per PBS item ($3.20 in January 1998) up to an annual maximum equal to 52 items. General beneficiaries receive a benefit only for items costing more than $20, in which case they pay a $20 contribution with a less generous safety-net operating for general users once they incur a specified out-of-pocket expenditure ($612.60 in January 1998) during the calendar year. For out-of-pocket expenditure above the specified amount, general beneficiaries become entitled to the concessional rate for all PBS items purchased for the rest of the year. All of the above-specified amounts are indexed annually in accordance with movements in the CPI, and are subject to periodic review.

Despite the government's ability to use its monopsonist purchasing power to keep the supplier cost of drugs listed on the PBS to one of the lowest levels in the industrialised world, several factors—including the open-ended nature of the scheme—have seen the PBS expenditure grow rapidly in real terms. Expenditures on pharmaceuticals grew by an average annual rate of 8.0 per cent in real terms for the period 1988/89–1994/95, significantly higher than the 3.5 per cent experienced by the health sector as a whole (AIHW 1997). An important contributing factor has been the rising proportion of new high-cost drugs being added to the PBS listing. Strategies adopted by the Commonwealth to slow the expenditure growth of PBS programs have included increasing the co-payments for both concessionary and general beneficiaries, basing the subsidy on the unit cost of the lowest-priced generic brand and subjecting new drugs scheduled for PBS listing to cost–effectiveness assessments. The Commonwealth is also attempting to secure more cost-effective prescribing of PBS medicines by doctors as part of the general practice reform strategies. (A detailed analysis of the pharmaceutical sector is provided in Chapter 6.)

Aged care

The ageing of the Australian population will have a significant impact on the demand for health care services, given that the elderly consume substantially more resources per capita than the non-elderly adult population. Further, increasing life-expectancy is changing the pattern of frailty and hence the composition and structure of services required for care of the elderly. For this reason, the past decade has seen substantial reform in aged care policy, with the expansion of community-based support programs and the containment of highly institutionalised residential care. Also, within residential care services there has been an effort to shift resources away from resource-intensive nursing homes towards greater support for the lower-dependency hostel sector. The Aged Care Reform Strategy, implemented in the mid-1980s, saw the number of nursing home beds reduced from 68 per 1000 persons over 70 in 1985 to 49 in 1996. For the same period hostel places per 1000 persons over 70 grew from 33 to 41. Planned target levels for residential services and intensive community-based support services were set at 10 per cent of those aged over 70: this represents 40 nursing home beds and 50 hostel places per 1000 persons aged 70 and over (CDHFS 1996a).

Residential care services are provided by both state government nursing homes and the private sector, but the Commonwealth government along with residents' contributions fund nursing home and hostel accommodation. Public funding accounted for 76.7 per cent of the $2.7 billion outlaid in the nursing home sector in 1994/95 (AIHW 1997). For the period 1988/89–1994/95, nursing home expenditure grew by an annual average rate of 1.8 per cent in real terms, about half the rate of the total health sector for the same period. Control of funding to nursing and hostel services was exercised through limits placed on the number of nursing and hostel beds and by strict entry requirements based on a formal assessment by aged care assessment teams.

Until recently (late 1997), Commonwealth funding for nursing homes comprised two components: the Care Aggregate Module (CAM), which linked funding to a five-level Resident Classification Instrument based (RCI) on the personal care requirements of patients; and the Service Aggregate Module (SAM), which provided infrastructure funding and also allowed a profit component for private providers. Residents contributed a daily fee, capped at 87.5 per cent of combined pension and rent assistance regardless of income. For hostel accommodation, residents' contributions were based on provider assessment of ability to pay with a minimum contribution of 85 per cent of combined pension and rent assistance. The Commonwealth provided subsidies for recurrent funding as well as for capital programs. Residents contributed to hostel capital maintenance through a negotiated capital entry contribution.

In 1996 the newly elected Liberal government announced the Aged Care Structural Reform Package. Implemented in late 1997, an important feature of the reforms was the removal of the distinction that existed between nursing and hostel facilities so that all residential aged care facilities would fall under a single classification instrument for funding purposes. The new instrument means that all providers will receive equal levels of funding for residents with similar needs, regardless of the type of facility. Another major change is the introduction of income-tested charges for part-pensioners and non-pensioners as contribution to the rental cost of accommodation in nursing homes and hostels. This is in addition to the basic contribution of 87.5 per cent of the combined pension and rental assistance that all residents must pay towards their accommodation costs. Residents were also expected to contribute to capital maintenance programs of both hostel and nursing homes by providing a lump sum entry contribution, which is mostly refundable when the resident leaves. However, in the face of a strong electoral backlash to lump sum capital contributions, this part of the reform was modified in early 1998. (The implications of these reforms and other policy issues are discussed in Chapter 7.)

The overwhelming majority of the elderly (83 per cent in 1993) live at home, however, not in institutions, and are cared for mainly by relatives with or without formal assistance (AIHW 1996). In 1985 the federal government placed most of the existing support programs for the non-institutional aged under one umbrella, the Home and Community Care (HACC) program. The aim of this program is to complement residential care by providing an integrated package of services within the community setting for those who want to remain at home. Services include home nursing, respite care, food services, aged daycare and transport services. HACC is administered by the states and the costs are shared by both levels of government: expenditure grew from $288 million in 1985/86 to $695 million in 1995/96 (Commonwealth of Australia 1997). The current Commonwealth government is negotiating with state governments for the implementation of a national fees policy, which will see the expansion of user charges for HACC services.

Current problems and issues of the Australian health system

Despite the relative strengths of (predominantly) publicly financed systems described above, most of the major developed countries are implementing, or are intending to implement, market-orientated health care reforms (van de Ven 1996). Institutional rigidities, perverse incentives, overbureaucratisation and inadequate consumer/patient response mechanisms, counter to *microeconomic efficiency*, have emerged as problems confronting publicly financed systems (Saltman & Otter 1992). In addition, growing pressure has been placed on the public purse by the impact of cost-enhancing technologies, an ageing population and lower economic growth rates

(post-1970s). As a consequence of perceived microeconomic inefficiencies and fiscal stringencies there has been a re-evaluation, in
many countries, as to whether the predominantly non-market social
institutions that characterise publicly financed health systems
continue to be the best response to the problems of market failures
and (in)equity.

Many of the problems experienced by the Australian health system
in general mirror those of other major developed countries;
consequently, the pressure for reforms has also been widely debated
in Australia. However, there are institutional and structural
characteristics peculiar to the Australian health system that have
compounded the problems associated with publicly financed systems
and that have to be looked at before future comprehensive reforms
can successfully be implemented. The two main problems, a perennial
source of concern and controversy to policy-makers, are Commonwealth–state responsibilities and structural financial instability.

Commonwealth–state responsibilities

The complex division of powers and responsibilities for the financing,
provision and regulation of health care services between Commonwealth and state governments remains a dominant feature of the
Australian health system. There are relatively few federations among
the OECD countries, with the partial exception of the USA, that
involve the same kinds of overlap in health service administration and
control. This division, a product of history and the Constitution,
continues to have major policy implications.

The Commonwealth had little jurisdiction over health and social
policies until 1946, when an amendment to the Constitution
conferred wide ranging powers to the Commonwealth with respect
(*inter alia*) to 'pharmaceutical, sickness and hospital benefits, medical
and dental services'. This power has underpinned legislation for cash
benefit programs to pay for doctor services, prescribed drugs and
nursing homes, which are overwhelmingly provided by the private
sector, and has enabled the Commonwealth to implement a national
health insurance program and to dictate the structure and regulation
of private health insurance. Further extensions of power to the
Commonwealth flow from section 96 of the Constitution, which
enables it to make grants to the states on conditions imposed by
Parliament. The use of this section has enabled successive Commonwealth governments to implement programs and policies outside the
scope of its explicit powers. The limited revenue-raising capacity of
state governments relative to their provision responsibilities, and their
consequent dependence on Commonwealth grants, has resulted in

what is known as vertical fiscal imbalance. The use of conditional grants to fund health programs administered by the states has been a source of continuing tension between the Commonwealth and states.

The compounding of jurisdictional overlap by a multiplicity of different programs at both Commonwealth and state level health care has resulted in a highly complex, fragmented and uncoordinated system. The resulting shortcomings in planning, financing and provision of health services have been described as 'the health jigsaw' by the National Health Care Strategy (NHS 1991), and as the 'balkanisation' of the health system by Paterson (1996). The institutional and historical rigidities that have resulted in health services lacking the flexibility and the responsiveness to meet the needs of particular individuals and communities adequately have been widely recognised (NCoA 1996; COAG 1995; NHS 1991). In particular, people with chronic illnesses and complex health care requirements were the ones for whom the system performed most poorly. Ironically, it is this group that consumes the bulk of health care resources.

In addition to duplication and overlap of programs and poor integration of services, there have been problems of cost-shifting. The dual (government) sources for funding public hospitals have created strong incentives for cost-shifting from capped budgets to uncapped areas under Commonwealth control, such as MBS and PBS programs. Facing budgetary constraints, state governments have an incentive to engage in cost-shifting rather than focusing on efficiency and on an optimal mix of services. In more recent times, cost-shifting has become so acute that it has prompted the Commonwealth to take its extent into account when determining future funding arrangements to the states in the Medicare Agreements.[3]

In recognition of the significant problems associated with Commonwealth–state arrangements, a major structural reform process was announced in April 1995 by the Council of Australian Governments (COAG). It was agreed to set up an agenda of major reform to realign the fundamental responsibilities in financing, planning, organising and managing of health and community services. On the agenda were proposals to explore ways of clarifying the funding and service responsibilities across all levels of government, to integrate better the array of health service programs and to eliminate duplication and cost-shifting. A consequence has been the implementation of a number of pilot studies known as 'coordinated care' trials which are designed to test alternative funding and delivery modalities for patients with on-going and complex needs (COAG 1995, 1996).[4] Given the chronic fragility of federal–state cooperation, it is unclear whether the COAG reform agenda will be able to overcome any of the major problems associated with the poorly structured federal arrangements (Healthcover 1997).

Structural financial instability

Approximately 32 per cent of the population hold some form of private insurance cover in addition to the universal coverage Medicare provides (PHIAC 1997). Private insurance offers coverage against accommodation costs of private patients in both public and private hospitals, benefits equal to 25 per cent of the 'gap' between Medicare benefits and scheduled fees for private medical services in hospitals, and cover for a wide range of ancillary services. Insurance funds are heavily regulated. They are required to keep their enrolments open and premiums community-rated. They are not permitted to cover any PBS-listed drugs or pay any medical benefits except the 25 per cent gap between benefits and scheduled fees for medical services provided to private patients in hospitals. Private insurance premiums contributed about 10.8 per cent of the total expenditure on health care in Australia in 1994/95 (AIHW 1997).

The introduction of Medicare resulted in an anticipated initial drop in the proportion of the population with private insurance, from 63.7 per cent in 1983 to 50 per cent in 1984 (PHIAC 1993). But the decline continued and has accelerated in recent years, with the participation rate in December 1997 down to 31.6 per cent (PHIAC 1998). The substantial decline in membership—and the subsequent rise in the number of people relying solely on Medicare—in the context of fiscal stringency has placed significant pressure on the public hospital system. It has been argued that in the absence of significant government expenditure rises, the long-term stability of the present financing arrangements is questionable (Scotton & MacDonald 1993: 275).[5]

The structural instability in financing derives from the lack of an appropriate role for voluntary private insurance in the context of a universal publicly financed health care system (Scotton & MacDonald 1993). In a private voluntary insurance system, substantial regulatory controls are required to mitigate the socially undesirable effects of competitive outcomes and market failures. When a universal public program is introduced, private voluntary insurance contracts to a supplementary role as the social welfare function is taken over by the public system. The need for cross-subsidisation, community rating and other anticompetitive regulations is greatly reduced (Deeble 1982; Scotton & MacDonald 1993). However, the issue of redefining the appropriate role for voluntary private insurance was never resolved with the introduction in 1984 of a universal health insurance system. The regulatory environment remains a legacy of the time when Commonwealth involvement was complementary to private insurance (Industry Commission 1997; Senate Select Committee 1990).

The Industry Commission (1997), in its recent report on private health insurance, explicitly highlighted the fact that the inherent tension between policies supporting a universal system and those supporting community-rated voluntary insurance can be solved only by having regard to the overall setting of the health policy in Australia. Unless the role of voluntary private insurance within the framework of a publicly funded universal health insurance system is clearly defined, the longer-term problems associated with structural financial instability will remain. The health care financing debate and associated reform issues are discussed in detail in Chapters 9–11.

Australian health policy: at the crossroads

The Australian health care system exhibits many of the positive features characterising other publicly financed systems. It has been relatively successful in controlling overall health care expenditure as a proportion of GDP and in providing universal access to high-quality medically necessary care which is guaranteed with financing linked to ability to pay. Further, the universal insurance system, since its inception, has enjoyed strong electoral support from the general population. However, the Australian health care system is also characterised by many of the problems associated with microeconomic inefficiencies and fiscal pressures currently confronting publicly financed systems. History and the Constitution have configured the federal–state relationship in a way that compounds many of these problems. In addition, the issue of the appropriate role for voluntary private insurance within the framework of a universal publicly financed system remains unresolved, contributing to structural instability.

It is unfortunate that 15 years since the introduction of a universal insurance system such fundamental problems have been permitted to remain. Little progress has been made in developing a coherent systemwide policy. Instead, health policy has been a mixture of short-termism, political expediency, and a preoccupation with minimising budget outlays. Future health care policy in Australia must meet the challenges of determining the appropriate levels of funding, improving microeconomic efficiency, enhancing consumer representation and maintaining equity, as well as providing long-term structural stability. To achieve these aims requires that policy direction be comprehensive, coherent and capable of transcending conventional political boundaries. While significant lessons can be drawn from overseas experience, reforms to the Australian health system must reflect the historical, political and social characteristics peculiar to Australia.

J. R. G. Butler

3   *Health expenditure*

This chapter provides a discussion of health expenditure in Australia, and has both descriptive and analytical components. The descriptive component is concerned with the behaviour and composition of health expenditures across countries and over time. It does not attempt to explain why health expenditures, in terms of either their level or their composition, differ between countries or fluctuate within a country over time. The analytical component takes this next step, considering hypotheses and arguments which are concerned with causality and which seek to deepen our understanding of what happens and why it happens. Ultimately, both components are necessary inputs in the formulation and implementation of informed health policy.

The remainder of this chapter has two main sections, one dealing with international comparison of health expenditures and the other with health expenditure in Australia in more detail. Given the range of data now available on health systems in various countries, it would not be difficult to devote the entire chapter to a comparative study of health expenditures in different countries, or to a study of health expenditure in Australia. Consequently, only selected aspects of this material are considered here.

Before proceeding, it is worth emphasising that health expenditure is only one side of the health system coin (health outcome being the other). Economics is concerned with the costs of health systems and with the benefits those health systems generate for their populations. A complete economic appraisal of the relative efficiency of alternative health systems would then consider not only the resources used but the relative health levels achieved by those systems, the latter measured in terms of both quantity of life (or life-expectancy) and quality of life. Although a consideration of the health levels attained by various health systems is outside the scope of this chapter, it should be remembered that any discussion of health expenditure not dealing with health outcome is telling only half of a complex story.

International comparisons

Data limitations

International comparisons of health expenditures in Western, industrialised countries have in recent years been facilitated by the health
data compiled by the Organisation for Economic Cooperation and
Development (OECD). This organisation now provides statistical
information on the health care systems of 27 member countries.
However, before considering the OECD data on health expenditures,
a number of caveats need to be borne in mind.

First, the definition of the boundary of the health sector can differ
between countries. For example, the Australian data exclude expenditures on defence force and prison medical services, education of
health professionals outside health institutions, and school health
services. Differences also exist between countries in what is classified
as a 'health' or a 'welfare' institution. For example, the OECD warns
that the Canadian data appear to include a larger array of long-term
care institutions than those of several other countries.

Second, even for institutions that appear to be similar between
countries, important differences can exist. For example, in recognition of the fact that long-stay patients are sometimes accommodated
in acute care hospitals, the OECD data include two measures of
average length of stay—one for inpatient care and the other for acute
care. However, for Japan the average length of stay in acute care
institutions is not available, while the average length of stay in
inpatient institutions in 1992 was 47.9 days. This compares with a
figure of 10.0 days for the same institutions in Australia, and suggests
that inpatient care institutions in the two countries may be
performing different roles.

Third, health expenditure data often exclude so-called 'tax
expenditures' which arise when governments subsidise health care by
allowing expenditure on various health care goods and services to be
claimed as a tax deduction. In Australia in 1996/97, for example, net
medical expenses in excess of $1250 incurred by a taxpayer qualified
for a rebate of 20 per cent of the amount of the excess. These tax
concessions, which result in a loss of tax revenue, amount to indirect
expenditure on health care goods and services but are generally not
included with direct expenditure in measuring health expenditure in
a country.

Fourth, even within an agreed set of definitions, cross-country
variations may reflect differences in the veracity of the data. For
example, the OECD reports that the figures for GDP in Belgium,
Greece and Portugal may be underestimates of actual GDP by as

much as 20 per cent or more. This has serious implications for any analysis relying on health expenditure related to GDP estimates for these countries.

Finally, because of national accounting limitations and measurement problems, the OECD data on health expenditure exclude non-monetary costs incurred in consuming health care. These costs take the form of time and travel costs to obtain health services, and the cost of time spent on waiting lists. In health care systems that rely more heavily on non-price rationing, time spent on waiting lists may constitute an important, unmeasured component of cost.[1]

Health expenditure and GDP

Despite these caveats, Table 3.1 presents the OECD estimates of total health expenditure as a proportion of GDP for 24 of the countries currently included in the data.[2] The ratio of total health expenditure to GDP is perhaps the single most commonly employed measure of the size of a country's health sector. This ratio, however, is subject to year-to-year fluctuation because of cyclical variations in GDP as well as fluctuations in total health expenditure. To minimise the influence of short-term variation in GDP, the data in Table 3.1 are presented in the form of five-year averages for the period 1960–1994.

Before considering the situation in any individual countries, two salient features of these data should be highlighted. First, without exception, the size of the health sector relative to GDP has grown in every country over the last 35 years. The mean proportion of GDP devoted to health across all countries grew from 5.0 per cent over 1960–1964 to 10.0 per cent in 1990–94; that is, on average, the size of the health sector relative to GDP has doubled since the early 1960s. Second, there is considerable variation in both the size and the growth of the health sector in different countries. In 1990–1994, the two ends of the spectrum with respect to size were Turkey (3.5 per cent of GDP) and the USA (13.8 per cent). Confining attention to countries for which estimates are available for 1960–1964 and 1990–94, Greece recorded the lowest growth in the size of the health sector (2.0 percentage points) and the USA the highest (8.3 percentage points).

Why has the health sector grown in these countries? Generally, the factors underlying this trend can be classed as either demand-side factors or supply-side factors. Considering first the demand side (which has received greater attention), a number of analyses employing earlier OECD data have consistently found evidence of a significant, positive association between per-capita expenditures on

Table 3.1 Total health expenditure as a proportion of gross domestic product, five-year averages for OECD countries, 1960–95[a]

Country	1960–1964	1965–1969	1970–1974	1975–1979	1980–1984	1985–1989	1990–1994	Change 1960–1964 to 1990–1994[b]
Australia	5.0	5.1	6.0	7.6	7.5	7.8	8.5	3.5
Austria	4.7	5.2	5.5	7.6	8.0	8.3	9.0	4.3
Belgium	3.5	4.0	4.4	6.5	7.3	7.6	8.1	4.6
Canada	5.8	6.3	7.0	7.2	8.1	8.6	9.9	4.1
Denmark	4.3	5.7	6.5	6.6	6.7	6.3	6.6	2.3
Finland	4.2	5.5	5.8	6.7	6.8	7.4	8.7	4.5
France	4.7	5.5	6.1	7.2	8.1	8.5	9.4	4.7
Germany	4.9	5.6	6.6	8.1	8.6	8.6	9.1	4.2
Greece	2.6	3.0	3.3	3.5	3.7	4.2	4.6	2.0
Iceland	3.5	4.7	5.2	6.0	6.9	8.1	8.1	4.6
Ireland	3.8	4.7	6.4	7.6	8.1	7.3	7.3	3.4
Italy	3.7	4.7	5.7	5.9	6.9	7.3	8.4	4.7
Japan	n.a.	n.a.	4.6	5.7	6.6	6.5	6.4	1.8
Luxembourg	n.a.	n.a.	3.9	5.6	6.2	6.2	6.1	2.2
Netherlands	4.1	4.9	6.6	7.5	8.1	8.1	8.7	4.7
New-Zealand[c]	4.3	5.1	5.5	6.8	6.5	6.8	7.5	3.2
Norway	3.4	3.9	5.3	6.5	6.1	6.6	7.2	3.8
Portugal	n.a.	n.a.	3.6	5.2	6.0	6.8	7.2	3.7
Spain	1.9	3.0	4.3	5.4	5.8	6.0	7.2	5.3
Sweden	5.0	6.4	7.4	8.7	9.5	8.6	8.0	3.0
Switzerland	3.5	4.8	5.7	7.2	7.5	8.3	9.2	5.7
Turkey	n.a.	n.a.	2.5	3.1	3.1	2.8	3.5	1.0
United Kingdom	4.0	4.3	4.8	5.4	5.9	5.8	6.7	2.7
United States	5.5	6.3	7.5	8.5	10.0	11.3	13.8	8.3
Average—all countries	5.0	5.8	6.3	7.2	8.2	8.8	10.0	5.0
Average—all countries excluding USA	4.5	5.6	5.4	6.4	7.0	7.2	7.7	3.2

Notes: n.a. = not available
[a] The Czech Republic, Hungary and Mexico have been excluded because of lack of data for most or all of this time period. Data for 1993 are semi-final, and for 1994 are preliminary estimates.
[b] For Japan, Luxembourg, Portugal and Turkey, change is from the most recent five-year average available.
[c] For 1960–64 and 1965–69, proportions are based on data for 1960, 1968 and 1969 only.

Source: OECD (1996).

health and per-capita GDP (e.g. Newhouse 1977, 1987; OECD 1987; Gerdtham et al. 1991, 1992). Furthermore, these studies commonly found that any given percentage rise in per-capita GDP was associated with a larger percentage rise in per-capita health expenditure, implying that the size of the health sector grows more than proportionately to GDP. In other words, wealthier countries tend to devote a greater proportion of their GDP to health than poorer countries. The upshot of these analyses, which are based on aggregate, national level data, is that health care appears to be a luxury good—that is, a good for which the income elasticity of demand exceeds unity.[3,4]

This same result characterises the more recent data presented in Table 3.1. To investigate this issue, the five-year average share of total health expenditure in GDP for each country for 1990–1994 was used as the dependent variable in a bivariate regression analysis in which average per-capita GDP for each country for this period (converted to US dollars using purchasing power parities) was the explanatory variable.[5] The data used in this analysis are shown in Figure 3.1, which also contains a plot of the estimated relationship between the proportion of GDP accounted for by expenditures on health and per-capita GDP (the solid line). The results indicate a statistically significant, positive association between the two variables, with 64 per cent of the variation in the size of the health sector relative to GDP between the 23 countries being 'explained' by differences in per-capita GDP (adjusted R-squared = 0.64). The analysis suggests that an increase in per-capita GDP of US$1000 leads to a growth in the health sector share in GDP of around 0.3 percentage points.[6]

Turning to Australia's position, the size of the health sector has grown from 5.0 per cent of GDP in the early 1960s to 8.5 per cent in the 1990s (see Table 3.1). Using the estimated relationship between total health expenditure as a proportion of GDP and per-capita GDP discussed above, the predicted size of the health sector in 1990–1994 is 8.1 per cent of GDP, suggesting that the Australian experience is in conformity with what would be expected for a country with our level of per-capita income (see Figure 3.1).

Another explanation of the growth in the size of the health sector relies on supply-side considerations. Inspired by the work of Baumol (1967) and Fuchs (1968), this explanation is based on the relatively poor growth in productivity in service industries in general compared with tangible goods industries. For personal services in particular (such as many health services), growth in labour productivity has been impeded by the difficulty of substituting capital for labour in the provision of such services. Fuchs (1968) found that, over the

Figure 3.1 **Relationship between observed and predicted ratio of total health expenditure to GDP and GDP per capita, 23 OECD countries, 1990–94**

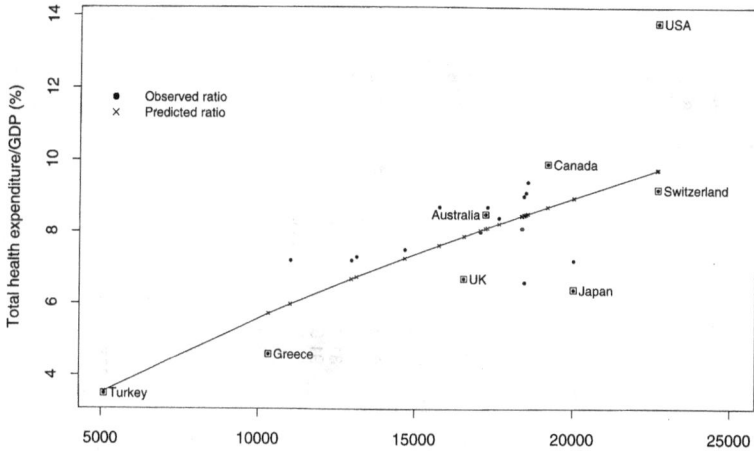

period 1929–1965 in the USA, the annual growth in labour productivity in goods industries of 2.2 per cent was double that in the service industries (1.1 per cent), and that this productivity differential was more important than either growing incomes or other demand factors in explaining the growing importance of service sector employment in the US economy. The productivity differential also implies that the unit costs of production of personal services will rise more rapidly than the unit costs of tangible goods, leading to growing shares of government budgets being devoted to services such as health and education. Baumol and Blinder (1985: 545) subsequently characterised this problem as 'the cost disease of the personal services'. Apart from a study by Haig (1975) of the service industry generally, which overall supported Fuchs' results, there has been no investigation of the importance of supply-side factors in explaining the growth of the health sector in Australia.

Publicly financed health expenditure

The extent to which health expenditures have been financed through the public sector in the OECD countries since 1960 is shown in Table 3.2. As with Table 3.1, the data are expressed as five-year averages. In the period 1990–1994, 58.9 per cent of all health expenditure in the OECD countries was publicly financed. If the USA is excluded from this average, the proportion is 76.0 per cent. There is

Table 3.2 Publicly-financed health expenditure as a proportion of total health expenditure, five-year averages for OECD countries, 1960–94[a]

Country	1960–1964	1965–1969	1970–1974	1975–1979	1980–1984	1985–1989	1990–1994	Change 1960–1964 to 1990–1994[b]
Australia	52.0	52.8	60.2	64.5	65.9	69.8	67.9	15.9
Austria	67.2	67.0	64.0	69.4	67.7	66.7	65.1	-2.2
Belgium	64.8	79.1	84.7	82.2	83.2	84.8	88.5	23.7
Canada[c]	42.7	52.1	73.5	76.0	75.6	74.7	73.6	30.9
Denmark	86.3	86.0	83.6	86.1	85.0	84.1	82.9	-3.3
Finland	57.5	70.7	75.1	78.3	79.2	79.4	78.8	21.3
France	64.7	68.7	75.3	77.3	78.4	75.8	75.4	10.7
Germany	68.3	73.2	73.8	75.9	74.2	73.5	73.2	4.8
Greece[d]	60.3	60.8	57.8	71.3	87.2	82.3	77.4	17.1
Iceland	82.6	82.4	84.6	89.0	88.3	86.9	85.3	2.7
Ireland	76.8	75.2	78.0	80.1	80.7	74.6	76.7	-0.1
Italy	87.7	87.5	88.6	87.0	78.7	77.1	75.0	-12.7
Japan	62.8	60.2	69.8	74.2	71.8	73.6	77.8	15.0
Luxembourg[d]	n.a.	n.a.	n.a.	92.1	91.2	93.9	98.8	6.7
Netherlands	52.0	78.1	73.8	74.6	75.4	67.8	76.0	24.0
New-Zealand[e]	80.6	77.2	83.7	86.3	86.1	85.3	78.0	-2.6
Norway	78.9	86.2	93.6	97.2	97.8	96.3	94.3	15.3
Portugal	n.a.	n.a.	60.9	67.1	56.2	52.3	55.6	-5.3
Spain	52.0	59.3	70.3	77.3	81.3	79.4	78.7	26.7
Sweden	75.4	82.2	87.3	91.1	91.8	89.7	86.1	10.6
Switzerland	61.7	62.3	65.5	67.9	68.2	66.6	70.3	8.6
Turkey[f]	n.a.	n.a.	37.9	24.4	38.5	38.7	55.4	17.5
United Kingdom	83.9	86.6	88.0	90.2	87.9	84.6	84.3	0.3
United States	25.2	34.4	39.1	41.7	41.1	40.8	42.8	17.6
Average—all countries	46.1	53.0	58.5	61.3	60.3	58.3	58.9	12.8
Average—all countries excluding USA	69.8	72.5	75.9	77.7	76.6	75.4	76.0	6.1

Notes: n.a. = not available

[a] The Czech Republic, Hungary and Mexico have been excluded because lack of data for most or all of this time period.
[b] For Luxembourg, Portugal and Turkey, change is from the most recent five-year average available.
[c] For 1960–64 and 1965–69, proportions are based on data for 1960 and 1965 only.
[d] Relevant data are unavailable for 1994.
[e] For 1960–64 and 1965–69, proportions are based on data for 1960, 1968, and 1969 only.
[f] Relevant data are unavailable for 1973, 1974, 1976, 1981, 1982 and 1983.

Source: OECD (1996).

also considerable cross-country variation in the relative importance of public financing of health, with public financing in 1990–1994 being least important in the USA (42.8 per cent) and most important in Norway (94.3 per cent).[8]

Two points about these data warrant emphasis. First, over the 35-year period 1960–1994 (or, for Japan, Luxembourg, Portugal and Turkey, from the most recent year for which data are available until 1994), publicly financed health expenditures as a proportion of total health expenditures rose in 18 out of the 24 countries shown in Table 3.2. Thus, in three-quarters of the OECD countries (including Australia), public sector financing of health care was greater at the end of this time period than at the beginning. Second, much of the growth in the relative importance of public sector financing took place in the 1960s and 70s. The average share of public financing in total health expenditure for all OECD countries grew from 46.1 per cent in 1960–1964 to 61.3 per cent in 1975–79 (or, excluding the USA, from 69.8 per cent to 77.7 per cent). Thereafter, public financing fell in relative terms for the next 10 years (1980–1984 and 1985–89), with a slight upturn in the average in 1990-94.

It is interesting to note that over the whole period 1960–1994 the share of total health expenditure in Australia that was publicly financed was low compared with other OECD countries. In many of the five-year periods shown in Table 3.2, Australia ranks among the five countries with the lowest publicly financed share of total health expenditure or, conversely, among the five countries with the highest privately financed share of total health expenditure. Particularly for the earlier years, however, it should be noted that these data exclude tax expenditures. Such expenditures were an important source of funds for health care in Australia up to the mid-1970s (see below).

The growing relative importance of publicly financed health care in the 1960s and 70s reflected a tendency in a number of countries to break the nexus between willingness/ability to pay and the demand for health care, and to pursue universal health insurance coverage for all citizens. The public sector, through the taxation and expenditure functions of government budgets, provides the vehicle whereby individuals' entitlements to health care can be divorced from their capacity to pay for such care. As a result, whereas seven out of 24 OECD countries attained coverage of 100 per cent of their populations against some level of health care costs in 1960, by 1985 this had risen to 16 countries. Since then, no additional countries have expanded the proportion of their population covered to 100 per cent. Another indicator of this expanded coverage is the mean level of coverage which, over 1960–1985, grew from 76 per cent to 96 per cent but has remained unchanged since then (OECD 1996).

The stagnation or decline in the publicly financed share of health expenditure in a number of countries since 1985 might indicate that those countries have now reached an upper bound on the extent to which their citizens are prepared to have their fiscs finance health care. Although public health insurance programs can sever the link between an individual's capacity to pay and the health care he/she receives, they cannot avoid making decisions as to the level of cover to be provided, and hence the co-payment to be imposed on consumers, and the range of services to be covered. With the range of services potentially covered growing rapidly in accordance with advances in medical technology, fiscs have increasingly been confronted with difficult decisions concerning the inclusion of new medical technologies and drugs on their benefit schedules and formularies. This has given rise to concern about growing rationing of services funded through public health insurance programs, and an explosion of interest in the economic evaluation of new drugs and medical services to ensure that the drugs and services included in these programs are 'cost-effective'.[9]

Two particular features of technological change in medicine underlie these developments. First, in contrast to technological change in a number of other industries, technological change in medicine generally appears to have had a strong cost-increasing effect (Weisbrod 1991). Second, the growing insurance coverage of health care services and consequent reduction in patients' out-of-pocket expenses may have provided a stimulus to R&D in medicine. In an environment where medical practitioners prescribe tests, investigations, drugs and other treatments on behalf of their patients, where the out-of-pocket expense to the patient is minimal or zero, and where third-party payers (government or private insurers) tended to be passive funders of those services provided or ordered by medical practitioners, the perspective of the cost–benefit analysis tends to be that of the medical practitioner/patient. There are obvious economic incentives for R&D in such an environment.

Developments in biotechnology, genetics, robotics and other areas of relevance to medicine suggest that technological change continues apace (Wyke 1997). Consequently, public health insurance agencies will continue to be confronted with difficult decisions concerning the services to be included in their programs and can be expected to become less passive in their role as third-party payers in the future. To the extent that governments are approaching the upper bound of public financing of health care in their jurisdictions, further stagnation or decline in the publicly financed share of total health expenditures can be anticipated.

Another issue concerning publicly financed expenditures on

health is the possible relationship between the share of publicly financed health expenditure in total health expenditure and the proportion of GDP devoted to health. Gerdtham et al. (1992) found that per-capita health expenditure was negatively related to the ratio of publicly financed health expenditure to total health expenditure. With per-capita GDP held constant, this implies that greater public sector financing of health care reduces the proportion of GDP devoted to health. This relationship was also found in an earlier study by Gerdtham et al. (1991), which used OECD data for several years.[10]

These results should be treated with considerable caution. The effect of the publicly financed share of health expenditure on the size of the health sector has not been studied extensively, and an earlier study by Leu (1986) found exactly the opposite effect. Gerdtham et al. (1991: 308) actually decline to draw any 'firm empirical conclusions' from their study on this issue, citing a lack of good data and measurement problems as reasons for their position.

Evidently, further empirical studies are required. The relationship between the publicly financed share of total health expenditures and the size of the health sector discussed above implies that, with a given level of GDP per capita, increasing publicly financed health expenditure by one dollar results in privately financed health expenditure falling by more than one dollar. In other words, an additional dollar of publicly financed health expenditure displaces, or 'crowds out', more than one dollar of privately financed health expenditure. Consequently, total health expenditure falls and the size of the health sector as a proportion of GDP shrinks.

Is it plausible that publicly financed health expenditures more than completely crowd out privately financed health expenditures? Perhaps, if greater public financing of health care also involves a greater degree of monopsonistic power in the markets for health care services (one or a few levels of government may be able to obtain lower prices for medical services and drugs than a multiplicity of private individuals and organisations). Another explanation may be that there are systematic differences between the two sectors in forms of remuneration for medical practitioners, with public financing being associated with a greater reliance on salary or capitation payment and private financing relying more heavily on fee-for-service payment. Different forms of remuneration may also be associated with different degrees of supplier-induced demand. Further empirical research will perhaps enlighten these issues.[11]

Health expenditure in Australia

Tax expenditure

Although the OECD data do include some information on tax expenditures on health in member countries, there are many gaps, with estimates being unavailable for most of the countries for most years. A consistent series has, however, been compiled for Australia for a number of years in the period 1960/61–1987/88 by Butler and Smith (1992). The authors integrated this series into the health expenditure data for Australia, providing revised estimates of publicly financed health expenditures for this time period. A comparison with the OECD data of the revised proportions of recurrent health expenditure that have been publicly financed is provided in Figure 3.2.[12]

It is immediately apparent that tax expenditure played an important role in health care financing in Australia from the early 1960s through to the mid-1970s. With tax expenditure included, the publicly financed share of total health expenditure rises to over 60 per cent of total health expenditure over this period, compared with a share in the range of 45–60 per cent based on the OECD data excluding tax expenditures. The reason for this is, of course, the heavy reliance placed on tax deductions for medical expenses and private health insurance contributions over the period 1960/61–1974/75.

Figure 3.2 **Publicly-financed recurrent health expenditures as a proportion of total recurrent health expenditures, with and without tax expenditures, Australia, 1960/61–1987/88**

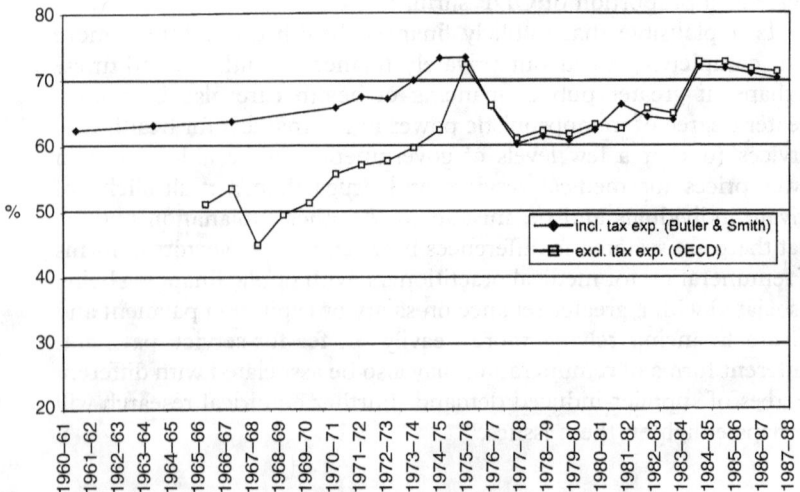

Source: Butler and Smith (1992); OECD (1996).

50

An effect of excluding tax expenditure from the health expenditure series is to overstate the rise in the importance of public sector financing in health care in Australia in 1975/76 consequent to the introduction of Medibank. While that scheme did result in some growth in public sector financing of health care, the comparison in Figure 3.3 suggests that to a significant degree there was a substitution of direct expenditure for tax expenditure, with tax deductions and tax rebates becoming much less significant as a source of health care expenditure after that time.

Sources of funds

Broadly, health expenditures are funded either by the public or the private sector. Within the public sector funds are provided by the Commonwealth, state and local governments. Within the private sector funds are provided by private health insurance organisations, individuals, and other sources such as workers' compensation and motor vehicle third party insurance. Table 3.3 presents data on the sources of funds for recurrent health expenditures in Australia for the period 1960/61–1995/96 (data for some years in this series are unavailable).

The importance of tax expenditure in Australia from 1960/61 through to 1974/75 is highlighted above. Also, before 1974/75 a disaggregation of funds sourced from the private sector according to whether such funds were provided by private health insurers, individuals or other private sources is unavailable (see Table 3.3). In discussing sources of funds for health, therefore, attention will be confined to the period from 1974/75 onwards. The relative importance of the various sources of funds over the period 1974/75–1995/96 is illustrated graphically in Figure 3.3.

The importance of the public sector in health care financing in Australia has been noted in this chapter (see Table 3.2). Within the public sector, the Commonwealth government has generally been a more important source of funds for health than state and local governments over the past two decades (see Figure 3.3). The exception to this occurred in 1981/82, when the Commonwealth's share of funding for recurrent health expenditure dropped to less than 30 per cent while the state/local government share rose to 35 per cent. This reflects a change in the intergovernmental funding arrangements in that year, with the effective absorption of the Commonwealth's specific-purpose payments for health into general revenue grants to the states.[13]

The extent of Commonwealth funding for health is significant in view of the fact that, in the Australian federal system of government,

Table 3.3 Sources of funds for recurrent health expenditure, Australia, selected years, 1960/61–1994/95[a]
(A$m, current prices)

	Government			Private				TOTAL[b]
	C'wealth	State/Local	Total	Private health insurance	Individuals	Other[c]	Total	
1960–61	191	161	352	70	247	24	340	692
1961–62								
1962–63								
1963–64	253	193	445	96	291	30	418	863
1964–65								
1965–66			528				504	1 032
1966–67	337	250	587	146	368	39	552	1 139
1967–68			561				689	1 250
1968–69			691				704	1 395
1969–70			809				768	1 577
1970–71	537	439	976				815	1 791
1971–72	658	511	1 169				922	2 091
1972–73	754	594	1 348				1 034	2 382
1973–74	892	796	1 688				1 190	2 878
1974–75	1 159	1 196	2 355	569	812	102	1 483	3 838
1975–76	2 494	1 152	3 646	412	908	126	1 446	5 092
1976–77	2 526	1 318	3 844	887	1 043	127	2 057	5 901
1977–78	2 564	1 494	4 058	1 438	1 068	198	2 704	6 762
1978–79	2 851	1 708	4 559	1 378	1 286	239	2 902	7 462
1979–80	3 109	1 918	5 027	1 535	1 432	303	3 271	8 297
1980–81	3 595	2 274	5 869	1 593	1 670	324	3 587	9 457
1981–82	2 921	3 878	6 800	2 114	1 784	351	4 249	11 049
1982–83	4 448	3 003	7 451	2 666	1 805	514	4 985	12 436
1983–84	5 612	3 316	8 929	2 367	2 196	504	5 067	13 996
1984–85	7 533	3 514	11 048	1 456	2 323	571	4 349	15 397
1985–86	8 350	3 975	12 325	1 767	2 665	415	4 847	17 172

Table 3.3 (continued)

	Government			Private				TOTAL[b]
	C'wealth	State/Local	Total	Private health insurance	Individuals	Other[c]	Total	
1986–87	9 170	4 646	13 817	2 178	3 012	521	5 711	19 528
1987–88	10 029	5 150	15 180	2 537	3 389	464	6 389	21 569
1988–89	10 949	5 747	16 696	2 783	3 987	809	7 580	24 275
1989–90	11 920	6 355	18 275	3 128	4 553	979	8 660	26 935
1990–91	12 887	6 709	19 597	3 512	5 227	1 010	9 749	29 346
1991–92	13 859	6 967	20 826	3 793	5 771	912	10 475	31 301
1992–93	14 996	6 991	21 987	3 979	5 893	967	10 839	32 825
1993–94	16 373	6 619	22 993	4 075	6 002	1 150	11 228	34 221
1994–95	17 321	7 152	24 473	4 201	6 594	1 324	12 119	36 591
1995–96	18 871	9 369	28 241				13 501	41 742

Notes:
[a] An empty cell in this Table indicates that the relevant datum is not available. For 1995–96, expenditures by the Commonwealth government and private sector include adjustments for tax expenditures.
[b] Differences between sums of components and totals due to rounding. For 1989/90, sum of components ($26 935m) differs from sum published in source document ($26 908m). Sum of private sector components ($8660m) also differs from sum published in source document ($8633m).
[c] 'Other' private includes payments made under Workers' Compensation and Motor Vehicle Third Party insurance, and contributions by various charitable organisations.

Sources:
1960–61, 1963–64 and 1966–67: Deeble (1970, Table 3.10)
1965–66, 1967–68 to 1969–70: OECD (1966)
1970–71 to 1973–74: AIH (1988, Table 3.01)
1974–75: Commonwealth Department of Health (1981, Appendix D, Table D1)
1975–76 to 1981–82: AIH (1988, Appendix H, Tables H.1–H.7)
1982–83 and 1983–84: AIHW (1992, Tables 9, 10)
1984–85: AIHW (1993, Table 9)
1985–86: AIHW (1994, Table 8)
1986–87 to 1988–89: AIHW (1995, Tables 10–12)
1989–90 to 1995–96: AIHW (1997a, Tables 5 and 12–17)

**Figure 3.3   Sources of funds for recurrent health expenditures,
Australia, 1974/75–1995/96 (%)**

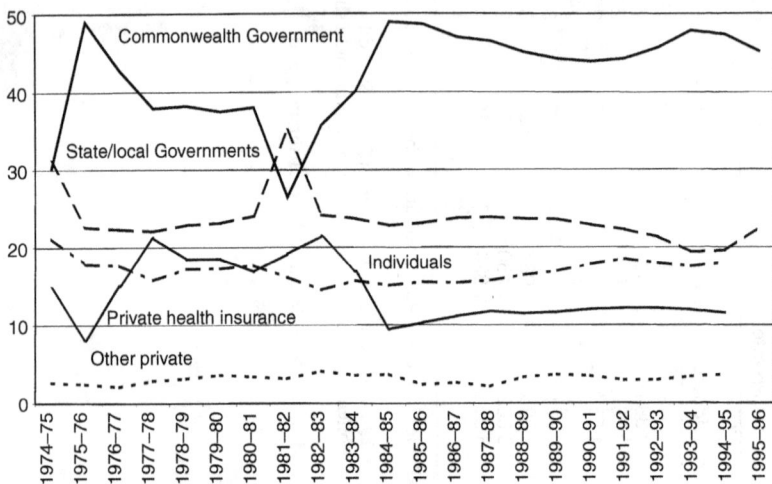

Source: Butler and Smith (1992); OECD (1996).

constitutional responsibility for the provision (as opposed to the
financing) of health services by the public sector lies with the states.
This undoubtedly explains why the vast bulk of publicly owned health
facilities (such as public hospitals) is owned by the states.[14] The
Commonwealth's role is confined for the most part to financing
health services rather than actually providing such services.

Within the private sector, the role of private health insurance as
a source of funds since 1974/75 is characterised by two main phases.
The first of these, from the late 1970s through the early 1980s, exhibited a more prominent role for private health insurance and followed
the termination of the original Medibank program by the Fraser
government. Over these years private health insurance funded around
17–22 per cent of recurrent health expenditures in Australia. The
second phase, which extended from the introduction of the Medicare
national health insurance scheme early in 1984 to 1994/95, exhibited
a less prominent role for private health insurance, its share being in
the range 9.5–12 per cent.

Of interest also is the share of recurrent health expenditure
contributed by individuals, as this indicates the extent of out-of-
pocket expenses met by individuals in purchasing health care services.
Since 1975/76 such out-of-pocket expenses have amounted to 14.5–
18.5 per cent of recurrent health expenditure. Three aspects of this
share warrant comment. First, it is considerably lower than the share
of recurrent health expenditure borne by individuals in the 1960s of

around 33 per cent (see Table 3.3). Second, it is currently greater than the share of health expenditure borne by private health insurance. Finally, since 1984/85 (the first full financial year after the introduction of Medicare), it has risen from 15.1–18.0 per cent in 1994/95.

To translate these data into per-capita terms, in 1994/95 recurrent health expenditure per head of population in Australia amounted to $2027 (using the ABS estimated population as at 30 June 1995 of 18 053 989). Of this, $1356 was sourced from government ($959 from the Commonwealth and $396 from the states/territories). Of the $671 sourced from the private sector, $365 was borne by individuals as out-of-pocket expenses and $233 was contributed by health insurance funds.

A disaggregation of the sources of funds for recurrent health expenditure by area of expenditure for 1994/95 is presented in Table 3.4. The major areas of expenditure by the Commonwealth are for private medical services funded through Medicare and through the Department of Veterans' Affairs ($6086m), hospitals ($5349m) and subsidies for pharmaceuticals prescribed under the Pharmaceutical Benefits Scheme (PBS) ($2086m). Together, these three areas account for nearly 80 per cent of recurrent health expenditures by the Commonwealth. As already mentioned, the Commonwealth government owns few health facilities. Commonwealth expenditure on hospitals is accounted for mainly by the Hospital Funding Grants to the states for their public hospitals. These Grants are made under the Medicare Agreements between the Commonwealth and the states, under which the states have agreed (among other things) to treat public patients at no charge.[15] In 1997/98 the Hospital Funding Grants are estimated to amount to $4103 million (Commonwealth of Australia 1997, table 11). These grants are block grants, or lump sum grants, with the states contributing the additional funds necessary to meet the costs of their public hospitals.

The main expenditure areas for state/local governments are hospitals ($4605m) and community and public health programs ($1312m), which together account for 83 per cent of state/local recurrent expenditure on health. Private health insurance funding is primarily for hospital treatment ($2440m), although a significant amount of funding from this source is also used for non-institutional health services ($1674m). For individuals, the main out-of-pocket expenses are incurred for pharmaceuticals that do not attract a subsidy under the PBS ($1630m), dental services ($1143m), other professional services ($901m) and the gap between the fees charged for medical services provided by registered private medical practitioners and the Medicare benefits provided by the Commonwealth

Table 3.4   Sources of funds for recurrent health expenditure by area of expenditure, Australia, 1994/95 (A$m, current prices)

Area of expenditure	Government sector			Private sector				Total expenditure
	C'wealth	State/ local	Total	Private health insurance	Individuals	Other	Total	
Recognised public hospitals	4 870	4 150	9 021	433	–	537	970	9 991
Private hospitals	240	–	240	2 004	434	168	2 606	2 846
Repatriation hospitals	233	–	233	3	–	–	3	237
Public psychiatric hospitals	6	454	460	–	–	2	2	462
Total hospitals	5 349	4 605	9 954	2 440	434	707	3 582	13 536
Nursing homes	1 860	243	2 102	–	641	–	641	2 743
Ambulance	43	238	281	87	123	32	241	523
Other institutional (nec)	128	–	128	–	–	–	–	128
Total institutional	**7 380**	**5 086**	**12 465**	**2 527**	**1 198**	**739**	**4 463**	**16 929**
Medical services	6 086	–	6 086	216	712	357	1 285	7 371
Dental services	105	141	246	546	1 143	8	1 697	1 943
Other professional services	171	–	171	205	901	166	1 272	1 443
Community and public health	507	1 312	1 819	1	–	3	4	1 823
Total pharmaceuticals	2 086	–	2 086	42	2 091	26	2 159	4 245
PBS benefit paid pharmaceuticals	2 086	–	2 086	–	461	–	461	2 547
All other pharmaceuticals	–	–	–	42	1 630	26	1 698	1 698
Aids and appliances	147	–	147	169	438	25	632	779
Administration	486	438	923	495	–	–	495	1 418
Research	340	176	516	–	111	–	111	627
Other non-institutional	14	–	14	–	–	–	–	14
Total non-institutional	**9 941**	**2 066**	**12 007**	**1 674**	**5 396**	**585**	**7 655**	**19 663**
TOTAL RECURRENT EXPENDITURE	**17 321**	**7 152**	**24 473**	**4 201**	**6 594**	**1 324**	**12 119**	**36 591**

Source: AIHW (1997a, Table 17).

($712m). These areas of expenditure account for two-thirds of all total out-of-pocket expenses for health services borne by individuals.

Uses of funds

Health expenditure is generally classified as being either for institutional or non-institutional purposes. The former encompasses expenditure on health care institutions such as hospitals and nursing homes while the latter includes expenditure on all other services such as medical and other professional services, pharmaceuticals, other outpatient services and research. A breakdown of recurrent health expenditures in Australia since 1960/61 in terms of these various uses is provided in Table 3.5, while the relative importance of the main areas of health expenditure is illustrated in Figure 3.4.

Considering first the overall division between institutional and non-institutional health expenditures, the relative importance of institutional expenditure grew from the mid-1960s to the early 1980s with a corresponding decline in the relative importance of non-institutional expenditure. Since then, however, that trend has reversed, and has now reverted to the situation of the early 1960s where the non-institutional expenditure share exceeds that of institutional expenditure.

The main changes in the expenditure patterns underlying these trends are evident in Figure 3.4, and can be summarised as follows:

- Up to the early 1980s, the share of pharmaceuticals in recurrent health expenditure declined markedly, from over 20 per cent to less than 10 per cent. From the late 1980s up to the present, the expenditure share of pharmaceuticals has been rising.
- Expenditure on medical services as a proportion of recurrent health expenditure has been rising steadily since the early 1960s, from 14.7 per cent in 1960/61 to 20.1 per cent in 1994/95.
- The expenditure shares of both public and private hospitals grew in the last half of the 1970s, with public and private hospital expenditure accounting for 36.1 per cent and 5.0 per cent of recurrent health expenditure respectively in 1977/78. Since the early 1980s the public hospital share has been falling, while the private hospital share stabilised for some years before beginning to rise noticeably in the late 1980s and early 1990s.
- The share of nursing homes in recurrent health expenditure grew from the early 1960s (4.4 per cent) through to the mid-1980s (9.0 per cent). Since then it has fallen to 7.5 per cent in 1994/95.

Table 3.5   Recurrent health expenditure by use of funds, Australia, 1960/61–1994/95[a] (A$m, current prices)

	Public hospitals[b]	Private hospitals	Nursing homes	Total institutional	Medical services	Pharma-ceuticals	Total non-institutional[c]	TOTAL
1960/61	262		30	310	102	154	382	692
1961/62								
1962/63								
1963/64	327		39	389	127	190	474	863
1964/65								
1965/66								
1966/67	425		62	514	177	241	625	1 139
1967/68								
1968/69								
1969/70								
1970/71								
1971/72								
1972/73								
1973/74								
1974/75	1 289	169	295	2 100	593	517	1 739	3 838
1975/76	1 774	230	379	2 795	919	560	2 297	5 092
1976/77	2 075	276	457	3 284	1 031	596	2 617	5 901
1977/78	2 443	335	516	3 846	1 152	631	2 916	6 762
1978/79	2 664	362	568	4 198	1 277	693	3 263	7 462
1979/80	2 949	394	646	4 678	1 461	694	3 620	8 297
1980/81	3 365	454	788	5 412	1 607	810	4 045	9 457
1981/82	3 851	533	969	6 276	1 873	950	4 773	11 049
1982/83	4 320	716	1 073	7 062	2 118	1 056	5 374	12 436
1983/84	4 651	803	1 257	7 760	2 416	1 221	6 236	13 996
1984/85	5 054	869	1 404	8 459	2 686	1 320	6 938	15 397
1985/86	5 518	969	1 546	9 221	3 091	1 491	7 951	17 172
1986/87	6 302	1 127	1 752	10 588	3 471	1 693	8 940	19 528
1987/88	6 908	1 216	1 905	11 579	3 887	1 864	9 990	21 569

Table 3.5 *(continued)*

	Public hospitals[b]	Private hospitals	Nursing homes	Total institutional	Medical services	Pharmaceuticals	Total non-institutional[c]	TOTAL
1988/89	7 675	1 335	2 085	12 626	4 351	2 164	11 649	24 275
1989/90	8 201	1 701	2 230	13 562	4 945	2 490	13 346	26 908
1990/91	8 663	2 008	2 529	14 751	5 491	2 782	14 595	29 346
1991/92	9 054	2 232	2 617	15 514	5 928	3 101	15 787	31 301
1992/93	9 276	2 384	2 648	15 862	6 422	3 432	16 963	32 825
1993/94	9 561	2 568	2 667	16 243	6 886	3 797	17 978	34 221
1994/95	9 991	2 846	2 743	16 929	7 371	4 245	19 663	36 591

Notes:

[a] An empty cell in this Table indicates that the relevant datum is not available.

[b] For 1960/61, 1963/64 and 1966/67, disaggregation by public and private hospitals is unavailable. Data for these years include all general and mental hospitals.

[c] For 1975/76 to 1981/82, expenditures on Health Promotion and Illness Prevention, Administration and Research have been added to 'Total Non-Institutional' as reported in source document to obtain statistics which are comparable with later years.

Source:
1960/61, 1963/64 and 1966/67: Deeble (1970, Table 3.10)
1974/75: Commonwealth Department of Health (1981, Appendix D, Table D1)
1975/76 to 1981/82: AIH (1988, Appendix H, Tables H.1–H.7)
1982/83 and 1983/84: AIHW (1992, Tables 9, 10)
1984/85: AIHW (1993, Table 9)
1985/86: AIHW (1994, Table 8)
1986/87 to 1988/89: AIHW (1995, Tables 10–12)
1989/90 to 1994/95: AIHW (1997a, Tables 12–17)

Figure 3.4   Uses of funds, recurrent health expenditures, Australia, 1960/61–1994/95 (%)

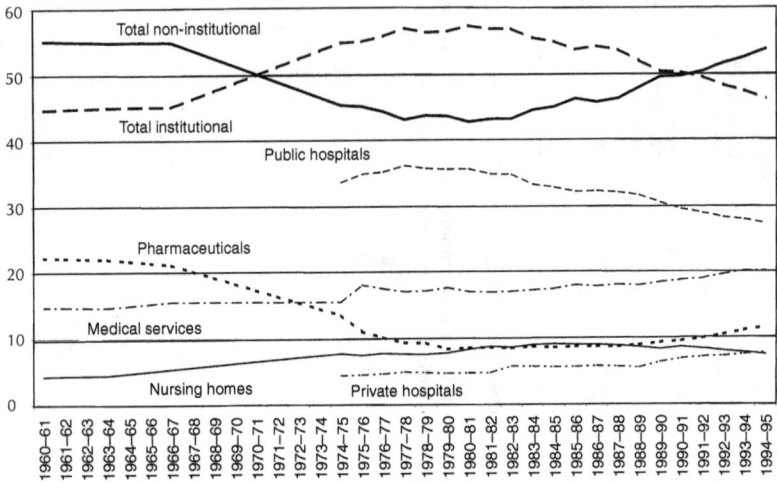

Source: Butler and Smith (1992); OECD (1996).

What factors are responsible for these changes in the expenditure shares of various health services in Australia?

Institutional features of financing arrangements

The declining share of pharmaceuticals in recurrent health expenditure through to the early 1980s is undoubtedly a reflection of the financing arrangements enshrined in the PBS, which bestowed monopsony power on the Commonwealth in negotiations with pharmaceutical companies concerning the price at which a drug was to be listed on the Scheme. Total expenditure on a good or service is calculated as 'price times quantity'. The PBS is open-ended in the sense that the Commonwealth cannot proscribe the quantities of drugs consumed in the 'price times quantity' equation. Although total expenditure on drugs in absolute terms has been rising in Australia for some time (see Table 3.5), the declining expenditure share of pharmaceuticals through to the early 1980s suggests that the monopsony power of the Common-wealth resulted in only moderate price rises, or even price reductions, for PBS-listed drugs over this period. Since the late 1980s, however, the introduction of new drugs combined with the open-ended nature of the Scheme have served to reverse this downward trend in the expen-diture share of pharmaceuticals.

The rising relative importance of medical services in recurrent health expenditure can also be ascribed, at least in part, to the open-ended nature of the subsidy schemes for these services. Although the Commonwealth does set the schedule fees and benefits for medical services, it cannot determine the quantities of medical services consumed by medical practitioners and their patients. The number of Medicare-funded medical services consumed per capita rose by nearly 50 per cent between 1984/85 and 1996/97, from 7.2 to 10.7 (CDHFS 1997, table A1).

In contrast to the open-ended subsidy schemes for pharmaceuticals and medical services, expenditure on public hospitals is budget-capped in that hospitals are provided with a budgetary allocation within which to operate, and their capacity to raise additional revenue is confined for the most part to the per-diem charge for those who choose to be treated as private patients (around $200 per day). This global budgeting arrangement confers greater power on governments to control total outlays on public hospitals than to control total outlays on pharmaceuticals and medical services. Hence, the rising expenditure share of pharmaceuticals and medical services and the declining expenditure share of public hospitals seen in Figure 3.4 is, in part, likely to be a reflection of these different financing arrangements.

For nursing homes, the declining expenditure share since 1984/85 indicates that the Aged Care Reform Strategy introduced around that time has had an impact. In 1985 there were 67 nursing home beds per 1000 persons aged 70 and over. By 1994 this had fallen to 52. This has been offset, at least to some extent, by a rise in the per-capita supply of hostel beds and in the availability of community care packages (AIHW 1996, section 5.5).

Another particular feature of health care financing arrangements in Australia is the division of responsibilities between Commonwealth and state governments and the consequent incentives for cost-shifting from state governments to the Commonwealth government. (This aspect is dealt with separately below.)

Technological change
Another factor likely to have exerted some influence on the changing expenditure shares is technological change in health care, which has resulted in reductions in the average lengths of stay in hospital, substitution of outpatient care for inpatient treatment for some conditions, and adoption of higher-cost pharmaceuticals in the management of various conditions.

The growth in day surgery is perhaps the most dramatic example of shortening lengths of hospital stays. In 1995/96 same-day separations accounted for 40 per cent of all acute separations from public hospitals, compared with 29 per cent in 1991/92 and 20 per cent in

61

1987/88. Overall, the average length of stay of acute patients in public hospitals fell from 6.9 days in 1985/86 to 4.6 days a decade later (AIHW 1996: 153, table 5.9; AIHW 1997b, table 3.1). An example of the substitution of outpatient care for inpatient treatment is provided by the introduction of the drug cimetidine in the management of peptic ulcers, obviating the need for surgery in many of these patients. These changes will have contributed to the declining share of public hospitals in recurrent health expenditure illustrated in Figure 3.4.

With respect to pharmaceutical expenditure, technological change is likely to have increased expenditure on drugs. This would be attributable to a range of new drugs such as angiotensin-converting enzyme (ACE) inhibitors, lipid-lowering agents and drugs used in the management of asthma gaining acceptance and replacing older, less expensive drugs on the PBS. This is not to suggest, of course, that such rises in expenditure are economically unjustified. In addition to providing improvements in quantity and/or quality of life, such innovations may reduce health care costs elsewhere in the system (as in the example of cimetidine). All such effects need to be considered in any economic appraisal of these newer agents.

Cost-shifting
Another factor that has contributed to the changing composition of health care expenditure in Australia is cost-shifting between the state and Commonwealth governments. Recall that, even though the Commonwealth contributes to the costs of states' public hospitals through the Hospital Funding Grants, these grants are block grants. Consequently, states must meet 100 per cent of the marginal cost of any additional services provided through their public hospitals. But they also reap 100 per cent of the cost savings that accrue from any reduction in service provision. This provides an economic incentive for states to substitute Commonwealth-funded services for services provided by their public hospitals, where possible. For example, services provided by private medical practitioners may be substituted for services provided in public hospital outpatient departments by referring patients to private practitioners for services such as pathology or imaging, or by simply closing the public hospital outpatient department altogether.

What evidence is there that cost-shifting of this type has occurred in Australia in recent times? Detailed quantitative evidence is not available, but some indication of the substitution of Commonwealth-funded services for state-funded services can be obtained from the data in Table 3.6, which provides information on the total number of Medicare-funded services for selected years between 1985/86 and

Table 3.6 Total and per capita numbers of services, Medicare-funded private medical services and non-admitted patient services in public hospitals, Australia, selected years

	Total number of services ('000)			Per capita number of services		
	Medicare-funded	Non-admitted patient services in public hospitals	Total	Medicare-funded	Non-admitted patient services in public hospitals	Total
1985/86	121 357	37 666	159 023	7.6	2.4	9.9
1987/88	134 839	43 711	178 550	8.2	2.6	10.8
1989/90	144 736	38 209	182 945	8.5	2.2	10.7
1991/92	156 579	30 676	187 255	9.0	1.8	10.7
1992/93	172 049	33 093	205 142	9.7	1.9	11.6
1993/94	180 226	30 562	210 788	10.1	1.7	11.8

Notes: Medicare-funded services are private medical services listed in the Medicare Benefits Schedule and subsidised by the Commonwealth government under the Medicare program, based on year of processing, and exclude MBS services funded by the Department of Veterans' Affairs. Non-admitted patient services in public hospitals refer to services provided by a functional unit of a public hospital to a patient who is not admitted as an inpatient.

Source: Medicare-funded services: Commonwealth Department of Health and Family Services (1997, Table A1)
Non-admitted patient services: AIHW (1996, Table 5.9)
Population: ABS population estimates as at 30 June for relevant years

1993/94, and on the total number of services provided by public hospitals to non-admitted patients in those same years.[16] These data are also shown in per-capita terms. Considering first the Medicare-funded services, both the total and the per-capita number of such services have increased over the time period shown, with per-capita consumption of medical services rising from 7.6 to 10.1 services per person between 1985/86 and 1993/94 (a rise of 2.5 services per person). However, the total number of public hospital services for non-admitted patients has, at least since 1987/88, shown a downward trend, with the per-capita consumption falling from 2.6 services per person in 1987/88 to 1.7 in 1993/94. When the two types of services are summed, the overall per-capita consumption of services actually declined between 1987/88 to 1991/92, from 10.8 to 10.7.

These data suggest that some cost-shifting from the states to the Commonwealth with regard to medical services has indeed taken place. To be sure, over the complete time period shown in Table 3.6, overall per-capita consumption of services did rise from 9.9 to 11.8, a rise of 1.9 services per person. However, this rise is about 25 per cent less than the rise in the per-capita consumption of Medicare-funded services alone (2.5 services per person), suggesting that substitution of Commonwealth- and state-funded services has taken place. And over the four-year period 1987/88–1991/92 the decline in the per-capita number of public hospital services for non-admitted patients was such that it more than offset the rise in per-capita consumption of Medicare-funded services. In short, the declining relative share of public hospitals, and the rising relative share of medical services, in recurrent health expenditure in the latter part of the 1980s and into the 1990s illustrated in Figure 3.4 is at least partly explicable by cost-shifting out of state-funded services in public hospitals into Commonwealth-funded medical services.

Private hospitals and private health insurance

A final area of expenditure that warrants attention is private hospitals and private health insurance. Although the private hospital share of recurrent health expenditure did rise slowly from the mid-1970s to the late 1980s, it has risen more rapidly since then, from 5.5 per cent in 1988/89 to 7.8 per cent in 1994/95. At first glance this might seem unexpected: the proportion of the Australian population covered by private health insurance has been declining since the introduction of Medicare, from 50.0 per cent covered by a hospital table at the end of June 1984 to 31.9 per cent at the end of June 1997 (PHIAC 1996, table 9; PHIAC 1997). Would not this decline in coverage lead one to expect the private hospital share in recurrent health expenditure to decline also?

One important reason why this has not occurred relates to the community rating requirement imposed on premiums for private health insurance in Australia. A community-rated premium is one that does not discriminate between individuals on the basis of their risk of becoming ill and requiring health care services. This is in contrast to a risk-rated premium, which would reflect such differences in risk. While community rating results in a uniform premium being charged by an insurer to all persons regardless of their risk, that premium is relatively high for lower-risk groups, and conversely for higher-risk groups. Lower-risk groups (which tend to comprise younger, healthier people) are then more likely to perceive private health insurance as a 'bad buy', while higher-risk groups (which tend to comprise older, sicker people) are more likely to perceive private health insurance as a 'good buy'. This results in private health insurance funds being left with an adverse selection of risks—that is, a clientele skewed towards the higher-risk groups. As lower-risk groups drop their insurance cover, the average level of risk of those retaining cover rises, resulting in a rise in the (community-rated) premium. This leads to more people predominantly from lower-risk groups dropping their cover, further rises in premiums, more people again mostly from lower-risk groups dropping their cover, and so on.

There is evidence to suggest that this problem has indeed characterised private health insurance in Australia over the past decade. Describing the problem as the 'vicious circle of falling membership', a recent Industry Commission report (1997: 179) on private health insurance found that:

> The age profile of the insured has been shifting away from the young (and healthy) and towards the old . . . For example, prior to the introduction of Medicare, about 70 per cent of the households with a head aged between 25 and 34 years were insured; that has now declined to about 30 per cent, representing a 60 per cent reduction in the membership ratio. In contrast, there appears to have been only a slight reduction in the coverage of older households.

If age-sex specific hospitalisation rates remain constant, adverse selection of this type will result in a higher overall hospitalisation rate among those remaining in the insured population. In Australia in 1995/96, the separation rate for private hospitals was 52.0 per 1000 population for persons aged less than 45 years, and 158.1 per 1000 population aged 45 years or over (AIHW 1997b, table 4.2, appendix table A1). Hence, any change in the age distribution of the insured population towards the over 45-year-old group will increase the separation rate in the insured population. However, if the absolute size of the insured population shrinks with the departure of the lower-risk clientele, the number of separations will fall even though the rate has risen.

Consider now the data in Table 3.7 relating to all private acute and psychiatric hospitals in Australia over the period 1991/92–1995/96. The average cost per separation for these hospitals has risen over this period. The number of insured separations in Table 3.7 is the number of separations where the patient had private health insurance,[17] while the insured population is the number of Australians covered by a hospital table with a private health insurer at the end of June each financial year. Note that the separation rate per 1000 persons in the insured population has also risen markedly over this five-year period, from 132.3 in 1991/92 to 184.3 in 1995/96. While part of this rise would be attributable to the adverse selection problem discussed above, it cannot all be attributed to this problem as the total number of insured separations has risen even though the size of the insured population has fallen. The combined effect of these changes has resulted in considerable rises in the total operating expenses for insured separations from private hospitals each year. It is these rises in total expenditures that explain at least a part of the rising share of private hospitals in recurrent health expenditure seen in Figure 3.4.[18]

Summary and conclusions

The size of the health sector, measured in terms of health expenditure relative to GDP, has grown in every OECD country since the early 1960s. On average, the proportion of GDP devoted to health has doubled over this time period. Perhaps one of the most consistent findings of studies examining this trend is the significant positive association between per-capita GDP and the per-capita health expenditure. Australia is no exception to this trend, with per-capita expenditure on health growing at an average annual rate of 10.3 per cent from 1960 through to 1995, compared with the corresponding per-capita GDP growth rate of 8.7 per cent.

Explanations for this trend may be found in both demand-side and supply-side considerations. Demand-side explanations interpret the association between the size of the health sector and income levels as being evidence that health is a luxury good with an income elasticity of demand greater than unity. As income grows, it is the resulting rise in demand for health that causes an increasing proportion of GDP to be devoted to health. Supply-side explanations argue that health expenditure as a proportion of GDP has been growing

Table 3.7 Private, acute and psychiatric hospitals[a], estimated expenditure and separations for privately insured population, Australia, 1991/92–1995/96 (current prices)

	Average recurrent cost per separation[b]		Total insured separations[c]		Insured population[d]		Separations per 1000 insured population		Total recurrent expenditure for insured separations[e]	
	($)	% change	No.	% change	No. ('000)	% change	No.	% change	($m)	% change
1991/92	1 689		947 638		7 164		132.3		1 601	
1992/93	1 703	0.8	997 452	5.3	6 967	–2.7	143.2	8.2	1 699	6.1
1993/94	1 780	4.5	1 021 187	2.4	6 632	–4.8	154.0	7.6	1 817	7.0
1994/95	1 859	4.4	1 098 046	7.5	6 304	–4.9	174.2	13.1	2 041	12.3
1995/96	1 944	4.6	1 133 195	3.2	6 149	–2.5	184.3	5.8	2 203	8.0

Notes:
a Excludes free-standing day hospital facilities.
b Averaged across all separations from private acute and psychiatric hospitals.
c The number of separations where the patient had private health insurance. For 1995/96, the ABS has reported data only for New South Wales, the ACT, Victoria, Queensland and Western Australia. The figure for this year shown in the Table has been obtained by extrapolating the per capita number of insured separations for these five States/Territories to Australia.
d The number of persons covered by private hospital insurance.
e Calculated as the average cost per separation multiplied by the total number of insured separations.

Source: Data on costs and separations: Australian Bureau of Statistics, *Private Hospitals Australia*, various years, Cat. No. 4390.0, ABS, Canberra. Data on insured population: PHIAC (1997).

because service industries in general, and the health sector in particular, have experienced lower rates of growth in labour productivity than the tangible goods industries. A consequence of this is that unit costs of production of services rise relative to those of tangible goods, and it is this change in relative costs that explains the rise in the share of GDP devoted to health. Only one Australian study has investigated this issue, and that study was concerned with service industries in general rather than the health sector in particular. It found that supply-side factors were more significant in explaining the growth in service industry employment in Australia.

Given the association between per-capita health expenditure and per-capita GDP, is it possible to infer that there is some 'correct' proportion of GDP that a country can be expected to devote to health, given its level of income? The answer to this is negative, for several reasons. First, the data on health expenditure generally include only direct expenditure on health, and do not include any allowance for time costs incurred by patients in receiving treatment, including time spent on queues. Hence, for any given level of income, countries that rely more heavily on non-price-rationing devices may attain lower levels of measured health expenditure but simultaneously impose greater unmeasured time costs on patients. Second, the size of the health sector alone does not convey any information about the health outcome that is attained for that expenditure. Even for countries with the same per-capita income and the same proportion of GDP devoted to health, health outcomes may differ because of differing levels of efficiency attained within their health sectors. Finally, although the empirical evidence suggests that wealthier countries devote a proportionately greater share of their income to health, this is not an economic 'law', nor does it necessarily have any particular normative significance. Citizens in different countries can choose, whether through market or political mechanisms, to commit larger or smaller proportions of their country's wealth to health. If citizens in one country have weaker preferences for health relative to other goods and services than another country, this is not particularly surprising and would not normally be a matter of concern to economists *qua* economists.

Another feature of a majority of OECD countries over the last 35 years has been the rise in the publicly financed share of health expenditure. Australia is in this majority, with the publicly financed share rising from 52.0 per cent over the five-year period 1960–1964 to 67.9 per cent in 1990–94. In Australia's case, however, this rise overstates the true rise in publicly financed share because of the exclusion of tax expenditure, which was a particularly important source of funds in the 1960s and 1970s. Although the publicly financed share of health expenditure in Australia has risen, in 1990–1994 it was ranked fifth-lowest among the OECD countries in terms of this share (or fifth-highest in terms of the privately financed share).

Most of the pronounced growth in the publicly financed share of health expenditure in many countries occurred in the 1960s and the 70s. The stagnation in the publicly financed share in the 1980s and 90s in the face of continuing and often cost-increasing technological change in medicine may indicate that many countries have reached an 'upper bound' on this share, with growing attention being devoted to economic appraisal of health interventions in an effort to ensure that only 'cost-effective' interventions are subsidised.

In Australia over the past two decades, the Commonwealth government has been the major source of funds for public financing, providing around two-thirds of all government funding for health. While the Commonwealth does not have constitutional responsibility for health service provision in the public sector, it has extended its influence through the payment of benefits to individuals for medical services and pharmaceuticals, and through the payment of grants to the states towards the cost of their public hospital systems. Interestingly, with respect to funds sourced from the private sector, individuals now bear a greater share of health expenditure as out-of-pocket expenses (18 per cent in 1994/95) than private health insurance (11.5 per cent).

Since the late 1970s Australia has experienced a significant decline in the proportion of recurrent health expenditure devoted to public hospitals. And since the mid-1980s there has also been a decline with respect to nursing homes. With regard to the latter, the Aged Care Reform Strategy goes some way towards explaining the decline. With regard to public hospitals, improvements in medical technology and the upsurge in day surgery have contributed to a reduction in the average length of stay in these institutions by one-third in 10 years (from 6.9 days in 1985/86 to 4.6 days in 1995/96). But cost-shifting from state-funded (at the margin) public hospital services to Commonwealth-funded medical services also appears to have played a role. Private hospitals have been consuming an increasing share of recurrent health expenditure since the late 1980s, notwithstanding the continuing decline in the proportion of the Australian population covered by private health insurance. Reasons for this include adverse selection resulting from community rating of private health insurance premiums, and a shift in the pattern of coverage within the insured group towards supplementary cover and consequently towards treatment in private rather than public hospitals. The structural imbalance between the public and private sectors in the market for hospital services is a continuing problem for health policy-makers.

What of the future? In the short to medium term it can be expected that insurance agencies, whether public or private, will become less passive in their role as funders of health care services. The continued flow of new products and services onto the health care market, some of which fare poorly in terms of cost-effectiveness, is likely to attract growing attention from third-party payers. These payers will subject such new products and services to closer scrutiny in terms of criteria such as efficacy, effectiveness and cost-effectiveness.

In the context of public sector financing, this will lead to more careful consideration of what products and services are to be subsidised and for whom. Those services which yield marginal health benefits, or which are considered to be 'elective' or 'cosmetic' and are of dubious cost-effectiveness from a societal perspective, are much less likely to attract public subsidisation in the future. Examples could include some forms of genetic testing, autologous blood donation and in-vitro fertilisation. The Commonwealth government in Australia has, since 1993, required pharmaceutical companies to submit an economic evaluation of drugs submitted for listing on the PBS. In 1998 a new Medical Services Advisory Committee was established to provide advice on the inclusion of new procedures and services on the Medicare Benefits Schedule (MBS) and to review existing MBS items. The criteria used by this Committee include safety, benefit to the patient and cost-effectiveness. These processes are resulting in more intensive screening of new drugs and medical services by regulatory authorities before public subsidisation is approved, and herald an era of constrained growth in public expenditure on health.

In the longer term, the acceptance of cost-effectiveness as a criterion in decision-making concerning subsidies for health care interventions can be expected to feed back into the R&D decision-making process. Organisations embarking on new R&D projects will factor the cost-effectiveness of the resulting product or service into their calculations concerning the profitability and rate of return from the investment. Health care interventions that do not offer much promise when assessed against a cost-effectiveness criterion are then less likely to move beyond the drawing board.

In closing, it is perhaps worth emphasising that, even with good-quality comprehensive data on the health sector that enable sources and uses of health expenditure to be ascertained and trends to be described, a considerable task remains. That task involves interpretation of these data and investigation of alternative hypotheses as to the underlying causal relationships. As the data are sometimes, if not often, consistent with two or more competing hypotheses about such causal relationships, there is scope for different interpretations of the data by researchers. Under these circumstances, we can be confident that health expenditure will provide fertile ground for future debate regarding health policy in Australia.

Richard Scotton

4 *The doctor business*

The medical profession is the core institution of a modern health care system, with prime responsibility for the development, transmission and application of medical knowledge and culture. Medical treatment has characteristics that distinguish it from most other production processes, and the special nature of health risks—and of the doctor–patient relationship—has given rise to singular norms and institutions that distinguish health care markets from the competitive model. These were analysed by Kenneth Arrow in an article that has become a classic in the health economics literature (Arrow 1963). Nevertheless, there are many aspects of medical care to which standard economic concepts and analysis can usefully be applied.

The explosion of medical science and of the technologies involved in its application have had radical consequences for the structure of the 'medical industry' over the past century, including the development of powerful professional associations, followed by more intense government intervention at state and federal level, growing specialisation and organisational complexity and, more recently, increasing corporatisation of medical care, both within and outside the profession.[1] Issues that might previously have been resolved privately within medical associations or negotiated between them and governments are now subject to the competing interests of a much wider set of stake-holders, with for-profit organisations growing in importance. In this context, the mix between custom, regulation and market forces is bound to change further.

Until about three decades ago, government intervention in the health care system was primarily directed at health protection and extending access to services. Since then—as real costs have risen to levels that impinge on other objects of public and private expenditure—policies designed to control health outlays and increase supply-side efficiency have received growing emphasis. The resulting policies, which include containment of public expenditures, restrictions on physical capacity and regulation of use/access, have wide-ranging implications for medical practice and its practitioners. Greater weight is also being given to market and quasi-market tools for raising efficiency, such as new methods of payment, more use of co-payments, contracting out, and removal of restrictions on competition.

Medical practice: a growth industry

In earlier times a significant proportion of Australia's medical services was provided by public agencies (predominantly public hospitals) and a smaller number of non-profit organisations employing salaried doctors. The latter have almost disappeared, and the role of public hospitals in supplying outpatient care has diminished. A substantial proportion of medical services in public hospitals is provided by trainee specialists, resident medical officers and interns; in 1995 they numbered some 9750 doctors, or about 21 per cent of all medical clinicians (AIHW 1997b, table 3). Most of the other providers of public care—senior hospital specialists with academic appointments and visiting medical officers (VMOs)—are engaged to a greater or lesser extent in private practice, which is the dominant mode of employment for the great majority of medical practitioners and the main subject of this chapter.

An ABS survey of the 'private medical practice industry' in 1994/95 identified 19 932 medical practices in which just under 34 000 doctors were employed (ABS 1997). Table 4.1 shows gross income and cost data from this survey and estimates (by the author) of average gross and net earnings of general practitioners and specialists. Mean gross earnings of specialists at $321 708 were 2.46 times the average for general practitioners, but when allowance was made for costs (other than medical salaries and superannuation contributions), estimated average net incomes of FTE general practitioners ($83 600–$94 900) were almost exactly half of those of their specialist counterparts. It should be noted that, while the GP income figures may be regarded as reasonably representative, the statistical averages for specialists conceal wide variations within and between different specialties.

The private medical practice industry has experienced rapid growth over the past few decades. Expenditure on private medical (i.e. doctors?) services is estimated to have risen from $173 million (0.71 per cent of GDP) in 1963/64 to $7371 million (1.77 per cent of GDP) in 1994/95 (Deeble 1978; AIHW 1997a). This constituted a rise from 15.7 to 20.1 per cent in the share of private medical services of total current health expenditure. As far as service volumes are concerned, changes in health insurance arrangements make it difficult to generate a strictly comparable series, but the overall rise in the use of treatment services shown in Table 4.2 almost exactly matches the rise in GDP share.

Table 4.1   Private medical practice 1994/95: income and expenses

	General practice	Specialist practice	All practices
Fee income	$2601.5m	$3960.2m	$6561.8m
VMO income	$69.9m	$213.3m	$281.2m
Total direct medical income	$2720.3m	$4234.0m	$6954.2m
Other practice income	$116.0m	$170.6m	$286.7m
Total practice income	$2836.3m	$4404.6m	$7240.9m
less			
Estimated expenses[a]	$1363.7m	$2429.5m	$3793.2m
Net practice income	$1453.0m	$1922.5m	$3375.5m
No. of doctors employed	20 825	13 161	33 987
(est. FTE[b])	(15 309–17 377)	(10 438–11 459)	(25 747–28 837)
Average net income per est. FTE	$83 616–$94 911	$167 777–$184 183	

Notes: [a] All costs except medical salaries and employers' superannuation contributions (estimated on the basis of total employer superannuation contributions less 10 per cent of non-medical salaries and wages).

[b] The conversion to full-time equivalents (FTE) is based on a range of 0.2–0.5 for the average participation of part-time medical practitioners.

Source: ABS 1997, tables 4–6.

It should be noted that the foregoing expenditure and utilisation statistics do not include remuneration earned from, and services involved in, the treatment of public patients in public hospitals. While shifts induced by Medicare are likely to have added significantly to doctors' remuneration from this source, the broad trend in service numbers would not have been markedly changed by their exclusion.

The medical workforce

The size of the medical workforce has grown at rates similar to per-capita service use. Exact comparisons over time are complicated by the lack of a totally consistent time series, with the number of active clinicians in 1996 above the census count but fewer than the broadly defined survey figure. The figures in Table 4.3 support the broad conclusion that the number of doctors per 100 000 population has roughly doubled over the last 30 years.

Most other OECD countries have also experienced rates of increase in the medical workforce well in excess of their population growth, to levels of supply approximating those shown in Table 4.2 (AMWAC 1996a). Although international comparisons should be made cautiously, the AMWAC figures indicate that the Australian

Table 4.2   Per capita use of private medical services, 1965/66–1995/96

Year	GP attendances[a]	Other treatment services	All treatment services	Diagnostic services	All services
1965/66[b]	2.40	0.64	3.04	0.42	3.48
1975/76[c]	3.80				5.60
1985/86[d]	4.29	1.44	5.73	1.85	7.58
1995/96[d]	5.58	1.62	7.20	3.50[e]	10.70

Notes and sources: [a] Includes unreferred specialist attendances.
[b] Scotton (1974: 56). Insured persons: average of NSW and Victorian figures.
[c] Barer et al. (1990).
[d] Commonwealth Dept of Health and Family Services (1997a), tables.
[e] Service count affected by restructuring of schedule.

ratio in 1993 was about the same as that of the USA and Canada, significantly above that of Britain and New Zealand, but closer to the lower end of the range in continental European countries, several of which had ratios above 300 per 100 000 population.

The underlying reason for the rise in doctor numbers was a rise in the number of Australian medical graduates, from 481 in 1961 (4.6 per 100 000 population) to more than 1300 in the years 1982–1985 (9.0 per 100 000 population), largely stimulated by the recommendations of the Karmel Committee (Committee on Medical Schools 1973, table 8.4; AIHW 1992, table A27). Since then medical graduations have stabilised at levels below 1250. However, the assumptions on which the Committee's recommendations were based were quickly confounded by a huge rise in medical immigration, from an average net permanent gain of 177 doctors in the five years to 1971 to around 600 in the three years to 1977 (Scotton 1984: 176–7). As a result, the Karmel Committee's 1991 target of 180 doctors per 100 000 population was attained by 1981.

In subsequent years, the inflow was stemmed by immigration restrictions first introduced in the late 1970s and the restriction of permanent registration to persons (other than New Zealand graduates) satisfying tests set by the Australian Medical Council (AMC). An official target of no more than 200 overseas-trained entrants to the medical workforce was endorsed by the Australian Health Ministers' Conference in 1992, but there has been difficulty in enforcing it (Birrell 1995). In 1994/95 and 1995/96 the number of medical practitioners arriving as permanent migrants were more than double the target, and the numbers satisfying the AMC requirements for

**Table 4.3   Doctor numbers and doctor population ratios,
1966–1996**

Year	No. of doctors	Doctors per 100 000 population
Census series		
1966	14 440	125
1976	21 150	156
1986	32 790	210
1996	44 010	241
Official surveys		
1987	36 610	228
1995	49 359	271

Sources: 1966–1996: Australian Bureau of Statistics census publications; 1987: Commonwealth Department of Health and Australian Institute of Health (1987); 1995: AIHW (1997b).

permanent registration were 317 in 1995 and 289 in 1996 (AIHW 1997b, tables 95, 98). These inflows have been supplemented in recent years by rising numbers of temporary resident doctors (AIHW 1997b, table 99; Birrell 1996).

Structure/composition of the medical profession

In addition to overall numbers, policy analysis relating to the medical workforce has to incorporate trends in its composition. Key dimensions in this context are gender balance, geographic distribution and specialisation.

Female participation

As in other areas of higher education and the labour force generally, the proportion of women in medical education and medical practice has risen markedly in recent times. The proportion of female medical students was 46.3 per cent in 1995, up from 14.4 per cent in the early 1960s, and is projected by the Female Working Party of the Australian Medical Workforce Advisory Committee (AMWAC) to rise further, to 50 per cent over the next 10 years (AMWAC 1996b: 43). As graduate cohorts age, the proportion of female practitioners may be expected to approach similar levels. In 1961 female doctors comprised only 11 per cent of the profession (Scotton 1974: 103). By 1981 the figure was 18.9 per cent and in 1991 had reached 28.6 per cent, including 44 per cent of practising doctors under the age of 30 (AMWAC 1996b: 42; AMWAC 1996a: 11).

The policy implications of this trend flow from differences between male and female doctors with respect to participation rates and location and type of practice. Female doctors have tended to have lower participation rates and, among those who practise, to work fewer hours. In recent years, the proportion of female graduates not in the medical workforce has declined to about 17 per cent—about the same level as for men (AMWAC 1996a: 11). However, their average hours worked has remained consistently below the male average—39.0 hours, as compared with 51.4 (AMWAC 1996b: 48). Female doctors also retire at a younger age. Gender differences in workforce participation partly reflect the fact that women are less well represented in the specialties and country general practice, two areas in which workloads and hours worked are relatively high.

The rising proportion of women has already had, and will continue to have, significant implications for medical workforce 'needs', as measured in terms of full-time equivalents: in other words, more doctors will be needed to produce any given level of output than if the proportion of women were not to grow. However, the force of this argument is weakened by observed declines in the workforce participation rates and hours worked by male doctors, which have resulted in the narrowing of the gap between male and female patterns (AMWAC 1996a: 11).

Specialisation

Spectacular advances in medical science and technology over recent decades across the whole spectrum of therapeutic and diagnostic fields have resulted in a relatively rapid growth in specialist practice. Not only have their numbers increased sixfold since 1961 but there has also been a continual evolution of new specialties and sub-specialties, of which 47 are listed in the classification now used by the Australian Institute of Health and Welfare.

Unlike the USA but as in many European countries, Australian health insurance arrangements have supported the role of general practice as the point of contact with the health system and as the dominant modality for delivery of primary care. Table 4.4 shows that general practitioners still comprise nearly 60 per cent of the medical workforce. Breaks in continuity of data make it difficult to track the precise course of events over the period; in particular, the GP figures may have been overstated in the Medicare series by the inclusion of a number of low-volume billers who were not in genuine general practice. An assessment based on full-time equivalents in 1992/93 suggests an overstatement of the GP share of about 2 per cent in the Medicare series.

Table 4.4   General practitioner and specialist ratios, 1961–1996/97

	GPs per 100 000 pop.	Specialists per 100 000 pop.	GPs as % of total
1961[a]	55.0	26.1	67.8
1971[a]	57.8	39.3	59.6
1982[a]	82.7	62.2	57.0
1984/85[b]	107.4	67.0	61.5
1994/95[b]	134.0	85.3	61.1
1996/97[b]	131.4	89.6	59.5

Notes and sources: [a] Permail series: Scotton (1984: 178).
[b] Commonwealth Department of Health and Family Services, unpublished tabulations of Medicare providers.

The broad picture appears to have been a rapid influx into specialist practice up to the mid-1970s, to the point that the future of general practice was seriously questioned. This process was halted at that stage by restrictions on the number of specialty training posts, with the result that the great majority of new entrants to the medical workforce were squeezed out into general practice. The restriction of entry to the specialties has been supported on quality grounds (i.e. the connection between volume of procedures performed and the maintenance of skills), but Deeble's analysis (1991: 43–8) of the relationships between doctor numbers, utilisation of services and fee levels indicates that most specialists achieved larger increases in their average gross earnings than GPs. At least in some specialties, the limitations on entry may have become too tight and recent evidence of rising levels of extra-billing has led to advocacy of increasing training positions in some of the specialties as a way of reducing market shortages and excessive fees (Paterson 1995).

Geographic distribution

In Australia, as in other countries, there are marked disparities between doctor/population ratios in various locations, with higher levels of provision in metropolitan than in rural areas and in higher-income than in lower-income locations. There are significant differences between states, with clinician/population ratios in 1995 ranging from 220 per 100 000 in Western Australia and 225 in Queensland to 303 per 100 000 in South Australia, the other states clustering around 250 per 100 000. The outliers to some extent reflect rates of population growth and age structure, but also the ratios of medical graduations to population.

However, the starkest differences in availability of doctors are not between states but within them, between metropolitan areas and other major urban areas on the one hand and rural and remote locations on the other. It is to be expected that specialists will tend to be concentrated in major centres where teaching and other large hospitals are located, and that country residents will have to travel to larger centres to receive tertiary and a substantial proportion of secondary services. But there is no reason why country people will have less need for primary care than city dwellers and, to the extent that they will call on general practitioners to attend to cases that would be treated in cities by specialists and public hospital outpatient departments, their needs for GP services would exceed that of their urban counterparts.

In fact, by every measure, country areas have substantially lower levels of specialist *and* primary care provision than the cities. On the basis of full-time equivalent (FTE) provision and age-standardised populations prepared for AMWAC, rural areas had a relative endowment of 33 per cent of specialists and only 70 per cent of general practitioners, compared with capital cities and other major urban centres (AMWAC 1996a, tables 10 and 13). However, capital city general practitioners managed to generate average levels of Medicare income per FTE practitioner remarkably similar to those of their rural counterparts by providing larger numbers of services per head to their smaller numbers of patients (AMWAC 1996a, table 4). Regardless of the level of provision that may be regarded as 'adequate', there is clearly a serious maldistribution of the medical workforce between larger cities and the rest of the country. Moreover, it is obvious that this maldistribution is facilitated by the system of open-ended fee-for-service remuneration for private medical services under Medicare.

Shortage or surplus? How many doctors is enough?

In a competitive market, the number of doctors would have little policy significance and would, in the long run, be efficiently determined by market forces. A shortage of doctors would cause prices and doctors' incomes to rise and would induce more doctors to enter training, or to migrate to Australia, until average doctors' incomes fell to a level just sufficient to induce the 'right' number of doctors to enter and/or remain in the workforce. The opposite process would occur in the case of a surplus. Although some economists in the past have suggested that the market might be left to correct 'shortages' and 'surpluses' of doctors, there are several reasons (given below) why this is very much a minority view.

The **lags between decisions** to change the number of medical school places and the impact on the supply of trained doctors are so great that the outcomes are likely to result in under- or overcorrections, with the result that the market may never reach equilibrium. The shorter-term adjustment falls on migration, which is heavily biased in the direction of oversupply. The proposition that doctors' incomes could be reduced to levels that would result in containment of immigration to acceptable levels is fanciful.

The **fee-for-service method** of remuneration embedded in Medicare limits the extent to which prices can act as equilibrating signals to providers and consumers. The very existence of medical benefits induces a higher level of demand than would otherwise be the case, and is conducive to higher levels of output at any given price. An important example of upward volume bias is provided by bulk-billed GP attendances (80.6 per cent in 1996/97), which put a floor under the price paid to doctors for an unlimited number of services supplied at zero cost.

The **ability of doctors to influence demand** for their services, through their socially accepted role as expert agents for their patients, is widely accepted by health economists and doctors, although rejected in whole or in part by market economists (Reinhardt 1991: 278–9; Phelps 1992: 211–4; Paterson 1995: 9–14). Whether 'supplier-induced demand' (SID) is motivated by financial maximisation or the desire to provide superior service to patients is irrelevant to the argument about its scale or existence. None of the proponents of SID suggests that doctors are untrammelled in their discretion to determine service use: they merely argue that constraints imposed by ethics, practice protocols and market forces leave room for considerable discretion on the part of individual doctors, the exercise of which is influenced by, among other things, the amount of time they have available and their views on appropriate levels of income (Evans 1984: 85–81). The evidence includes:

- remarkable variations in per-capita service use in areas with different population ratios and different methods of payment, and
- rates of growth in service use over time that correlate more closely with increases in doctor numbers than with population growth.

The generally accepted implication of these propositions is that, far from having a capacity for self-correction by market forces, the medical practice industry in Australia has a chronic tendency to develop excess capacity and for increments to its workforce to generate additional utilisation of its own services and other inputs to care. This is not to say that there are *no* relevant market signals:

the extent of extra-billing and levels of medical income may be useful indicators of excess demand or supply (Deeble 1991; Paterson 1995). However, in the absence of self-correcting market mechanisms, the avoidance of surpluses and shortages of medical practitioners requires purposive government intervention, on the basis—wholly or substantially—of non-market criteria.

Medical workforce planning models that are capable of being applied in practice fall well short of the requirements of an adequate theoretical framework (Reinhardt 1991). Most of them involve a 'needs-based' reference level, together with forecasts of changes in demand or 'needs', and additions to and withdrawals from the medical workforce. There is a long history of such forecasts turning out to be wildly wrong in Australia, as well as other countries—the most common source of error being unforeseen fluctuations in medical migration.

The other (and more important) problem with these pragmatic models is the basis on which the 'adequacy' criteria are based. Needs-based models start from consensus or expert views on the volume of services needed to respond to projected patterns of morbidity, at expected levels of technology, and the number of doctors needed to provide them. The arbitrariness of needs-based estimates is illustrated by the wide range of doctor/population ratios found within and among developed countries with similar levels of health status. Their methodology takes no account of supplier-induced demand, or the question of whether society will be willing to finance all the 'needed' treatments. An alternative modelling method—characterised by Reinhardt as 'demand-based'—attempts to predict what will happen (starting from the present supply) without the normative content of the 'needs-based' approach.

The perils of the 'needs-based' approach were illustrated by the outcome of the Karmel Committee, whose perceived 'need' to increase the doctor/population from 140 to 180 per 100 000 led to the 25 per cent increase in medical school places during the 1970s which the Commonwealth government now aims to reverse. Since then the forecasting sights have been lowered. In its 1988 report, the Committee into Medical Education and the Medical Workforce (Doherty Committee) carefully avoided any opinion on the 'correct' ratio, but by implication accepted the existing ratio (then about 230 per 100 000) as acceptable. At the same time Doherty expressed surprise at the number of cases in which the various methodologies of the specialist groups had led them to believe that the 'correct' ratios corresponded almost exactly with those in existence (Paterson 1995: 14).

Medical workforce policy made little subsequent progress until the mid-1990s when, alarmed by the burgeoning number of doctors, Commonwealth and state ministers established the Australian Medical Workforce Advisory Committee (AMWAC). The Committee's first action was to establish a working group to determine (if possible) 'appropriate benchmarks for the supply of general practitioners and medical specialists', a task that was completed in the following year (AMWAC 1996a). Using better databases than had been available to its predecessors, the working group was able to build up a detailed picture of GP and specialist supply, in relation to standardised populations, for capital cities and other statistical areas within each state. Using pragmatic benchmarks of 'need'—based on doctor/population ratios in localities in which demand and supply seemed to be in balance—the working party found very large (34 per cent) surpluses of general practitioners in capital cities, barely offset by small overall shortages in other areas. There were large individual variations within both of these groups (AMWAC 1996a, table 6).

No similar measure of adequacy was constructed in the case of practising specialists, even though very large (and only partly justifiable) differentials were observed between capital city and non-capital city practitioner/population ratios. Some submissions cited waiting lists and failure to fill specialist training positions in public hospitals as evidence of 'shortages', but the working party took a cautious view of their utility as measures of adequacy—opting for lack of effective demand (i.e. public expenditure) and inefficient incentives rather than 'unmet need' as the problem. Explanations of 'shortages' of specialists in non-metropolitan locations and in the public sector are clearly to be found in factors that influence their location decisions, such as income, professional satisfaction and residential desirability, rather than in the overall 'adequacy' or otherwise of their numbers.

As in the case of general practitioners, while overall 'shortages' in some specialties (as evidenced, for example, in extensive extra-billing) could be relieved by increases in doctor supply, the ability to earn good livings in capital city private practice might result in little if any spillover to less well-served areas. It is clear that the most effective—and probably the only—way to increase the supply of doctors in underserved locations is through policies specifically focused on those locations. Such policies will almost certainly require limitation of the rights to earn incomes in the more favoured locations.

Controlling expenditure growth

The major thrusts of current health care policy in developed countries are containment of the inexorable growth of total health expenditure and implementation of incentive and structural changes designed to improve the efficiency with which specific health services are produced—that is, to obtain better health outcomes for each dollar spent on them. It is widely agreed that both arms of policy are necessary to the efficient operation of the health care system as a component of the broader economy. Because of the central role of doctors in decisions about the use of health services generally, policies relating to the medical profession are in effect a subset of overall government health policies.

Administrative containment of health expenditure is a widely used means of achieving an important aspect of allocative efficiency— that is, maintaining the health system's claims on the national resources at a level at which the marginal returns are in keeping with those available from their application to other purposes. Production of health services is subject, like that of most other goods and services, to diminishing returns, and there is a systemic bias among both doctors and patients towards applying resources well beyond the point at which the additional benefits no longer justify the additional costs—that is, into 'flat-of-the-curve medicine' (Evans 1984: 16–21).

While the thrust of the cost-containment argument applies equally to public and private outlays, the tendency has been for governments to focus more directly on the public sector, for pragmatic budgetary as well as ideological reasons. Cuts in public expenditure affect private medical practice in various ways: on the one hand they limit the resources (public hospital admissions, expensive drugs, nursing home care) that doctors can order, especially for their less well-off patients; on the other, they underpin private health insurance and directly stimulate the demand for private hospital treatment. This has no doubt worked to the advantage of the profession, in particular of specialists, who have the largest share of hospital work. On balance, the transfer of demand from the capped public sector to the uncapped private sector is likely to raise unit costs.

Capping benefit outlays

The open-ended reimbursement of fee-for-service benefits has contributed to above-average rates of expenditure growth in Medicare and the PBS, compared with other public programs, as well as to inefficiencies and inequities resulting from geographic maldistribution. At the individual level, fee-for-service payment induces a welcome willingness to provide care. However, over the long term, at the systemwide level, it is conducive to excessive levels of service provision, to unequal levels of provision to different populations and to excess doctor supply. Under Medicare, total medical benefits rose at an average annual rate of 4.7 per cent between 1984/85 and 1995/96. Within this total, pathology benefits rose by an average of 7.9 per cent and radiology benefits by 11.1 per cent, while the rise in all other benefits averaged 3.0 per cent.

It is the open-endedness of the system as much as fee-for-service itself which is the genesis of the problem. In other countries where fee-for-service is the dominant mode of remunerating doctors under national health insurance programs, there have been attempts to impose ceilings on the total amount paid to doctors. The most comprehensive move in this direction has taken place in Germany, where the health insurance system has progressively moved toward a capped pool, by which annual rises in total payments to doctors are limited to the rate of growth of the insurance levies paid by the covered population (Henke 1994). Several Canadian provinces have gone down a similar path.

The German and Canadian measures have been facilitated by the fact that in their systems insurance payments cannot be supplemented by extra-billing of patients: that is, the insurance payments constitute the total remuneration of doctors. In Australia, because of the tenacious adherence by the organised profession to the unilateral right of doctors to set their own fees, and political and constitutional barriers to the prohibition of extra-billing by the Commonwealth government, capping of the Medicare benefits pool has not been considered until recently to have potential as a cost-control strategy.

Against this background, an agreement covering total pathology benefits, negotiated between the Commonwealth government and organisations of pathology providers in 1996, can only be interpreted as a significant breakthrough. Under the agreement, total pathology expenditure growth is to be capped at around 6 per cent annually over the three years to June 1999, primarily by a range of measures to monitor and manage utilisation; to the extent that these measures fail in their objective, automatic discounting of fees will occur (CDHFS 1996). Despite the modesty of the projected expenditure reduction target, the precedent is important in terms of the future viability of fee-for-service remuneration under Medicare.

Nevertheless, it is important to remember that the agreement was greatly facilitated by economies of scale available in pathology through new technology and concentration of ownership—increasingly in the hands of the for-profit corporate sector. These developments are not matched elsewhere in private medical practice, except in the field of diagnostic imaging. A package of measures including a one-year fee freeze, restructuring of the fee schedule and changes to billing rules was developed in 1996 in consultation with representative organisations of radiologists and nuclear medicine physicians (CDHFS 1996). While it is possible that a capped pool of funding on the pathology model may eventuate for imaging services, the small scale and high labour intensity of most other areas of medical practice make it an unlikely model for more general application in the Australian health system.

Capacity limitation

Keeping the lid on industry capacity in key areas of the health system is an essential aspect of expenditure control. In the case of the medical profession, capacity means the number of trained doctors eligible to practise. As the only sources of additions to it are Australian medical schools and immigration of trained doctors, the size of the medical workforce may be thought of as amenable to—if not a function of—government decision, rather than as a response to market factors.

In 1995, on the basis of the consensus concerning the excess of doctors in Australia, the Commonwealth government announced its intention to reduce the number of new entrants to medical schools to a number that would bring annual graduations down to 1000. This will be an interesting test of wills: medical schools have been very reluctant to downsize, and the logical course of closing one or more of the smaller schools is off the scale of political feasibility. In the 1996 Budget, the government announced that it would terminate automatic entitlement of newly registered medical practitioners to Medicare provider numbers, by which their services are eligible for Medicare medical benefits. In future, provider numbers will be allocated only to doctors recognised as general practitioners and specialists by virtue of requisite postgraduate qualifications, and to occupants of recognised training placements in the course of obtaining these qualifications. Given the limited number of training positions, this opens the prospect of many Australian-trained doctors having little prospect of becoming principals in private medical practice. Trainee doctors have threatened industrial action and Birrell (1997) has argued strongly for Australians to have priority in accessing professional opportunities in medical practice.

On the face of it, levels of medical immigration appear to be more amenable to Commonwealth government control, if only because most of those affected directly have no votes. However, immigration controls have proven difficult to implement because of the many paths by which people born and/or trained in other countries may find their way into medical practice in Australia (Birrell 1997). Partial success in containing the inflow of permanent immigration has been followed by substantial rises—to nearly 1000 annually—in the number of foreign-trained 'temporary residence doctors' (TRDs) entering Australia for employment (AIHW 1997b, table 99). Most of the TRDs are recruited on 'area-of-need' grounds to public hospital positions in rural and remote public hospitals. However, many of them have private practice rights involving Medicare billing, and some have been able to convert their status from temporary to permanent residence (Birrell 1997). After failing to secure adherence to a 1993 agreement by state health ministers to reduce TRD recruitment, the Commonwealth government decreed that from 1 November 1997 TRDs would not be accorded provider numbers unless they had relevant overseas postgraduate qualifications, and that no TRDs at all will be eligible to bill Medicare after 1 January 2000 (CDHFS 1996). This means that they will be limited to salaried public hospital and locum positions.

Given the evidence of past failures, it will be interesting to observe the effectiveness of the new regulatory barriers to entry to the Australian medical profession in the face of financial incentives operating in the opposite direction. At the same time, while market approaches could improve efficiency in many aspect of the health sector, the apparently irresistible extension of the global economy makes it impossible to conceive of market solutions that would reduce career opportunities to levels that would deter medical immigrants from major source countries.

Price control

In many of its benefit programs, notably those covering prescribed drugs and nursing home beds, the Commonwealth government is able to contain costs by directly fixing prices. However, there is a widely held view (not tested in the courts) that the 'civil conscription' clause in subsection 51(xxiiiA) of the Constitution prohibits the Commonwealth government from fixing medical fees. Consequently the Medicare legislation contains no direct constraints on the extent to which doctors may bill above it, nor on the quantum of their services on which benefits are payable. In this respect Medicare is almost uniquely open-ended, compared with medical payment arrangements in other countries (Deeble 1991: 61).

Nevertheless, the legislation does contain some provisions designed to restrain doctors' ability to raise their fees. One is the gap (currently 15 per cent, subject to a maximum of $50 per service and an annual family safety-net of $276) between the fees listed in the Medicare schedule and benefits paid for out-of-hospital services, which sets an officially sanctioned co-payment for services billed to patients. Another is the prohibition on private insurance coverage of any amounts billed above the schedule fee: this is designed to inhibit extra-billing by exposing patients to its full cost, and perhaps inducing them to look for another provider. A third constraint is contained in the direct billing option, under which doctors are able to bill the Health Insurance Commission direct for services provided, on condition that the Medicare benefit is accepted as full payment. These provisions have supported a Commonwealth government policy of limiting rises in scheduled fees (and hence benefit rates) to rates at or below the movements in the CPI.

The force of these persuasive sanctions on actual fees charged depends on the market balance for various services. Their effect is greatest in general practice in which, as Table 4.5 shows, the proportion of direct-billed services rose substantially during the Medicare period. However, the percentage of direct-billed GP services remains much lower in the less well-supplied rural areas, where average co-payments in 1995 were almost double the metropolitan figure (AMWAC 1996a, table 4). Pathology tests recorded similar levels of direct billing and scheduled fee observance. But the picture with respect to specialist medical services was very different (see Table 4.5).

No recent figures are available for the magnitude of over-schedule billing, but it could be expected to vary in line with the

Table 4.5 **Fee observance, Medicare medical services, 1984/85 and 1996/97**

	Direct-billed (%)			At or below scheduled fee (%)		
	1984/85	1990/91	1996/97	1984/85	1990/91	1996/97
GP attendances	52.5	70.3	86.8	76.9	76.7	84.5
Specialist attendances	21.2	25.5	32.4	73.8	57.1	57.2
Obstetrics	16.2	26.8	22.9	66.6	40.2	45.4
Anaesthetics	4.8	6.2	10.2	60.1	29.6	31.3
Pathology	43.7	63.2	77.8	95.6	80.9	89.8
Diagnostic imaging	34.3	45.7	62.6	84.8	65.5	77.5
Operations	27.5	38.0	44.5	78.0	63.0	66.3
Assistance at operations	5.4	3.4	1.9	75.4	52.6	51.1

Source: CDHFS 1997a, tables C3 and C4.

observance percentages. Deeble found that in 1989/90 average fees charged by obstetricians, anaesthetists and surgeons were, respectively, 20.1, 18.6 and 11.5 per cent above the scheduled fees—all margins being well above the 1984/85 figures. While the observance figures in Table 4.5 suggest a modest improvement in recent years, the real picture is complicated by substantial differences (not revealed by the statistics) between specialties.

This analysis illustrates the limitations on the cost-control options available to a government under an open-ended fee-for-service remuneration arrangement. Although it is going too far to depict the system as (in popular parlance) 'spiralling out of control', the long-term rate of growth in medical expenditure is cause for some concern. It appears that utilisation growth slowed markedly during 1997, but this is too short a period on which to project the future. At this stage there are grounds for doubting the long-term viability of a system of open-ended fee-for-service remuneration, and for suggesting that effective limitation on medical care use and expenditure must involve significant structural change in payment and delivery arrangements.

Co-payment

The term 'co-payment' is generally applied to out-of-pocket payments (by patients) related to individual services, but is sometimes extended to include other types of patient charges such as global deductibles and percentage coinsurance. Under Medicare, co-payments are expressly prohibited in the case of directly billed claims, but in the case of services billed to patients, there is no onus on doctors either to charge more than Medicare benefits or to limit their charges to the scheduled fees. In other words, there has been no official policy on the role of co-payments in Medicare—except for the short-lived mandatory co-payment of $3.50 on direct billed claims for non-holders of health care cards introduced by the Labor government in 1991.

Some economists have argued that the obligation of patients to share in the cost of medical services would constrain the growth of medical expenditures, and improve the efficiency of the health system and the economy generally, by reducing the consumption of needless and/or less valued services (Arrow 1963; Feldstein 1973). It is not surprising to find support for their view from medical associations whose members stand to gain additional income by charging fees in excess of insurance benefits, and from finance ministers and bureaucrats looking for ways to reduce public outlays.

On the other hand, many health economists are sceptical of the extent of welfare losses resulting from arrangements that involve medical services being provided at less than their 'market' price (Evans 1984: 49–52; Feldman & Morrisey 1990). Many more share concerns expressed by non-economists at the distributional consequences of patient charges. Findings from the Rand Health Insurance Experiment (the multi-million-dollar research project which constitutes the definitive study of the demand for medical care) were that co-payments reduced the use of out-of-hospital medical services significantly, but by the poor relatively more heavily than the non-poor. The Rand study also found that cost-sharing resulted in adverse health outcomes for the sick poor, and imposed disproportionate cost burdens on people with chronic health problems (Newhouse et al. 1993: 338–45).

Moreover, as Evans (1984: 90) and Richardson (1991: 19–22) point out, if we are interested in the impact of co-payments on the *use* of medical services, the impact on *demand* is only part of the story. The volume of services consumed is the product of both the demand and supply sides. The design of the Rand study was such that the providers of services would not have noticed the reduction in demand. Consequently, its results would not necessarily predict the outcome of imposing co-payments across an entire health system, especially in the presence of SID.

The most relevant evidence on this point is provided by research into the effects of substantial co-payments in the Canadian province of Saskatchewan between 1968 and 1971, in which it was found that the overall fall in use of doctors' services of about 6 per cent was composed of a fall of 18 per cent in use by the poor and elderly, while the use of services by people in higher-income groups actually grew (Beck & Horne 1980). As in the Rand results, the reduction primarily occurred in initial visits, and in Saskatchewan it was offset by a rise in the number of subsequent (i.e. primarily doctor-initiated) visits.

It appears that as a device for reducing utilisation of medical services, and hence their overall cost, co-payments are relatively ineffective: Richardson (1991: 24) estimates that a 50 per cent co-payment would reduce utilisation by only 7.6 per cent. Co-payments at much more modest levels than this would have adverse effects on the poor and chronically ill; on the other hand, if they were exempted from the co-payments, the overall reductions in use would be minimal. Of course, a government could still achieve substantial budget savings by reducing benefits payable to the non-poor, and the case of introducing them would have to be made on the grounds that the resulting budget savings could be applied more usefully elsewhere.

In fact, it should be borne in mind when considering the role of financial incentives in health service efficiency that their application to service providers is likely to produce more positive results than their application to consumers. Acceptance of SID strengthens the implication that policy action should focus more heavily on the supply side—in this context, on doctor numbers and behaviour—than on the demand side.

Strategies for future reform

The strategic objectives of public policy relating to the medical practice industry involve improvement of efficiency, clinical effectiveness, and access of all Australians to needed and useful care. To a substantial degree, achievement of these objectives will depend on reforms to the financing and public program framework rather than measures aimed directly at the structure and operation of medical practice. These broader issues, which are at the centre stage of health policy and health politics, are dealt with extensively in Chapters 5, 10 and 12.

In recent years, successive Commonwealth governments have implemented a number of low-key but useful incremental reforms, directed specifically at containing costs and improving efficiency in the medical practice industry. These include measures to restrain doctor numbers, slow down the growth of expenditure on diagnostic services, encourage negotiation of fees to cover services to private inpatients (referred to in Chapter 5) and promote more comprehensive care through coordinated care trials (see Chapter 10). One can sense the strategic direction underlying these changes, without being confident of the political will to carry them through to implementation on a scale that will have a major systemic impact. The aspect of the 'doctor business' for which the strategic pathway has been most clearly enunciated and the program follow-through most effectively pursued is structural reform of general practice.

General practice reform

The role of private general practice as primary care provider and gatekeeper to the wider health system is arguably the most enduring and best supported feature of the Australian health system. Fears of its erosion in the 1970s in the face of burgeoning specialisation have proved unfounded. In recent years perceived problems have included overcrowding, isolation from other services, and the need for higher levels of training and broader ranges of skills to cope with new responsibilities. These issues were examined in the early

1990s by the National Health Strategy (1992) and a General Practice Consultative Committee (1992) established by the AMA, Commonwealth Department and the Royal Australian College of General Practitioners. The thrust of their two reports was similar, in supporting:

- vocational registration based on postgraduate training at the fellowship level;
- the widespread establishment of general practice 'divisions' as agencies through which general practices would be involved with each other and other health professionals in community-oriented functions; and
- supplementation of fee income by practice-based payments to cover services other than those to individual patients.

These features were incorporated in a Commonwealth government 'General Practice Strategy', for which funding is scheduled to grow to more than $300 million a year by 1999/2000. In financial terms, the largest components of the Strategy are the Better Practice Program and grants to the Divisions for carrying out their functions as geographically based GP cooperatives and as agencies for promoting the coordination of care between general practitioners and other providers in their designated areas.

The Better Practice Program is the most dynamically expanding component of the Strategy, with expenditure scheduled to rise from $40 million in 1994/95 to $92 million in 1997/98, and to more than double again over the following three years to more than $200 million. These outlays consist primarily of grants to individual general practices, based on the demographic composition of their patients. The long-term objective is to progressively increase the share of general practitioner incomes being paid in the form of grants, as against fees for individual items of service. This was to be accelerated by paying only a proportion of indexation rises in the form of higher fees, and allocating the remainder to the Better Practice Program. In November 1997, the estimated 1.7 per cent rise was split 50-50 between a 0.85 per cent rise in GP fees and an increased allocation to the practice grants pool, but in the 1998 Budget the Commonwealth government announced its intention of reserving full indexation of GP fees.

Other important features of the General Practice Strategy are designed to support rural practice and improve the availability of services to country populations. The formula for Better Practice Program grants provides a loading of about 20 per cent in favour of rural practices; additional payments totalling $15 million annually are designed to attract doctors to rural locations and, one hopes, to keep them there.

Pending completion of an evaluation still in progress, it is difficult to make any judgement about the outcomes of the General Practice Strategy. It represents a cautious and evolutionary approach, constrained by the need to develop consensus for change in a basically conservative constituency, with a historic commitment to the present payment structure (CDHFS 1996: 12–14).

In the long run, the promotion of 'better' patterns of practice is likely to require further reform of financing arrangements. In particular, to the extent that better practice involves continuity of care and sharper focus on the health of subpopulations rather than individuals, the obvious method of promoting it is implementation of population-based payments in place of at least some of the item-based fee revenue. In other developed countries, a trend has been observed towards replacement of reimbursement benefits in medical insurance by contracts between payers and providers, for specified ranges of services to the populations covered by the payers (Hurst 1991; van de Ven et al. 1994). These contracts may include budgets for prescribed, bought-in and referred services, giving positive expression to the gatekeeping role of primary care practitioners. It is possible that the current evaluation of the General Practice Strategy will give some attention to these longer-term[2] issues.

5   *Economics of hospital care*

Hospitals are without doubt the key institutions of the health sector, accounting for over one-third of total health expenditure. The public often frames health care in terms of hospital care, and the images of the hospital operating theatre and hospital emergency department are regularly used as images of health care generally. However, the nature of acute health care services is changing. Patients are increasingly being maintained in the community with support from a hospital, and quite sophisticated surgical procedures can now be done without an overnight hospital stay.

Hospital inpatient capacity and utilisation

In 1995/96 Australia had 1209 hospitals, 62 per cent being public and providing 83 029 beds, of which 72 per cent were in public hospitals (see Table 5.1). Public hospitals are generally larger (mean: 79 beds) than private hospitals (51 beds). There is significant concentration of ownership of private hospitals: 8510 beds (36 per cent of all private hospital beds) are in hospitals owned by five large for-profit chains (Health Care of Australia, Australian Hospital Care, Ramsay Health Care, Benchmark, and Healthscope). Although there is a greater proportion of private hospital beds in larger hospitals able to deal with more complex procedures than a decade ago, the average complexity of cases treated in private hospitals is still substantially less than in public hospitals (depending on the data source, the difference is between 10 per cent and 50 per cent).

Overall, Australia has 4.6 acute beds per 1000 population (see Table 5.1). There are substantial differences between the states in hospital provision, in terms of both the relative role of the private sector (32 per cent of all beds in Victoria being in private hospitals compared with 24 per cent in New South Wales) and overall provision. South Australia has a bed/population ratio of 5.3 beds per 1000 population, 23 per cent higher than the Victorian provision of 4.3. The different level of provision is also associated with different levels of utilisation: South Australia has a separation rate of 310.6 per 1000 population and bed day utilisation of 1294.6 per 1000, this being

Table 5.1 Provision and utilisation of hospitals, 1995/96

	NSW	VIC	QLD	WA	SA	TAS	ACT	NT	Total
Provision									
Public acute general									
Number	218	138	192	98	82	20	3	5	756
Beds	21560	13139	11113	5547	5543	1468	780	570	59720
Beds/1000 pop.	3.50	2.91	3.35	3.18	3.76	3.10	2.56	3.22	3.29
Beds/hospital	98.90	95.21	57.88	56.60	67.60	73.40	260.00	114.00	78.99
Private acute general									
Number	169	134	63	47	30	10			453
Beds	6806	6241	4890	2438	2274	660			23309
Beds/1000 pop.	1.11	1.38	1.47	1.40	1.54	1.39			1.28
Beds/hospital	40.27	46.57	77.62	51.87	75.80	66.00			51.45
Total acute general									
Number	387	272	255	145	112	30			1209
Beds	28366	19380	16003	7985	7817	2128			83029
Beds/1000 pop.	4.61	4.29	4.83	4.57	5.30	4.50			4.57
Beds/hospital	73.30	71.25	62.76	55.07	69.79	70.93			68.68
Utilisation									
Public acute general									
Separations/1000 pop.	202.7	191.8	190.6	190.5	216.5	152.1	186.4	260.1	196.7
Bed days/1000 pop.	1058.8	809.5	835.1	769.9	920.5	802.3	760.9	1050.9	905.2
Private acute general									
Separations/1000 pop.	78.9	93.6	105.5	65.3	94.1	111.6	45.3		87.7
Bed days/1000 pop.	253.5	355.0	455.3	248.5	374.1	395.9	155.3		327.7
Total acute general									
Separations/1000 pop.	281.6	285.4	296.1	255.8	310.6	263.7	231.7	260.1	284.4
Bed days/1000 pop.	1312.3	1164.5	1290.4	1018.4	1294.6	1198.2	916.2	1050.9	1232.9

Note: ACT and NT private hospital data are included in NSW and SA respectively.

Source: Australian Institute of Health and Welfare, *Australian Hospital Statistics, 1995/96*, tables 2.2 and 3.2; and AIHW periodical communications.

Figure 5.1 **Separations, patient days and costs by major diagnostic category, 1995/96**

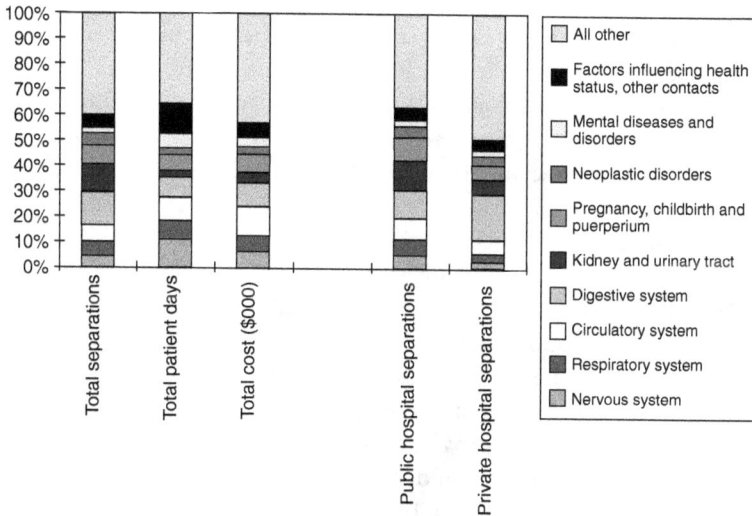

9 per cent and 11 per cent above Victorian levels. (A separation is a discharge, death or transfer.)

Figure 5.1 shows the major diagnostic categories (MDCs; body systems) for which patients were admitted to hospitals in 1995/96, together with proportions of bed days and costs. Over 10 per cent of all admissions were for diseases and disorders of the digestive system, the principal reason for admission being for an endoscopy, a procedure normally done on a same-day basis. This MDC thus accounts for a much lower proportion of bed days.

The major reason for admissions in the kidney and urinary tract MDC is renal dialysis, almost always involving a day-only admission. Admissions for MDCs relating to the nervous system, circulatory system and mental health disorders have longer lengths of stay, and so these MDCs account for a larger proportion of bed days than separations.

Figure 5.1 also shows the difference in the proportion of separations for public and private hospitals. Significant differences can be seen here, for example, in the larger proportion of digestive system admissions, again probably reflecting the prevalence of day-only endoscopies in the private sector.

Trends in inpatient provision

Table 5.2 shows that in the last decade or so there has been a substantial decline (22 per cent) in the number of public acute hospital beds, with a smaller decline in private acute beds. The decline in public provision is the result of specific government policies to reduce bed provision, particularly in rural areas (where the decline has been almost 30 per cent). However, the admission rate for public hospitals has risen by 22 per cent, with the result that the bed reductions have not led to a reduction in access because of the significant growth in productivity in terms of both an increased occupancy rate (over 10 per cent in public hospitals) and the decline in length of stay (30 per cent in public hospitals). Reductions in average length of stay have occurred because of the reduction in stays of long duration and a significant increase in day-only patients. Both these trends have been facilitated by improvements in medical technology (e.g. anaesthetic agents and flexible endoscopy).

Most states regulate the number of private hospital beds. Bed licences are tradeable commodities and so, although there has been a redistribution of private beds, few private beds have been closed. The reduction in private hospital provision per capita has been caused principally by a growth in the population with only marginal changes in private bed provision. As Table 5.2 shows, there has been a rise in the per-capita provision of private hospitals in non-metropolitan areas, reflecting partly reductions in population but partly also the development of new private hospitals in major rural centres. Private hospitals have also experienced substantial productivity growth (as reflected in increased admissions per 1000 population), with the productivity principally occurring through reduction in length of stay and, to some extent, higher occupancy rates.

The most dramatic trend in service provision over the past decade has been in provision of public psychiatric services, where there has been a reduction of over 60 per cent. This has been caused by two key factors. First, advances in psychotropic medication have meant that patients who previously required very long-stay care in psychiatric institutions are now able to be maintained in community settings. A second trend has been the 'mainstreaming' of psychiatric services: acute psychiatric provision is increasingly provided in acute general hospitals, with dedicated psychiatric admission wards being incorporated in the mainstream service.

Table 5.2   Provision and use of acute hospitals, 1985/86–1993/94

	1985/86	1987/88	1989/90	1991/92	1992/93	1993/94	Growth 1985–1994
Beds per 1000 population							
Metropolitan areas							
Public acute general	3.3	3.2	3.1	2.9	2.7	2.7	−18.18%
Private acute general	1.4	1.5	1.4	1.3	1.3	1.3	−7.14%
Public psychiatric	0.9	0.6	0.5	0.5	0.4	0.3	−66.67%
Non-metropolitan areas							
Public acute general	5.5	5	4.6	4.1	3.8	4	−27.27%
Private acute general	0.7	0.7	0.8	1	1	1	42.86%
Public psychiatric	0.6	0.5	0.5	0.4	0.3	0.2	−66.67%
Whole population							
Public acute general	4.1	3.9	3.7	3.3	3.1	3.2	−21.95%
Private acute general	1.3	1.3	1.3	1.2	1.2	1.2	−7.69%
Public psychiatric	0.8	0.5	0.5	0.4	0.4	0.3	−62.50%
Admissions per 1000 population							
Public	157	160	165	174	177	191	21.66%
Private	55	54	60	65	68	70	27.27%
Total	212	214	225	240	246	261	23.11%
Average length of stay (days)							
Public	6.9	6.5	6.0	5.3	5.2	4.8	−30.43%
Private	5.5	5.2	4.6	4.2	4.2	4.1	−25.45%
Total	6.5	6.2	5.6	5.0	4.9	4.6	−29.23%
Occupancy (%)							
Public	72	73	75	79	87	80	11.11%
Private	62	58	60	64	66	67	8.06%
Total	69	69	71	74	81	77	11.59%

Source: Australian Institute of Health and Welfare, *Australia's Health 1996*, tables 5.5., 5.7 and 5.9.

Hospital funding

In 1994/95 Australia spent over \$13.5 billion on hospital services including public, private and psychiatric hospitals, about 80 per cent going on public hospitals (including repatriation and psychiatric hospitals). Figure 5.2 shows the sources of this hospital expenditure. The principal source of public hospital funding is government.

Commonwealth involvement in public hospital funding commenced with the Curtin government's postwar social policy initiatives (Kewley 1973). The Curtin scheme had many similarities with later Labor initiatives to eliminate financial barriers to access: it subsidised hospitals (in 1946 at 60¢, or 6s, per bed day), on the basis of a five-year agreement with the state, in return for states (and hospitals) agreeing that all persons could be treated in public hospitals (in public wards) without a means test. This policy did not survive the change of government in 1949: the Coalition government from 1949 de-emphasised direct Commonwealth involvement in and responsibility for access to hospital services, and pursued policies to encourage private health insurance as a way of consumers covering the cost of hospital care. The ramshackle arrangements that developed for both hospital and medical insurance in the 1950s and 60s led to a series of reviews and attempts in the late 1960s to rectify the inherent anomalies and complexities of such schemes.

The Whitlam Labor government saw a short-lived return to universal hospital coverage via Medibank. The Medibank hospital arrangements provided for relatively generous 'cost-sharing' agreements between the Commonwealth and the states. Despite this

Figure 5.2   Sources of hospital finance, 1994/95

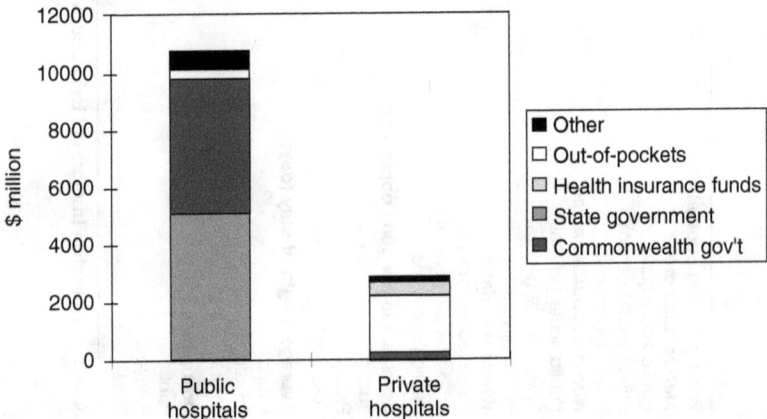

generosity, conservative states were initially reluctant to participate in them, principally for ideological reasons (Scotton & Macdonald 1993). The cost-sharing arrangements required substantial systematisation of the existing public hospital funding arrangements, including identification of all the public hospitals in Australia (to be known as 'recognised hospitals') and setting of agreed budgets for those hospitals.

With the dismissal of the Whitlam government and the election of the Fraser government, the cost-sharing arrangements were renegotiated and eventually terminated. As with its conservative predecessors, the Fraser government pursued voluntarist policies emphasising private health insurance.

The return of Labor to office in 1983 led to a re-emphasis on Commonwealth government responsibility for ensuring access to hospital services. Labor's hospital Medicare policies were, like their 1946 and 1974 precursors, implemented through Commonwealth–state agreements. The three five-year Medicare Agreements negotiated since 1984 have varied in their policy emphases. The structure of all three Agreements has been similar, with four key obligations on states:

- that all Australians (together with others covered by the scope of the Medicare Agreement, such as persons from countries with which Australia has a reciprocal health care agreement) are entitled to elect, at the time of admission to hospital, to be treated as a public patient;
- that public patients are treated without any fees or charges;
- that all Australians are entitled to treatment for a broad range of outpatient services without any fees or charges; and
- that the states do not bill Medicare or the PBS for medical and pharmaceutical services provided to either inpatients or outpatients.

The Medicare hospital Agreements have not emulated the generous cost-sharing arrangements of Medibank: the Medicare Agreements provide that states are responsible for the full marginal cost of any rise in hospital budgets during the term of the Agreement. Conversely, states accrue the full benefit of any reduction in hospital budgets over this period. Commonwealth Medicare funding is formula-driven during the course of a Medicare Agreement, with the formula being unrelated to actual hospital budgets. This places a strong incentive on states to achieve efficiency improvements or to reduce hospital budgets through other strategies.

The first Medicare hospital Agreements (1984–88) were

designed to compensate states for specific additional costs incurred as a result of the introduction of Medicare and, because of this focus, were known as Medicare Compensation Agreements. Compensation was provided for revenue losses associated with reduction in inpatient revenue (both price and volume) and for other revenue forgone (e.g. when lower numbers of private patients reduce the revenue stream for public pathology services). Compensation for cost increases was based on the number of 'shift bed days', which was based on the proportionate charge in the public/private bed day ratio, assuming no rise in volume (Duckett 1988 describes both the 1984–88 and 1988–93 Agreements). Funding under the 1984–88 Agreement supplemented the ongoing Commonwealth funding known as the 'Identified Health Grant'.

The two subsequent Medicare Agreements (1988–93 and 1993–98) have attempted to address perverse incentives in Australia's health care system and to achieve specific Commonwealth policy objectives (see Table 5.3).

The current (1993–98) Agreement was negotiated in the runup to the 1993 election; indeed it was signed on the day the writs for the election were issued (see Butler 1993; Pearse 1994, for detailed discussion). From the Commonwealth government's perspective, the Agreement was meant to ensure Medicare's continuance even if Labor lost the election: they were enshrined in legislation and major changes to them had to be approved by the Senate.

In an attempt to deal with the continuing political problem of waiting lists (or 'access to public hospitals') and the emerging problem of cost-shifting, the 1993–98 Agreement initially had five key components:

- a base grant analogous to that in the 1988–93 Agreements;
- funding for nominated services, essentially rolling over funding for the 'AIDS component and incentive packages' of the 1988–93 Agreement;
- a new 'incentives package', a mishmash of somewhat conflicting initiatives, including promotion of area health management and devolution of clinical budgets; waiting list reductions ('hospital access'); and strategic capital planning;
- funding to redevelop state mental health services;
- 'bonus payment' (not subject to Grants Commission equalisation) for improved public access, involving two key elements, a 'base provision pool' and an 'annual adjustments pool'.

The bonus payments under the 1993–98 Medicare Agreement were designed to tackle explicitly perceived problems of access for public

Table 5.3   Key elements of Medicare Agreements

Agreement	Political objective	Key principles
1984–1988	• Introduction of Medicare	• Compensation for cost increases and revenue losses
1988–1993	• Consolidating Medicare • Growth and reform of public provision	• Incentives for system reform • Penalties for lower public/private bed day shares and excess private medical service use
1993–1998	• Entrenching Medicare • Expansion of public provision	• Reward for relatively high levels of public provision and for growing public provision relative to other states • Post 1996, accountability for negotiated outcomes

patients. The 'base provision pool' rewarded those states with higher levels of public bed day shares (over 51.5 per cent) at the commencement of the Agreement, in a sense a reward for past good performance. The 'annual adjustment pool' was designed as an encouragement to states to increase their public bed day share. The total amount of funding in the pool was fixed, and a state's share depended in part on the extent to which its public bed day share increased and the extent to which public bed day shares increased in all other states. Funding from the 'annual adjustment pool' was heavily influenced by behaviour of the larger states, but even the amount of funding these states would receive was unpredictable, with estimates exhibiting high volatility.

Over the course of the 1988–93 Agreement it had become clear that although states had acceded to the key obligations of Medicare outlined above, both politically and in the form of the signed Agreement, states and/or their hospitals had attempted to circumvent their obligations through cost-shifting and other stratagems. The principal mechanism for cost-shifting is the 'privatisation' of outpatient clinics, whereby hospital outpatient clinics are terminated but replaced by 'private clinics' run by hospital specialists that raise a fee for the medical services either directly from patients or through direct billing on the (Commonwealth) Health Insurance Commission. Hospitals also reduced the pharmaceuticals provided to patients on discharge and the extent of pharmaceuticals available to outpatients, each of which strategies requires provision by the PBS. This led to inefficiencies in health care in Australia overall (it is probably cheaper to provide pharmaceutical services in outpatients rather than through all the markups associated with retail provision) and to inconvenience for the consumers (by requiring additional visits to GPs to obtain prescriptions post-discharge) and in some cases inequity through the introduction of direct consumer payments. With respect to the first point, the 1993–98 Agreement introduced a requirement that states advise hospitals of the states' obligation to the Agreement and that states ensure that the recognised hospitals implement the commitments the state has made. (This requirement was introduced to stop states from claiming that the hospitals were totally autonomous in their cost-shifting activities.)

The 1993–98 Medicare Agreement was revised mid-term to incorporate more directly objectives related to the expected negotiated levels of throughput and performance in other key policy areas, such as waiting lists and emergency department waiting times. This was done by replacing the (by now discredited) 'annual adjustment pool' with specific payments to each state, conditional on achieving negotiated objectives in areas such as public provision and waiting lists. Failure to reach the negotiated targets could lead to the Commonwealth's withholding a component of the funding. This new structure of the Agreement thus allowed the Commonwealth to impose direct incentives on states with respect to many aspects of hospital policy. Table 5.4 shows the structuring of the negotiated targets for Victoria.

Importantly, the Commonwealth has more than maintained its share of hospital funding since the introduction of Medicare. Although the Medicare Agreements rest on the assumption that hospital services are a 'state responsibility' and the Commonwealth leaves the detailed control of hospital policy to the states, the Commonwealth share of hospital funding in 1995/96 was slightly more than half (52 per cent) of government outlays for services in recognised hospitals.

Figure 5.3 shows the pattern of change in hospital funding in the six states and the ACT. (The Northern Territory is not included because Commonwealth funding has grown so dramatically—almost 300 per cent—that it distorts the scale for all other jurisdictions.) These data are taken from Commonwealth Grants Commission sources and represent the most authoritative independent data on hospital spending available. Over the period 1990/91–1995/96, total hospital expenditure rose by 18 per cent, with total Commonwealth hospital expenditure rising by 31 per cent and also rising in each state and territory, the range being 17 per cent (Vic) to 272 per cent (NT).

Unlike the uniform pattern across states of increased Commonwealth total expenditure, there are significant differences

Table 5.4 Victorian Medicare targets, 1995/96

Target area	Bonus pool funds attributable to target (%)	Performance bonus		
		Target	Bonus payable ($m)	Penalty threshold
Inpatient activity	59	145 weighted separations per 1000 weighted population (0.5% increase on 1994/95)	31.561	113 weighted separations per 1000 weighted population
Non-inpatient activity	3	1418 occasions of service per 1000 weighted population (same as 1994/95)	1.605	1106 occasions of service per 1000 weighted population
Elective surgery waiting times				
• category 1	13	'Effectively zero' (i.e. no. waiting >30 days is <1% of total admissions)	6.954	>5% waiting >30 days
• category 2	7	<20% admissions waiting >90 days	3.745	>40% waiting >90 days
Emergency department waiting times				
• category 1	4	100% seen immediately	2.140	90% seen immediately
• category 2	3	60% seen <10 minutes	1.605	30% seen <10 minutes
• category 3	1	60% seen <30 minutes	0.535	30% seen <30 minutes
Developmental activities				
• Implementing casemix funding for non-inpatients	3		1.605	
• Participating in ambulatory care data development	1		0.535	
• Provision of nationally comparative data on waiting times	5		2.675	
• Progress towards national data on hospital emergency services	1		0.535	
Total	**100**		**$53.495**	

Figure 5.3   Change in Commonwealth, state and total hospital expenditure, by state, 1990/91–1995/96

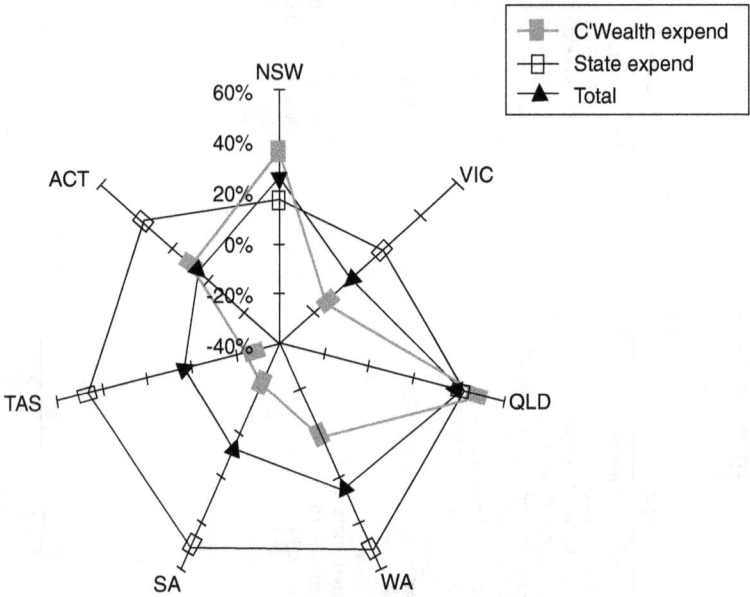

between states in both expenditure and state expenditure on hospitals. On average, states and territory expenditure grew by 11 per cent, but there were significant declines in state expenditure in Victoria (14 per cent), South Australia (23 per cent), Tasmania (29 per cent) and the Northern Territory (14 per cent). These changes are affected by the year chosen as the base: in Victoria's case, for example, total expenditure declined marginally (1 per cent) for 1990/91–1995/96; if 1991/92 were the base year, the decline would be 7 per cent. Health prices grew by 9 per cent from 1990/91 to 1995/96 (AIHW 1997); New South Wales and Queensland were the only states in which state expenditure growth exceeded growth in health prices.

In only one state, New South Wales, did total expenditure rise faster than Commonwealth expenditure. However, the states would argue that this analysis, concentrating on relative shares of hospital expenditure, distorts the true nature of Commonwealth perfidy, as the Commonwealth's untied general revenue assistance to states has reduced substantially. This argument is essentially a political one. Notwithstanding such comments, the general pattern for hospital expenditure thus developed is clear: the Commonwealth has assumed identified responsibility for an increased share of hospital expenditure and the states have used this as an opportunity to withdraw their own source support for hospital services.

The states have adopted different strategies to tackle the pressures on hospital expenditure, the most notable being the introduction of case-mix funding.

Paying for hospital services

Currently there are four broad approaches to paying for hospital activity: capitation; historical/negotiated payment; per-diem funding; and per-case funding. In the longer term it may be possible to pay hospitals on the basis of their outcomes—the extent to which they contribute to improving health status. However, the technology for this does not yet exist.

Unlike the USA, where many hospitals have capitation-based contracts as a key source of funding, none of the Australian states or territories has adopted a capitation approach to funding public hospitals. Further, health insurance funds are prohibited from paying for private patients on a capitation basis. In New South Wales, hospitals are the responsibility of Area Health Authorities, with the Authorities' budgets being in part determined by the weighted population for which they are responsible. However, this capitation approach is not used for hospital funding: Area Health Authorities generally fund their hospitals on a historical or negotiated basis.

A number of states fund their hospitals, either directly or indirectly, on the basis of historical funding (with marginal annual adjustments) or through negotiation as to appropriate funding levels, with cost per patient treated as only one of the factors to be taken into account. A particular variant of the negotiated basis is to set a hospital budget based on the prior year's budget, with or without a standard adjustment, raising the budget for inflationary effects or reducing it on a standard basis across the state for deemed productivity improvement. Such historical budget-setting is now generally not pursued, and standard across-the-board cuts have been replaced by tailored budget cuts. Similarly, increasing budgets usually has some form of service rationale. The historical budgeting approaches have thus evolved to be equivalent to a negotiated basis.

Generally, negotiated budgets for public hospitals are formalised in a contract or 'agreement' between the state health authority and the hospital. These agreements often also include negotiated goals covering a range of aspects of hospital administration—broad targets for number of patients treated, number of outpatient attendances and so on, together with a specification of the funds that would be available to that hospital in that year. However, negotiated budgets do little to change historical funding arrangements in terms of either patient flows or efficiency.

The third approach to paying hospitals is to base payments on the number of patient days. Per-diem payment approaches are most commonly applied to nursing home and non-acute institutional provision and hospital provision with longer durations of stay (e.g. rehabilitation services), where the bed day is an appropriate measure of the product. However, private hospital reimbursement (and charges to private patients in some states) has been on a tiered per-diem approach since 1987. The Commonwealth government has prescribed a tiered per-diem model using differential bed day payments for patients in each of five bands: advanced surgical; surgical/obstetrics; psychiatric; rehabilitation; and other (see Table 5.5).

The tiered per-diem funding model also recognises that longer-stay patients in each of these bands have lower costs per bed day. The Commonwealth-prescribed payment is the minimum payment that insurers must make for private patients, and these payments are probably lower than costs in even efficiently operating private hospitals. Most insurers make higher per-diem payments in the early days of stay but introduce multiple stepdowns of stay. These stepdown arrangements make longer stays uneconomical to private hospitals, and essentially provide the same type of incentives for efficient provision as is provided under the fourth form of hospital payment, per-patient or case payments.

Table 5.5 Patient categories and stepdowns for minimum private hospital payments

Patient category	Payment steps
Advanced surgical	0–14 days
	over 14 days
Surgical and obstetrics	0–14 days
	over 14 days
Psychiatric	0–42 days
	43–65 days
	over 65 days
Rehabilitation	0–49 days
	50–65 days
	over 65 days
Other	0–14 days
	over 14 days

Hospital payment should place incentives on hospital management to provide appropriate care efficiently. Hospitals cannot usually influence the number and type of patients presenting at the hospital, but should assume responsibility for the number of days of stay and number of services provided (pathology tests, nursing interventions), as well as the costs of each day of stay and of each service (Saltman & Young 1981; Young & Saltman 1985). Under 'case-mix funding' or per-patient reimbursement policies, the funder or purchaser assumes the risk for cost variations caused by variations in the number and type of patient treated, by setting differential prices for different types of patients and allowing budgets to vary with volume. The hospital therefore becomes more clearly accountable for variation in the efficiency of the services it provides.

Generally, case-mix funding is seen as being able to yield efficiency improvements more rapidly than negotiated funding: negotiated budgets could achieve greater levels of savings by being based on a continual improvement approach, with efficiency improvement targets being set for even the most efficient hospital and larger efficiency gains being expected of less efficient hospitals. The overt justification for negotiated budgets may stress this potential for greater level of efficiency improvements. However, it is often difficult to ascertain whether such overt justification is simply masking a covert justification to allow more flexibility in budget-setting to respond to non-economic factors, such as the perceived need to provide adjustments to hospital budgets for political reasons. In these circumstances an objective payment formula may mitigate the ability for political adjustments to budgets.

The move to case-mix funding

Australia has a long history of case-mix development. The first consultancy in this area was undertaken in 1985, and aimed at testing whether the Diagnosis-Related Group (DRG) classification system as developed by Professor Fetter in the USA was relevant to Australian clinical practice (Palmer et al. 1986). The consultancy also attempted to assign costs on a DRG basis in a sample of three Victorian hospitals. Since that small beginning Australia has embarked on an ambitious case-mix development program, and a number of states have now implemented case-mix funding in a variety of forms.

The key events in the transition to case-mix funding occurred in 1993/94, when Victoria adopted the system for public hospitals (for an analysis of the original Victorian funding policies, see Duckett 1995; Health Solutions 1997; for a discussion of the policy process leading to the introduction of case-mix funding, see Lin & Duckett

1997). South Australia introduced case-mix funding in 1994/95 (for an evaluation of the South Australian experience, see Brooker 1997). All other states except New South Wales have now adopted case-mix funding arrangements for hospital inpatient care.

A prerequisite for case-mix funding is greater clarity in describing hospital activities. Clarification of hospital products occurs through 'unbundling' of hospital activity by first defining broad product lines. Case-mix funding also requires, for each of the major *product lines*, specification of *prices* and *volumes* of activity and specification of *quality* standards.

Typically, three broad streams of hospital product can be identified: inpatient services, outpatient services, and 'teaching and research'. Naturally, these broad streams cannot specify the full range of other activities provided by hospitals, including home care services. The latter services are normally captured in 'specified grants' or 'site-specific grants' made on a negotiated basis. (Examples of specified grants are home dialysis, and funds for special wards for treatment of prisoners.)

Inpatient services

Inpatient services have been the main focus of case-mix development, partly because they are the core business of hospitals, accounting for over three-quarters of all hospital expenditure, but also because inpatient case-mix classifications are the best developed.

Prices

One of the key advances in health economics and health services research over the past few decades has been the development of Diagnosis-Related Groups. Hospital services in Australia can now be described in terms of Australian national DRGs (version 3), with 667 separate DRGs. Because of their design characteristics—in particular, because patients in the same DRG are expected to consume similar amounts of resources—DRGs are able to be used to standardise for differences in the case-mix of hospitals to allow comparisons of hospital efficiency and for payment purposes (Fetter 1991).

Case-mix funding normally provides for a statewide standard contract and a standard base price across the state or for broad classes of hospitals. The contract also provides the rules under which funding varies with volume. Under case-mix funding, payments to hospitals are based on relative weights developed using 'cost-modelling' or data extraction from hospital clinical costing systems. Cost-modelling is a relatively simple costing approach, which takes general ledger data and patient activity data to estimate hospital-specific prices by DRG (Chandler et al. 1991). It uses 'service weights' (e.g. pathology and theatre weights) to estimate service costs in each DRG, which are then summed to yield an estimated cost and relative weight for each DRG. Initial cost-modelling in Australia used US service weights, but the Commonwealth government, through the Case-mix Development Program, funded the development of Australian service weights to be used in calculating DRG relative weights for public and private hospitals at state and national level (Commonwealth Department of Health and Human Services 1995). The alternative approach to deriving cost weights uses data from hospital clinical-costing or patient-costing systems. These systems, which are used for internal management purposes (Stoelwinder & Abernethy 1989), provide costing information at the patient level which can be aggregated by DRG to provide cost relativities on a DRG basis. Data from Victoria's 13 largest hospitals (accounting for 48 per cent of the state's separations) are used to set Victorian price relativities (Health Solutions 1997).

There are two broad approaches to case-mix funding in Australia: fixed and variable payments, or full-price payment. Victoria, Queensland and South Australia have adopted a fixed and variable model. This system, which emulates many other public sector pricing arrangements, follows standard economic theory in aiming to set the marginal price for additional volume as being equal to marginal costs (Scotton & Owens 1990). A 'fixed grant' is paid to hospitals to cover overhead and other costs; hospitals also receive a 'variable payment' for each DRG weighted 'separation'. The alternative, full-price model does not distinguish fixed and variable elements but pays the full (average) price for each separation.

DRGs are developed to represent the 'normal case' for that grouping; therefore, in addition to the standard or base payment, 'outlier' payments are paid for unusual cases. Outliers are cases which are statistically different from the norm, falling outside high and low boundaries, or 'trim points'. Australian funding formulae generally set trim points using the 'L3H3' approach: the low trim point is one-third the average length of stay for that DRG, the high trim point is three times the average length of stay (McGuire et al. 1995). High outliers (cases above the high trim point) receive an additional per-diem payment, while low outliers (cases below the low trim point) get less than the ordinary base payment.

The payment system adopted in the case-payment states involves extremely low transaction costs. All discharges from all hospitals in Australia have diagnoses and procedures recorded in computerised databases, with diagnosis and procedure coding being undertaken locally. The development of a payment system relies on this routine production and transmission of data, and the low transaction costs of the payment system occur because the information flow on which the system is based is already in place. The information on the number of patients treated is aggregated by the state health department, the relative weights and hence relative prices are applied on a monthly basis through a simple spreadsheet-type program, with adjustments to cash flow to hospitals being made on a quarterly basis. Because locally coded data are being used for payment purposes, coding audits are generally conducted to monitor coding accuracy (Reid 1992).

Given the capped nature of public sector spending, case-mix funding incorporates expenditure-capping systems, either through declining marginal payment for additional value or through explicit volume caps.

Quality
Partly because measurement of quality is poorly developed in Australia, the ability to incorporate quality into the new case-payment systems is also weak. Common quality-related policies include a special additional payment to hospitals accredited by the Australian Council on Healthcare Standards, and use of patient satisfaction or patient experience questionnaires.

A number of states have also introduced new measurement systems to monitor unplanned readmission rates, on the hypothesis that case-mix funding might lead to too early discharge with a consequent increase in the risk of readmissions. However, readmission rates have not changed significantly since the introduction of case-mix funding (MacIntyre et al. 1997). Governments in all states are placing emphasis on better measurement of quality through commitments to the production of comparative quality indicators or league tables in the same way that they have published comparative efficiency indicators in the past. The new indicators are partly based on those incorporated in the accreditation system, including unplanned readmissions, return to theatre, hospital-acquired infection and hospital-acquired bacteraemia.

Outpatients
The second major broad product line of hospitals comprises 'outpatient' or 'non-inpatient' services. Relatively little progress has been made in developing case-mix measures for outpatient services, with the result that current funding approaches are generally based on occasion of service counting within 10–15 broad areas (e.g. medical, surgical, allied health).

There are two main strands of development work taking place in Australia on case-mix categorisation for outpatient services: 'clinic' categorisation, and an individual patient-based classification. The latter approach relies on substantial investment in data collection systems in outpatient services (including diagnosis coding), which may make it unfeasible for introduction in the foreseeable future.

Victoria and Queensland have a systematic 'clinic' categorisation system as part of case-mix funding arrangements for outpatient care. The Victorian Ambulatory Classification System (VACS), developed using patient-level costing data, identifies 46 clinic types and associated relative weights. Payments (and relative weights) for episodes of out-patient care in VACS incorporate the clinic visit and any associated investigation and pharmaceuticals ordered in a 30-day window around the clinic visit. Because of heterogeneity in some areas (especially allied health) and because of the distinct nature of the product of emergency departments, Victoria has implemented a case-mix funding system only for medical and surgical clinics. Clinic-based systems involve an audit process to ensure homogeneity of clinic types between hospitals (Jackson & Sevil 1997).

Training and development
Teaching hospitals are more expensive than non-teaching hospitals. This difference is in part explained by the fact that teaching hospitals produce another product, variously called 'training and development' or 'teaching and research'. Generally, this has been measured in terms of the number of junior medical staff (interns, registrars etc.), together with a recognition that the first year on the job of many health professionals includes a training component. Hospitals in Australia still participate in a range of post-registration educational programs for nurses, and these too attract payments.

Conclusions

The hospital system in Australia has changed dramatically over the past two decades, in terms both of average length of stay and occupancy rate as shown earlier in this chapter, and in more recent times of the move from historical to case-mix funding in most Australian states.

The past decade has seen growing use and specificity of payment incentives in hospital policy, both in the relationship between Commonwealth and state governments as articulated in Medicare Agreements and between states and hospitals as evidenced by the introduction of case-mix funding. This transformation has been made possible in large part by developments in the technology of measurement of hospital activity (especially measurement of inpatient activity using DRGs) and in the necessary infrastructure for performance measurement. The next decade is likely to see a sharpening of the incentives for states and hospitals as part of a drive for improvements in the efficiency and effectiveness of the hospital system.

The decline in length of stay in hospitals presages a change in the focus of hospital management. A much higher proportion of activity in hospitals of the future will be performed on an ambulatory basis. Further, a decreasing proportion of hospital activity will require immediate access to the expensive infrastructure associated with the hospitals of today. A growing proportion of procedures will be undertaken on a day-to-day basis and ambulatory care centres will become increasingly important components of health care. Hospitals will need to develop close organisational arrangements with such facilities (Robinson 1996), either through organisational integration or tight contractual arrangements.

The hospital of the future will probably aspire to be the hub of a network of hospital and ambulatory care services. A pessimistic scenario for hospitals might be that they become simply one element of a broader health care network. As the organisational structure of hospitals changes, it will be increasingly important that our tools for describing hospital activities reflect the contemporary organisational realities: as care becomes better integrated across organisational boundaries, classification and payment systems that are defined in terms of historical boundaries will become irrelevant—or, worse, will create perverse incentives and inhibit appropriate microeconomic reform (Duckett & Jackson 1993).

An increased reliance on economic incentives to drive efficiency improvements can be achieved only if the tools for measurement are developed at the same pace as organisational practice changes. Case-mix measures, such as DRGs, were developed in the context of a particular structuring of health care and pattern of care. A critical factor that needs to be closely monitored with the introduction of case-mix funding is whether the very definition of the product of health care is changing: that is, whether hospitals achieve efficiencies by changing the definition of when 'patient care' is completed by hospitals so that more recovery is undertaken post-discharge than prior to discharge, thus transferring the costs of hospital care to community or rehabilitation providers or to the family. To the extent that these transfers of costs have occurred, the significant recorded perceived improvements in efficiency associated with the introduction of case-mix funding may simply record changes in payer rather than improvements in efficiency. It is essential that measurement of hospital activity take into account these changing product definitions.

Improvements in measurement will also be necessary to respond to the ideologically inspired wave of privatisations of hospital care.

The *sine qua non* of any contract is specification of what is being bought and sold. Hospital privatisation contracts must therefore specify in sufficient detail the services to be provided by the privatised organisation. Subject to the constraints outlined above, inpatient services are able to be well specified, but this is not the case in many other aspects of hospital care, such as ambulatory services or the teaching and research activities of hospitals. To the extent that the services are not specified, these important aspects of the health care system may suffer through privatisation initiatives.

The changes in technology that underlie many issues of change in hospital practice will drive many aspects of hospital reform. State governments (the principal providers of public hospital capital) are now ideologically less well disposed to using state capital funds for hospital refurbishment and upgrading and are increasingly turning to the private sector to capitalise public hospitals. The benefits of privatisation are often presented in terms of capital savings (less money to be borrowed) and improvement in recurrent cost (as it is argued that private providers are able to operate more efficiently than public providers). The research evidence for these claims is non-existent, and privatisation initiatives can be regarded as a high-risk natural experiment of strategies to improve the efficiency in health care in this country.

The focus of most hospital reform programs in Australia has been on improving hospital efficiency. Tackling this problem and thus removing it from the policy agenda means that attention can now be paid to other critical issues of hospital performance, such as measurement of quality of care. Such measurement is complex, and just as there have been improvements in measuring hospital product and efficiency over recent decades so too has there been improvement in the ability to compare the quality of hospital care. This is an important issue in Australia, as Wilson et al. (1995) have revealed substantial levels of iatrogenesis associated with health care treatment. A related issue will be the one of ensuring not only that what is performed in hospitals is of high quality but that the admission or operation was necessary at all. This separate question of appropriateness is highlighted by the high levels of unexplained variations in utilisation rates for a number of medical and surgical conditions across Australia (Renwick & Sadkowsky 1991). This is an extremely complex issue (Evans 1990), and will also need to be the focus of policy attention.

Many of the contemporary issues of hospital policy can thus be seen to be about efficiency and the allocation of resources. These are the very areas in which health economics can make an important contribution. The economics of hospital care is a rapidly developing science. A mere five years ago no state was involved in case-mix funding. But there are still many challenges. No state is currently involved in systematic measurement of hospital quality and the outcomes of hospital care, and there are currently no exogenous arrangements for utilisation review of hospital activity. Measurement of the output of many key components of hospital activity is still weak (e.g. for geriatrics and rehabilitation services). The next five years could well change that, and it is in these areas that the challenges for R&D in the economics of hospital care lie.

6   *Pharmaceuticals*

On any given day of the year, more Australians will consume a prescribed medication than any other type of health care good or service (ABS 1996). This is the result of decades of government involvement with the supply of medicines. Australians have been promised timely, reliable, safe and affordable access to necessary medicines, and that is what they now expect.

For nearly 50 years the supply of drugs to the Australian community has been administered by the Pharmaceutical Benefits Scheme (PBS). Australians now have a long experience and high expectation of affordable access to medicines. However, the cost of maintaining the current equity of access has risen markedly over the last two decades; due to increasing per-capita consumption of drugs listed on the Commonwealth's schedule of the PBS, rising drug prices, population growth, the growing number of retail pharmacy outlets and the addition of the oral contraceptive pill to the PBS (Harvey & Murray 1995). By 1987 government expenditure in providing drug price subsidies was rising at an exponential rate. Total Commonwealth payments on benefit prescriptions (for general and concessional beneficiaries) and miscellaneous payments in the period 1980/81–1985/86 almost doubled, from $309 million to $616 million (Commonwealth of Australia 1997a).

This rise in government expenditure triggered an amendment to the *National Health Act, 1953* in 1987 and subsequently one of the most innovative developments in the application of economics to health care policy. For the first time, the Pharmaceutical Benefits Advisory Committee (PBAC) was required to (Commonwealth of Australia 1987):

> take account of comparative effectiveness and cost in recommending drugs as pharmaceutical benefits and in considering any change to prescribing restrictions applying to pharmaceutical benefits.

Prior to 1987, in the absence of legislated criteria the PBAC had formed its own criteria, which focused on the comparative clinical performance and community need for the drug. Cost was an optional consideration. The addition of economic data as a 'fourth hurdle' to successful marketing now presents a major challenge to both the methods of economic evaluation and the development of health care policy (Drummond 1994). It also places the onus on each manufacturer to demonstrate the comparative cost-effectiveness of its drug. If a manufacturer seeks a higher price on the PBS schedule for a new drug (and this subsidy is an essential requirement for the successful marketing of most drugs), it has to prove that the drug has a significant therapeutic advantage over current therapy (Drummond 1994; Mitchell 1996a).

Background

This chapter focuses on the major economic initiative in the pharmaceutical arena: that is, the economic evaluation of drugs as a statutory requirement as set out initially in the 1987 amendment to the *National Health Act, 1953*. We present a descriptive analysis of this requirement for economic evaluation, against a background of the contextual influences on the decision-making process.

Adding a drug to the drug subsidy mechanism

To understand the contextual influences on decision-making first requires an appreciation of the Australian listing process. This is illustrated in Figure 6.1.

A prerequisite to listing a drug on the PBS is that it is registered for marketing in Australia. Applications for registration of new drugs are made to the Therapeutics Goods Administration (TGA) within the Commonwealth Department of Health, which considers evidence on pharmaceutical chemistry, toxicology, clinical pharmacology, clinical efficacy and safety (Hall 1989). An expert committee, the Australian Drug Evaluation Committee (ADEC), then advises the TGA regarding the registration of new products based on assessment of data relating to quality, safety and efficacy, but not cost (Hall 1989), and the TGA thereafter proceeds to register the product (or not).

Listing a drug on the PBS is a two-step process. In the first stage the PBAC decides whether to recommend that the drug be listed. In doing so, the Committee considers the need for the drug in the community, and the effectiveness and safety of the new product in comparison with drugs already listed for the relevant indication(s) (Henry 1992). As noted above, legislation passed in 1987 now requires the PBAC to consider comparative costs as well as comparative effects. In the second stage, the Minister of Health decides whether to accept any positive recommendation to declare the drug

Figure 6.1   Process for considering submissions for PBS listing

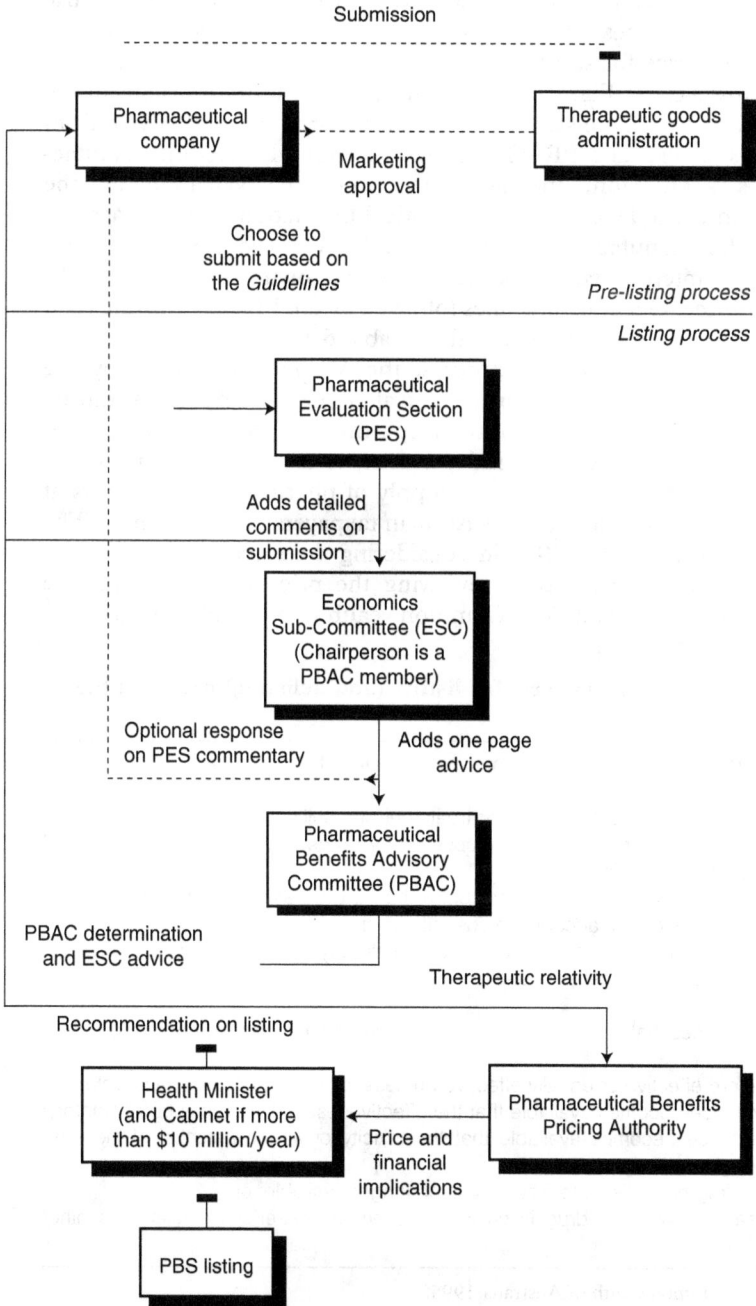

Source: Glasziou & Mitchell 1996.

to be a pharmaceutical benefit and hence eligible for subsidy. The Minister also considers whether to restrict the drug's subsidised use to specified types of patients and whether to accept the drug's proposed price for subsidy.

However, as Figure 6.1 illustrates, the statutory decisions of the PBAC and the Minister are based on information and advice from other sources. The PBAC is provided with the relevant manufacturer's submission, the associated in-depth evaluation by the Department of Health's Pharmaceutical Evaluation Section (together with the manufacturer's brief rejoinder on this evaluation) and concise interpretive assessment by its own Economics Sub-Committee. General guidelines followed by the PBAC for listing (and delisting) drugs are summarised in Table 6.1.

Following the PBAC process, the Minister is assisted by the deliberations of the Pharmaceutical Benefits Pricing Authority (PBPA) and the activities of the Department of Health's price negotiators. The PBPA is an independent, non-statutory body whose objective is to secure a reliable supply of pharmaceutical benefits at the most reasonable cost to Australian taxpayers and consumers. The criteria used by the PBPA in considering the price of items recommended for listing and in reviewing the price of listed items are summarised in Table 6.2 (Commonwealth of Australia 1996a).

Table 6.1   PBAC criteria for listing (and delisting) drugs on the PBS

A new drug entity may be recommended for listing if:

- it is needed for the prevention or treatment of significant medical conditions not already covered or inadequately covered by drugs in the existing list and is of acceptable cost-effectiveness;
- it is more effective, less toxic (or both) than a drug already listed for the same indications and is of acceptable cost-effectiveness; or
- it is at least as effective and safe as a drug already listed for the same indications and is of similar or better cost-effectiveness.

Circumstances that may result in removal of a drug from the list include the following:

- if a more effective or equally effective but less toxic drug becomes available;
- if evidence becomes available that the effectiveness of the drug is unsatisfactory;
- if evidence becomes available that the toxicity or abuse potential of the drug outweighs its therapeutic value;
- if the drug has fallen into disuse or is no longer available; or
- if treatment with the drug is no longer deemed cost-effective relative to other therapies.

Source: Commonwealth of Australia 1995.

The main mechanism to determine initial prices for drugs is the advice from the PBAC arising from the cost-effectiveness information supplied by the sponsor and evaluated by the PBAC. The PBPA also reviews prices of pharmaceutical products supplied through the PBS by considering the gross margin on the cost of manufacture or on the landed cost (Commonwealth of Australia 1997b). From 1 January 1993, submissions for listing of new drugs or for substantial changes to current listing are required to have information on the cost-effectiveness of the drug as detailed in the '*Guidelines* for the pharmaceutical industry on preparation of submissions to the Pharmaceutical Benefits Advisory Committee' (Commonwealth of Australia 1990, 1992, 1995).

Commonwealth government expenditure on pharmaceutical benefits

Drugs listed on the PBS have consistently been priced below the world average. The Bureau of Industry Economics (BIE) estimated that in 1991 the prices of drugs in Australia were 30 per cent below the EEC average and about 50 per cent below the world average (BIE 1991). Australia, along with a majority of developed countries, has an extensive system of price control (Elgar 1992).

Despite generally low drug prices by world standards, the cost of pharmaceutical services and benefits to the government rose by 12 per cent (nominal) a year or 5.5 per cent (real) in the years 1982/83–1991/92. (See Figure 6.2 for a breakdown of Commonwealth expenditure from 1980/81–1996/97.) Reasons for this growth include

Table 6.2   Factors considered by the PBPA

In reviewing the price of listed items and in considering the price of items recommended for listing, the Authority takes account of the following factors:

- PBAC comments on clinical and cost-effectiveness aspects of items;
- the prices of alternative brands of a drug;
- comparative prices of drugs in the same therapeutic group;
- information on costs, when provided by the supplier or estimated by the Authority;
- prescription volumes, economies of scale and other factors such as expiry dating, storage requirements, product stability and special manufacturing requirements;
- the level of activity being undertaken by the company in Australia, including new investment, production, R&D;
- the price of the drug in reasonably comparable overseas countries;
- other relevant factors which the applicant company may wish the Authority to consider; and
- any direction of the Minister.

Source: Commonwealth of Australia 1996a.

continuing increases in service volumes, listing of new (and expensive) drugs (Shiell & Salkeld 1997), an ageing population (80 per cent of total government expenditure is on concessional prescriptions) and drug complexity (Grant & Lapsley 1996; Commonwealth of Australia 1997a). More recently, rises in drugs costs have been attributed to doctors changing their prescribing for common conditions from relatively cheap to more expensive treatments (Henry 1997; Hill et al. 1997).

Although these factors affect the government's capacity to afford to add drugs to the PBS and hence the main policy, a complete analysis of each is beyond the scope of this chapter. Three of the most important factors are summarised below (see Commonwealth of Australia 1997b for further detail).

First, patient co-payments have been introduced and increased, necessitating the introduction of safety-nets to protect patients with chronic illnesses who are prescribed relatively large quantities of medicines. Co-payments have been maintained at a lower level for welfare recipients than for the remainder of Australians.

Second, the government now only subsidises to the level of the lowest price brand for any group of products containing the same quantity of active ingredient in the same type of formulation. A patient choosing to use a more expensive brand must pay the difference in price. This policy has been strengthened by giving

Figure 6.2   Annual government expenditure on the PBS 1980/81–1996/97

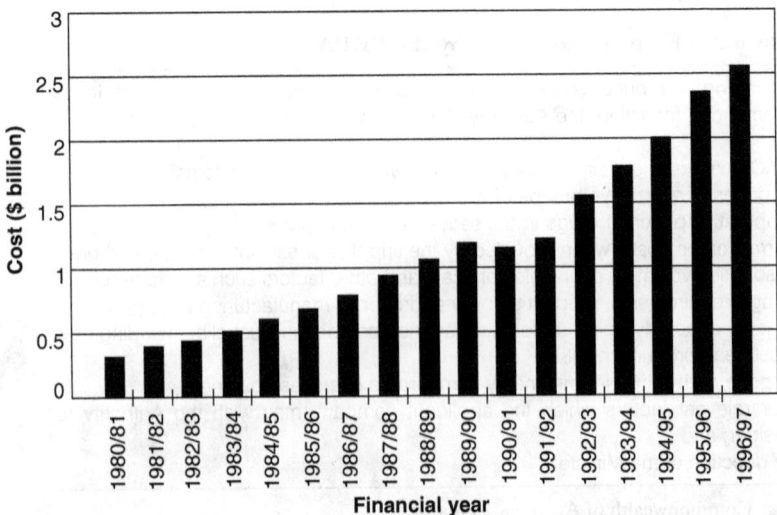

pharmacists the authority to switch brands with patient agreement (i.e. generic substitution). In its May 1997 Budget, the government announced its intention to extend this concept to a limited number of drug groups where different active ingredients exert equivalent therapeutic effects.

Third, with the support of the pharmacy profession, the number of community pharmacies in Australia authorised to dispense pharmaceutical benefits has been reduced in order to achieve economies of scale in the pharmacies that remain.

Thus, even though the cost of the PBS to the government is still rising, the net effect of each of these policies has been to reduce the extent of potential government expenditure on the PBS.

The world in which policies are made

There is no doubt that escalating Commonwealth government expenditure on pharmaceutical benefits provided the impetus for the 1987 amendment to the *National Health Act, 1953.* But neither the legislation per se nor sustained cost pressure on its own created subsequent drug policy. This came through the interplay of values (an amalgam of interests, beliefs and ideologies) and information (in the form of technical *Guidelines* for economic submissions) working through the institutional structure for decision-making (the committee and political process) to achieve public policy outcomes (Lomas 1996). The outcomes are the changes in the way in which the PBAC decides what drugs to recommend for listing—in essence, whether their listing represents an efficiency gain while retaining a balance of other objectives such as equity. Balancing the different goals of a national medicinal policy of efficiency, equity and quality of use aspects of the drug subsidy program requires two things: first, developing policy that articulates clearly the desired objectives; second, making decisions that are consistent with these stated objectives. To that end, the 1987 amendment was intended to tip the balance towards efficiency.

A schema of the world in which policies are made is presented in Figure 6.3. The analytic framework in this schema contains an institutional structure which mediates the interplay of values and information (Davis et al. 1993). The sections of this chapter follow the main components of this analytic framework.

Having assessed how economic evaluation influences reimbursement decisions for drugs in Australia, at least three questions emerge: has the requirement for economic evaluation been successful; if so, can it be applied to other health care interventions; and are there

Figure 6.3 The world in which policies are made

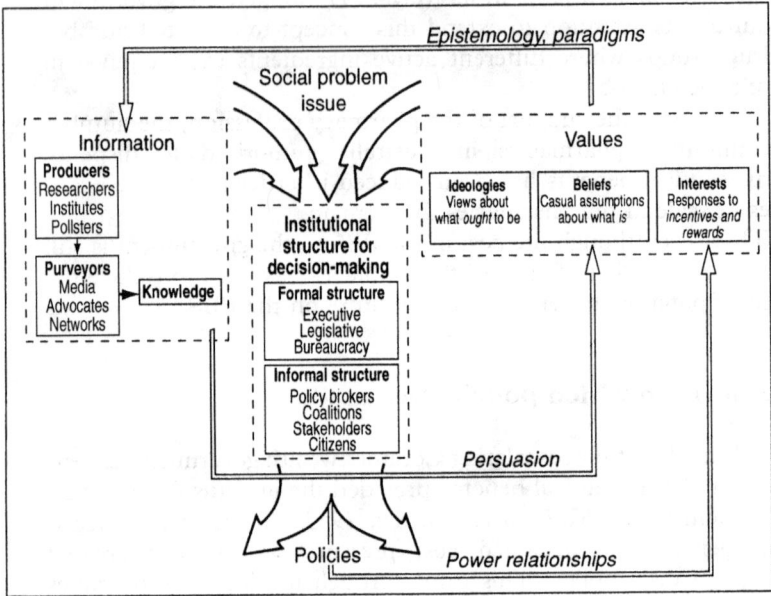

Source: Lomas 1996.

signs of other countries also applying economic evaluations to reflect and influence their policy on pharmaceuticals?

The social problem

Australia, along with many other industrialised countries in the 1980s, experienced marked rises in government expenditure on drugs. The primary concern has been about cost and rising health care expenditure and not cost-effectiveness. There was no systematic approach to evaluating whether successive drugs listed on the PBS represented a good use of public money. This was unsustainable in an open-ended Commonwealth pharmaceutical budget.

In seeking the passage of the 1987 amendment to the *National Health Act, 1953* the Minister specified that the requirement for cost-effectiveness was to achieve 'value for the taxpayer's dollar and improve efficiency' (Commonwealth of Australia 1987). (Interestingly, the legislation does not specify explicitly the efficiency objectives of the PBAC.) The central questions for the PBAC in developing cost-effectiveness policy for its decision-making were:

- What are the efficiency criteria to be used by the PBAC?
- What perspective should be adopted? (Only the health services or something broader?)
- What types of economic evaluation are appropriate to meet the efficiency criteria? Hence
- On what basis are the outcomes of new pharmaceuticals to be valued?

A climate for change

In a review of the policy change process, Duckett (1997) cites a study by Milio (1988) on progressive policy change in four countries in which she identified a number of common elements in the policy process:

- the political climate was ripe for change;
- the policy was created by a small elite;
- there was political backing at high level prior to any consultation;
- the selling of the policy relied on extensive use of information;
- timing and leadership were critical elements; and
- resources were available for implementation.

All of these features are to be found in the process of introducing economic criteria to PBAC decision-making.

In the leadup to the passing of the 1987 amendment of the *National Health Act, 1953* Commonwealth expenditure on pharmaceutical benefits had continued to grow exponentially. There was considerable political will to reduce the rate of growth in health spending. In the second reading speech of the *National Health Amendment Bill (no 2), 1987*, the Minister for Veterans' Affairs claimed that if further cost-control measures had not been introduced in the 1986 Budget (which, among other measures, doubled the co-payment for general beneficiaries from $5.00 to $10.00 per script with a safety-net threshold of 25 scripts, after which scripts in the remaining calendar year would attract a lower co-payment), expenditure on the PBS would have risen by 59 per cent in the two years since 1985/86. Government concern about increasing prescription of expensive drugs led to an 'efficiency scrutiny' being conducted in early 1987 into the payment of pharmaceutical benefits.

The open-ended nature of government expenditure on pharmaceuticals added to the political climate for change in the way that the PBAC made reimbursement decisions about new drugs. There was political backing within the health portfolio for economic data to be included as criteria for deciding the list price of a new drug.

Additional resources were made available to support the PBAC. These were initially used to better assess drug utilisation patterns and to draft guidelines for conducting economic evaluation in submissions. Subsequently they were to establish the Pharmaceutical Evaluation Section, whose responsibility it was to implement and review these guidelines and, once economic submissions had been received, to appraise critically these submissions.

Industry gave support in principle for the provision of information on cost-effectiveness, with most people in the industry reserving judgement until they could see how it would work in practice. The industry was also assured that the draft economic guidelines for submissions would be reviewed and revised in response to consultations with the industry (which they were). A further revision of the guidelines took place in 1995, and the revision process was initiated again in 1996 (Carmine 1996; Grobler et al. 1996; Langley 1996; Mitchell 1996b). The message from the pharmaceutical industry concerning this latest revision of the guidelines is that greater account must be given to the production effects and wider economic impact of new drugs. The question of the extent to which these effects ought to be considered remains to be answered.

Values

Ideologies and interests

Grund (1996) postulates that drugs generate two sets of values for society, one as a health care product and the other as an industrial product. The Commonwealth government must balance the different and potentially conflicting arms of national medicinal policy that deal with these two sets of values. The health-related aspects include the supply of medicines of acceptable quality, safety and efficacy, and affordable access to necessary medicines. The addition of cost-effectiveness criteria suggests that efficiency is an underlying value. The industry-related aspects of pharmaceutical policy include the extent to which government provides incentives for increasing local production and distribution of drugs, encourages exports, and promotes local research and development.

Within government, the 'health' interests are the responsibility of the Department of Health and Family Services; the 'industry' interests lie with the Department of Industry, Science and Tourism. For its part, the PBAC has adopted *Guidelines* for economic analysis, with the primary objective of maximising the health of Australians. The Department of Industry has a voice in pricing policy and general government assistance to the pharmaceutical industry. For example, following the recent Industry Commission review of the pharmaceutical industry (Commonwealth of Australia 1996b), the government decided that the 'Factor f' scheme would be extended into the next century, with about $300 million allocated over three to five years beginning in 2002 (Commonwealth of Australia 1996b).

The Commonwealth government simultaneously decided to change the patent protection laws to extend them beyond the recent GATT agreements, in keeping with the USA and most European countries. Instead of the patent protection commencing from the date the chemical is registered, under the new laws the protection will start from the date of the product launch. This effectively extends the number of years that a new drug is protected, thereby offering industry greater returns for its R&D.

The main players in the pharmaceutical market are citizens, industry, health care providers and government. As well as being an active participant, the government extends its role to establishing the 'rules of the game'. Where there is conflict between the policy recommendations of 'health' and 'industry' these are resolved at Cabinet level. Government must also manage these competing interests through the best use of taxpayers' dollars.

Pharmaceutical companies are responsible to their shareholders to try to maximise the return on their investment. The aim of R&D, production and distribution of new drugs is primarily to generate profits and secondarily to maintain goodwill within the local market. In doing so, the companies contribute to the wealth of the nation and the health of its citizens.

For their part, as taxpayers and as patients the citizens of Australia have a stake in pharmaceutical policy. As taxpayers they require that the government be accountable for expenditure and use their dollars efficiently. As patients and beneficiaries of public price subsidies, people want affordable access to necessary medicines. As informed citizens, health care providers have particular influence both in advising on the clinical place of new drugs and in advocating their listing. Consumer associations recognise the need to strike a balance between what is best for the 'common good' and what is best for the 'individual'. Yet until the recent addition of a consumer representative to the PBAC, consumer involvement in that body's decision-making had been limited. Specific consumer groups also advocate the interests of patients with particular diseases such as multiple sclerosis and HIV/AIDS, particularly when a new drug is being reviewed by the PBAC. Public pressure can be brought to bear through media coverage of PBAC decisions on individual drugs as well as organised lobbying activities.

Beliefs

The PBAC's values are heavily influenced by its beliefs about the likely implications of a recommendation that a drug be subsidised on the PBS. There are three reasons for this. As noted above, the PBAC sits at the end of a rigorous evaluation process which is unique among all health care interventions. Drug regulation has created an evaluation culture founded on strict scientific principles. This culture is supported by the pharmaceutical industry (regulatory approval offers protection against litigation) and ensures that there is scientifically rigorous evidence to support claims against the three decision criteria of quality, safety and efficacy. The drug evaluation process has arisen from concern built up this century about the safety of agents that are ingested with the intention of healing or ameliorating disease but which also carry unintended risks of possibly unacceptable adverse effects. Public outcries with the sulphonamides in the 1930s and thalidomide in the 1960s generated the impetus to develop the extensive drug regulatory process that has to be completed before a new drug can enter the market.

The implementation of a requirement to consider cost-effectiveness preceded worldwide interest in evidence-based medicine (especially through the Cochrane Collaboration), which depends on a systematic review of all relevant evidence of acceptable scientific rigour. The purpose of providing information on incremental cost-effectiveness is to help justify the increased expenditure on the PBS. Consequently, failure to provide supporting evidence to support a claim of benefit is regarded very unfavourably.

There is an emphasis on measurement of all quantifiable and relevant costs and benefits. Although the edges remain blurred, such measurement extends beyond the perspective of the PBS to society more generally, and beyond health care resources and health outcomes to equity and indirect outcomes. Measurements of incremental differences are assessed for random error (could they have occurred by chance?) and for systematic error (is there another explanation for the difference that cannot be excluded?). Evidence that minimises these errors is most preferred, but the PBAC promotes an explicit hierarchy that sets no general minimum standard. Modelled economic evaluations are encouraged to allow generalisation beyond the acknowledged limitations of randomised trials using assumptions that are examined through the use of sensitivity analyses.

Information

It is one thing to enact legislation requiring the use of economic analyses in PBAC decisions for reimbursement of new drugs. It is quite another to specify how this can be done, and the Australian authorities were the first to make an attempt. The principles and methods of economic evaluation had never previously been subjected to such scrutiny and high expectations in a major health policy initiative (Salkeld et al. 1995). The success of the addition of economic criteria to PBAC subsidisation decisions regarding new drugs depended on a sound theoretical basis for conducting economic evaluation of drugs as well as guidelines for the technical execution of specific economic analyses.

With the assistance of a team of international experts and the federal Department of Health, the PBAC released a set of 'draft guidelines' in August 1990 to indicate to the pharmaceutical industry its information requirements so that the Committee could adequately meet this legislative intent (Commonwealth of Australia 1990). A second document describing the theoretical underpinnings for these *Guidelines* was also made available. A revised set of *Guidelines* was released in August 1992 (Commonwealth of Australia 1992). The requirement for economic analyses in new drug submissions came into effect in January 1993. Prior to that, there was a 'phasing-in' period, during which the inclusion of economic analysis in a submission was optional. In this way the industry, the Department of Health and the PBAC all gained valuable experience in, respectively, preparing, evaluating and using the information as requested by the *Guidelines*.

The current Australian *Guidelines* are quite prescriptive in how to prepare a submission containing an economic evaluation. The PBAC emphasises the need for a transparent and evidence-based approach to comparing the incremental costs and benefits of a new drug. The *Guidelines* provide an explicit hierarchy of levels of evidence, with randomised controlled trials preferred to lower levels of evidence such as expert opinion. In that respect, the *Guidelines* for economic evaluation remain firmly within a clinical framework for decision-making. Thus, economic data are seen as an aid to decision-making and not as the sole arbiter of drug subsidy decisions (Neumann & Johannesson 1994).

On an operational level, the Pharmaceutical Evaluation Section, whose job includes evaluating each submission critically, recognises the need to adopt a pragmatic approach, at least in the short term, to the PBAC's stated preference for trial-based data to establish comparative clinical performance as a prerequisite to considering comparative economic performance (Mitchell 1996a; Mitchell & Menon 1996). The PBAC's request for a preliminary trial-based economic analysis is a major area of concern within industry. Industry spokespersons feel that the balance between a trial-based cost–efficacy and modelling approaches to 'real world' estimates of cost-effectiveness is weighted too heavily towards trial-based methods. Carmine (1996) argues that controlled trials are usually not predictive of the 'real-world' situation. Further, it is the industry's view that the intention of the 1987 amendment was 'cost-effectiveness' analysis, which 'blends the use of data from well-controlled studies with the realities of the actual treatment process' (Gorham 1995).

Getting the balance right is tricky. On the one hand, the rigour and credibility of trial-based economic evidence may come at an increased cost to industry. On the other, the use of modelling techniques provides greater flexibility for industry but increases the risk for the PBAC of making decisions based on less reliable evidence. Longer-term, the answer lies in designing randomised trials that reflect better the use of new drugs in routine clinical practice. For example, they should include active comparators where appropriate, measure patient-relevant outcomes, and follow patients for a sufficient duration.

The content of the *Guidelines* has been described elsewhere (Aristides & Mitchell 1994; Glasziou & Mitchell 1996; Freund 1996; Langley 1996). From a policy perspective, the more interesting aspects of 'information' concern the way in which the values of the key players (government and industry) have influenced the development and subsequent revision of the *Guidelines*. This is apparent in several key areas, including: the choice of a *comparator* as the basis for incremental analysis; the *perspective* adopted within the *Guidelines*; the *definition of efficiency* criteria used by the PBAC; and how to *value the benefits* of new drugs.

Choice of comparator
The *Guidelines* require the systematic evaluation of *incremental* costs and benefits of a new therapy. It follows that the choice of a comparator influences the results. This was recognised early in the development of the *Guidelines*. They state that the comparator (which could be a non-drug therapy) should be 'the therapy which most prescribers would replace in practice'. This avoids the possibility of a bias from the selective choice of comparator drug.

Efficiency criteria
The 1987 amendment requires the PBAC to consider 'value for money' in its decision on the level of reimbursement for a new drug. While this translates easily to an efficiency objective, the *Guidelines*

do not specify the efficiency criteria. Rather, they specify the perspective of the analysis (societal) and which evaluative techniques can be used: cost–effectiveness analysis (including cost-minimisation analysis), cost–utility analysis, and cost–benefit analysis (though the last, which addresses the question of allocative efficiency, is neither promoted nor encouraged in the *Guidelines*).

Technical efficiency is usually concerned with meeting a given objective at least cost. If the primary objective of the PBAC is to maximise health gains, then the question becomes how to maximise health at least cost, and cost–effectiveness and cost–utility analysis are the relevant techniques.

If, on the other hand, the objective of the PBAC were to decide whether, for a new drug, the increased benefits outweighed the increased costs, then this is a matter of allocative efficiency, and cost–benefit analysis is the appropriate evaluative technique. To date, the PBAC has discouraged the use of cost–benefit analysis, implying that the PBS has already answered the question of whether it is worthwhile providing health gains by subsidising access to pharmaceuticals. Therefore the (unstated) objective of the *Guidelines*, even with an 'uncapped' pharmaceutical budget, is to consider technical efficiency. In practice, however, the PBAC consecutively considers many drugs, each of which can promote a different health gain in a different patient group. It also recommends drugs that promote further health gains even though they disproportionately raise costs when it judges that the health gains outweigh the increased costs. Assimilating these elements of maximising allocative efficiency is a matter being considered in the current revision process.

Perspective
Virtually all economic guidelines for the economic appraisal of pharmaceuticals adopt a societal perspective. Notable exceptions include proposed Italian guidelines, which suggest adopting a payer perspective (Garattini et al. 1995), and proposed US HMO guidelines, which suggest adopting a health system purchaser perspective (Langley & Sullivan 1996). The perspective of a study is important because it defines the scope of costs and outcomes to be included in the analysis. A societal perspective includes all costs and benefits no matter where they fall or accrue. The Australian *Guidelines* clearly state that an economic evaluation should be conducted from a societal perspective. Despite this, there has been some controversy about the inclusion of indirect costs and effects. Assumed changes in productive capacity as an outcome of therapy are not encouraged in submissions to the PBAC. The *Guidelines* state that '*productivity estimates give the misleading impression that additional*

output in the economy will pay for the additional drug consumption'
(Commonwealth of Australia 1995). Therefore companies are
required to justify the inclusion of indirect benefits in their economic
appraisal and to present the results with and without the indirect
benefits and costs included. This provides the PBAC with some
measure of freedom to decide what, if any, importance may be
attached to production gains and losses in its deliberations about
reimbursement decisions.

There are implications for priority-setting in pharmaceuticals if,
for example, drugs for patient groups with high earnings are given
priority over other groups with low earnings. While equity in the
sense of 'affordable access to necessary medicine' remains an explicit
objective of the PBS, the equity objectives of the PBAC are probably
considered on a case-by-case basis.

Valuing outcomes

The *Guidelines* require a preliminary economic evaluation based on
the evidence from comparative randomised trials. Companies may
also submit a modelled economic evaluation, which allows for the
extrapolation of surrogate outcomes from trials to final outcomes.
The former evaluation specifies that each outcome should be
described in terms of a natural unit of measurement (such as life-
years saved—if available—or the number of successes or failures of
treatment) with 95 per cent confidence intervals. Survival as a
measure of outcome is comparable across different therapies, and can
be used in league tables to assess relative value for money across
different therapeutic groups (for a review of PBAC decisions using
life-years saved, see George et al. in press). Disease-specific measures
of outcome are comparable within therapeutic groups, where it is a
matter of choosing drugs within diseases. For example, the cost of a
drug that achieves a ≥50 per cent decrease in seizures among patients
with refractory epilepsy is comparable to other drugs used to treat
epilepsy.

Ideally, these and other drugs where quality of life is an important
outcome would be subjected to cost–utility analysis. The current
Guidelines do not prescribe the methods for deriving QALY utility
weights in deriving quality-adjusted life-year (QALY) measures. A
question for the current revision is: 'To what extent is it possible (or
even desirable) to standardise methodology, and standardise to
what?'.

It must be recognised that, while there is considerable diversity
in the practice of deriving utility weights, there is a well-developed
theoretical foundation for deriving QALYs. As practice moves further
away from theory it becomes difficult to assess what is being done

and how to assess the worth of different utility-based preference weights. If it can be established that there is some conceptual and technical 'common ground' for the derivation of QALYs, it might be feasible to develop a set of guidelines for measuring and valuing utility weights for PBAC submissions.

Institutional structure for decision-making

We have seen how ideologies, beliefs and interests interact with the provision of information to influence decisions. These decisions are mediated through the institutional structure for decision-making, that is, the political process. Institutions matter because they define possibilities and shape outcomes according to their interpretation of the underlying values.

After receiving expert advice, the PBAC has specified the information it needs to meet this legislative requirement in a set of *Guidelines* (Commonwealth of Australia 1995) offering detailed technical advice to sponsors of drugs on how the relevant information should be identified, combined and presented. Generating the contents of this document entails a complex amalgam of paradigms from diverse disciplines such as health economics, clinical science and biostatistics. A collaborative tension has ensued, which takes the apparently contradictory theoretical foundations of each discipline and forges a pragmatic approach which minimises the risk that any critical foundation will be contravened. This multidisciplinary approach has attracted some criticism (Langley 1996; Grobler et al. 1996).

Given the quantity and complexity of the information provided by sponsors in response to these *Guidelines*, the Department has established a team of evaluators to appraise critically each submission in depth (Glasziou & Mitchell 1996). The tasks of the team are to check the information provided for accuracy, relevance and adequacy and to provide a written commentary on the submission. The PBAC has also established an Economics Sub-Committee of experts in appraising clinical and economic information, to review and interpret each submission and related commentary and to advise the PBAC on its quality, validity and relevance.

The generation and use of a more explicit evidence basis for decision-making improves the consistency and transparency of the listing process. The sponsor now receives the Department's commentary in time to provide a written rejoinder on any matters in dispute prior to consideration by the PBAC. Sponsors are also encouraged to discuss proposed submissions with secretariats of both committees and to obtain additional feedback on PBAC outcomes.

However, the secrecy provisions of the *National Health Act, 1953* effectively curtail the provision of information by government officers involved in the listing process to any other stakeholder, including the sponsor of any comparator drug, or to potential prescribers and consumers of the drug. Given the public impact of listing or not listing a major new drug, there have been a number of calls (Marley 1996; Hill et al. 1997) for these provisions to be amended to meet the public's right to know the basis of the decisions.

Methods for eliciting the consumer's voice in the decision-making process are being encouraged. These range from having a consumer representative contribute at PBAC meetings to supporting more formal research into the participation of the public in resource allocation decisions.

The use of economic evaluation in other countries

Since the PBAC *Guidelines* were first released in 1990, many other guidelines have been and are still being promulgated. The content of the earliest of these has been reviewed elsewhere (Genduso & Kotsanos 1996; Neumann et al. 1996), so we focus here instead on the other aspects of the worlds in which any of these subsequent guidelines influence or reflect policy relating to health care resource allocation.

Some guidelines are likely to influence and reflect such policy indirectly. For example, the *Principles for the Review of Pharmacoeconomic Promotion: Draft Guidelines* (FDA 1995) relate specifically to US policy on the promotional activities of drug companies. Likewise, the *Report of the Panel on Cost-Effectiveness in Health and Medicine* (Gold et al. 1996) is intended to apply generally across the US Public Health Service rather than to any specific decision-making body.

The guidelines which can directly influence and reflect such policy are those which have been promulgated under the authority of the relevant drug subsidy agency. Only the guidelines from Ontario (Ontario Ministry of Health 1994) and France (Agence du Médicament 1995) meet this criterion. Although the other drug subsidy programs administered by each province in Canada are prepared to receive economic evaluations of drugs, only British Columbia has specifically requested that these follow the Canadian guidelines (CCOHTA 1994), promulgated by an independent agency with Canadian government funding.

The listing processes of all three of these jurisdictions have an institutional structure featuring political decision-makers receiving advice from independent expert committees in addition to the advice of the supporting bureaucracies. Their guidelines tend to reflect the values and information that have been shown to exist in the world in which PBS listing policies are made, although specific details do vary. One difference is that no revisions have been released by the decision-makers to reflect developments in understanding these values and information needs, possibly because these guidelines have been more recently promulgated.

In common with the Australian experience, the Ontario Drug Benefit program subsequently established a defined evaluation process to assess the extent to which the information provided meets the values of the institutional structure. Likewise, in establishing its therapeutic and pharmacoeconomic initiatives, the Pharmacare program in British Columbia subsequently established a defined evaluation process. In contrast, although the listing process of the drug subsidy system in France has a similar advisory committee process, a process to evaluate the submitted information does not appear to have been established. Chalanson (1997) reports that the advisory committee process gives this as a reason why, from September 1997, it is no longer mandatory for economic evaluations of drugs to be submitted in France. The introduction of more detailed information requirements in the form of guidelines appears to be a necessary but not sufficient prerequisite to developing a broader and arguably more robust world in which to form policies for health care resource allocation decisions.

The systematic use of economic evaluation in pharmaceutical price decision-making: Can it work for other types of health care interventions?

Health policy is not created in a contextual vacuum, nor does it change rapidly. In the pharmaceutical arena, a confluence of events, circumstances and political will have brought about the legislative requirement for change. Maintaining the desire for change towards more efficient use of the pharmaceutical benefit dollar sustained the impact of economic evaluation on decision-making. There was a commitment from government, academia and industry to make it happen and make it work. It took several years to develop the *Guidelines* to support the use of economic evaluation in decision-making. In its May 1997 Budget the Commonwealth government announced that it would extend its experience in appraising pharmaceuticals to health care interventions covered under other Medicare programs. In implementing this announcement, the Department of Health faces at least three major challenges.

Within the institutional structure of policy-making the PBAC has a long history of critically appraising new drugs. It and the pharmaceutical industry also have a culture of evaluation. For economic appraisal to work in other settings, a culture of evaluation is an important requirement for change. Once that is in place, the rest is a matter of timing, political will and a commitment to change.

Setting up the institutional framework for evaluation is one thing; making it happen is another. Someone has to pay for the generation and presentation of the necessary information. The question of who pays may be an impediment to the application of systematic economic evaluation to other health care interventions. Unless the sponsor of the evaluation perceives a direct link between the evaluation and its potential benefits, the case for systematic evaluation will be weakened. The difficulty lies in assessing the counterfactual. The opportunity cost of not performing systematic economic evaluation may be greater than would be the case with systematic evaluation. Indeed, the need for economic evaluation is based on the premise that it will yield efficiency gains. How these efficiency gains are then distributed among the agencies bearing the cost of information-gathering will, most likely, influence the acceptability of economic evaluation wherever it is applied. The Commonwealth announced a total of $21 million over the first four years following the Budget announcement.

The measurement of outcomes may not be straightforward in other health care settings. Drugs always induce a direct health outcome, but this is not necessarily so for other health care interventions. A new diagnostic agent may have a health impact only if it has an effect on the therapeutic management of a disease. The fact that outcomes in other health care settings may be difficult to measure or value is an impediment to evaluation but not a reason to abandon it. Requirements for systematic economic evaluation may have the effect of encouraging development of measurement techniques for outcomes where previously there were few such incentives.

Conclusion

How successful has the scheme been? The first answer to such a question is surely another question: What would success mean and how would that be measured? Presumably what would be needed in any such evaluation would be to examine the incremental costs of the scheme and compare these with the benefits. While some assessment of the former could probably be made now, the latter—the benefits—are much less easily identified at this stage of the process. Even in the longer run the extent to which the benefits will be measurable has to be questioned. We do not know enough about the counterfactual (what would have happened otherwise) to reach any definite conclusion.

There can be few, however, who would doubt that the idea of weighing up the costs and benefits of new pharmaceuticals for listing for public subsidy was a good thing. There cannot be an open-ended commitment from the public purse to subsidise pharmaceutical products: some form of rationing has to occur. Once that is admitted and accepted, the question becomes what form that rationing should take.

It is difficult to envisage a system that did not take explicit account of the costs and benefits being superior to that introduced in Australia. So, what system of economic evaluation is to be preferred?

This debate now lies in the international arena, with various countries going through the same process. But at an international level there is only one system that has moved beyond the initial implementation stages—the Australian. What is noteworthy is the extent of interest internationally in operations on this front in Australia.

We would submit that legitimate answers to this debate are now being generated in Australia. There is no doubt scope for improving the current scheme, and as we have indicated there have already been various changes since its inception. However, the Australian experience shows that the necessary mix of values, information and structures for decision-making can be developed. A scheme along these lines is here to stay.

By reviewing the world in which the policies were made to introduce the requirement for economic evaluation of new pharmaceuticals, we have also shown that this baseline is important for the successful implementation of the initiative. In other words, there are lessons to be learned that might be relevant to getting major changes in policy in somewhat similar vein in other parts of the health sector or indeed beyond that.

The background of rising public expenditure with no overt mechanism of control created a climate in which the need for more visible accountability was apparent. This desire for 'value for money' coincided with the rise in popularity of economic evaluation, both in academic and policy circles—largely it would seem because of the greater willingness to put actual measures on health in the form of the QALY. The encouraging climate for economic evaluation was further aided by the era of evidence-based medicine, in which evidence-based pharmaceutical trials led the way. It is hardly surprising then that it was in pharmaceuticals that such economic evaluation supported by trial evidence paved the way.

There is little reason to think that the advances that have been made in pharmaceutical policy-making and which have been documented in this chapter cannot be emulated in other areas of health policy. But it is unlikely that all the circumstances will be quite so favourable. Any lack there, however, is likely to be more than compensated for by the fact that any other policy area will have an example to go by.

7 *The economics of aged care: achieving quality and containing costs*

At the same time as ageing of the population is seen as threatening to impose intolerable costs for health and long-term care on the community, actual levels of expenditure never seem to be regarded as sufficient to provide high quality care for the frail and vulnerable. The tension between controlling cost and maintaining quality was evident throughout the decade of Labor's Aged Care Reform Strategy, from the mid-1980s to the mid-1990s, and was at the fore in radical new policies proposed by the incoming Liberal government in March 1996. The justification for these policy changes, particularly with respect to nursing home funding, came largely from the National Commission of Audit, which identified population ageing as a major source of pressure on Commonwealth expenditures and likely to burden future generations. It recommended that (National Commission of Audit 1996: 140):

> While maintaining universal access to nursing homes for those in need, the government should change funding arrangements so that those able to contribute more towards their own care do so. This could be achieved by introducing means testing for nursing home benefits and, for income poor but asset rich clients, providing scope for the government to recover the cost of nursing home benefits from their estates.

There is nothing new in these concerns, and this chapter begins with a brief history of the changing views of responsibility for cost control and quality of aged care since the 1970s.

Identifying responsibility for cost control and quality

Historically in Australia there have been periods of rapid escalation in the cost of aged care at the same time as major concerns were expressed about quality. From the mid-1960s and through the 70s long-term care in Australia was effectively nursing home care, which absorbed close to 90 per cent of expenditure. The widespread dissatisfaction with quality of care has been recounted by Kewley (1973).

Several reasons for past rapid cost escalations have been identified, and these shortcomings have become the focus of policy attention at different times (Howe 1986). Prior to 1972 there were no controls on bed numbers, so rapid bed growth combined with periodic fee increases saw costs escalate. When growth controls were introduced in early 1972 the planning ratio, set at the average of current provision, still allowed considerable additional development. Further, there was little effective fee control: neither the participating scheme that applied to private sector providers nor the deficit financing scheme that applied to the voluntary sector created incentives for cost control. A final reason for the escalation of expenditure was the lack of alternative forms of care, and hence continuing excess demand for nursing home care. Even in the voluntary sector, the superior support for and returns to nursing homes limited the effectiveness of several attempts to expand hostel care as an alternative (Howe & Sharwood 1989).

The one factor that could not be identified as creating pressure for escalating outlays to the mid-1970s was growth of the aged population. The population aged 65 years and over grew only slowly by 34 per cent from 1961 to 1976. Mainly due to sustained immigration, the proportion aged 65 years and over grew only marginally, from 8.5 per cent to 8.9 per cent over that 15 years.

The reasons for the persistence of poor quality of care, notwithstanding the growth of expenditure, have been addressed less often. The most commonly identified reason is the perceived avariciousness of nursing home operators, especially in the private sector. Despite constant protestations that nursing homes were on the brink of financial disaster, the past profitability of the industry is evidenced by a sustained rate of capital inflow, the high levels of goodwill paid when beds were sold, the virtual zero risk associated with government underwriting, and negligible business failures. Twenty years on, none of these factors has changed sufficiently to make nursing homes an unattractive investment.

Attributing poor quality of care to greedy proprietors is too simplistic an explanation and begs the question as to why government took so little responsibility for the outcome of its substantial expenditure on nursing home care. The course by which this changed has been traced from a period of laissez-faire policy in the 1960s through a period of policy by regulation in the 1970s, to the major restructuring undertaken by the Labor government from the early 1980s (Howe 1990). The full extent of responsibility that the Commonwealth then assumed is seen in the range of measures taken through the Aged Care Reform Strategy (DHHCS

1991, 1993). The controls over spending on residential care that were implemented in concert with measures to protect residents' rights, monitor outcome standards and promote good care practices are set out in Table 7.1.

Just as the early history of aged care showed that uncontrolled expenditure did not necessarily result in high quality care, the Reform Strategy recognised that additional expenditure would not automatically achieve better quality care. The most obvious reason for this is that funds could be siphoned off and not spent on care at all. Second, funds could be poorly or unwisely spent on areas that contributed little to quality of care. A third reason is that it might not be possible to buy the inputs needed to provide good care; shortages of qualified staff are a case in point. Finally, there is a need for incentives to improve care and penalties for providing poor care, including a regulatory framework designed to promote quality of care.

Although the margins for ongoing change narrowed and the momentum of the Reform Strategy overall flagged by the mid-1990s (Howe 1997b), the nursing home funding system came under continuing pressure from the industry, particularly the National Association for Nursing Homes and Private Hospitals. Recognising that the broader economic climate made additional government funding unlikely, attention turned to means of loosening the controls

Table 7.1 Aged care reform strategy: measures implemented to control cost and improve quality of care

Protection of residents' rights	Standards of care
• Charter of residents' rights • Resident–proprietor agreements • Complaints units • Community visitors • Advocacy services	• Outcome standards defined • Standards Monitoring Teams • Publicly available reports • Declaration of 'homes of concern' • Imposition of sanctions
Financing measures and cost controls	**Promotion of appropriate care**
• Care funding based on resident needs • Validated rating of care needs • Acquittal of care costs • Infrastructure costs paid at flat rate • Control of provision by planning ratios • Fee control through standard resident contribution • Exempt homes	• Training • Staff mix and skills • Clinical guidelines (e.g. medication) • Special-care programs (e.g. dementia care) • Special needs groups (e.g. ethnic aged) • Residential respite care • Preadmission assessment

within the funding structure and the scope for increased user charges.

A review of the structure of nursing home funding was commissioned by the Labor government in late 1993 (Gregory 1993a). The terms of reference of the Funding Structure Review noted that options for structural reform would need to ensure that funding provided for direct care was used for that purpose, to complement labour market efficiencies through reforms in industrial relations, and to provide incentives and scope for greater efficiencies in the operation of nursing homes. The review was extended to a second stage specifically to investigate the adequacy of capital funding for nursing homes, including interaction with the hostel funding system, which allowed resident entry charges and variable fees related to residents' incomes (Gregory 1994).

The Funding Structure Review did not result in any major changes being made by the Labor government, but some of the options canvassed were taken up in the Opposition's policies leading up to the 1996 election. The change of federal government then brought a fundamental redefinition of the issues requiring attention in aged care policy and of the approaches to be taken to them.

The structural reform package focused on residential care, with the aim of bringing about an integration of the separate hostel and nursing home systems. The rationales for integration were that substantial numbers of hostel residents were as dependent as those in nursing homes, and that hostel residents who came to require nursing home care would be able to 'age in place'. The move to an integrated residential care system also carried with it the extension of hostel variable fees and entry contributions to nursing homes. With both these measures having the capacity to inject additional funds into the nursing home system from users while relieving government outlays, the more fundamental motives for integration are evident. The 1996–97 Budget Estimates showed that over the next four years, the Commonwealth stood to save $244.69 million in capital outlays from the introduction of resident entry contributions for nursing homes, with increased fees generating a further $253.08 million savings in recurrent payments (Commonwealth of Australia 1966). While these savings made a substantial contribution to the government's immediate budget targets, the proposed measures were justified in terms of the need to control escalating costs over the long term. Given these ostensible grounds for the changes, a brief account of expenditure trends over the past decade is needed to set the scene for analysis of the effectiveness of the measures adopted to date and those now proposed in controlling costs and promoting quality of care.

Recent trends in expenditure on aged care

From 1985/86 to the time of the *Mid Term Review* of the Aged Care Reform Strategy in 1990/91, total expenditure on Australia's aged care program grew in real terms by 28 per cent, well ahead of the 16 per cent growth in the population aged 70 years and over (the base population used for planning aged care services). For the next five years to 1995/96, the real growth in expenditure moderated slightly to 25 per cent, yielding even lower relative growth, given an 18 per cent growth in the aged population.

Within these overall trends, there were major shifts in the balance of expenditure between residential care and community care, and within residential care, between nursing homes and hostels. In brief, from 1985 to 1997 the share of all funding going to nursing homes declined from 80 to 63 per cent while expenditure rose on hostels from below 5 to 13 per cent, and on community care from 15 to 21 per cent, with the remainder on assessment and some innovative programs substituting community care for hostel care. Detailed accounts of these trends compiled by the Australian Institute of Health and Welfare (1995, 1997) show that the shift in the balance of care was achieved by injections of additional funding, as it was not until the mid-1990s that savings from reductions in nursing home outlays began to be realised.

The decade of steady but contained growth in aged care expenditure from the early 1980s to the early 90s spanned the period of the most rapid growth in aged population in Australia's history and projected for the short- to medium-term future. It is not until after 2016 that the population aged 70 and over is projected to increase at a rate reaching, but not exceeding, the 21 per cent increase seen between the 1981 and 1986 censuses. The rate of increase drops slightly to 1996, and then falls more steeply, to less than 10 per cent for each of the intercensal periods from 2001 to 2011. While these projections call for the maintenance of the strong central controls that contained growth of outlays through this recent period, population ageing in Australia does not threaten doomsday.

The modest increase in aged care expenditure occurred against a stable level of expenditure on health overall as a proportion of GDP over the longer term. In noting the stability of these expenditure trends in comparison to the growth of aged population, three recent reviews have concluded that the relationship between demographic trends and expenditure levels is mediated by many other factors, including the nature of policy decisions taken by government (Goss et al. 1997; Taylor & Salkeld 1996; Howe 1997a). Gregory (1994) has also observed that growth in expenditure has been erratic, reflecting policy changes, rather than moving in line with the steady growth of aged population.

The Australian experience has been similar to that of the other OECD countries, with the notable exception of the USA (Johnson 1996). The comparative analysis made by Goss et al. (1997) identifies Australia as a high spender on health care generally relative to its youthful age structure; they calculate that health outlays would drop by 30 per cent if the age-adjusted expenditures of the UK applied in Australia. Taylor and Salkeld (1996) emphasise the similarity of outcomes among the OECD countries in improvements in life-expectancies notwithstanding variations in the proportion of GDP spent on health care over the past two decades, and argue strongly against Australia adopting health care reforms from systems with markedly higher costs but no better outcomes. The evidence is that it has been, and presumably will continue to be, possible for governments to make policy decisions that deliver health and long-term care to older age groups without losing control of expenditures.

Cost control and quality improvement in nursing home recurrent funding

A number of macro and micro level measures related to recurrent funding of nursing home care have been used to control cost and improve quality of care concurrently.

Control of bed numbers

One of the first steps taken in the Aged Care Reform Strategy was to strengthen control over the growth of nursing home beds and thereby change the balance of residential care towards hostels. The introduction of bed controls in the early 1970s had stabilised provision at around 70 beds per 1000 aged 70 years and over, but an upswing in growth from 1979 saw the ratio rise to 74 beds per 1000 in 1982. The change of government in 1983 brought a pause in approvals for new beds and, allowing for an adjustment that removed homes catering for younger people with disabilities from the aged care program, there were 67 nursing home beds per 1000 aged 70 and over in 1985. The 33 hostel places per 1000 brought the total residential care ratio to 100 places per 1000. The planning ratios of 40 nursing home beds and 60 hostel places per 1000 were set in 1986 with the intention of reversing the balance between the two forms of residential care over the next 20 years. The effectiveness of the planning ratios is seen in the outcome realised by 1996, when there were

50 nursing home beds and 41 hostel places per 1000 population aged 70 years and over.

Outlays on nursing home care did not, however, fall in line with this pronounced decline in provision, as there were offsetting rises in costs per bed. Gregory (1994) has demonstrated that the additional resources more than compensated for increases in resident dependency and the higher cost of some inputs, and that additional care hours and enhanced staff skills lead to improvements in quality.

Case-mix funding of care costs

Improved quality of care was pursued through several features of the nursing home funding arrangements introduced from 1987 that addressed the threats arising from the practices commonly labelled 'skimming' and 'skimping'. Skimming is a response to incentives to admit residents who can be cared for at a cost below the level of reimbursement, ahead of high-cost, more dependent residents. Skimping occurs when funds are not spent on care as intended, and standards fall.

The two main components of the 1987 funding system were an amount for nursing and personal care, the Care Aggregated Module (CAM), and a separate component for infrastructure or hotel costs, the Standard Aggregated Module (SAM). The rationale for separating these components and the way in which they operated has been detailed elsewhere (Department of Community Services and Health 1987; Gregory 1993b). In defining levels of funds prospectively and allocating care funds on the basis of individually assessed resident dependency, and other hotel and infrastructure costs at a fixed rate, CAM/SAM effectively constituted a case-mix system. The similarities between the CAM/SAM system and the Resource Utilisation Groups developed for funding of nursing home care in the USA have been noted (Duckett et al. 1995).

CAM was paid at five levels, according to dependency and care needs categorised on the basis of the Resident Classification Instrument (RCI), which was completed and documented by the director of nursing. To guard against gaming, this documentation was used in validation of the RCI and the overall distribution of the categories was monitored. CAM was acquitted and unspent funds were recouped, with only a small tolerance margin allowed. These features of CAM worked together to create incentives to admit more dependent residents and to provide care services relative to care needs, thus overcoming the skimming that had occurred when there were only two levels of benefit.

The SAM component was paid at a flat rate for all residents.

SAM was not acquitted and homes were allowed to retain surplus CAM funds, creating an incentive for efficiency. The third component of the CAM/SAM system covered 'other cost-reimbursed expenditure' (OCRE), such as payroll tax. Also within OCRE, payment of workers' compensation premiums at the industry average drove cost control and improvements in care, as occupational health and safety practices impinge directly on quality of care. Again, any surplus from OCRE could be retained by the home, and with SAM and OCRE together accounting for around 45 per cent of total average income per bed there could be a reasonable margin for profit. But homes could not skimp on care by excessive underspending on SAM, as to do so would risk failing the 'outcome standards' that were applied in formal monitoring of quality of care.

Standards monitoring

Failure to comply with the 'outcome standards' posed a threat to income first if a home's reputation fell and residents expressed a preference for other homes, resulting in empty beds. If standards did not improve, the imposition of sanctions meant that homes could not admit new residents, thereby losing income from the empty beds, although funding continued for existing residents. Combined with mandatory assessment that contained demand for nursing home care by directing clients to alternative forms of care and limited the supply of residents to the most dependent, the standards monitoring process created a small but sufficient buyers' market to give prospective residents and their families a margin of choice, and prompted providers to improve quality of care in order to maintain full occupancy.

The effectiveness of the standards monitoring system can be seen in the growing proportion of homes meeting the outcome standards over time; these figures also provide one answer to the question as to whether the CAM/SAM funding was sufficient to provide high quality care. In 1989/90, 13 of the 31 standards were met by fewer than 70 per cent of homes and only one standard was met by more than 90 per cent. By 1993/94, only the standard covering safety of environmental design, equipment and practices was not met by at least 70 per cent of homes, and 13 standards were met by 90 per cent or more (Braithwaite et al. 1993; AIHW 1995: 384). As all homes received the same funding relative to the dependency mix of residents, it follows that the source of variation in quality had to lie in factors other than the level of funding.

It was arguably the existence of the CAM/SAM system per se that had as much effect on controlling costs and improving quality of care as the detail of its operation. The contribution of the CAM/SAM split to improving quality of care by protecting funding for nursing and personal care was acknowledged in the Funding Structure Review (Gregory 1994). Two other options were considered—one involving the abolition of requirements for acquittal of CAM funds, the other moving the boundary between acquitted and non-acquitted funds. The former was seen to be the more radical option: while it allowed for increased profits from improved operational efficiencies and from reductions in the provision of nursing and personal care, these reductions put quality of care at risk. It was considered that the kind of regulation required to guard against such skimping would probably be more burdensome than the existing standards monitoring system (Gregory 1994). Notwithstanding these criticisms, this option was the one adopted in the funding arrangements that were to come into operation from 1 October 1997.

Resident fees and quality of care

The role assigned to resident fees in funding nursing home care has varied over time, reflecting differing views of government responsibility to protect access for those with limited means, the responsibility of individuals to pay for services, and the role of consumer choice as a means to improving quality. Prior to 1987 fees paid by residents were controlled at a level that ensured access to 70 per cent of beds for those who had pension-only income. Maintaining this level of cover had a ratchet effect on Commonwealth outlays, as benefits had to rise in line with fee increases. While fee increases had to be approved for each home, applications were rarely refused. There was, however, no necessary relationship between the level of fees and the quality of care.

From 1990, the amount paid by residents was limited to a Standard Resident Contribution (SRC), set at 87.5 per cent of the age pension plus rent assistance, which was paid to all residents with pension-only income. Some 65 per cent of nursing home residents were full pensioners, and only 10 per cent had income and assets at a level that made them ineligible for any pension. Resident contributions were in effect means-tested, as means-testing of the age pension meant that those who were part-pensioners and non-pensioners had to meet the difference between any pension they received and the SRC from their own income. Income from fees was offset against CAM/SAM and OCRE, and accounted for about 25 per cent of the total average cost per bed.

While the SRC was designed to protect access for low-income residents and to protect others from excessive charges, it was recognised that some nursing home residents might wish to purchase a higher level of optional services. Provision was thus made to exempt some homes from fee control, with the Commonwealth benefit reduced by 50 cents for every dollar charged above the SRC. Allowance was made for 6 per cent of beds to be exempt, but only half this number was ever taken up. While providers argued that the requirement for a whole home to be exempt was inflexible and that they would prefer to offer an exempt wing, it appears that satisfaction with the standard of care generally was such that few residents or their families saw value in paying the premium for an exempt bed.

The SRC also applied in hostels, but a system of variable fees enabled providers to charge higher fees provided residents were left with a minimum disposable income and the maximum level of assets that could be held without affecting entitlement to a full age pension. The family home was exempt from the assets test, and it appears that hostel residents who had been home owners either rented that house and paid higher fees from the income generated or sold the house to finance an entry contribution and then paid only the SRC. A survey of hostels conducted in late 1993 by Aged Care Australia, the major industry body representing the voluntary sector, found that some 75 per cent of hostel residents were paying only up to the SRC, and the range of fees above this amount was limited, with only 8 per cent of residents paying as much as 20 per cent more (Aged Care Australia 1994).

The system of variable fees now proposed for nursing homes differs from the hostel arrangements in several ways. First, the fees to be charged are not at the discretion of the nursing home operator but will apply to all residents on the basis of the age pension means test. Second, while the 65 per cent of residents who are full pensioners will continue to pay only the SRC, the level of charges above that amount will be greater, to a maximum of $63.30 per day. Third, 'personal care subsidies' paid to hostel residents were not affected by the level of fees paid, and the extra fee income was available to the hostel to improve the quality of care. Fees to be paid in nursing homes are to be offset against benefits paid to generate savings to government. Full integration of the funding systems for nursing homes and hostels would presumably see hostels lose their advantage in this respect.

Capital funding and quality of care

To address the need for capital improvements in nursing homes, it was planned to extend the system of entry contributions that applied to hostels to nursing homes. This move was a radical shift in policy, as entry payments had never been a part of nursing home funding. In introducing her restructuring package, Minister Moylan proclaimed ingoing capital payments for hostels as uniquely successful among all the Labor government's initiatives, and their success provided the grounds for extension to nursing homes. But several factors limited this transferability, and it was these differences that ultimately made the entry charges for nursing homes unsustainable.

Balance of accommodation and care services

There are substantial differences between the balance of accommodation and care services in nursing homes and hostels. The history of the hostel ingoing payments shows them to be linked to the provision of housing rather than health care, originating as they did under the Menzies government's *Aged Persons' Homes Act, 1954*. Thirty years on, the Aged Care Reform Strategy tackled widely recognised inequities in the scheme by removing subsidies for independent living units and modifying the remaining scheme applying to hostels. The level of capital grants, which had previously been paid at a flat rate per hostel place, was varied to take account of entry contributions. To preserve access for financially disadvantaged persons (FDP), hostels existing prior to 1987 were required to provide access to 20 per cent of places free of an ingoing capital payment, and the proportion of FDP residents in new hostels was determined in accordance with the proportion of the regional aged population that was financially disadvantaged. Variable capital funding was also able to address the special needs of rural and remote areas, and of Aboriginal and Torres Strait Islander communities and ethnic groups that had limited capacity to raise resident contributions.

The difference in the balance of care and accommodation services is also evident in the characteristics of residents and the circumstances of their admission. The arguments for integration of nursing homes and hostels based on the similarities of the resident populations are not particularly robust, and analysis of dependency and other characteristics of resident populations and their patterns of utilisation of the two forms of care has found them to be more different than similar (Howe 1997b). In particular, transfers to nursing homes accounted for only about one in five of all residents leaving hostels, and an even smaller share, about one in 10, of all nursing home admissions.

Most importantly, hostel entry is essentially a choice about a place to live. Realising assets, including the family home, for this

147

purpose provides the means to securing another home; the average hostel stay is about four years. A range of other accommodation and care options are available for those who make other choices. Nursing home entry is less a matter of choice and more a matter of need for the level of care that can be found only in that setting; two-thirds of admissions occur on discharge from acute care and half of all residents exit within six months, most through death; only some one in four stay for two years or more. Thus, notwithstanding the label 'accommodation bonds' applied to entry charges to nursing homes, the balance of care over accommodation services makes nursing homes essentially health care facilities.

Extent and nature of capital need

The area of difference of most relevance to financing is the extent and nature of capital needed for hostel and nursing home development over the past decade and into the next. With the planning guidelines for hostels introduced in the Reform Strategy allowing for almost a doubling of places over the decade, a sustained and substantial inflow of capital was needed. Formalisation of arrangements for entry contributions provided the Commonwealth with a means to this end at the same time as limiting expenditure.

On the basis of figures from the survey conducted by Aged Care Australia (1994), it is estimated that residents contributed about 25 per cent of the total funding going to hostel construction and upgrading from the mid-1980s to the mid-90s. Commonwealth grants were thus effectively 3:1 for every dollar raised by provider organisations, making the variable capital arrangements more generous than ever before and providing a strong incentive for hostel development. The effectiveness of this incentive is seen in the construction of some 27 760 hostel places over the decade to 1996.

It was in recognition of the large number of hostel places that were required to meet the planning ratios that the private sector was encouraged to take up hostel provision from 1990. Private sector providers could charge entry contributions if they met outcome standards, but they were not eligible for capital grants. Hostels did not, however, prove attractive to the private sector: by 1996, it had provided only some 10 per cent of the additional hostel places established over the preceding five years.

In contrast to some 3000 hostel places to be constructed annually, the planning guidelines allowed for only around 600 new nursing home beds each year and, with a much larger stock of older facilities, the main capital requirement was for refurbishment and renewal of existing beds. The total level of Commonwealth capital grants for residential care declined substantially over the decade to the mid-1990s, and nursing homes received only about 20 per cent of these funds, with private sector providers having access to only a small program for upgrading and replacement. The industry itself was thus the main source of capital for nursing homes.

The adequacy of capital available from all sources for nursing homes was extensively examined in the second stage of the Funding Structure Review, which reported in mid-1994. It was estimated that $103 million a year was required to maintain the quality of the nursing home stock (Gregory 1994: 5). With this estimate based on a nursing home being replaced over a 40-year lifetime, the industry could reasonably be expected to generate most of the capital required.

While the main grounds for the introduction of accommodation bonds for nursing homes was a claimed capital crisis, there are several indicators to the contrary. First, the rate of increase in nursing home beds up to the mid-1990s was readily realised in line with projected requirements for new beds, and there seems little reason to doubt that sufficient capital would continue to become available. Second, there has never been any evidence of a shortage of capital for the purchase of nursing home beds: through the early 1990s especially, a ready market developed as state governments scaled down their nursing homes, with the government sector declining by 2066 beds between 1990 and 1996. A third indicator that a significant level of capital funding was going into nursing homes is the standard of maintenance of the majority of buildings. Ratings from the first certification survey conducted in preparation for the new capital funding arrangements, released by the Department of Health and Family Services in late 1997, show some 81 per cent of nursing homes met the standards, with more of those that failed being in the public than the private sector.

Given that all voluntary and private sector nursing homes operated under the same funding scheme over the past decade, and that only a small proportion of total provision was newly constructed over that time, it can be suggested that funding was adequate for maintenance and that outcomes were more a matter of management of funds than an inadequate level of funding. Proprietors' reluctance to spend on capital improvements is not the same as a shortage of capital funds, and given the variable performance of proprietors in maintaining their facilities, it is debatable whether there was a 'crisis' in capital funding. It might even be surmised that some proprietors had postponed refurbishment in the expectation that additional capital funds would become available after the 1994 Funding Structure Review and the 1996 change of government.

Prudential arrangements

The final and most striking area of difference in funding of nursing homes and hostels concerns the prudential arrangements governing resident capital payments. In hostels it was left to providers to negotiate with each resident on whether a capital contribution would be charged, the amount, and conditions of repayment within broad Commonwealth guidelines. In these circumstances there was no need for income- or assets-testing by the Department of Social Security. Some 40 per cent of hostel residents paid entry contributions averaging $25 000, and only 14 per cent paid more than $50 000. These funds went direct to the hostel provider and their use was not subject to any special external scrutiny.

The loosely defined prudential provisions for hostels contrast markedly with the complexity of the arrangements developed to protect the accommodation bonds. A series of fact sheets was released in early 1997 announcing the new arrangements (Department of Health and Family Services 1997), but numerous adjustments were made before the bonds were implemented some 16 months later and abandoned soon after. The consumer pressure that generated many of these changes indicated that private sector nursing home providers were not held in the same trust as the voluntary sector has traditionally been. That trust appears to have been well placed. Neither the complaints units established by the Commonwealth in conjunction with the monitoring of hostel outcome standards nor other consumer bodies reported frequent difficulties relating to refunds of entry contributions or other money matters.

While nursing home providers, especially those in the private sector, hoped to gain access to the full amount of entry contributions, the prudential provisions requiring trust funds to be established limited access to a 'draw down' of $2600 a year and interest on the bond funds. Periodic payments that could be made as an alternative to payment of a bond would generate around the same amount. With the same provisions also to cover hostels, hostel providers were set to lose access to the full capital they had previously had from entry contributions.

Rather than being discretionary as in hostels, all those entering residential care were to be required to make an ingoing payment on the basis of formally assessed capacity to pay. The income and assets test was, except in some specific circumstances, to include the family home. Residents had to be allowed to retain assets of $22 500, but the provider was then free to charge whatever level of bond they saw fit given the intending resident's assets. As the need for conservative investment combined with present low interest rates limited the income generated, some providers responded by seeking the maximum bonds that could be secured from intending residents. The paradoxical outcome would have been that if all assets went to the payment of a bond, the resident would escape the means test applying to fees, and savings to government from means-tested fees would have been reduced accordingly.

The bonds were at the centre of contention about the restructuring package, and it was not long after the proposals were announced that it became apparent that they would not have an easy passage. The legislation embodying the changes was referred to the Senate Community Affairs Reference Committee (1997) and even after being passed, implementation was subject to a series of delays. Objections to the proposals emerged and, shortly before the new arrangements were due to take effect from 1 October, Minister Moylan was replaced. The new minister, Smith, faced a barrage of media attention and heated debate in the House of Representatives, and while the accommodation bonds came into effect on 1 October, the introduction of means-tested fees was first delayed to 1 November and then for a further six months. The immediate experience of the bond scheme saw a rapid escalation of expressions of concern on the part of providers and older people. Prompted by electoral pressures, a group of backbenchers approached the Prime Minister and, despite protestations that only some 'fine tuning' to the policy was required, the bond scheme was abandoned in the first week of November and a variant on the periodic payments seemed set to emerge as a fallback option. This was the eventual outcome, to a maximum charge of around $4000.

The continuing search for solutions

A number of lessons that can be learned from this excursion into the turbulent waters of health care financing should inform the continuing search for solutions. First, aged care financing is as politically fraught as any other area of health care financing. In passing responsibility for capital funding to the industry, government ran the risk of sacrificing its own interests to the interests of the industry. These conflicting interests mean that, even if the restructuring package had proceeded as proposed, it might not have secured either the projected savings to government or the long-term viability of the industry. Proprietors' interests lay in maximising the amount of the bonds from which they could earn income, potentially removing the capacity of residents to pay means-tested fees and incurring a cost to government, as savings on recurrent expenditure would not have been realised.

Second, the injection of substantial additional capital funds was as likely to distort investment in the industry as to ensure its long-term viability. Proprietors able to charge the highest bonds had the least need for capital to upgrade their already high standard facilities, while those with most need of upgrading had least access to bonds. The former proprietors might judiciously have set aside bond income to meet future capital requirements, or used it to buy up and improve lower standard homes and then gain access to profits from benefit payments, enhanced by the removal of acquittal requirements. A nursing home bed would have become an increasingly valuable asset, and it is likely that pressure to approve more beds would ultimately have arisen.

The third lesson concerns recognition of the potential for perverse behaviour on the part of consumers and providers. Faced with bonds and higher fees, potential residents might have decided not to pay for residential care but to seek alternatives, leaving residential care facilities with empty beds. A higher demand for HACC services and an extra cost to government would follow, especially as these individuals would qualify for community service programs providing levels of funding equivalent to hostel or even nursing home care. Some of the decline in demand for hostel places over the past decade can be attributed to intending residents faltering at having to pay an entry contribution, and a similar outcome was a real possibility for nursing homes. This outcome eventuated in a very short time in New Zealand after the introduction of full cost recovery charges for rest homes; after protests from providers faced with empty beds, the charges were dropped (Howe 1996).

The repercussions of the adverse response to the proposed bonds and the continuing uncertainty about the proposed alternatives are likely to reduce the demand for residential care more than any other measure could have done. The collapse of the restructuring package and the considerable uncertainty generated in the industry is likely to see reduced interest in hostel construction. Together these outcomes will create pressure for government to expand community care.

Fourth, the political reaction that triggered the reversal of policy should not obscure the want of sound analysis that characterised the proposed measures. Apart from the extensive field surveys carried out in the development of the new Resident Classification Scale (Rhys Hearn 1997), which survived as a relatively uncontentious element of the restructuring package, there was remarkably little detailed empirical information. Economic modelling of the outcomes of the proposed measures appears to have been limited, and certainly no scenarios for different conditions were publicly presented. With reference to the central question of the quality of buildings and the need for capital upgrading, for example, no new data were produced from the time of the limited survey conducted for the second stage of the funding structure review in 1993 until the certification survey was instigated in late 1997.

The dramatic collapse of the main financing elements of the 1996/97 restructuring package was not due to the difficulty of selling the message or to consumer resistance, although these certainly played a part. Fundamental weaknesses in the proposed measures meant they were unsustainable, but once the commitment was made to them there was little critical policy analysis and even less economic analysis. The policy vacuum that now exists means that the financing of long-term care will remain on the political agenda in Australia for some time. Beyond the immediate need for short-term options that recover some semblance of credibility in government policy, the need to develop a sound means of financing aged care over the long term should attract more interest from health economists than it has to date. Options for long-term care social insurance that have already been canvassed briefly (DHHCS 1993; Walsh & De Ravin 1995; Howe 1997a) are likely to be a particular focus of attention.

8 *Evaluation of health services*

The Australian health system, like many of its OECD counterparts, has passed through a number of distinct phases since the end of World War II. Richardson (1991) described three: (i) a period of strong expenditure growth from the 1950s to the late 70s; (ii) a period of expenditure control during the 1980s; (iii) an anticipated period of economic evaluation in the 1990s. The first period generated a concern that increasing outlays were not being matched by similar improvements in health outcomes, the second a concern whether continuing cost containment was starting to jeopardise the quality of the health services being provided. By the third period, the ever-growing availability of new health care technologies (particularly on the diagnostic side), continuing pressures to control health care spending, and a sharpening focus on health care outcomes, underpinned the expectation of extensive health service evaluation. There was a growing awareness that few interventions had been evaluated on the basis of their costs and benefits, also that the effectiveness of many established treatments had not been proven and that wide variations existed in the rate of use of many interventions (Harvey 1991).

Economic evaluation (or appraisal as it is often called) is one of a number of tools that have been developed by various disciplines for the purpose of assessing the relative merits of health services. The focus of economic evaluation is as an aid to decision-making in resource allocation. In theory, it allows decision-makers to be more rational in determining which projects to fund or expand and which to cut or contract. At the very least, it encourages decision-makers to clarify their objectives and to be aware of the consequences of decisions for costs and outcomes.

The aim of this chapter is to provide an appreciation of the main concepts underpinning the economic evaluation of health services. It is not intended as a guide on how to do an evaluation, on which there are a number of excellent texts and articles (Drummond et al. 1987; Hall and Mooney 1990a, b; Gold et al. 1996; Elliot and Harris 1997). Rather, it examines some of the theoretical underpinnings of economic evaluation and the key concepts that distinguish economic evaluation from other forms of evaluation in health.

What distinguishes economic evaluation from other approaches to evaluation? Some key concepts

Social efficiency

A peculiar characteristic of economic evaluation is its emphasis on social efficiency. Much of health care involves social decisions about the use of society's resources to achieve social goals. There are of course debates over what those goals might be, as well as how resources should be used to achieve them. This societal perspective means that decisions will be recommended based on economic appraisal that may be at odds with the wishes of individuals, or with particular groups in society. While this may on occasion present difficult ethical issues, it is the only perspective that never counts as a gain something that is really another person's loss.

There are various ways in which changes in society's welfare might be identified and measured. One particular criterion—the potential Pareto improvement criterion—lies at the heart of economic appraisal. A change that makes at least one member of a community better off and makes none worse off is a simple Pareto improvement. While unambiguously an improvement in social welfare, such changes do not present themselves very often. Usually decisions about resource allocation involve both winners and losers. Undertaking a project provides a 'potential Pareto improvement' if it is possible *in principle* to ensure an actual Pareto improvement by linking the project with an appropriate set of transfers of money between gainers and losers—even if in fact these transfers will not take place. In essence, the potential Pareto improvement criterion requires that changes in people's welfare should be measured by the 'willingness to pay': that is, by the amount they are willing to pay for the benefits of the project and by the amounts they are willing to accept as compensation for harm inflicted on them.[1] These benefits and costs borne by individuals are aggregated into 'social benefits' and 'social costs' by simple addition. A project is warranted from an economic perspective if its 'net social benefit' is positive. The fundamental value judgement on which the Paretian approach rests is that social welfare is only an aggregation of individual preferences (Arrow 1963): hence, the notion of 'consumer sovereignty' and the importance of 'willingness to pay' in much of economic theory. Such a value system is certainly appealing when the product and its costs, benefits and risks are easily understood, and there is the possibility of what Richardson (1991) calls 'error learning'. The assumption that individuals understand all available options and implications is sometimes taken to the extreme libertarian view, that any interference with consumer sovereignty by governments must reduce utility. As Richardson (1995) comments:

> It is sufficient to note that only the most sterile exercise of 'welfare theory' would lead to such an uncompromising position in the health sector. (It must, however, be acknowledged that some economists do adopt this position.) . . . the economics profession has, in fact, had two traditions. 'Welfarism' comes close to the sterile stereotype sketched above (Culyer 1991) . . . By contrast, in the 'material welfare' tradition of Pigou and Marshall (Robinson 1986) or extra welfarism (to use Culyer's term), external criteria such as objective health status have been considered the legitimate objective in cost effectiveness analysis.

It is the extra-welfarist tradition that most health economists would espouse (Williams 1993). This recognises the characteristics of the health sector, particularly that there is inadequate information for individuals, left to their own devices, to be able to make decisions in their own best interests.[2] It raises the issue of whether the value judgement of consumers being sovereign (being the best judge of their own welfare) should be replaced, or at least be complemented by, a paternalistic judgement about what is desirable for the individual or the society. From the perspective of social welfare, is it appropriate to accept individual preferences for health vis-à-vis other commodities, or should social policy be based on the assumption that the goal of health policy is to maximise health?

One manifestation of a special concern with health is the common assumption that the appropriate objective in health policy and its economic evaluation is health maximisation. This derives from two sources. First, with a large public sector budget in health, there is a tendency to view the health budget as separate, fixed, and directed towards health production. Public sector decision-making is such that there is little opportunity to consider intersectoral transfers of resources or common goals. Second, many argue that health has a special status as a 'merit good'—that it has importance independently of how much weight individuals place on it and that individual preferences for other commodities over health care should be overridden by decision-makers representing social values.[3]

The definition of 'social benefit'—whether based on an aggregation of individual utility or health gain—and the role of experts in defining health gain, can be linked to two schools of thought as to what constitutes the theoretical foundations and ambit of economic appraisal. The two schools can conveniently be defined as the 'decision-making approach' and the 'Paretian approach' (Sugden & Williams 1978; Gold et al. 1996).

With the decision-making approach, economic appraisal is seen as a process for evaluating decision problems in the light of objectives chosen by the decision-maker. The decision-maker (often the government or government authority) is responsible for making decisions in the public interest. The perspective is 'societal' in that economic appraisal is used to aid decisions that affect society as a whole. The decision-maker is assumed to be entrusted with the task (usually via the political process) of making choices on behalf of the general public, and this trust implies the formation of objectives on their behalf. Most government intervention in health care, for example, has been to ensure that access to necessary services is not determined by income. It seems unfair to many that those with the same level of medical need (however defined) should receive less treatment simply because they have less income. Thus, while governments may pursue efficiency in the provision of health care services, they consider other social objectives such as fairness and equity. The broader concept of 'benefit' raised by the decision-making approach poses important challenges for economic appraisal. If, in addition to health outcomes, equity and issues associated with the process of care are important objectives (and therefore important dimensions of benefit), how are they to be incorporated into the cost–benefit matrix?

With the Paretian approach there is a long tradition of considering social welfare as having essentially two dimensions, those of economic efficiency and distributive justice. Its exponents generally argue that economic appraisal should focus on changes in economic efficiency. If a project were to involve a decrease in efficiency, for example, it would be up to others to argue that the improvements along other dimensions of social welfare (e.g. distributional justice) justify the decrease in economic efficiency. The exclusion of equity considerations from the formal analysis sets the Paretian approach apart from the decision-making approach. For a discussion of the equity implications of the two approaches, see Wagstaff (1991).

While this discussion of theoretical underpinnings to the concept of 'benefit' may sound esoteric, its impact on the way in which economic evaluation is (and should be) conducted is quite profound. It affects not only the way in which 'benefit' itself is conceptualised and measured but the choice of comparator (next-best option or comparator relevant to the decision context), the approach to resources (society's resources or the decision-maker's budget) and many other dimensions of methodology. It is one reason why economic methodologies adopted by various researchers have varied so widely.

Opportunity cost

Economic evaluation starts from the fundamental premise that resources are scarce. If this were not the case, economic evaluation would be irrelevant (Birch & Gafni 1991) and all that would matter is whether the interventions work (i.e. their effectiveness based on clinical, behavioural or epidemiological evaluation). The existence of resource scarcity has important implications: it means that the use of resources in one program automatically denies their use in alternative applications—the notion of 'opportunity cost'. For example, the real cost of expansions in high-technology care for very-low-birthweight infants may be that community care programs for the elderly do not expand.

The concept of costs as forgone opportunities (or sacrifices) provides the logic for two important characteristics of economic appraisal: first, that it considers both costs and benefits; and second, that it involves a comparison of alternatives. It is possible to distinguish economic appraisal from other forms of appraisal using these two characteristics (Drummond et al. 1987).

Sometimes decision-makers are attracted by methods other than economic appraisal, precisely because they do not wish to include a consideration of costs. Indeed, some regard consideration of cost to be unethical. They would prefer to ration on the basis of 'medical necessity', 'clinical efficacy' or other such criteria. These criteria are commonly perceived to be technical statements—objective and free-of-value judgements—rather than economic decisions. In practice, however, as Gold et al. (1996) argue, they usually involve important value judgements, and costs often play a part, albeit without explicit acknowledgment.

While some forms of appraisal focus on outcomes (and ignore or try to avoid costs), others look only at costs and ignore outcomes. One common type is described as cost of illness (COI) studies: these focus attention on diseases or risk factors that impose large costs on the community, but say nothing about whether it is worth implementing programs to reduce that burden. The main danger with COI studies is that they may be taken out of context and used by decision-makers as a pragmatic alternative to economic appraisal. Like epidemiological or clinical studies, they can provide important input into an economic evaluation (in this case by describing resource flows associated with the status quo), but they are not substitutes for economic evaluation. It is important that COI and disease impact studies be kept in perspective and not allowed to dominate the evaluation agenda or consume a disproportionate share of evaluation resources.

Marginal analysis

Economic evaluation stresses the marginal costs and marginal benefits of a health service as fundamental concepts for policy analysis. If the objective is to maximise health for a given budget, then the task is to ensure that the last dollar spent on each program improves health by the same amount. The rationale is simply that if this criterion were not met, resources could be transferred between programs to improve total health with the same total resources. As Mooney (1993) explains:

> If no budget constraint exists, then a programme should be expanded or contracted to the point where marginal benefit equals marginal cost; if there is a budget constraint, then all programmes should operate at a level whereby the ratio of marginal benefit to marginal cost is the same for all.

This is an important principle, even if in practice it is difficult to achieve.[4] Often decisions relating to health services are not about whether to introduce a health service per se, rather whether to have a little more or less of it (e.g. whether to have two-yearly screening or annual screening; which age groups to target).

Marginal analysis as a way of thinking is vital, as basing a decision on the marginal analysis concept will give very different answers from basing it on notions of clinical effectiveness, absolute need or average cost.

Decisions based on 'clinical effectiveness', for example, reflect evidence of whether a treatment or procedure works or not. They are seldom informed by a careful analysis of the incremental benefits associated with design options and their opportunity cost. Where increments are considered, the tendency is for program designs to maximise total benefits (i.e. to be expanded as long as the marginal benefit is positive), which may be well beyond the point at which marginal benefits equal marginal costs. An often-quoted case study is the recommendation of the American Cancer Society that six sequential tests of stools be carried out to test for cancer of the colon. Six tests were recommended to ensure positive predictive value for the screening program, even though the incremental gain in cases detected in moving from five to six tests was known to be slight. It was only when the marginal costs were calculated by Neuhauser and Lewicki (1975) and compared to the incremental benefits that it was realised that each additional case of colon cancer detected by the sixth test was costing over $47 million! The issue for decision-makers here was not whether there was benefit in detecting each additional case of cancer (there undoubtedly was) but whether more benefits could have been achieved with $47 million than the detection of one case of colon cancer.

Case studies illustrating the importance of marginal analysis, as well as factors limiting its acceptance, are available closer to home. Decisions based on national evaluations of the breast and cervical cancer screening programs (AIHW 1990, 1991), for example, illustrate the trade-off between efficiency (and the importance of marginal analysis in achieving it) and other objectives (such as equity of access and political acceptability). The interval for cervical cancer screening was modified from one year to two years as the evaluation identified that significant cost savings were available with minimal impact on health gain. On the other hand, women aged 18–24 were not excluded from the cervical cancer screening program, even though the cost per additional life saved was calculated to be approximately $17 million for this age group! The improvement in efficiency flowing from the change in screening interval was more acceptable than the age group change, as it did not challenge the equity of access objective. The choice of interval and target age group for the national breast cancer screening program reflected a similar balancing of efficiency and broader objectives.

Techniques

The term economic evaluation encompasses three main techniques—cost–benefit analysis (CBA), cost–utility analysis (CUA), and cost-effectiveness analysis (CEA). While CBA has its origins in welfare economics, CEA and CUA are often referred to as the 'decision-maker approach' to economic evaluation (Johannesson 1996). The choice of which of these techniques to use is not arbitrary but depends primarily on what question is to be answered. This involves distinguishing the question of how best to allocate scarce resources across quite different programs (termed 'allocative efficiency' by economists) from the question of technical performance, or how best to pursue a chosen objective (often termed 'technical efficiency').

Cost–benefit analysis (CBA)

CBA adopts 'market-like' appraisal techniques for measuring costs and benefits, based on the 'potential Pareto improvement' criterion referred to earlier. The defining characteristic of CBA is its attempt to reduce all benefits and costs to a single measurement unit, the dollar.[5] This is both its key strength and its key weakness. The strength is that CBA can be applied to a wide range of choices. With everything valued in monetary terms, it could be used to compare different health care services with quite divergent outcomes, or with projects in other sectors of the economy. CBA is thus the only economic technique available to answer the question: Is it 'worth' providing this health service? A CBA measures worth in terms of the net social benefit of the program or service (i.e. the incremental social benefit of the program less the incremental social cost, all measured in dollars).

The advantages of CBA in determining worth (i.e. allocative efficiency) come at the expense of difficult measurement issues, such as the assignment of dollar values to life, illness, clean air, and other non-marketed goods and activities. The most common approaches to assigning dollar values to health consequences are an output-based approach and a preferences-based approach. The output-based approach (or 'human capital' approach, as it is often called) values life and health in terms of the contribution people make to the economy. The value of life is seen as something external to the individual in the tradition of the material welfare school referred to earlier. Because of its simplicity, it has been the most commonly used measure in the CBA literature and was the original method recommended by the US Public Health Service (Hodgson & Meiners 1982). Two defects of the human capital technique led to its demise, although more recently interest has again focused on its use in measuring production effects in the economy, as opposed to placing a dollar value on human life (Olsen 1993; Koopmanschap & Rutten 1993). First, it has strong and, to most, unacceptable equity consequences (such as the low value of life it attributes to the elderly, unemployed people, people on low incomes, or 'home-makers'). Second, the view among most economists has been that the appropriate measure of value is the intensity of individual preferences, and that this is not reflected by future labour costs (Richardson 1991).

The preference-based approach to the monetary valuation of outcomes is normally based on individual maximum willingness to pay (WTP) for a health gain (or maximum willingness to accept compensation to forgo that gain). WTP can be assessed direct, by survey (called contingent valuation), or it can be inferred from decisions actually made that involve trade-offs (called revealed preference) between health and money (Viscusi 1978, 1993). As with the human capital approach, however, WTP has been criticised on both its equity implications (i.e. WTP is affected by ability to pay) and its theoretical foundations (Richardson 1991).

The revealed preference approach requires either observation from a direct market for health or an identifiable relationship between health and the price of a substitute or complement. With the possible exception of mortality risk (Viscusi 1993), examples are rare in health.

Contingent valuation has a number of theoretical and empirical problems. As a number of authors such as Richardson (1991) have pointed out, it might be regarded as paradoxical that we have rejected market valuations of health care by providing public funding, yet are willing to consider individual surrogate market values in economic evaluation of social programs. Individual monetary values of health care may take into account aspects of health that are irrelevant from a societal perspective. Thus, while the typical WTP survey asks about individual maximum willingness to pay for a program, Olsen and Donaldson (in press) ask about willingness to contribute to a public program. What to ask and how to ask it are the key areas of debate in the contingent valuation literature.

Even if we know what to ask, the validity of the WTP values are critically determined by the reliability of the survey instruments. The NOAA panel (Arrow et al. 1993) made a series of recommendations for the construction of contingent valuation instruments in order to minimise bias in responses. There remains, however, a vigorous debate among economists. Diamond and Hausman (1994) and their co-authors in Hausman (1993) claim that contingent valuation produces results responsive to theoretically irrelevant considerations (e.g. the order of questions or the payment vehicle) and insensitive to theoretically relevant considerations (e.g. the size of risk or health effect), while Hanemann (1994) is a spirited defender of the technique. It is probably true to say that in spite of a qualified endorsement by a number of eminent economists (Arrow et al. 1993) many remain sceptical of the technique's potential to offer policy guidance. It is as yet unclear the extent to which the issues raised in this debate, centred on the environment, are relevant to health policy. Given the uncertainty over the validity, reliability and sensitivity of the results at this stage, the literature on WTP in health can only be classed as experimental. The continued development of survey approaches to WTP in environmental and transport economics, however (Cummings et al. 1986; Jones-Lee 1989), has led to renewed interest in the application of CBA in health care (Tolley et al. 1994; Johannesson et al. 1991, 1992, 1993; Donaldson et al. 1995; Chestnut et al. 1996; O'Brien et al. 1995).

In practical terms the consequence of early attempts to derive a dollar equivalent to the value of human life led to a widespread perception, among non-economists and many health economists, that CBA was not a very useful technique in the health sector (e.g. Abel-Smith 1985). It reflected a more general view that many program benefits (not just in health care) could not sensibly be converted into dollars. It led to the development of cost–effectiveness analysis.

Cost–effectiveness analysis (CEA)

CEA avoids the need to value benefits in money terms, but at the expense of reducing the range of problems it can legitimately address. CEA is based on the idea that we want to meet a given objective at least cost. It addresses the question of how. The central measure used in CEA is the cost–effectiveness (C/E) ratio. Health effects might be life-years saved, cases diagnosed, functional status, symptoms avoided or any clinical occurrence. A decision rule based on adopting all interventions with incremental C/E ratios less than or equal to a particular value is optimal in the sense that (Gold et al. 1996: 27):

- the resulting set of health services will maximise the aggregate health effects achievable by the resources used; and
- the resulting aggregate health effects will have been achieved at the lowest possible cost.

The main limitation of CEA is that it can only compare health services or interventions whose benefits are measured in the same units of effectiveness. The measure of outcome in CEA is unidimensional, and as a consequence CEA usually does not have the ability to capture all relevant dimensions of benefit in the C/E ratio. While a number of C/E ratios can be listed for a health service (e.g. cost per life saved, cost per cancer detected, cost per woman attending) and these can be meaningful within the context of that program or very similar programs (e.g. cancer screening programs), their relevance to broader-based comparisons is more tenuous. CEA nonetheless can be quite powerful, where the treatment or prevention objective is not being questioned directly and where there is a single unambiguous objective for the interventions (or where the outcome measure is considered to be a reasonable proxy for the benefits). The frequency with which CEA is the method of choice in the health sector suggests that this is not an infrequent occurrence.

While there are cases where a single dimension of outcome is valid, the limitations of CEA need to be recognised. An important limitation is that CEA treats all life-years as having equal value, no matter what the quality of life. It would be difficult, for example, to compare the relative value with CEA of a cancer screening program that prevented premature death and provided reassurance, with a rehabilitation or pain relief program that improved the quality of life but had no impact on its quantity. In principle, CBA could include both morbidity and mortality issues, but with its decline a suitable measurement technique for capturing both mortality and morbidity was lacking until the development of cost–utility analysis (CUA) and the notion of quality-adjusted life-years (QALYs).

Cost–utility analysis (CUA)

CUA lies somewhere between CEA and CBA in terms of the problems it can tackle, exactly where being an issue of some debate (Butler 1992; Gold et al. 1996). It can be seen as either a form of CEA that can cope with more than one form of output (i.e. combining quantity of life and quality of life); or as a form of CBA where QALYs are the criteria of value (rather than dollars) and where rankings can be made for setting priorities within a fixed health sector budget. The conventional approach to QALYs is to multiply the preference or quality of life weight for health states, with and without the intervention(s); by the time spent in those states. Preference weights are normalised on a zero (death) to one (perfect health) scale.

Whether CUA is a suitable technique to assess 'worth' (i.e. allocative efficiency) is unclear. In some circles it is thought to do this—but within a constrained environment (i.e. outcomes in the health sector) (Mooney 1988). All else being equal, the most desirable options are taken to be those which result in the cheapest QALYs (or the most QALYs, if the budget is fixed). CUA does not, however, tell us what a QALY is 'worth' and therefore defines no threshold value of cost per QALY beyond which a given intervention is not worthwhile. Whether or not this is a serious limitation depends, among other things, on one's view about the method of determining the size of the health care budget. If it is accepted that the size of the health budget is politically determined, then the main task for economic appraisal is to advise on how the assigned budget can be spent efficiently. If, on the other hand, the task for economic appraisal is to help to determine the size of the allocation of funds to health care, then CUA has serious limitations.

Assuming the former position, the question that remains is how good a measure of benefit QALYs are. The issues surrounding the measurement and application of QALYs have been reviewed by Torrance (1986), Loomes and McKenzie (1989) and Richardson (1994). There are two basic problems: first, the issues surrounding the specification of health states associated with and without the intervention(s); second, the issues surrounding the measurement of preferences for those health states. Both stages involve issues of validity. The former in what concepts to include in 'health' and the latter in the validity and reliability of measurement techniques.

On the first issue, there are considerable challenges in specifying what constitutes 'health' and capturing its various dimensions in health state descriptions. There is also the related issue of what we want from our health care system. Mooney (1988) has argued that we want more from health care than just health. Diagnostic technologies, for example, often provide information and reassurance, but may not alter treatment or health outcomes.

The second issue involves not only the psychometric properties of the measures, but the way in which QALYs are aggregated and expressed (i.e. cost per QALY), which limit the role given to individuals' intensity of preference. As noted by Torrance (1986), the basic assumption in CUA is that:

> the difference in utility between being dead and being healthy is set equal across people. In this way the method is egalitarian . . . each individual's health is counted equally!

This allows QALYs to be simply summed, but means the maximand is not total health-related utility but a weighted average of individuals' utilities, 'where the weights are designed to treat individuals equally irrespective of the absolute intensity of their preferences' (Richardson 1991). That is to say, the marginal social utility of one year of quality-adjusted life-expectancy is assumed equal for all individuals, irrespective of their present health status, social standing or preferences for health.

Moreover, as Garber and Phelps (1995) point out, if we are concerned to maximise individual utility, and health is but one argument in the utility function, then we should want individuals to equate their own personal marginal benefit and marginal cost of a health care intervention. They note the difficulty that this entails for public policy (1995: 29):

> The variability of the optimal cost effectiveness ratio across persons leads to a fundamental tension in using it to guide the allocation of health care resources: insurers, and policy makers may wish to equate cost effectiveness across interventions and across populations, yet members of the population have very different optimal cost effectiveness ratios. Cost effectiveness analysis applied at the population level may give the most efficient egalitarian distribution of health resources, but it is not likely to be Pareto optimal.

The weight given this issue would depend on whether one saw CUA from the perspective of the welfare economics school or from that of the decision-making school. While attempts have been made to place CUA in the former tradition (Garber & Phelps 1995), most health economists see it as belonging to the latter (Sugden & Williams 1978; Gold et al. 1996; Johannesson 1996).

A final, although obvious, point about CUA methodology is the importance of understanding the various instruments on which QALYs can be developed. A large number of instruments are now available, and many have demonstrated poor, if any, evidence of validity or reliability. Care should be taken to ensure that the QALY instrument is appropriate to the problem being considered (Donaldson et al. 1988; Richardson et al. 1990; Richardson 1991).

Apart from the efficiency implications of the aggregation method, some oppose QALYs on ethical grounds. Harris (1987) argues, for example, that the only priority in health care should be the preservation of life, and that all have an equal right to life no matter what its length or quality. But Williams (1987) and Richardson (1991) see a variety of ethical bases that could underpin the way our health system works. We simply have to stand up and be counted on which view we take. As an alternative, changes in QALYs could be weighted more heavily for members of society whose level of health is poorer (Nord 1992), but the problem is to justify a weighting scale in a principled or morally acceptable way.

While there are certainly conceptual and practical questions associated with CUA, the technique can no longer be considered as being in an experimental stage, and should merit serious consideration by decision-makers and funding bodies. The work by Richardson and colleagues (Hawthorne et al. 1997), to develop an instrument with Australian weights and values that has strong psychometric properties, is particularly important in this respect.

Concluding comment on techniques

While economists can be rather evangelistic at times, the power of these techniques should not be overstated. None provides a magic formula for the removal of judgement, responsibility, or risk from decision-making. They are, in essence, methods of critical thinking, of approaching choices, of pursuing consistency and quality in decision-making. They provide a framework for comprehensive identification of relevant costs and benefits within which some quantitative statements about the costs and consequences can be made.

While our discussion has focused on the key microeconomic techniques for developing the quantitative statements (i.e. the C/E ratio, the C/U ratio, or the net social benefit), it is important to realise that other economic techniques are available to complement the arithmetic. Techniques such as the 'social audit' (BTCE 1984) and 'cost consequences analysis' (Gold et al. 1996) provide a qualitative description of the parties affected by health service options, the way in which their interests are affected by the options, together with a description of arrangements for public participation. Such techniques, which often focus on issues associated with implementation, can be an important complement to conventional microeconomic analysis. Further, the broader notion of 'benefit' raised earlier (i.e. that benefit can be more than mere efficiency or health gain) can also be accommodated by innovative techniques such as 'program budgeting and marginal analysis' (PBMA)[6] and the associated technique of 'options appraisal', which link the measurement of benefit to organisational objectives (Mooney et al. 1992; Peacock et al. 1997).

Applications

Interest in the economic evaluation of health services began in the 1960s when CBA, first developed by the US military some 30 years earlier, was applied to measles vaccination (Weisbrod 1961). The methodological development of CEA in the 1950s, again developed by the US military, did not find its way into the health sector until the late 1960s (Klarman et al. 1968), while CUA, a distinctively health-oriented form of appraisal, was first applied in the early 1970s (Bush et al. 1973).

In his first volume of *Studies in Economic Appraisal in Health Care,* Drummond (1981) reviewed 101 studies published before 1980 (i.e. covering roughly a 20-year period). The second volume, on the next five-year period, contained a review of another 100 published studies (Drummond et al. 1986). Most of these studies were CEAs. Gerard (1992) surveyed the CUA studies published in the English language over the period 1980–1990, and estimated that the 51 studies she found constituted less than 10 per cent of all published economic evaluations in health care. Similarly, only a small percentage of published studies would be CBAs. Zarnke et al. (1997) report that most studies described as CBAs do not measure outcomes appropriately. Continued development of survey approaches to WTP, however, has led to renewed interest in CBA. Berwick and Weinstein (1985) were among the first to use WTP to assess the benefits of non-health attributes of health care. They found that patients do attach value to ultrasound in pregnancy in spite of the fact that it provides information that has little or no medical significance. Donaldson et al. (1995) have used contingent valuation techniques to measure the money value of screening for cystic fibrosis, while Lindholm et al. (1994) have examined the WTP for a community-based primary prevention program. There have also been a number of studies of the monetary value of drug treatments for hypertension (Johannesson et al. 1991, 1992, 1993), angina (Chestnut et al. 1996) and depression (O'Brien et al. 1995).

Turning to the Australian health care system and published Australian studies, Salkeld et al. (1995) reviewed 33 economic appraisal papers published between 1978 and March 1993. Interestingly, almost half of the studies were in the area of health promotion or illness prevention although, as Drummond (1983) also found, appraisal of 'non-medical' choices were largely overshadowed by the focus on screening, immunisation and chemoprophylaxis. The most common single intervention was drug therapy (10 out of the 33). Of the 33 studies, 17 were classified as CEA, seven as CBA, and eight as CUA, while one study performed both CEA and CBA. Salkeld and colleagues noted, however, that the appropriateness of the method applied was often debatable.

The relatively small number of published studies over a 15-year period poses important questions of the role envisaged for economic evaluation in Australian health care policy. It could be interpreted to suggest that both economists and governments envisage a modest role, such as a series of ad hoc and randomly selected studies. Richardson (1993) has questioned (rightly, in our view) how it is possible that Australia could have a $33 billion industry with so little economic evaluation of its products. What happened to the 1990s as the anticipated period of economic evaluation? One explanation is that the 1980s and early 90s saw an emphasis in health policy on restructuring the financial organisation of health care to ensure that there were incentives to purchase and provide efficient services (Richardson 1993). Such financial reorganisation, however, while important in its own right, will not solve the question of what are the most efficient services to purchase and provide.

Economists worldwide have long bemoaned the lack of acceptance of economic appraisal in health policy (Ludbrook & Mooney 1984; Drummond 1987, 1990). A number of Australian authors have also commented on some of the reasons for this (Hall 1993; Ross 1995). The general lack of influence could be explained in terms of quality, timeliness and the applicability of studies. There is then the lack of in-house expertise and lack of knowledge about economic appraisal, together with academic health economists being preoccupied with rigour of their methods rather than communicating the principles involved to decision-makers (Ross 1995).

Some authors are less pessimistic. Drummond et al. (1991) reviewed nine Australian studies in health technology assessment and concluded that six had had an influence on government decisions. There is some comfort in the fact that, of the 33 studies reviewed by

Salkeld, half were published between 1991 and 1993, providing evidence of a rapid growth in the Australian literature (albeit from a tiny base), with a particularly rapid growth in CUA in that period. There is also evidence to suggest that the role of economic appraisal is becoming more widely recognised. Many working parties of the National Health and Medical Research Council (NHMRC) and evaluations of the Australian Health Technology Advisory Committee are now including health economists. Initiatives such as the NHMRC general practice guidelines (NHMRC 1995) and the Commonwealth government's public health partnership are also seeking an input based on economic appraisal. While this recognition and a steady flow of one-off studies is encouraging, the most important development is undoubtedly the mandatory use of economic evaluation in decisions to reimburse pharmaceuticals in Australia.[7] George et al. (1997) report on 110 CEA or CUA studies considered by the Pharmaceutical Benefits Advisory Committee (PBAC) from November 1993 to March 1996—an average of over 40 per year (although few are published in the refereed journals). There is some limited evidence that the use of economic evaluation has led to consistent decisions in line with the notion of health maximisation subject to an implied budget constraint (George et al. 1997).

It is apparent that the mandatory economic evaluation of pharmaceuticals for reimbursement in Australia has had an impact, not only on drug policy in other countries but in the acceptance of economic evaluation of other health technologies. There was an indication in the Commonwealth government's 1997/98 Budget, for example, that some form of mandatory economic evaluation of new medical services was likely to be considered in Australia. It may be, as Hall (1993) suggests, that 'economic evaluation as a way of thinking is becoming increasingly accepted as part of institutional and regulatory processes'.

Conclusions

Culyer (1991) claimed that in the field of economic evaluations 'the variance in quality is extremely high'. Drummond et al. (1993) suggested that, while the quality of economic evaluations has improved, there are still unresolved methodological issues. Six issues were listed on which they held that there is still a low level of agreement:

1. inclusion of indirect costs and benefits;
2. choice of discount rate for health benefits;

3. method of measuring the utilities of health states;
4. incorporation of considerations of equity in economic evaluations;
5. inclusion of health care costs in added years of life; and
6. inclusion of intersectoral consequences of health care programs;

to which could be added:

7. monetary valuation of health outcomes; and
8. accounting for the nature of the health care program and the appropriate objectives of health policy, including issues of outcomes other than health such as 'process utility' (Olsen 1993; Mooney 1996; Salkeld 1997) and community level benefits (Shiell & Hawe 1996).

A discussion of these various issues would warrant a chapter in its own right. They are raised in order to increase awareness that, while there is a high level of agreement between economists on most of the key methodological issues (i.e. terminology of economic evaluation, need to consider alternatives, superiority of marginal costing, importance of specifying viewpoint, need for discounting, use of sensitivity analysis), methodological standards either do not exist or are not fully specified on some aspects.

We have argued that there seems to have been an improvement in the quality of economic evaluation studies in health care in the past decade. Such an improvement has no doubt been the result of such textbooks as Drummond et al. (1987), and in Australia the PBAC *Guidelines* (Commonwealth of Australia 1995) and the introduction of tertiary courses in health economics and economic evaluation. Salkeld et al. (1995) and anecdotal evidence (Mitchell 1996; Drummond et al. 1991) suggest that the quality and sophistication of studies has improved over time. In particular, the use of modelling techniques to extrapolate from clinical trial evidence has been encouraged in Australia by the PBAC (Drummond & Davies 1991; O'Brien 1996; Johnson & Weinstein 1997). There have also been recent developments in the literature (O'Brien et al. 1994; Laska et al. 1997; Polsky et al. 1997) on the use of classical and Bayesian statistical techniques in CEA in dealing with uncertainty and a growing use of Decision Analysis and Markov models (Keeler, 1995).

Yet as Salkeld et al. (1995) also found, basic errors are still being made, such as in the choice of economic method or of comparators, the failure to use marginal analysis or to employ sensitivity analysis. The continuing development of standards for economic evaluation methods will help to maintain the scientific quality of studies, facilitate the comparison of evaluation results for different health care interventions and assist in the interpretation of study results from setting to setting. A concerted effort to disseminate the principles and methods of economic evaluation to policy-makers and non-economic evaluators would also be an important aid to improving the credibility and usefulness of economic evaluations in priority-setting. If economic evaluation is ever to become a major contributor to health care policy, the right questions have to be asked. Current evidence (Drummond et al. 1991; Ross 1995) suggests that the impact of economic analysis is enhanced when it is linked directly to the policy and the decision-making process.

9 *Health insurance*

The theory

Insurance and risk

Insurance is a collective device which offers individuals protection against risk. On the principle that individuals face uncertainty, whereas society as a whole can face approximate certainty, insurance provides a means by which individuals can trade or pool their risks in order to acquire the levels of certainty attainable by larger populations.

Individuals purchasing insurance are able to exploit gains from trade by agreeing to pool risks. Because most people are risk-averse, it might be rational for them to insure even when the expected payout is less than the premium charged. A risk-averse person will be prepared to pay a net price for insurance (gross premium—average payout) so long as it does not exceed the value to him or her of securing certainty.

Under market conditions an insurer will charge an actuarial premium, reflecting the individual's expected loss plus the insurer's transaction costs (comprising administrative costs and normal profit). The setting of actuarially fair premiums rests on a number of preconditions:

- that the probability of the insured event for an individual is independent of that for everyone else;
- that the relevant probability is less than one;
- that the relevant probability is known and estimable;
- that there is no adverse selection (where the contributor is able to conceal his/her high risk from the insurer); and
- that there is no moral hazard (where the contributor can manipulate the probability of an insured event or its cost).

Some at least of these conditions are rarely satisfied in the case of health insurance.

Insurance and subsidy

Health insurance is a form of insurance with special characteristics. On one definition, health insurance is described as 'the pooling across a defined population of losses arising from ill health and its consequences' (Scotton 1997). As it operates in the real world it may be viewed as a broader concept than pure insurance, with three distinct components (Scotton 1997):

- *'pure insurance'*: pooling of random deviations from the expected health costs incurred by people in various risk groups, the average of which can be calculated from known factors, such as age and health status;
- *transfers between risk groups*: pooling across risk groups under which people with higher expected costs pay less than actuarially fair premiums and those with lower expected costs pay more;
- *transfers between income groups*: people on low incomes who cannot afford actuarially fair premiums are cross-subsidised (partly or wholly) by others.

Thus the transfers under the last two involve cross-subsidies between different groups to supplement the pooling achieved from pure insurance. The need for a combined approach of pooling and cross-subsidisation arises from the uneven and unpredictable need for health care, the size of the potential costs to individuals, and the universally accepted principle that necessary services should not be denied because of inability to pay. Such social objectives require much greater pooling than insurance alone can provide, although the balance between these different elements will differ markedly between health systems.[1]

Health insurance as a social and political issue

The emergence of health insurance as a major social issue is the consequence of enormous advances in the efficacy of medical care. However, this progress has been achieved at ever-increasing economic cost, to the point that developed countries now spend up to 10 per cent of their gross domestic product on health services. The combined results of these two factors are that not only are the benefits from health care more highly valued by their actual and potential recipients, but that individuals in those countries stand to incur much larger financial losses from ill-health than their forebears. The combination of more costly medical care with rising incomes has generated a growing demand for pooling risks through insurance in order to reduce the potentially large financial burden on individuals and families.

The special features of the health care 'industry', along with the social benefits of risk-pooling and disparities in health needs and incomes, have long necessitated some form of government intervention in all countries. The forms of this intervention have been diverse, depending on a wide variety of social, cultural and political factors, but historically there have been two distinct approaches—one based on support for and regulation of private (but usually non-profit) insurance, the other involving direct public provision and subsidisation (Scotton 1997). More recently, as the scale of necessary cross-subsidisation has grown, these approaches have tended to converge. The role of government in the pooling of health care costs has been a prominent political and public policy issue in Australia for half a century, with the solution reflecting a 'mixed system' compromise between voluntarist and public sector models. On the subject of insurance, there has been vigorous debate on the extent to which a private insurance market can meet the needs of the community to reduce risk in regard to health care, whether the government should intervene in this market and, if so, what form this intervention should take (Scotton & Macdonald 1993).

Until very recently the political parties were divided between the merits of a voluntary insurance system and compulsory national insurance, but since 1995 Australia has moved closer to the consensus around the social insurance approach which characterises most of the European OECD countries. However, there is still a strong attachment among many on the conservative side of politics to a substantial role for private health insurance, as both a supplement and an alternative to Medicare.

Health insurance in Australia[2]

In Australia, the government intervenes in health care financing both through the provision of universal social insurance under Medicare, covering both medical and public hospital services, and the regulation and subsidisation of private health insurance, which covers private inpatient care in hospitals and some other privately provided services. The Medicare program is described in Chapter 2 and issues relating to it appear in Chapters 5, 10 and 11. The focus in this chapter is on private health insurance.

Private health insurance remains a significant feature of the Australian health care system, but less so than in the past. Prior to the introduction of Medicare in 1984, private insurance was in effect

Australia's national health insurance scheme, providing cover for medical services as well as hospital and ancillary services, with about as much as 78 per cent of the population enrolled as contributors and dependants. With Medicare providing universal coverage of medical services and access to free public hospital care, the role of private insurance was substantially abridged, and its membership contracted.

In 1994/95 private health insurance funded 11.5 per cent of Australian current health expenditure. While the Commonwealth and state governments are the source of over 80 per cent of the expenditure on public hospitals, medical services and pharmaceuticals, private health insurers are the source of funds for around 70 per cent of private hospital expenditure (AIHW 1997, table 17).

The regulatory environment

The private health insurance industry operates within a highly regulated environment, largely laid down in the *National Health Act* which, when originally enacted in 1953, defined the functions of the health funds as carriers of the voluntary insurance scheme. The conduct of the insurers is also governed by provisions of the *Health Insurance Act*. The Commonwealth Department of Health and Family Services administers the regulatory framework, including registration of funds and oversight of fund rules, while the Private Health Insurance Administration Council (PHIAC), a Commonwealth statutory authority, monitors reserves, administers reinsurance, provides information to consumers and monitors the impact of the government's financial incentives.

Many features of the regulatory system were designed to limit competitive behaviour in order to promote social objectives—in particular, to provide access to all members of the community on equal terms. Health insurance can be offered only by organisations registered under the *National Health Act*. Under the Act, insurers must accept all applicants and may not discriminate in setting premiums and paying benefits on the basis of health status, age, race, sex or use of services. The requirement that insurers may not have regard to differences in risk in setting contribution rates is known as 'community rating'. In order to underpin this massive distortion of market signals, and to reduce the financial impact on funds with relatively high proportions of older members, registered funds must participate in reinsurance arrangements for their hospital tables. These arrangements pool across all funds the hospital costs of contributors aged over 65 years and those hospitalised more than 35 days, which constitute 48 per cent of total claims costs.

Other requirements are designed to assure contributors of basic and uniform coverage of services. For example, funds must offer minimum default benefits for all public or private hospitals; they must also include in-hospital psychiatric, rehabilitation and palliative care services in all tables and cover nursing home-type patients at the acute rate for 35 days. On the other hand, funds cannot offer no-claim bonuses, non-smoker discounts, nursing home cover, gap insurance above the scheduled fee (unless a contract is in place) or gap cover for drugs listed under the Pharmaceutical Benefits scheme. Maximum waiting periods for hospital cover are specified in the Act. A maximum of two months is generally applied, with higher maximum periods of 12 months for pre-existing ailments and, until recently, nine months for obstetrics.

Most of these provisions carry over from the voluntary health insurance scheme, when the government heavily subsidised the health funds as the agencies for delivery of national health benefits. This function is now substantially undertaken by Medicare, but the implications have been only partly reflected in government policy. As a result, the regulatory framework governing private insurance is an amalgam of some components designed for its past social agency role and others appropriate to a competitive, market-based industry.

The supply side

Structure of the industry

There were 48 registered health insurance organisations in Australia as at 30 June 1996. Of these, 30 were open to anyone to join and 18 were restricted membership organisations (RMOs) or closed funds. Only three operate on a for-profit basis (National Mutual Health Insurance Pty Ltd, NMHI; FAI Health Benefits Ltd, FAI; and SGIO Health Pty Ltd). The rest are tax-free mutual funds, for which any surplus must stay within the fund and be used for the benefit of contributors.

The largest three funds cover more than half the market. Medibank Private is the largest, with nearly 890 000 members in mid-1996. It is operated by the Health Insurance Commission, but the government has recently announced its intention to hive it off as a separate organisation—presumably as a candidate for eventual privatisation. Details of fund membership and market shares are given in Table 9.1.

Two or three organisations cover the bulk of membership in each state and territory, reflecting a high degree of concentration in each market. In fact, in all the state markets except NSW and Victoria,

Table 9.1 Membership and market shares of major health organisations, 30 June 1996

Organisation	Membership (*n*)	National market share (%)	Cumulative market share (%)
Medibank Private	889 474	25.9	25.9
Medical Benefits Fund of Australia	660 270	19.2	45.1
National Mutual Health Insurance	396 110	11.5	56.6
Hospitals Contribution Fund of Australia	291 395	8.5	65.1
Hospital Benefit Fund of WA	267 646	7.8	72.9
NIB Health Funds	186 238	5.4	78.3
Other open organisations	436 716	12.6	90.9
Restricted membership organisations	312 055	9.1	100.0
National total	**3 439 904**	**100.0**	

Source: IC 1997, based on PHIAC 1996.

more than 50 per cent of members are enrolled with the largest insurer. There are also several regional funds, such as Yallourn Medical and Hospital Society, which dominate local markets.

Coverage

Private health insurance funds generally offer hospital cover for up to 100 per cent of charges levied by public and private hospitals, together with 25 per cent of the Medicare schedule fee for medical services provided to private patients in hospital (public or private). More recently they have been permitted to provide medical cover beyond the scheduled fee, for services covered by contracts between them and the doctors providing the services. In addition, funds provide cover for a variety of ancillary services, including dentistry, optical and physiotherapy.

Hospital benefits comprise about 73 per cent of private health insurance payouts. Various levels of cover for hospital stays are available, ranging down from 100 per cent cover to tables offering fixed benefits per day and 25 per cent medical benefits, which often leave patients facing substantial out-of-pocket costs. Most contributors are covered for intermediate levels of benefit: in September 1997, 31 per cent of members were insured on tables involving front-end deductibles and less than 2 per cent on recently introduced 'exclusionary' tables, under which benefits are not payable for certain services.

Financial performance

During the first half of the 1990s, despite declining membership, the health funds were able to build their reserves by raising prices and marketing higher tables. Total reserves rose from $0.5 billion in June 1985 to $1.4 billion in June 1996. However, in 1995/96, with benefit payments amounting to $3.9 billion or 95 per cent of contribution income, they reported a combined operating loss of $81.3 million (PHIAC 1996). Their deteriorating experience reflected rising use of private hospitals and adverse selection, and in 1997 most of the major funds implemented substantial rate rises.

Funds are required by regulation—subject to certain exemptions— to hold reserves equivalent to two months' benefit to meet unexpected demand and ensure solvency. In aggregate, funds hold about the equivalent of three months of contributions for reserves, although there are significant differences between funds. For example, in June 1996 there were six organisations with reserves of less than the required two contribution months, while seven funds held reserves equivalent to more than five contribution months.

The share of administration costs to contribution income is around 12 per cent, and compares relatively favourably with general insurance (averaging over 24 per cent) and life insurance (averaging 16 per cent). However, the circumstances are not strictly comparable. For example, PHIAC has noted that there are underwriting costs in general insurance that are not present in health insurance, and general insurers operate their business on a risk basis which involves actuarial costs. Administrative costs compare much less favourably with Medicare, at around 4 per cent. In this case also the figures are not strictly comparable, as health insurers face marketing and premium collection costs not incurred by Medicare.

The Industry Commission undertook an analysis to examine whether economies of scale were present. It found that among a group of major funds the larger funds achieved lower management costs as a proportion of contribution income (IC 1997, appendix G).

Market structure

The traditional functions of private health insurers in Australia have been premium collection, claims processing and payment, with virtually no influence over service use or prices charged. Their role has been described as that of passive conduits of funds from service users to health care providers (Richardson 1995). The payment method of open-ended reimbursement of provider charges is conducive to inflation of health costs, and attempts to raise benefit coverage have led to cycles of price and premium rises.

In an attempt to break the cycle, and its inevitable consequence of further shrinkage of membership, insurers have endeavoured since the late 1980s to move progressively towards negotiation of contracts with private hospitals. This process was accelerated by legislation introduced by the Labor government in 1993, in consequence of which some at least of the health insurance funds are now beginning to see themselves as active financial intermediaries between consumers and providers of hospital and medical services. In 1995 further legislation was introduced to facilitate contracting between funds and providers. It allowed for three types of contractual arrangements (IC 1997, box 3.12):

- *Hospital Purchaser–Provider Agreements (HPPAs):* may be made between funds and hospitals and/or day-procedure centres. The hospital must accept the agreed price as full payment for the episode of care;
- *Medical Purchaser–Provider Agreements (MPPAs):* refer to agreements between funds and doctors relating to the provision of medical services to contributors in hospitals or day hospitals. Where a MPPA is in place, a fund can pay medical benefits in excess of scheduled fees; and
- *Practitioner Agreements (PAs):* refer to agreements between hospitals and doctors. Initially, these agreements did not enable reimbursement above the MBS rates.

Contracts between funds and hospitals (HPPAs) can allow insurers to offer nil or predetermined out-of-pocket expenses to contributors. By mid-1996, 9700 HPPAs had been signed, of which two-thirds were in Victoria and NSW. There has been limited progress in agreements between doctors and funds (MPPAs), with fewer than 100 signed by mid-1996. Even with respect to private hospitals, the bargaining position of the insurers remains weak. The essence of market power is the ability to contract selectively with providers, but successive Commonwealth governments have severely limited insurers' freedom in this respect. The 1995 legislation provided for minimum default benefits of about $210 per day to be paid to patients in non-contracted private hospitals. In 1997, despite the recommendation of the Industry Commission that the funds no longer be required to pay default benefits to non-contracted private hospitals (IC 1997: 375), the government legislated a 'second-tier' level of default benefits at rates expected to be 80–85 per cent of average benefits paid to contracted funds.

Competition

The geographic segmentation of the private health insurance market on a state basis, with a small number of participants in each market, would suggest that competitive pressures might be weak. However, it is not just the number of competitors that is relevant in assessing the degree of competition in this market: rather, observed behaviour is influenced by other factors—the threat of potential competition, and features of the broader regulatory environment in which insurers operate.

Health funds seek to compete on the basis of price, product differentiation, marketing and contracting. Funds appear to be more effective in competing in marketing, while product and price competition are tempered by regulatory constraints. Another significant source of competitive discipline is the existence of Medicare as a 'free' alternative.[3] While there appear to be few entry barriers to potential rivals, low profitability and community rating render the industry unattractive to entrants.

The Industry Commission found a reasonable degree of competition among the funds, within the bounds of regulatory constraints that affect incumbents and potential entrants alike.

The demand side

Membership trends

In June 1997 there were just under 2.8 million contributors to hospital insurance, covering 5.9 million people, or 31.9 per cent of the total population (PHIAC 1997). Coverage varied between states, with relatively low proportions of the population covered in the Northern Territory (24.4 per cent) and Queensland (30.0 per cent). In the Northern Territory this may reflect younger demographics, a substantial Aboriginal population, and a greater proportion of people living in rural locations. Queensland's low coverage reflects its long-term policy of free hospitalisation, but the gap between it and other states has progressively narrowed over the last decade, in the context of uniform conditions relating to access to public and private services under Medicare.

Figure 9.1 depicts the pattern of demand for insurance since 1970/71. It indicates a long-term downward trend, with occasional upward shifts reflecting different policy and regulatory regimes over time.

Since June 1984, when Medicare was introduced, the proportion of the Australian population covered by private health insurance has

Figure 9.1 Proportion of population covered by private hospital insurance (%)

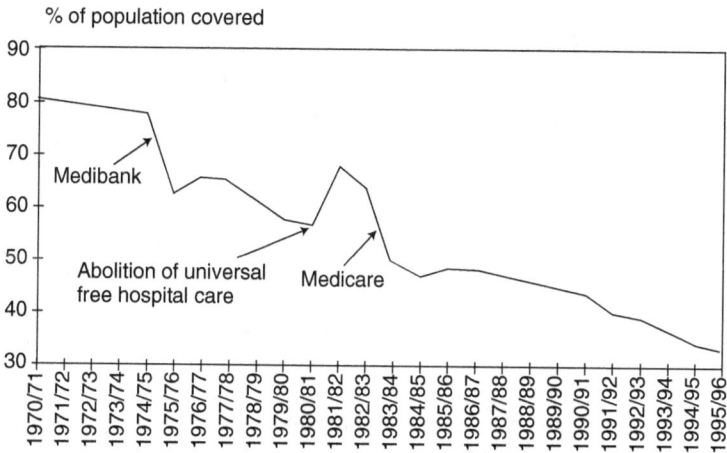

% of population covered

Source: IC 1997, based on PHIAC data for the year ending June, 1971–1996.

declined from around half to less than a third. A slight rise (from 31.9 to 32.0 per cent) in the September 1997 quarter reflected a small positive response to government incentives introduced in July, but it subsequently dropped back to 31.1 per cent by the March 1998 quarter. Prior to Medicare's introduction the rate of decline was accelerating, reaching 5.5 per cent per annum in the past three years—a trend, if it were to continue, would result in only around 11 per cent of Australians having private health insurance by 2030. Whether such a figure will be reached is debatable. The concept of an eventual 'natural floor' to private insurance coverage is purely hypothetical, and in any case its level would depend on the type and extent of structural change to the system, as well as the working out of incentives inherent in the present structure.

The demand for private health insurance is influenced by a range of interacting conventional socioeconomic factors, including age, ethnicity and income, and these factors go far to explaining the patterns of coverage—in terms of levels of coverage of various groups in the population at any point of time (Wilcox 1991; Schofield 1997). However, these factors contribute relatively little to explaining changes in coverage over time. A major contributor to the decline in membership of private health funds since the introduction of Medicare has been undoubtedly a steep rise in real prices. Since 1990 the price of private health insurance has risen inexorably, at a rate averaging three times inflation: as Figure 9.2 shows, affordability—as

Figure 9.2 Private health insurance premiums and affordability

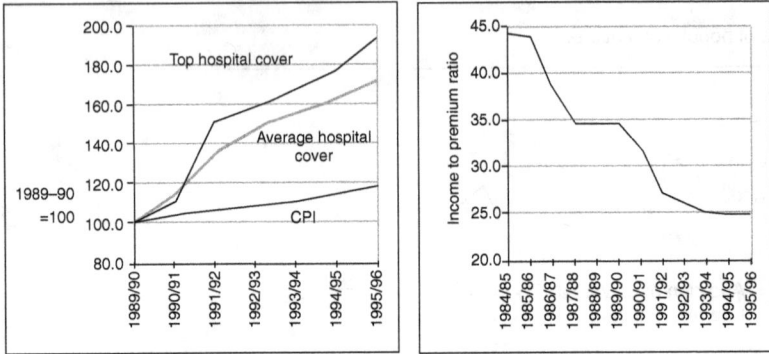

Source: IC 1997.

measured by the ratio of household income to contribution rates—has almost halved since the introduction of Medicare.

The pattern of decline in membership and coverage cannot be explained as simply a result of price changes. Despite the removal of government subsidies in 1986, membership held up well until about three years later. The subsequent decline can be interpreted as a response to the economic downturn of 1989/90, with an attendant rise in unemployment, and the subsequent pattern of income redistribution which eroded the position of middle-income groups.

Underlying all these 'economic' factors is another, which could be particularly important in the long term: generational change, in the form of the ageing and death of cohorts of people who regarded private health insurance as the 'natural' method of securing protection from health risks—and their progressive replacement by cohorts for whom Medicare has always been around. To the extent that this concept of a 'natural floor' has any validity, it will be the preferences of the post-Medicare generation that will determine where it lies.

Market imperfections and actuarial games

The beginning of this chapter laid out the conditions for the setting of actuarially fair premiums in insurance markets. In the real world these conditions are never perfectly satisfied. *Moral hazard*, in the sense of observable differences in experience between insured and uninsured people, is widely observed in most forms of insurance. The classical response of insurers has been to oblige the insured to share the risk, by contributing to losses incurred, in the form of coinsurance and/or front-end deductibles included in policies. Moral hazard is probably not so great a problem in health insurance as in many other areas of insurance, as a large part of health expenditure is non-discretionary. However, this is not the case with regard to levels of amenity in hospital care, and some part of the increased costs incurred by health insurers in recent years stems from the marketing of 100 per cent tables covering the high-cost end of the private hospital market.

Adverse selection, namely the chance of an insurer attracting a higher than expected proportion of bad risks, is a much greater problem than moral hazard in health insurance, as individuals tend to have a better knowledge of their present and likely future health status than is available to insurers. It is observed universally that, other factors being equal, people with worse health status are more likely to be insured, and if insured more likely to have higher coverage, than those with smaller chances of requiring medical services. As premiums set in a competitive market will be related to the average experience of an insured population, the underwriting result of an individual insurer will depend critically on how the experience of *its* policy-holders compares with that of the population on which the rates are based.[4]

How do insurers protect themselves against adverse selection? In unregulated markets one method is to make the best effort to ascertain risk factors, to categorise risk levels and to differentiate premiums accordingly. As Arrow (1963) pointed out, welfare optimality in insurance markets depends on the maximum possible degree of risk discrimination. In practice it is more cost-effective for insurers to stop well short of the maximum, and instead use other strategies, ranging from refusal to renew policies to the manipulation of coverage, terms and conditions (e.g. no-claim bonuses, exclusions, waiting periods) in a manner designed to attract good risks and deter bad risks. These strategies are referred to as 'cream-skimming'.

Under the regulatory system applying to private health insurance in Australia, nearly all these defences are denied to the health funds. Despite the general policy direction toward a more deregulated regimen, the central pillars of the old system remain, in the form of community rating of contributions and compulsory participation in the reinsurance pool. While community rating in its present form remains, the reinsurance pool is an essential prop, as the proportions of elderly and other high-use contributors vary so widely across the health funds that some would not remain solvent without it. However, the reinsurance pool itself compounds the inefficiency of the health care system, most obviously by weakening incentives to control costs associated with the elderly through the use of lower-cost community-based alternatives.

However, the most serious consequence of community rating is that it intensifies adverse selection, which is manifested in a number of ways identified in the Industry Commission report: so-called 'hit and runs', in which people opportunistically take out insurance ahead of a known episode of illness or confinement and leave thereafter, and 'hit and stays', which occur when people delay entry into insurance until they reach an age at which they expect higher health costs. In the longer run, the most obvious effect of community rating has been to institutionalise incentives for the low risks to drop out, with the consequence of weakening the risk profiles of those continuing to be insured. This has been a major cause of rises in contribution rates, which in turn strengthen incentives for low risks to drop out, resulting in the vicious circle illustrated in Figure 9.3.

The sustainability of community rating was arguably the most important issue considered by the Industry Commission in its recent inquiry, which is dealt with later in this chapter.

Government subsidies

The private health insurance industry was basically brought into existence by Commonwealth subsidies, in the form of benefits payable through health funds under the *National Health Act*. Subsequent expansion of the industry over the next two decades was supported by rising levels of these subsidies and income tax deductions on contributions. Most of these were terminated when the original Medibank program was introduced in 1975. However, that program

Figure 9.3   The vicious circle of falling membership

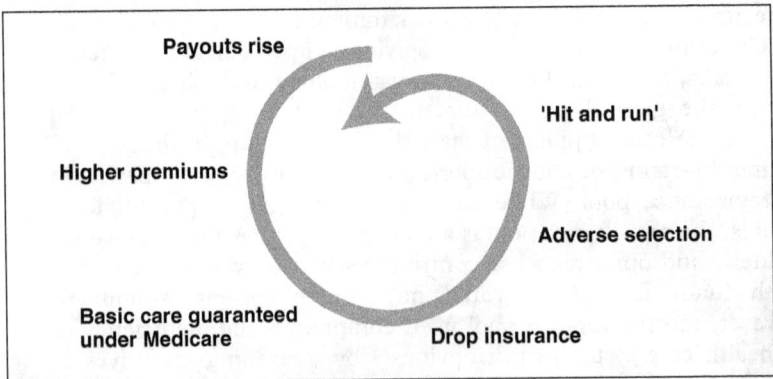

Payouts rise

'Hit and run'

Higher premiums

Adverse selection

Basic care guaranteed under Medicare

Drop insurance

Source: IC 1997.

and its successor Medicare incorporated daily bed payments to private hospitals, on the principle that private patients should be entitled to benefits comparable to those extended to public patients of public hospitals. When implemented in 1984, Medicare also included a substantial subsidy to the reinsurance pool, which meant that the additional costs of high-use contributors were not fully borne by the young and healthy insured.

These subsidies had the practical effect of lowering the cost of hospital insurance and containing the pressures on public hospital systems which would have resulted from a precipitate decline in private health insurance coverage. Two years later, for budgetary reasons unrelated to the health system, both these subsidies were terminated, and the costs of private insurance rose further by making health funds liable for benefits equal to 25 per cent of scheduled fees for medical services billed to private inpatients. These measures resulted in rises of up to 50 per cent in health insurance contribution over the following two years (PSA 1993, fig. 2). Although their full impact on private insurance membership was not felt immediately, they laid the foundation for the subsequent downward spiral. In addition, they created a sense of grievance among people who were privately insured, through the perception that they were obliged to 'pay double' for their health coverage.

What constitutes equity in the relative levels of subsidy available to users of public and private health services is a complex and controversial issue. Without making any judgement on the ethical or political considerations involved, the practical consequence of the 1986 decision to withdraw subsidies—adverse selection, rising contribution rates and growing pressure on public hospital systems—all helped to feed perceptions that the health system was in mounting trouble. The belief that the accelerating decline in private health insurance membership was central to the problem was most strongly held by people on the conservative side of politics, but came to be widely shared by Labor politicians—especially, but not solely, at the state level.

In formulating its policies for the 1995 election, the Liberal–National Party coalition abandoned the opposition to Medicare which had cost it so heavily at previous elections, but at the same time included as a 'core commitment' a substantial level of subsidy to private health insurance. In government, its 1996 Budget announced financial measures costing $600 million annually, to take effect from 1 July 1997, to encourage people to maintain or take out private health insurance. The incentives take the form of income tax or cash rebates for people on lower incomes, and Medicare levy surcharges imposed on higher-income individuals not privately insured. The details are:

- *rebates* payable to single people earning less than $35 000 a year and couples and families earning less than $70 000; annual threshold rises by $3000 for each additional child. Rebates of up to $125 are paid to singles, $250 for couples and $450 for families;
- a *Medicare levy surcharge* of 1 per cent of taxable income payable by single people earning over $50 000 and families earning over $100 000 if they fail to take out private cover.

The main objectives of these financial measures were stated to be to relieve pressure on public funding; to encourage private service provision; and to widen choice of public and private services. It is too early at time of writing to properly assess the overall impact of these incentives on fund membership, the health budget or the community as a whole. As mentioned above, there are early indications that the uptake of private health insurance has been largely unaffected, although the industry has suggested that fund membership would have been even lower without the incentives. It is likely that most of the benefit will be derived by people who are already insured, in which case it may prove a costly way of retaining or attracting contribution revenue.

The Industry Commission estimated that there could be a net cost to the budget in the short term of $320 million, after allowing for savings in costs to Medicare from the transfer from public to private hospitals and the cost of the rebate (IC 1997, box 3.14). The IC argued that the rebate constituted a partial solution to the inequity of 'double payment', but pointed out that this inequity did not apply to the part of the rebate associated with ancillary insurance (IC 1997: 382).

As far as *new* contributors are concerned, the impact of the rebate has been substantially offset by subsequent premium rises. Any ongoing incentive effect will be eroded further in the longer term unless the rebates are indexed. The overall community benefit arising from any shift of financing and provision from the public to private sector will depend on the extent of such a shift and the relative efficiency of the two sectors.

The Industry Commission inquiry

In August 1996 the government announced that the Industry Commission would undertake a six-month inquiry into the private health insurance industry. This announcement was in part a response to concern that substantial rises in contribution rates following the

Budget announcement could greatly weaken the impact of the rebates. It was also hoped that the inquiry would present some longer-term solutions for a troubled component of the health care system.

Consumer concerns

The main symptom of the problems to be examined by the Industry Commission was decline of consumer confidence in private health insurance. While lack of affordability is probably the most important reason for consumers relinquishing insurance, there are other significant factors. Concerns raised during the inquiry (IC 1997) included:

- perception of poor value for money;
- large and unpredictable out-of-pocket costs;
- proliferation of bills and cumbersome billing arrangements;
- complexity of the insurance product, resulting in difficulties when comparing funds and tables; and
- lack of equity, especially for long-term contributors cross-subsidising the 'hit and runs'.

Policy background

These factors are underpinned by the existence of a 'free' substitute in Medicare, which reduces the risk associated with dropping out. When viewed from a longer-term perspective, the underlying inconsistency between Medicare and a relatively highly priced (private health insurance) substitute remains an inherent source of instability. Moreover, since 1986 at least, there has been no serious attempt to resolve the ambiguous role of private health insurance in the Australian health care system. In the course of the Industry Commission inquiry there was a considerable debate on what was seen as the core issue, namely the extent to which private health insurance can be seen as

- *topping up* public funding to provide optional extras (i.e. a complement to Medicare), or
- *replacing* public funding (i.e. an alternative to, or substitute for, Medicare).

On the former view, private health insurance could be regarded as being of little consequence in terms of public policy. There would be no need for public regulation, beyond the prudential supervision applying to insurance in general, and even less justification for public subsidy. On the other hand, it would logically involve a greater degree of government commitment to giving Medicare adequate capacity to provide adequate access to care for the whole population.

Versions of the latter view range from the 'freedom of choice' position—that is, as stated in some early Medicare publicity, people should have (more or less) equal access to public and private hospital care—to the 'free enterprise' position—that private health insurance is not only an alternative to Medicare, but a substitute which *should* be used by those who are well enough off to afford it. Proponents of these positions would be more inclined to justify a regulatory system incorporating community rating and government subsidy as means of ensuring equitable access.

The Industry Commission was able to draw attention to the wider implications of these alternative positions, but its terms of reference did not allow it to pursue them. The reality is that to do so may have reawoken political divisions concerning universal health insurance which, at the time, the government wished to avoid.

Recommendations and proposed reforms

In fact, the Industry Commission's terms of reference were circumscribed in such a way as to prevent it from considering reform options which extended beyond the confines of the private insurance system: they specified that the inquiry be conducted 'against the background of the Government's policy to retain Medicare, bulk billing and community rating, and to provide financial incentives for individuals with health insurance'. Nevertheless, in framing its policy recommendations the Commission tried to ensure that its proposals would improve community welfare without getting in the way of wider, possibly more beneficial, changes to the health system in the future.

Given the circumstances that gave rise to the inquiry, the Commission had to give particular attention to explaining why premiums had risen so much more rapidly than the general level of inflation in recent years. In simple terms it was found that premiums are rising fast because payouts to members are rising fast. Funds are not making excess surpluses and administrative costs remain relatively low. The main contributors to rising premiums were identified as:

- a substantial rise in the proportion of fund members using private rather than public hospitals;
- rising average private hospital admission charges, due in part to changing technology and clinical practice;
- increased admissions by private patients; and
- adverse selection.

The Commission concluded that the most important cost-drivers behind premium rises are not under the direct control of the funds, but tend to reflect decisions by governments, doctors, patients and hospitals about what treatment to provide, where, and at what price. Table 9.2 summarises some key Commission recommendations and

Table 9.2   Industry Commission inquiry: key recommendations and government response

Objective	Recommendation	Government response
Reducing adverse selection	• unfunded lifetime community rating	• support, subject to further analysis
	• increase waiting periods for obstetrics	• increased from 9 to 12 months
	• maintain restrictions on no-claim bonuses	• support
Facilitating innovative products	• drop compulsory coverage of rehabilitation and palliative care (but retain for psychiatric)	• retain in all 3 areas, subject to admission/ quality criteria
	• introduce composition-based reinsurance	• disposed to support, subject to review of impact
Enhancing competition	• improve governance by facilitating hostile takeovers	• support principle, subject to further review
	• allow other private funds to act as Medicare agents	• support; introduce 1 July 1998
	• separate Medibank Private from HIC	• support
	• competitive neutrality between public/private hospitals via full economic charging	• resolve in Medicare Agreement negotiations
Improving cost-effectiveness	• improve incentives within contracting by eliminating default benefit	• reject; introduced second tier default benefit
Alleviating other regulatory burdens	• drop regulation of premium changes	• reject; introduced annual premium rises on common date (1 March)
	• improve regulation of reserves	• support
Meeting other consumer needs	• billing reforms	• support; introduced simplified billing
Maximising the value of the incentives	• improve rebate/levy administrative arrangements	• not support

Source: IC 1997.

the government's response on release of the report in April 1997 and in subsequent legislation (*Health Legislation Amendment Act No. 2 1998*).

The most significant of the Commission's recommendations, which drew on a large number of submissions, was replacement of the form of community rating that has characterised private health insurance for more than four decades by an unfunded version of 'lifetime community rating', in which the premium paid by a contributor would vary according to age at entry. For example, a 65-year-old who entered at age 35 years would pay a lower premium than someone who entered at age 60 but the same as someone entering today at age 35. The main objective of this approach would be to deter late or strategic entry and as such is fairer to existing and long-term members. It would also produce a more balanced pool of risks, which would relieve the upward pressure on health fund premiums and hence make private health insurance more affordable to a wider cross-section of the population (IC 1997: 314–25).

This recommendation received wide-ranging support from participants in the Industry Commission inquiry, and was agreed to in principle by the Commonwealth government, subject to a detailed assessment of implementation issues by the Department of Health and Family Services. Actuarial work has been undertaken and there is a widespread expectation that some form of unfunded lifetime community rating will be introduced.

The way ahead?

The future of private health insurance in Australia depends on a number of factors. First, it depends on the response of the community to the government's financial incentives to take out, or stay in, private health insurance. Second, it depends on the successful implementation of the Industry Commission's recommendations and the response of the 'stake-holders' and the community to the changed incentives. Third, it depends on the willingness of the insurance industry to continue to innovate by adopting new approaches, such as managed care, and the willingness of other stake-holders—the AMA and private hospitals in particular—to adapt to this new environment. Finally, it depends on the government's future agenda for reform of the health system as a whole.

Although significant in their own right, the Industry Commission's recommendations were of necessity incremental in nature, and designed to alleviate some of the problems of the health insurance industry in the short term. They may serve to improve the stability of the private health care system and alleviate some of the pressure on the public system. But their implementation will not resolve the inherent and ongoing tension between universal access under Medicare and voluntary community-rated private health insurance. Nor will they resolve the inherent tension between the stake-holders—between medical practitioners, insurers, private and public hospitals—or between the Commonwealth and state governments arising from cost-shifting.

As the Commission made very clear, any long-term solution will require much more substantial reform of the broader health care system. It noted that: 'Private health insurance is a cog in a machine. One can burnish the gears of that cog, but ultimately its performance and functioning depend on the rest of the machine' (IC 1997: 384). Because private health insurance is a component of an interdependent system, piecemeal reform can be hazardous. Many participants recognised this concern, urging a more fundamental examination of policy options across the health system. As a result, a wider public review was recommended by the Commission, encompassing the whole health system and the interactions between the parts. At this stage the government is more disposed to continue focusing on specific issues of concern.

10   *The health care financing debate*

'Would you tell me, please, which way I should go from here?' Alice asked the Cheshire Cat. 'That depends a good deal on where you want to get to,' said the Cat.

Lewis Caroll, *Alice in Wonderland*

Issues, interests and ideologies

Even in principle the financing of health care is a complex issue, and its reform has been persistently on the political agenda. This reflects the all-pervasive importance of health care financing in achieving often conflicting objectives. The source of funds—government or private sector—determines the balance between individual and collective responsibility for the financial burden of health care, and is an important determinant of access and equity. Funding arrangements influence the level of health expenditures and the overall pattern of costs and benefits in the health sector. Each of these issues affects powerful interests or is the subject of strong ideological and ethical beliefs. Expenditure growth increases the cost to the state and federal governments, taxpayers and patients; it increases the incomes of doctors, hospitals and providers generally.

With billions of dollars at stake it is not surprising that these interest groups have actively participated in the health funding debate. Until recently there was a de facto alliance between the medical profession, private health insurance (PHI) and the coalition parties for the promotion of private health insurance and for the circumscription of the government role in the health sector. For the political right this position is consistent with its advocacy of individual responsibility and the private market as the preferred method for allocating resources. For doctors, the preservation of private health insurance ensures the economic viability of private hospitals and professional and economic independence for doctors. More generally, providers believe that increased government involvement in the health sector is likely to facilitate control of expenditures and, in the longer term, to lead to interference with the clinical freedom that Australian doctors have enjoyed to date. Their desire to limit government involvement has been supported by some economists both inside and outside government, partly to reduce the government deficit by cost-shifting to the private sector and partly because of their (incorrect) belief that the greater use of unregulated market forces will control expenditure growth.

The alliance was forged by opposition to the universal insurance scheme, Medibank, in 1975 but the controversy over health care financing was not ended by the endorsement of Medicare by the Liberal Country Party in the 1995 election. Since about 1990, a combination of economic pressures and government policy has resulted in the emergence of persistent hospital queues and in a decline in private health insurance membership. These symptoms indicate that, even in the short run, the health system is not in equilibrium. Growing attention has also been given to structural defects and the evidence of allocative inefficiency.

The coincidence of providers and private insurer interests has recently been threatened by the advent of managed care. In the USA, the American Medical Association is increasingly looking to government intervention to protect providers from market forces. In Australia, the first tentative movement towards managed care (the 1995 legislation to promote individual bargaining and contracts between health funds, doctors and hospitals) created a rift between doctors and the private health funds. As in the USA, doctors have sought government protection from contractual arrangements which could affect clinical autonomy, irrespective of the outcomes that these controls might have for patients.

The purpose of this chapter is to outline these problems and to discuss the options available for reforming health care financing.

Achievements and problems

The health system may be evaluated both by benchmarking against other health systems and by comparison with what is theoretically achievable. The first criterion might be defended as being more realistic; the second as providing a clearer indication of the direction of appropriate reform.

Achievements
By international standards the Australian health care system appears to perform well, whether this is judged by the level and growth of expenditures, by the provision of services or by health outcomes as

measured by mortality rates. (For a more detailed discussion, see Chapter 2.)

Problems

Despite this conclusion, there have been numerous criticisms of Medicare.[1] Some of these reflect the visible signs of disequilibrium within the system, such as hospital queuing and declining membership of the private health funds. Other criticisms are based on a comparison between the structure and performance of Medicare and what is theoretically possible. These criticisms focus on the cause and symptoms of allocative inefficiency and inequity—the multiplicity of uncoordinated health programs, the division of responsibilities between the federal and state governments, and the variation in access and service use between rural and urban areas. Despite universal coverage by Medicare there are charges of inequity relating to access to hospital services and levels of subsidy received by private insurance contributors. Finally, there are claims that Medicare is structurally ill-equipped to control future cost pressure.

Some of these concerns are better founded than others. For example, the claim that the public hospital system is dependent on the viability of private hospitals and PHI is untrue. The public sector could expand to absorb the entire private sector if resources were transferred to it. The relative size of the public and private sectors is entirely a matter of social choice. This depends as much on the preference for individual or collective responsibility for hospital funding as it does on the economic performance of the two sectors.

Similarly, the propositions that neither the nation nor the government will be able to afford the future cost of health services are gross simplifications. The first assumes that the marginal benefits of health care are less than the opportunity cost of spending elsewhere. If this is not the case (i.e. if further spending on health produces greater wellbeing than other forms of spending), the nation's health budget should increase. The truth of the second proposition depends on the unstated assumption that taxation should not rise. However, the issue of whether increased spending should be individually or collectively financed through higher taxation is a matter of social choice. The often-repeated assertion that the electorate is opposed to higher taxation is not supported by the evidence in the case of revenue sources (such as the Medicare levy) earmarked for health care (Withers et al. 1994; Hayes & Vanden Heuvel 1995).

Concern over hospital queuing is better founded. A non-trivial proportion (11 per cent) of category 1 patients (those for whom admission within 30 days was clinically desirable) were not admitted within this time in 1995, and a significant number of category 2 patients (others) were forced to wait more than 12 months before admission. There is no suggestion that these figures have improved since 1995.

While some queuing is inevitable (even desirable), these figures suggest that Australian queues are too long. However, the significance of this problem needs to be placed in context. Twenty years ago there was almost universal agreement that public hospitals were highly inefficient, and that the rapid growth of health expenditures was largely driven by spiralling hospital costs. The decision to limit these expenditures was entirely responsible, but the only available policy was the capping of public hospital budgets. In Australia and most other countries this was the means by which aggregate cost control was achieved in the 1980s. Present waiting lists may be seen as a consequence of a continuation of the policy of using aggregate hospital budgets to achieve internal reform.

However undesirable in itself, excessive queuing is an indicator of the difficulty of achieving internal reform in hospitals. It will, of course, represent a serious failure if it becomes a permanent feature of the public sector, but the use of more sophisticated techniques, such as case payment and the greater understanding of each hospital's behaviour made possible by management information systems, should produce efficiencies that modify the impact of global caps on patient access.

Structural problems

There are several structural problems. First, and as noted in preceding chapters,[2] Commonwealth and state governments and private sector jurisdictions overlap. The adverse effects of an almost arbitrary division of responsibility, shown in Table 10.1, is compounded by a lack of coordination both between and within jurisdictions. Patterson (1996), for example, has claimed that the Commonwealth alone has no fewer than 60 programs (medical, pharmaceutical, nursing home, multiple disease-specific, educational, child care, maternal care, technology-specific, artificial limb programs, etc., etc.).

There is no economic rationale for most of these divisions, which not only raise costs but, more seriously, impede coordination and planning of service delivery. Before the AHMAC Coordinated Care Trials were proposed in 1995 (see below) there were few attempts at providing an integrated service to patients across jurisdictional and program boundaries.

The second structural problem is the inefficient pattern of incentives running through the system. In the public sector these follow largely from the patchwork of program funding already described.

Table 10.1 **Responsibilities for the finance and provision of health care**

Provision	Finance		
	Commonwealth government	State government	Private sector
Commonwealth	• Quarantine service • Rehabilitation hospitals		
State	• Public hospitals • Nursing homes	• Public hospitals • Ambulance • Community health centres	• Public hospital (private beds)
Private	• Out-of-hospital medical • In-hospital private medical care • Drugs/pharmacy • Nursing homes	• Workers' compensation (medicine) • Traffic accident compensation (medical)	• Dental • Private hospital • 'Alternative' medicine

The private sector is different, but little better. Protected by insurance-underwritten fee-for-service remuneration, private medical practice remains a cottage industry. There has been little movement towards the development of integrated multispecialty clinics that characterise many health systems, and some of the doubtful entrepreneurial developments stimulated by the private sector have met with justified opposition. The potential for patient benefit that more integrated structures might afford has not been realised (Richardson 1987b).

On the financing side, the chief source of private, third-party funds is the private health insurance industry, which has seen itself as a passive financial conduit between patients and health care providers and has not attempted to coordinate health service delivery or to secure cost-effective care for its contributors. This role was largely forced on it by a regulatory framework designed to make it operate as a public welfare agency. As pointed out in Chapter 9, both government and the industry have had difficulties in adjusting to the new role of private insurance as a supplement to Medicare.

A related problem is the structural imbalance between the public and private hospital systems in the form of zero or below-cost charges to public hospital patients and—since the abolition of the bed day and reinsurance pool subsidies in 1986—fees covering the full cost charged to private hospital patients. Rising contribution rates, in the context of community rating, have led to a cycle in which adverse selection, with the young and healthy abandoning health insurance, has led to a worsening experience and further price rises.

Despite the declining demand for PHI this disequilibrium has not yet had a significant impact on private hospital use. On the contrary, between 1989/90 and 1994/95 private hospitals increased their share of hospital expenditure from 15.6 to 21 per cent, partly as a result of a growing number of self-insured patients using private hospitals and partly because insured patients made growing use of private hospitals as the access to public beds was reduced. The result is an uneasy—and probably unstable—equilibrium, in which rising price differentials are offset by deteriorating access to public beds.

The fourth structural deficiency in Medicare is the open-ended fee-for-service benefits for medical services and pharmaceutical drugs, which contrast with the capped budget allocations to public hospitals and most other areas in the public sector (Paterson 1996). Between 1989/90 and 1994/95 the share of the health bill absorbed by private medical services and prescribed drugs has risen from 18.4 to 20.1 per cent and from 9.3 to 11.6 per cent respectively. While the rising drug bill has been largely driven by changes in composition associated with technical progress, the main driver in the case of medical services has been the growing number of doctors, now at levels which constitute a substantial overall surplus (see Chapter 4).

The fragmentation of authority, planning, financing and delivery and the paucity of coordination described here would be expected to result in service use that does not reflect best possible practice with the available resources. In fact, international evidence suggests that health systems generally are extraordinarily inefficient in this respect. Between similar developed nations, the rate at which well-defined procedures are delivered per 1000 population vary by an astonishing amount: 519 per cent for hysterectomy; 579 per cent for cholectys-tectomy and 431 per cent for appendectomy (McPherson 1990). Small-area analysis within the USA reveals even greater variation.

These differences suggest that, relative to best practice, some populations are being significantly overserviced, others under-serviced, or both, and that there is an unrealised potential for a significant improvement in allocative efficiency. The first of these hypotheses has been tested in at least one study (Leape et al. 1990). Analysis of rates of coronary angioplasty, cataract, endarterectomy and upper gastrointestinal tract endoscopy among Medicare enrollees in 23 counties in one state of the USA found that inappropriate use varied by up to 75 per cent, 67 per cent and 25 per cent respectively, which indicates both the inability of the patient to judge the need for medical procedures and the extent of overservicing that is possible.

The only study of practice variations to date in Australia has been Renwick and Sadkowsky (1991). This revealed highly significant variation in the age/sex adjusted rate of surgery for different elective procedures between states (e.g.—and excluding the NT as an outlier—81, 113 and 71 per cent differences for tonsillectomy, lens implantation and thyroidectomy respectively) and, generally, an even larger variation between the statistical divisions within each state. Results from a recent analysis of age/sex standardised rates of delivery of various procedures in statistical local areas in Victoria are reported in Figure 10.1 and Table 2.

While the maximum and minimum rates may be in part the result of random statistical variation, this evidence suggests that significant overservicing and/or underservicing are also prevalent in Australia. There is no mechanism for the systematic detection of such misallocations, nor incentive for their reduction. Except in the case of fraud, there has been no system of medical accountability to ensure that patients receive best practice or the most cost-effective care.

Figure 10.1 Standardised rate ratios for various operations in the statistical local areas in Victoria, compared with the rate ratios for all Victoria[1]

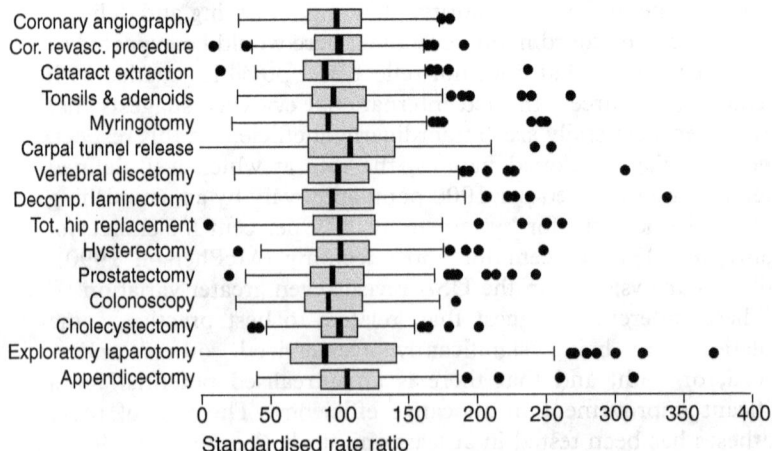

Note: Median, range, 25th & 75th centiles for statistical local areas, standardised to Victorian state ratio = 100. Extreme values greater than three times 50th–75th and 25th–50th centile intervals are recorded as separate points.

Table 10.2 Variation in the age/sex standardised two-year use of various operations: Victoria 1995/96[a]

Statistical local area ratio[a]	Minimum (1)	25%[b] (2)	Median (3)	75%[b] (4)	Maximum (5)	Max./min. (6)	75%/25% (7)	Variance ÷ expected variance[c]
Appendicectomy	15.3	86.55	106.2	128.1	314.5	20.56	1.48	5.2
Exploratory laparotomy	0	64.8	89.6	142.5	374.5	∞	2.20	1.5
Cholecystectomy	38.3	86.9	101	114.25	200.9	5.25	1.31	3.6
Colonoscopy	25	74.5	92.5	116.9	185.5	7.42	1.57	21.0
Prostatectomy	18.1	78.05	96.1	117.95	243.8	13.47	1.51	2.2
Hysterectomy	24.6	83.9	101.1	121.8	248.5	10.10	1.45	4.4
Total hip replacement	4.7	81.9	101.3	126.2	262.6	55.87	1.54	2.1
Decompression laminectomy	0	74.25	94.5	125.25	338.3	∞	1.69	0.6*
Vertebral discectomy	24.4	76.5	99.2	121.05	306.9	12.58	1.58	0.2**
Carpal tunnel release	0	77.5	109	140.8	255.5	∞	1.82	4.6
Coronary angiography	27.7	77.8	99.3	116.15	181	6.53	1.49	7.7
Coronary revascularisation procedures	8.4	83.25	100.5	115.85	191.2	22.76	1.39	3.0
Cataract extraction with lens implant	13.9	75.1	90.3	111.1	237.2	17.06	1.48	7.6
Myringotomy	23.8	76.5	92.4	112.8	249.3	10.47	1.47	6.1
Tonsillectomy +/- adenoidectomy	26.8	79.75	96.5	121	268.6	10.02	1.52	5.1

Notes: [a] Each entry is the *ratio* of the actual to the age/sex predicted rate of at which SLA residents received procedures, times 100.
[b] 25% and 75% represent the ratio at the top of the 25th percentile and the bottom of the 75th percentile respectively.
[c] Variance between SLAS divided by the variance predicted from state average use by age and sex.
* Total statewide procedures, n = 1047;** n = 1585 only.

Source: Victorian Department of Human Services, Hospital Morbidity Data file.

These data give strong *prima facie* support to the belief that in Australia, as elsewhere, there is a significant misallocation of resources, and that the reform of financial incentives may achieve a correspondingly large improvement in allocative efficiency.

The reform of health care financing

There have been numerous suggestions for the reform of health care sector financing. These vary in scope, in their time frame and, reflecting different social values, in the principal objectives of the reform. In Table 10.3 there is a non-exhaustive list of options, which are broadly classified as either 'ad hoc' or 'radical' reforms. The first group contains reforms intended to overcome specific problems, which may or may not be consistent with the evolution of the health system towards some long-term objective: options 1–5 are concerned primarily with private financing of health services; options 6 and 7 with private-sector efficiency; and options 8–10 with funding and efficiency in the public sector. In the second group four 'radical' options are outlined: two promoting the private sector and two that are consistent with a mixed public/private system.

Ad hoc private reforms: funding PHI (options 1–3)

Subsidising private health insurance (PHI) (option 1) and private hospitals (option 2) would have a similar impact. As the chief outlay of PHI is the reimbursement of private hospital fees, a subsidy that reduced fees (option 2) would lower (or at least retard the growth of) PHI premiums. The chief difference between the options is that the private hospital subsidy would also benefit those who elect to self-insure but pay for private hospitalisation out-of-pocket. In the 1996 Budget the federal government adopted option 1, and introduced a $560 million subsidy to PHI for people on low to middle incomes. Its immediate objective was to stem the decline in PHI membership, and to ensure that this decline did not result in a reduction in the use of private hospitals and a corresponding rise in the demand for public hospital care.

From a long-run perspective there is a twofold rationale for either option 1 or 2. First, those who elect to purchase PHI or private hospital care at present are forced, in effect, to pay for their hospitalisation twice. They must by law pay for public hospital entitlement through the Medicare levy and through general taxation. They must in addition pay the full cost of private hospitalisation through their PHI premium. That this choice is voluntary does not alter the fact

Table 10.3   Policy options

✓✓✓	Strong positive effect
✓	Weak positive effect
X	Weak adverse effect
XXX	Strong adverse effect
?	Unknown

Key to columns:

1 ↑ PHI subsidy
2 ↑ Private hospital subsidy
3 ↑ Levy on wealthy
4 ↑ Patient co-payments
5 Health savings accounts
6 Privatise hospitals
7 Empower PHI
8 ↑ Public hospital funding
9 Rationalisation Fed State division
10 Co-ordinated care
11 Total Privatisation including deregulation
12 Privatisation + voucher + Private Premium
13 Managed care (MC)
14 MC & Managed Competition

	1	2	3	4	5	6	7	8	9	10	11	12	13	14
Structural														
Fed/state imbalance									✓✓✓	✓	✓✓	✓✓	✓?	✓✓✓
Allocative efficiency									✓✓	✓✓	XX	XX	✓✓✓	✓✓✓?
Uncoordinated programs			X				✓?			✓✓	?	?	✓✓✓	✓✓✓
Patient empowerment										✓	X	X	✓?	✓?
Medical accountability	X	X					✓?				XX	XX	✓✓	✓✓
Equity														
Financing	✓	✓?	✓	X	XXX			✓				✓✓		✓✓
Equal access	X	?	XX	XX	XX			X		✓	XXX	✓	✓✓	XX
Level playing field (pub/pte)	✓✓	✓✓✓	✓											✓✓✓
Private health insurance														
Inequity to members	✓✓✓	✓					✓✓✓	X			✓	X	✓✓✓	✓✓✓
Historical complacency	XX	XX	XXX				✓				X			✓✓
Public hospitals														
Queuing, excess D	✓	✓	✓			✓	✓	✓✓✓	✓	✓			✓?	✓?
Technical efficiency	X	X	X			✓?	✓	XX	✓	✓	?	?	✓	✓
Overuse of hosp.	X	X	X	✓		X	✓	XX		?			✓✓?	✓?
Medical														
Open-ended ffs	XX	XX									XXX	XXX	✓✓	✓✓
Excess doctor supply														
Cost and finance														
Total cost control	XXX	XXX	XXX	✓	XX	?	?	X	✓✓		XXX	XXX	✓?	✓?
Govt budget	XX	XX	✓	✓✓	✓			XX	✓		✓✓✓	X		?
Health outcome				X	✓		✓?		✓	✓✓	XX		✓✓?	✓✓?

of double payment; consequently, a subsidy could be defended with the equity argument that such double payment is unfair to those with a preference for private hospital care.

The second and related argument is that double payment creates an 'unequal' playing field between the public and private health sectors. The distortion of individual choice reduces individual utility: that is, some who may have maximised their welfare by selecting private hospitalisation will be induced by the distorted out-of-pocket prices to select public care. The result is that for the same (or similar) economic cost a less preferred product is purchased. A third common argument for a subsidy—and one that has commonly been used to justify the 1996 budgetary measures—is that increased PHI will inject more private money into an underfunded system and 'allow governments to target scarce public funding at those genuinely in need' (Industry Commission 1997: 303). As noted earlier, this form of argument is invalid unless the improbable assumption is made regardless of circumstances that governments will maintain the same level of public funding of the public hospital system.

If the primary objective were to ease pressure on an underfunded system, options 1 and 2 are likely to be inefficient depending upon which of two 'leverage' effects was quantitatively more important. First, if a 25 per cent subsidy to PHI resulted in additional membership, the increase in health sector revenue from each new member would be four times the subsidy paid to that member. Second, if the subsidy increased membership by 20 per cent, then for each new member five old members would receive the subsidy and only one-sixth of the subsidy would be to new members. With these numerical parameters the net rise in health sector funding would be $(1/6 \times 4)$, or two-thirds of the value of the subsidy, and greater health revenue would be achieved by direct expenditure of the subsidy in the public sector. This will almost certainly be true for the 1996 budgetary measures, as it has been estimated that the subsidy will increase membership not by 20 per cent but only by 3.7 per cent (Industry Commission 1997).

The third option in Table 10.3 was also adopted by the Commonwealth government in the 1996 Budget. From 1 July 1997, individuals and families earning above $50 000 and $100 000 respectively have had to pay a Medicare levy surcharge of 1 per cent if they do not have PHI. The effect will be to make the marginal cost (of PHI) very low or even negative for many high-income families. Not surprisingly, high-income-earners will find negative or near-negative costs a more than satisfactory price for PHI, irrespective of its value. Despite this, the Commonwealth Department of Health has estimated that the surcharge will raise the funds' membership only by 275 000 or 1.5 per cent (Industry Commission 1996). This limited impact reflects the fact that most families with annual incomes above $100 000 already have PHI.

As judged by either efficiency or equity criteria, it is hard to justify this option. As a method of injecting additional resources into either the private or total health sector, the levy surcharge is also inefficient. First, about 12 per cent of the additional revenue from reluctant new members will be lost in administrative costs. Second, distorted price signals induce behaviour that would not otherwise occur; they alter consumption patterns and induce an 'excess burden' (a loss of utility in excess of the loss from the direct dollar cost). More generally, long-term microeconomic reform cannot be achieved by the imposition of arbitrary and distorted net prices. An important part of recent microeconomic reform has been the elimination of internal cross-subsidies within an industry such as those which this option creates.

Ad hoc private: privatising funding (options 4 & 5)

Option 4

A persistent theme in the Australian financial debate has been the desirability of raising patient co-payments (out-of-pocket expenditures at the point of service). The simple economic model of the marketplace suggests that this might decrease demand and cost, and therefore discourage patients from seeking expensive care for trivial complaints.

The simple economic model represents a plausible description of behaviour in many markets, but it is highly implausible in the health sector. The asymmetry of information between providers and patients, the uncertainty about optimal treatment among providers and the desire of distressed patients to believe in their doctor's integrity combine to ensure provider dominance and the likelihood of a low price-elasticity of demand.

The actual behaviour of the medical marketplace should, of course, be the subject of empirical investigation, and the effects of co-payments have been more thoroughly researched than any other topic in the economics of health. A detailed summary and application of this information to the Australian health sector may be found in Richardson (1991). Numerous studies confirm that patient co-payments have the expected effect on the demand for health care but that the effect is quantitatively small, and associated with impaired access for the poor.

Option 5
Health savings accounts give tax advantages and possibly a subsidised rate of return for funds that individuals set aside for their own health care. For the reasons given above, it is unlikely that they would increase the individual's capacity to evaluate the benefits of alternative therapies or the quality of different providers. Unless accompanied by additional measures, they would simply shift costs back to the individual in such a way that access and the quality of care would depend on the individual's wealth and income. This latter affects appears to conflict with prevailing ethical values.

Ad hoc: contracting and efficiency (options 6 and 7)

There has been a worldwide trend towards the use of contracts to increase the cost-effectiveness of service delivery (Saltman & von Otter 1995). The underlying belief is that the likelihood of improving productivity and achieving the purchasers' objectives will be greater when these objectives are explicitly stated in a contract and when there is the possibility of terminating the contract and negotiating with an alternative service provider. This trend has been reflected in two recent policy developments in the health sector: the separation of hospital management from the purchasing authorities, and the requirement that PHI funds form individual contracts with doctors and private hospitals.

Option 6
The first of these policies requires the (partial) autonomy of service providers. It is for this reason that states like Victoria and South Australia have created separate purchasing authorities within their state departments, increased the independence of their hospitals and imposed contract-like 'agreements' based on case payment. For the same reason there has been limited experimentation with the contracting of public hospital services to private hospitals and (in one case) the partial privatisation of a public hospital. For example, New South Wales has entered a long-term 'build–own–operate and retain asset' contract for a hospital in Port Macquarie. New South Wales and Victoria have build–own–operate and transfer (BOOT) agreements with Hawkesbury and Latrobe Hospitals respectively, and South Australia has privatised the management of Modbury Hospital in Adelaide. While the evidence from these and similar experiments to date is not encouraging, it is too soon to draw strong conclusions. State health departments have almost no experience with this form of contracting, and subsequent experience may demonstrate the benefits of skilled negotiation.

There is also doubt concerning the superiority of contracts for individual hospitals over 'global contracting' as used by the Victorian government when it introduced case payment based upon DRG-weighted separations. As shown in Table 10.4, 'apparent' productivity growth between 1991/92 and 1994/95 rose by an astonishing 36 per cent. The apparent gain was almost certainly the result of the run-down of existing resources; the 21.8 per cent apparent gain between 1991/92 and 1996/97 is more likely to indicate true productivity growth. Even discounting this improvement for unobserved adverse effects on productivity (e.g. decline in the quality of care or patient inconvenience), it indicates the capacity of a large purchaser—the state government—to exercise significant market power when it chooses to do so. There is no reason why a government that is capable of 'tough' negotiation with individual private hospitals is not equally capable of 'tough' negotiation with its own public hospitals.

Option 7

The requirement for PHI to negotiate individual doctor and hospital contracts introduced in 1995 was an attempt to 'empower' the private health funds and to induce them to exercise their market power to negotiate more cost-effective care for their members. Some funds had already entered purchaser/provider agreements with selected hospitals (generally to cover the entire hospital bill and thereby encourage their members to use the hospital) in exchange for a negotiated and (perhaps) lower price. By 1997 all of the major funds had hospital (but not doctor) contracts. Because of the need for 'commercial confidentiality' there is no public information available on the hospital contracts, but it is believed that they have not achieved

Table 10.4   Victorian hospitals, 1991/92–1996/97

Year	Acute care budget	Cost index	Real budget ($) 1989/90	WIES (000)	WIES/$ index
1991/92	2037	108.2	1882.6	595.0	100
1992/93	1892	110.2	1716.8	621.5	114.5
1993/94	1836	111.7	1643.7	667.5	128.4
1994/95	1890	112.8	1675.5	718.5	136.0
1995/96	2138	114.4	1868.9	724.4	122.5
1996/97	2203	114.5	1924.0	741.0	121.8
1991/92– 1996/97 (%)	8.1	5.8	2.2	24.5	21.8

Note: WIES = Weighted inlier equivalent separations.
Source: Hospital data: Victorian Dept of Human Services costs, ABS December quarter, VIC. 1989/1990 = 100.

significant cost savings and, as a consequence, have had little impact on premiums.

The apparent failure of the legislation to create a competitive marketplace probably reflects three factors. First, there has been no history or experience of competitive price-setting by Australia's health insurers. At best, the transition to an industry that competed in the medical and hospital marketplace on behalf of its members would have taken time. Second, specialist doctors in Australia have exercised significant market power and, in the short run, have succeeded in a de facto cartel-like preservation of high fees. Third, the 1995 legislation required PHI funds to pay non-contracted hospitals a minimum default fee of at least $200 per day (compared with an average $450–$500 per day for contracted hospitals). This is analogous to a requirement that manufacturers purchase inputs from any producer irrespective of the quality of the product. As this significantly reduced the bargaining position of the funds, the Industry Commission (1997) recommended its termination. The reforms announced in August 1997 raised the minimum default fee to 80 per cent–85 per cent of the average contract fee, and ended the requirement that funds form contracts with doctors. This will ensure that private health insurers are unable to exercise effective market power on behalf of their members.

Long-term options

While each of the short-term reforms discussed above may be more or less desirable, none represents a clear movement towards a coherent health system which will be stable and more cost-effective in the long term. In broad terms, there are three long-term options: that is, schemes in which the funding and purchasing of health services are (i) predominantly public; (ii) predominantly private; or (iii) mixed, as with the present Australian scheme. This classification is based on funding and purchasing as distinct from ownership and management of service provision, as it is now generally accepted that it is the former and not the latter which is the determinant of efficiency and equity in the health sector.[3]

Public financing (options 8, 9, 10)

If the present mixed system were rejected as a long-term option, the transition to a predominantly publicly financed system could easily be effected by the withdrawal of all life-support systems from the PHI and private hospital industries. This would ensure the continued decline of the former and would require a transfer of resources into the public sector as the private hospital sector contracted. Based on Queensland and overseas experience a residual private sector would survive to cater primarily for the wealthy. Its size would depend, *inter alia*, on the size of the 'steady-state' queuing which the government determined.

This option would have to resolve two major issues, relating to allocative efficiency. The first is the level of government that would be primarily responsible for funding and purchasing services. A prerequisite for efficiency is the existence of a single funding body capable of negotiating cost-effective and coordinated care. There is almost universal agreement that either the Commonwealth or the state governments should take over the entire funding role (option 9). There is less agreement about which is the better level of government for the task. Advocates of the centralised option emphasise the potential economies of scale and scope at the national level, the greater negotiating power, and the constitutional superiority of the Commonwealth. Advocates of the state-based system emphasise the increased potential for experimentation and benchmarking, the greater sensitivity of states to local issues, and the greater constitutional power over doctors' fees.

Coordinated care

The second issue requiring resolution is the achievement of service coordination within the public system. One approach to this is currently being trialled. Following an initiative from the Council of Australian Government (COAG), interested bodies were invited to tender for support in the establishment of a 'coordinated care trial'.

Shortlisted tenderers were required to develop a model of health financing and coordinated delivery for a designated population with complex or chronic care needs. In October 1997 nine of the 12 groups that submitted protocols were proceeding with patient enrolment, including two trials in remote communities with predominantly Aboriginal and Torres Strait Islander populations. In theory, each trial's budget is determined by all of the health services that enrolled participants would have been expected to use, and actual patient costs and the cost of care coordination are to be subtracted from the pool. In practice, the range of services included varies, with each trial including at least medical, hospital and some pharmaceutical services. The extent of inclusion of community-based services varies, as does the basis on which hospital services are evaluated. Participants in the trial have unrestricted access to Medicare services. The objective of each scheme is to provide an opportunity to achieve a better mix of services for no additional budgetary costs, by the substitution of low-for high-cost care and by the use of case managers or protocols for the provision of more effective care. New services are to be financed from any savings arising from reduced hospitalisation, from better monitoring of pharmaceutical use and from improved patient health. Trials are being evaluated to determine the factors that increase the likelihood of success in these tasks.

While demonstrating the capacity of the government sector to innovate, the COAG trials are limited in their scope and in their potential for correcting allocative inefficiency. First, they exclude the general population and the allocative inefficiency associated with their use of acute care. Second, trials generally exclude nursing home care and services received from the private sector. These omissions mean that global allocative efficiency cannot be achieved and, as in the case of aged care, the major benefit of service substitution—reduced nursing home use—cannot be observed. (A budgetary adjustment might be made if a reduced use of nursing homes could be demonstrated.) Third, GPs must be used as the coordinators for medical problems, and alternative models cannot be trialled. Finally, the requirement of immediate budget neutrality means that trials have not been provided with short-run funding to establish alternative services and programs with the potential for long-run cost savings. This limits the extent of substitution to services that provide immediate cost savings. The trials are therefore in the same position as a new enterprise which attempts to establish itself with no initial capital or access to the capital market. Few such enterprises succeed. Finally, as the evaluation of the trials must be completed in less than 18 months, long-term health improvement and the long-term cost savings cannot be observed.

Radical privatisation (options 11, 12)

The option of a deregulated, privatised, free and voluntary market for health services and health insurance has been rejected by every developed country and (to my knowledge) by every functional government in the world. The fundamental reason for this is that the social consequences of such a market are unacceptable. To a greater or lesser extent every society accepts collective responsibility for at least basic health care for the most needy. From the considerable body of empirical evidence available the overwhelming majority of health economists have also concluded that unregulated markets of the sort envisaged in the economist's model of perfect competition will be inefficient and inflationary (Feldman & Morrisey 1990). By contrast with the assumptions made in the model, individual consumers cannot objectively evaluate the product (health care) either before or after its delivery, and there is a knowledge and experience-based asymmetry of power between the purchaser and provider.

Despite this near consensus, proposals for a simple market keep recurring (e.g. Macleod 1997). Most recently the Industry Commission (1997) has listed a deregulated private and voluntary market as one of the options for Australia. It argues that such a system requires sophisticated insurers that will actively bargain on behalf of their consumers, but gives no indication of whether or how such a change in the industry will occur. The Commission acknowledges that its proposals may significantly increase costs and leave some parts of the population uninsured, but argues—without supporting evidence—that such a scheme has the potential for significant efficiency gains. In the absence of such evidence the proposal should be judged as a 'first worst' solution. Its basis and rationale conflict with established health economics theory, evidence and social values.

Managed care, managed competition (options 13, 14)

Market competition may, however, have an important role in the health sector, and the 1990s have witnessed the development and application of sophisticated competitive models. 'Managed competition' is discussed in detail in Chapter 11 by Scotton, its chief Australian advocate. It differs from the simple competitive model in several important respects. First, health services are purchased not by relatively uninformed and powerless individuals but at full cost by well-informed and powerful agents acting on behalf of patients. Second, agents compete for patients. Third, for each enrolled patient agents receive a premium from the government which, as far as possible, reflects the expected health care costs of the patient. Fourth, the government assumes responsibility for enforcing and reforming procompetitive regulation and the other measures required in the model to achieve social objectives. In principle these four structural features could ensure respectively: (i) the purchase of the most cost-effective health services (technical and allocative efficiency); (ii) responsiveness to patient needs and preferences and technically efficient intermediation; (iii) equity in the financing and access to services; and (iv) constant revision of the rules, as the key players identify illegitimate ways of competing.

In the Australian context this model is attractive, as it resolves many of the structural problems discussed earlier and reconciles the coexistence of a mixed private/public system with efficiency and equity objectives. However, the success of the model is unproven. It depends on the one hand on the magnitude of the additional trans-action costs arising from the proliferation of contracts between providers and agents, and on the other hand on the benefits arising from increased competition and from the fact that agents will be implementing various forms of 'managed care'. The social accepta-bility of managed competition will be determined not only by its effects on efficiency but on the possibility that the emergence of numerous and varied private health plans will suborn the public health system. As with US Medicaid, this could leave the public program as an unsatisfactory safety-net for the politically ineffective, poor and disabled who, unlike the present beneficiaries of Medicare, are unable to protect their public benefits in a political forum.

Managed care represents the second major development of the 1990s. It may prove to be the greatest threat to date to doctors' financial and professional dominance of the health care sector, while simultaneously providing major benefits to health care consumers. It is chiefly associated with the astonishing growth of managed care intermediaries in the USA in the 1990s (Rosenman 1996). Like managed competition, managed care involves an agent assuming full responsibility for the provision of health services for its members. These may be provided either directly (as in the case of vertically integrated health maintenance organisations) or indirectly via a series of contracted services. In theory, efficiency is achieved (i) through the negotiation of lower prices; (ii) through allocative efficiency in the choice of (a possibly enlarged range of) services; and (iii) through reduced access to some (usually costly) services. In managed care this latter restriction may, in principle, reduce the quality of care. In managed competition it would be the government's role to ensure that this did not occur.

The long-run significance of managed care arises from its poten-tial impact on allocative efficiency and, in particular, its potential for rationalising the variation in service use noted earlier through insistence on accepted and (one hopes) best practice protocols. As noted earlier these variations suggest a quantitatively huge misallo-cation of resources. Weinberg has described this as arising from an 'intellectual crisis' in the scientific basis of clinical practice (Weinberg 1988)—a situation in which clinicians commonly do not know the best treatment regimen and in which clinical decisions are based on personal (doctor) preferences or inadequately justified judgements. The present organisation of health care provides little incentive to any of the major participants—except disempowered patients—to alter this pattern. In principle, managed care provides this incentive and, if translated into practice, could have a profound impact on efficiency and the quality of care. The last would depend on how efficiency was improved: by the elimination of unnecessary services while holding quality fixed, or by higher quality while holding health care costs constant.

It is an empirical and not theoretical issue whether or not managed care will realise its potential and whether it is more likely to do so in a model of government, doctor or agent domination. US evidence to date indicates that its chief impact has been on cost (Luft 1995; Reinhardt 1996; Rosenman 1996; Wilton & Smith 1997). With regard to quality, systematic analyses indicate that it has had a mixed effect, sometimes improving and sometimes harming outcome (Miller & Luft 1997). The US results are not surprising and may not be transferable to Australia. US managed care is being driven by a cost crisis, and costs have been the first (and easier) target for managed care. In the Australian environment control of cost is less important. If the balance of evidence indicates the superiority of managed care over the present Medicare model then, in principle, Medicare could be incrementally modified to incorporate the benefits without the framework of managed competition. Governments and medical organisations are able to encourage the development of best-practice protocols, but the evidence that this may occur at a satisfactory speed is not encouraging. It is known that doctors typically disregard information about best practice when it conflicts with their existing practice (Sackett 1995; Lomas 1990), and this will almost inevitably occur if best practice threatens to leave existing doctors underemployed.

To date, the Australian Medical Association has failed to take leadership on this issue or to take steps to incorporate the potential benefits of managed care into the existing scheme. Rather, it has attempted to pre-empt debate and stigmatise 'US-style managed care', which it incorrectly portrays as inevitably threatening the quality of care in Australia (Nathan 1997). The right of the individual doctor to practise any form of medicine has been defended as 'clinical freedom'. The right of the patient to best practice has been subordinated to this goal. In July 1997 the Commonwealth government supported the doctor's position by announcing legislation to prohibit any attempt by PHI funds to influence medical practice—including, therefore, regulated attempts to encourage best-practice medicine. In the longer run it is likely that patient interests will prevail. It is when these are frustrated by doctor interests that the model of managed competition and the exercise of managed care becomes most appealing.

211

Conclusions

The task of health care financing is to create a set of financial incentives that will assist with the achievement of social objectives, which economists often equate with efficiency and equity. There are two major obstacles to achieving these apparently simple goals. The first is our limited ability to predict the impact of various options and our limited knowledge about the quantitative significance of many of the key parameters. Undoubtedly one of the most important unknown factors with respect to efficiency is the long-run impact of managed care. If it realises its full potential, it must inevitably be included in the health system. The only question is the framework within which it will operate.

The second obstacle is the ambiguity surrounding social objectives in the health sector. With the possible exception of options 9 and 10 (rationalisation of Commonwealth/state financial relations and coordinated care), each of the ad hoc options is value-laden and would move the health system towards one of the three long-term options. There is, however, no consensus concerning which of these should be the long-term goal. The reason for this ambivalence is that social objectives are more complex than implied by the simple interpretation of objectives in terms of efficiency and equity.

There is clear evidence that, for many, the financing and delivery of health care raise a number of important issues of social justice and the nature of our society that are difficult to include in the simple equity–efficiency dichotomy. This is exemplified by the introduction to one report on the Canadian health system, in which it is stated that (Evans 1995):

> Canada's system of universal public insurance for health care is . . . widely regarded as an important symbol of community, a concrete representation of mutual support and concern. It expresses a fundamental equality of Canadian citizens in the face of disease and death . . . As David Petersen, the Premier of Ontario, pointed out . . . 'There is no social program that we have that more defines Canadianism or that is more important to the people of our country.'

In Australia, as elsewhere, health financing choices reflect, *inter alia*, the relative importance of a communal versus individualistic approach to social problem-solving. The vigour with which governments interfere with private decision-making in order to promote health as an end in itself reflects the division between the 'welfarist' belief that individual utilities (preferences) are the basis of social

welfare and the 'extra-welfarist' position that in addition to preferences social welfare must take into account considerations such as
health per se. In principle, these ethical issues can be traded off
against the achievement of efficiency. However, in the absence of
clear evidence concerning the type of health system that best achieves
efficiency, it is likely that these ethical issues will be decisive in determining the nature of the health system and its financing.

11   *Managed competition*

The general objective of managed competition is to establish structures in which market incentives can increase economic efficiency—that is, make better use of resources to improve health outcomes and satisfy consumer wants. It is a complex concept, with implications for every aspect of the health care system.

While managed competition involves the use of market tools to guide resource allocation, it also includes a regulatory framework designed to eliminate sources of market failure found in unregulated markets for health services. Its most obvious structural innovation is the establishment of competitive, at-risk budget-holders as the purchasers of health services on behalf of defined populations of consumers enrolled with them. In terms of detailed applications it comes in many forms, to meet the diverse needs of the various health care systems in which its operation has been proposed.

Background

Perhaps the best way to introduce the concept of managed competition is in terms of its historical context. The development of health care financing arrangements in developed countries can be thought of as taking place in three stages. The first stage saw the establishment of national health/health insurance programs designed to secure universal access and equitable incidence of costs, with varying degrees of direct government involvement in funding and service delivery. While the European origins of this intervention took place as early as the 1880s, the process continued until the 1970s in some countries. The second stage was the application in the 1970s and 80s of budgetary ceilings to control unsustainable rises in health expenditure. These fairly gross measures were effective in abating the rate of expenditure growth and, in some cases, in actually reducing the proportion of GDP allocated to health services.

The third stage, which commenced in the 1980s and is still current, is dominated by responses to continuing rises in real costs of state-of-the-art health care resulting from advances in medical knowledge and technology. The impact of cost increases is sharpened by declining rates of sustainable economic growth in the developed world. Global cuts in government health budgets have already been pushed, in many countries, to the stage of threatening access, equity and even quality of care. In this context, raising health service efficiency has become the overwhelming policy imperative.

For this reason, microeconomic reforms involving some aspects of managed competition are being increasingly looked to as the most promising means of continuing to provide first-class health care to all citizens at a sustainable cost (Chernichovsky 1995; Van de Ven 1996). Policy-makers in most countries are aware that there is not a direct trade-off between the social and economic objectives: in particular, publicly financed national health and national health programs, which are primarily designed to secure access and equity, are also an essential tool in controlling total health care expenditures. It is in this context (i.e. of national health systems involving management by governments of global health care budgets) that aspects of managed competition can be contemplated in the great majority of OECD countries, including Australia.

The major exception to this historical pattern is the USA, where the impetus to national health insurance (other than for the elderly and the very poor) has stalled, and where successive governments have lacked the authority to implement global expenditure controls. Precluded by political factors from the path of strong public intervention followed by other countries, American health economists and policy analysts have given much greater emphasis to approaches based on pluralism and microeconomic reform than their counterparts elsewhere. It is in the USA that the concept of managed competition originated and has been most vigorously developed.

There have been two streams in the US-managed competition literature. The first of these involved an explicit public framework, starting with Somers and Somers' (1972) proposal and culminating in the abortive Clinton plan (White 1995). The other, which emphasised the power of competitive markets, dated from Enthoven's (1978) initial formulation of a 'consumer-choice health plan', and culminated in the latest version of the Jackson Hole plan (Ellwood et al. 1992; Reinhardt 1994). Although no significant reform at the federal level has eventuated, pressure from private employers and state payers has lifted managed care coverage on the part of competing insurers and health care providers from 18 per cent of the insured population in 1988 to an estimated 73 per cent in 1995 (EBRI 1994; Jensen et al. 1997).

The relevance of European experience of managed competition to Australian health policy is that it relates to its development *within* a national program. In this context it is seen as a devolution of decision-making, through the use of financial incentives and commercial contracting, in hitherto single-payer systems relying heavily on regulatory and administrative machinery as the means of achieving efficiency and cost control. When seeking examples on which to draw for the broad financing and regulatory structure, European precedents, such as the arrangements being implemented in the Netherlands, are clearly the most relevant (Netherlands 1992; Van de Ven & Rutten 1995).

However, when looking at the all-important consumer/provider nexus, the hothouse growth of managed care and managed competition in the USA is the best source of evidence on the shape of purchasing, risk management and service delivery arrangements under managed competition. The very diversity resulting from the lack of public intervention in the USA—not to mention the ready availability of research funding—has resulted in its being the source of the overwhelming bulk of information of the responses of consumers, providers and funders to the incentives incorporated in managed competition.

The Australian context

There is a widespread feeling among Australians at all levels that our health system is in progressively worsening trouble. However (and despite the litany of problems cited in this chapter), Australians have much to be pleased about, in terms of the quality of care generally provided, the accessibility of services to people at all levels of income, health outcomes and the overall cost of health services to the community. The deficiencies that give rise to dissatisfaction, such as hospital waiting lists, high costs of private insurance and arbitrary cost-sharing, do not presage an early collapse of the system, but reflecting as they do the working out over an extended period of inherent contradictions in the way health services are financed and organised they flag the need to reconsider the structural features that generate them.

The Australian health care system is far from unique, and is best thought of as our particular version of a national health insurance model common to most developed countries. Within this model, differing political and cultural contexts have resulted in health care systems with distinct national characteristics. By comparison with most of its counterparts, the distinguishing features of the Australian system are:

- overlapping Commonwealth and state powers and programs to an extent unique in federal systems and, by definition, unknown in unitary systems of government. The consequences include poor coordination of planning and service delivery; barriers to efficient substitution between alternative types and sources of care, and wide scope for cost-shifting, to which considerable ingenuity and resources have been devoted (National Health Strategy 1991; Paterson 1996);

- a relatively large private sector (if the USA is excluded from the comparison), with 33 per cent of total health costs met from private sources, 32 per cent of the population privately insured and about 43 per cent of hospital inpatients privately treated. The scale of the private sector is of less significance than the inefficient financing and payment systems within it, and the lack of articulation between public and private sectors, which adds considerably to the opportunities for cost-shifting and cost inflation. The cost-enhancing tendencies built into existing private sector arrangements are overlooked by most of the advocates of substituting private for public sector services as a means of containing public outlays;

- a dynamically unstable balance between public and private sectors, due to the coexistence of free and universal access to the public hospital system and an unsubsidised private health insurance system with escalating premium costs (Industry Commission 1997: 291–311). The erosion of private insurance to the point at which it constituted no more than a minor supplement to a basically public system, as in UK and Canada, would not be a disastrous outcome but would require a corresponding expansion of public sector provision, funded by higher Medicare levies and/ or taxation. More importantly it would resolve few of the inherent inefficiencies in current payment arrangements.

The COAG initiatives discussed in Chapter 4 are too tentative yet to offer a pathway to serious reform. The limited scope for remedying the basic causes of our problems through incremental change is the reason for contemplating more radical structural change. The structural inefficiencies embedded in the present arrangements mean that Australia could stand to gain more than most other countries from a well-designed system of managed competition.

On the basis of the foregoing analysis, the features to be incorporated in such a system would include:

- defined and distinct roles for Commonwealth and state authorities;

- a private sector basically operating within the national system—subject to incentives designed to achieve national program objectives—and not (as now) outside it;
- efficiency-promoting incentive systems, including
  - all government subsidies taking the form of risk-related capitation payments to purchasers or budget-holders (to inhibit risk selection, or 'cream skimming'),
  - all costs incurred in the treatment of any individual being financed out of a single budget (to prevent cost-shifting),
  - the income of all service providers consisting of payments by budget-holders for services provided to their enrollees, at prices reflecting the full costs of efficient production (to promote internal efficiency).

The sweep of the structural changes involved emphasise the point that managed competition is not designed (like, for example, Medicare) primarily to affect the way in which services are paid for. Rather, it is deliberately designed to bring about significant behavioural change on the part of funders, providers and consumers, by means of financial incentives that bear on their decision-making.

The elimination of cost-shifting between different programs and payers would focus the corporate objectives of funders and providers on cost reduction, subject only to the need to satisfy consumers and to meet whatever outcome and quality standards are required by the regulators. The capitation basis of budget-holders' income would inevitably lead in the direction of provider remuneration based on populations served rather than on items of service rendered, and toward cost containment through selective contracting and managed care. What would *not* be affected by reforms involving these features would be the universality of coverage and equitable incidence of existing programs such as Medicare.

A managed competition model for Australia

Without going into a good deal of detail, it is difficult to explain the full ramifications of a complex and elastic concept such as managed competition, and in particular what it might mean for the participants in our health care system. One way to do this is to set out an explicit model, which has the additional benefit of testing whether a workable design incorporating the principle is capable of being specified. On the other hand, the presentation of a model runs the risk of appearing unduly prescriptive and of focusing attention on inessential details. It is therefore important to note that the model which follows is to be regarded as no more than illustrative. It is certainly not advanced as a blueprint for an implementable program.

The model can be outlined in terms of the roles of three participants—Commonwealth government, state governments and private sector—in carrying out the functions of financing, budget-holding and service provision.

Commonwealth government

The Commonwealth government would be responsible for funding and overall direction, through the amalgamation of all existing publicly funded programs into a *single program*, incorporating Medicare, pharmaceutical benefits, nursing home benefits, home and community care (HACC), mental health and diverse community health programs. The Commonwealth functions in the model would be:

- to prescribe basic coverage by budget-holders and mandate outcome and quality control standards;
- to collect revenue, calculate adjusted capitation rates, and pay these to budget-holders for people enrolled with them; and
- to set the rules for budget-holders so as to promote competition, and to minimise cost-shifting and risk selection.

This would involve Commonwealth government withdrawal from many existing functions related to the administration of specific benefit and grant-supported programs. However, it may be necessary to remove the existing panoply of regulation progressively over what could be an extended transition period. One would need to be satisfied, for example, that a workable competitive market had been established before dismantling controls over prices and benefit levels in key industries such as pharmaceuticals and private medicine. Most of the administrative machinery functions involved in statistical and payment operations could be undertaken by the Health Insurance Commission.

State and territory governments

State and territory governments would be responsible for *public sector* service provision and for the establishment and management of *public sector* budget-holders. These functions would include:

- planning, regulation and (subject to delegation) operation of public providers of health services. These providers would depend for revenue on selling their outputs to budget-holders and, as far as possible, would receive no public subsidies for service provision; and

- establishment, policy direction and prudential supervision of public (*area*) budget-holders. Public agencies must be financially accountable to elected governments, and the states would exchange their present liability as residual funders of public hospital systems for liability as guarantors of the public budget-holders.

The private sector

Under the model presented in this chapter, a large proportion of private insurance and the services currently financed by it would be brought within the framework of the national program. This would enlarge the opportunities for existing health insurers to function as competitive budget-holders for *all* services covered by the program and for private providers to compete for the care of patients enrolled with public budget-holders.

It is proposed that private budget-holders satisfying prudential and other requirements set by the Commonwealth government would:

- receive risk-adjusted capitation payments, at the same rates as public budget-holders, for individual members of their enrolled populations;
- provide all benefits and services covered by public budget-holders under the national program; and
- collect premiums to cover administrative costs and additional services, of which limited access to private hospital care (e.g. elective services, in a restricted number of contracting hospitals) would be a mandatory component.

Budget-holders

Budget-holders funded on a capitation basis and being at risk for costs incurred by their enrolled populations are central to any managed competition or purchaser/provider regimen. The conditions under which public and private budget-holders would operate (especially the requirement to meet the full costs of services covered, less any applicable co-payments and deductibles) would subject them to much more rigorous budget constraints and efficiency incentives than now apply to private health insurers.

Public budget-holders would be the funders in their designated geographic areas of all services now covered by Medicare and the other public programs folded into the basic package. In order to ensure large risk pools and to secure economies of scale, it is suggested that their target populations should be in the range of 500 000 to 1 000 000 persons. Universal coverage would be maintained by the provision that all people not contracting for coverage by a private budget-holder would be automatically covered by the public budget-holders in their areas of residence.

The criteria for registration of *private budget-holders* would be based on financial viability and capability of delivering services to consumers. Although it is assumed that many organisations currently registered under the *National Health Act* would wish to become budget-holding health plans, the conditions of registration would be such as to encourage new types of intermediary (e.g. as health maintenance and preferred provider organisations, coalitions of community health centres and other organisations catering to different styles of care) to enter the system.

Both private and public budget-holders would have the widest possible freedom to contract (or not contract) with public and private providers, in order to provide access to their enrollees to the full range of services at the lowest possible cost. The only exceptions would relate to hospital services. First, because of the central importance of public hospitals in the health system, it is essential that all packages offered by all budget-holders include full coverage of the costs of all treatment as a public patient in any public hospital. Second, it is proposed that coverage of in-hospital treatment as a private patient would continue to be available only under private plans, for an additional premium. Private budget-holders would be required to provide a minimum table covering all services in the basic public package plus a minimum private cover.

With *sub-budget-holders*, it would not be necessary or desirable for primary budget-holders to contract directly with every kind of health service provider for services to all of their enrollees. On the contrary, it is envisaged that management and provision of various classes of care used by subpopulations would be devolved on a contractual basis to others. Fund-holding general practices on the British model are an obvious example. Another might be managed care organisations covering broad ranges of services to the aged, disabled and chronically ill. Diffusion of risk-bearing among a network of more or less specialised sub-budget-holders would provide scope for diversity and initiative in matching needs and services in an efficient manner.

Figure 11.1 is a simplified diagram showing the financial flows between the three sectors in this model. The major simplification is

Figure 11.1 Managed competition model: financial flows

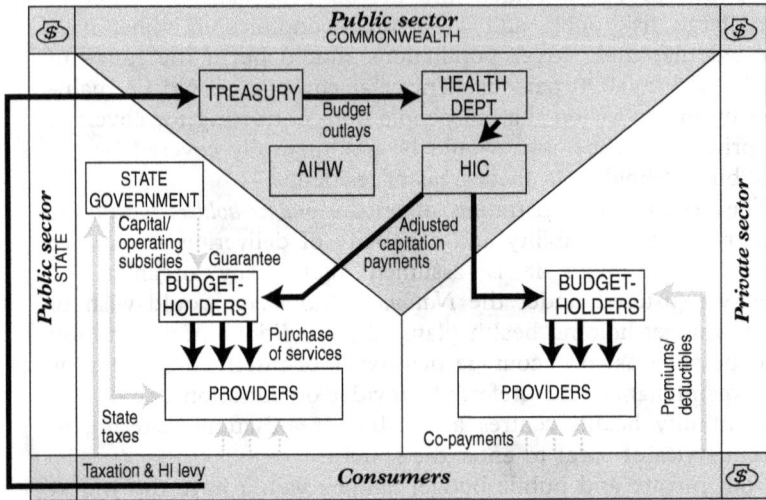

the interface between the budget-holders and service providers: it does not show the cross-contracting arrangements between public and private sector budget-holders and providers. It also omits entirely the network of sub-budget-holders and subcontractors that would in time constitute the most substantial outcome of the reforms to the delivery system.

Some design issues

Defining service coverage

Given the centrality of purchaser/provider contracting in market-oriented reforms of national health insurance programs, health authorities in some other countries devoted a good deal of time and effort to the definition of the services covered by their proposed programs. In the Australian model, this would translate into the services a public budget-holder would have to provide to enrolled persons in return for the capitation payment. Despite the ease with which a few services of limited social and medical value could be identified (as possible exclusions), the goals of developing functional definitions of use in priority-setting proved elusive.

What does this mean in the Australian context? In the proposed model, the services involved are defined broadly as those currently covered under Medicare and other public programs. This would include institutional care in nursing homes and state psychiatric facilities, admission to which is now confined to people with major medical diagnoses. It could be argued that their inclusion in the adjusted capitation payment system would provide budget-holders with incentives for substitution wherever possible of community-based services, and providers with incentives to technical efficiency. However, Van de Ven and Schut (1994) have presented a compelling case for the exclusion of residential homes for the aged and handicapped (i.e. hostels) from a managed competition program to cover health care risks.

Competition between budget-holders

Competition between multiple payers (budget-holders) is the feature of managed competition distinguishing it from less radical reforms involving the introduction of purchaser/provider arrangements into single-payer systems. Promotion of a multiple competing payer model appears to fly in the face of the conventional wisdom that a single-payer regimen has substantial advantages in terms of eliminating adverse selection, increasing bargaining power vis-à-vis service-providers, gathering information for service planning and management purposes, and minimising administrative costs. Concerns on these accounts are the basis of vigorous opposition to managed competition by White (1995) and reservations expressed by influential European policy analysts (OECD 1995; WHO 1996).

It can be argued that the advantages of single-payer systems have been greater in the past than they are likely to be in the future, and that the proposed Australian model, in particular, incorporates features specifically designed to minimise them (Scotton 1995). It could be argued that the amalgamation of public sector program streams and the inclusion of private sector funders in a budget-constrained envelope would be in effect a move towards, rather than away from, the benefits claimed for a single-payer system.

However, the prime argument in favour of competition is that it is likely to increase the effectiveness with which budget-holders act as the agents of their enrolled populations, and that the motivation for their doing so arises from consumers having a real choice between them, involving the right to vote with their feet. The incentives would apply to both public and private budget-holders. Indeed, the greatest benefit might lie in the resulting incentives on the public budget-holders to be responsive to the expressed needs of their populations. In the long term the proportion of the population opting for private coverage could be expected to reflect the relative levels of efficiency with which public and private budget-holders met the demands of their covered populations. Public and private shares would have little or no public policy importance.

Risk adjustment of capitation payments

Incentives to compete on grounds of efficiency will be effective only if the way is barred to easier paths to profitability, involving preferential recruitment of low-risk customers. Indeed there is general agreement that the prevention of 'cream-skimming' is a key condition for a workable competitive market. One requirement—to which Enthoven (1978) accorded great emphasis—is a framework of continually monitored and revised regulation to minimise cream-skimming by penalising discriminatory tactics designed to attract good risks and discourage bad risks. A second necessary element is the risk adjustment of capitation payments to budget-holders. To the extent that these rates accurately reflected the expected costs incurred by people in these categories, the rationale for cream-skimming would disappear. Equity and efficiency objectives would both be met, in that budget-holders would receive income on a basis corresponding to the risks they incurred, while people in high-risk groups would not be required to pay the full expected costs.

The question then becomes whether it is possible in practice to categorise health risks sufficiently well to reduce the incentives to budget-holders to use cream-skimming tactics. The complex issues involved have been analysed by several US and Dutch health economists, in the context of reforms involving devolution of public programs to capitated budget-holders. The most significant statistical findings are that only 15–20 per cent of individual variance in annual health care costs is potentially explicable in terms of systematic demographic and health status measures, and the proportion of variance that can be explained by a set of prospective factors relating to health status is probably less than 7 per cent (Newhouse et al. 1989; Van de Ven et al. 1994).

On the basis of these figures (i.e. 80–85 per cent of individual variation being random, with a substantial fraction of the predictable variance being explained by objectively derivable factors) one could be optimistic about the possibility of devising a formula for risk-adjusted capitation payments which would reduce the scope for cream-skimming to workable proportions. However, there is no general agreement on this point. Van de Ven and Schut (1994) believe this to be the case, but only for services other than those involving 'catastrophic' risks. Newhouse (1996) has concluded, for several reasons, that pure capitation adjusters would have to possess much higher explanatory power than any yet analysed to inhibit cream-skimming by insurers and budget-holders. He advocates a mixed-payment formula, involving a blend of risk-adjusted capitation and reimbursement of individual beneficiaries' previous year's costs.

My view is that, under Australian conditions, the services covered by capitation payments should include most of the 'catastrophic' risks that are proposed to be excluded from the Dutch program (Scotton 1995). However, Newhouse's arguments for a mixed-payment system are compelling. One might therefore aim over time to increase the share of the capitated component in payments to budget-holders. In the context of an annual review process which could periodically change budget-holders' revenues so as to reduce the prospective returns from cream-skimming, a mixed-payment formula as advocated by Newhouse could reduce it to acceptably low levels.

Cost-sharing by patients

It is proposed that the services covered by the managed competition model be predominantly financed, as at present, by income-related earmarked levies and general taxation. At the same time, it is legitimate to consider the extent to which the costs of the public program should be borne by the users of services—that is, by individuals as consumers rather than as taxpayers. As an equity objective, meeting 100 per cent of the health care costs of the non-poor would not rank high in the priorities of most taxpayers. To the extent that public outlays on the program were constrained, contributions by service recipients would enable a wider range, or larger volume, of services to be provided than would otherwise be the case.

At any level of out-of-pocket payments, aggregation of programs under the managed competition model would offer the opportunity to rationalise the present mix of co-payments, safety-nets, exclusions and mandatory patient contributions, the effect of which is that out-of-pocket costs may largely depend on which services a patient receives. One way of rationalising out-of-pocket payments in a manner consistent with equity and efficiency would be to replace all or most of them by a uniform global deductible, from which health care card-holders (and selected others, such as infants) could be exempted. However, in some cases—notably the patient contribution to nursing home costs—it would be reasonable to retain separate service-specific co-payments.

Policy on patient contributions to service costs may differ with respect to private and public sectors. With regard to public budget-holders, there would no doubt be spirited debate on the appropriateness of any deductible, while in the case of private budget-holders there could be an expectation, on the general grounds of containing moral hazard, that all tables would incorporate deductibles and that higher-benefit would generally carry larger deductibles than lower-benefit tables.

Implications of the model

Consumer interests

Meeting the felt needs of consumers, as well as advancing their health status, are twin goals of any heath care system. In the real world, consumer sovereignty in health care choice is limited by relative ignorance vis-à-vis providers and the bewildering complexity of the health care system. In cases of serious illness the critical issue is not one of control over treatment but of engaging the most effective manager of the process. To the extent that managed competition is conducive both to managed care of the whole patient/patient episode, and that budget-holders are constrained to incorporate quality assessment in their contracting and payment arrangements, they and their sub-contractors will have incentives to act as enlightened agents for consumers.

However effective these arrangements may turn out to be in terms of health outcomes, they would not satisfy the need for consumer choice as an end in itself. It is therefore necessary to ask what the critical aspects of consumer choice are. The managed competition model has several answers to this, in the terms of *real* choices between packages offering various options in *styles of care*, and in the level of choice in service provision.

Managed care will be an inevitable tool of cost control in many packages offered by budget-holders. At the same time it is important that consumers have the option of avoiding the consequent limitations on freedom of choice of provider and services used, *subject to the proviso that the additional costs of doing so would be met by the user*. Under the model, private budget-holders would be able to offer packages giving unconstrained choice of provider, but with the proviso that they be priced in a way that involves no cross-subsidisation from more basic tables. As it might be expected that these higher tables would be subject to adverse selection, the additional premiums required might be very high indeed.

Equity for high-risk consumers

In unregulated markets for private health services, it is likely that the composition of output would be oriented toward demands expressed by the well-to-do at the expense of people with more pressing health needs and less income. This orientation is entirely reversed in the managed competition model presented here, in which the spending power—in the form of risk-rated capitation revenue—is weighted in favour of the most ill. There would be no more 'healthy singles' tables, for which low-risk capitation payments would yield slim pickings. On the contrary, if the risk-adjustment formulae are accurate, budget-holders' offerings would be designed to attract the high users, and the result might well be the development of specialist (sub-budget-holder) organisations geared to meet the needs of various high-risk/high-need subpopulations.

Regional (non-metropolitan) populations

There is a chasm between the levels of service available to health care consumers in the major cities and other areas of the country. To some extent this is the inevitable product of distance, the dispersal of non-metropolitan populations, and the economies of scale relating to the production of many secondary- and most tertiary-level specialist services. However, it is also partly the product of payment methods, which make it possible for doctors and other health service providers to live and work in their preferred locations and make good livings by providing higher volumes of services per head to their relatively small catchment populations.

By comparison, a risk-adjusted capitation formula would automatically build in equity between populations living in different areas. (Depending on costs, there might even be a loading in favour of regional/remote populations in the risk-adjusted capitation formula.) The redistribution of revenue in accordance with the needs of populations would raise the incomes of regional providers serving larger numbers of patients and cap the amounts available to metropolitan providers. There would always be a flow of rural patients referred to higher-level services in metropolitan centres, but the capitation formula might stimulate greater innovation in meeting the needs of regional populations.

Implications for delivery systems

Managed competition is designed to have a profound impact on the structure and functioning of the health care delivery system. It can be considered as a serious program of microeconomic reform, analogous to others which have been implemented in formerly protected areas of economic activity during the past decade. Typically, the changes in regulatory environment and incentives would result in a continuing process of dynamic change. While the pace of such change is difficult to predict, it is possible to project some of the directions in which managed competition would steer the Australian health system by reference to the rapid changes that have occurred in many parts of the USA over the past five years.

It could be expected that preferred provider and exclusive provider arrangements would increasingly become the norm for contracts between budget-holders, sub-budget-holding intermediaries and health care providers. This substitution of contractual freedom for anticompetitive regulation would bring about a new balance of market power between the purchasers and providers of services. The 1995 amendments to private health insurance constituted some tentative steps in this direction. The much wider scope of contracting and the stronger incentives to cost reduction under managed competition would greatly accelerate this process. A concomitant outcome would be the widespread implementation of managed care as a key cost-containment strategy, especially in 'basic' packages. Managed care comes in many forms, but basically involves processes by which the choices available to some patients and their treating doctors are constrained by care managers, who intervene in the planning and coordination of service use. It should be an objective of the AMA to ensure that the medical profession is properly represented in the formulation and administration of protocols governing these processes.

Another logical consequence would be a transition from fee-for-service to population-based remuneration as the basis of budget-holder contracting. In the Australian context, this would most likely develop through the sub-budget-holding network, as intermediaries came forward to contract for ranges of services to defined subpopulations, who might be the residents of particular localities, members of particular age groups or sufferers from defined chronic conditions. Such intermediaries would inevitably seek to contract with their providers so as to devolve the sharing of risks further. This process has progressed so rapidly in California that capitation has largely replaced fee-for-service as the basis of physician remuneration (Trauner & Chestnutt 1996).

In the USA these trends have been accompanied by substantial restructuring of service providers, both defensively (to maintain market share in the face of rising surplus capacity) and offensively (to gain the benefits of economies of scale in risk-bearing). The result has been the development of integrated provider organisations, based around hospitals and/or multispecialty groups, contracting directly with ultimate funders (employers) on a capitation basis and cutting out the intermediaries (budget-holders) altogether. It is hard to say what the implications might be in the Australian context, but there is no doubt that our large metropolitan conurbations would provide scope for considerable vertical (or 'virtual') integration along the lines depicted by Robinson and Casalino (1996).

Given the key role of general practice in the Australian health system, the consequences for it carry considerable weight in any assessment of the managed competition model. In fact, the implications are bullish for primary care in general and general practice in particular. On cost grounds budget-holders can be expected to favour primary care, for its relatively low cost both as a care modality and as a gateway into the health system. It would be logical for budget-holders to place progressively greater emphasis on the gatekeeping function, and to restructure their contracting arrangements on this basis, perhaps along the lines of the GP fund-holders in the reformed British NHS.

This would involve patients being induced to enrol with practices that would receive budgets—at least partly determined on a capitation basis—to cover services such as pharmaceutical drugs, diagnostic tests and ancillary professional care, in addition to the services personally rendered by them. The resulting incentives would encourage the practitioners to substitute lower-cost for higher-cost inputs to care, which might induce more discriminating patterns of prescription and referral, and would promote patterns of practice more consistent with evidence-based medicine and continuing care than the current fee-for-service arrangements. Another likely effect would be an increase in practice size, with greater opportunity for peer review and linkage with other elements of the health system.

Has managed competition a future in Australia?

This is a complex question, which needs to be answered in several steps. Does the Australian health system have problems requiring remedial action? If so, are they of a kind requiring systemic, as distinct from incremental, reform? If the former, does managed competition offer the best solution? Finally, even if it does so *in principle*, are the barriers to its implementation surmountable?

Only an outline sketch of the answers can be offered here. With regard to the first question there is a general consensus that, despite a high level of community and bipartisan political attachment to its basic structure, the Australian health system is becoming stressed to a degree that puts at risk its ability to meet access and quality objectives. On the second, while a description of the system as being 'in crisis' is not supported by evidence, there are widely held views that the problems are not susceptible to remedy by incremental and piecemeal reforms of the kind seen over the past decade. The Industry Commission report on private health insurance (1997, ch. 9) reviewed the many submissions relating to system-wide policy options and went beyond its terms of reference in recommending (p. lvi) a broad public inquiry into the health system—which the Commonwealth government was quick to reject.

It may well be that such an inquiry would not be the best way to work towards an agenda for systemic reform. But the case for putting managed competition on such an agenda is probably stronger in Australia than in almost any other country one might nominate. On the benefits side, the programmatic maze and the scope for cost-shifting between Commonwealth, state and private sectors described by Paterson (1996) and epitomised as the 'health jigsaw' means that we have more to gain from major reform that systematically tackles these problems than countries with more integrated program and governmental structures. On the costs side, the advanced development on a nationwide basis of infrastructure components such as information systems (Medicare, pharmaceutical/nursing home benefits, hospital morbidity), DRG categories and case payment experience, and private health insurance organisations means that the development and implementation effort (and hence costs) could be expected to be lower than elsewhere.

The case for managed competition is that it deals (at least potentially) with specific structural features that are widely held to underlie the observed problems of our health care system, and that the institutional barriers to its implementation are lower than elsewhere. However, neither it nor any other structure will solve all problems, although some will do better than others. What *can* be claimed for a managed competition regimen along the lines of the model presented here is that it provides a framework within which many problems that now seem intractable could be more successfully tackled.

What are the chances that the systemic reform will be seriously considered, or that managed competition will be placed on the agenda? This is a political rather than an economic issue. However, even an economist can observe that the barriers are substantial. First, health care reform is characterised by a great diversity of views on the direction it should take. The disparate positions held by stakeholders are strongly driven by ideology and self-interest. Second, a reform as radical as managed competition involves a big step into the (largely) unknown. The normal path of incremental change is not applicable, and the potential for electoral damage from a sceptical and easily sensitised voting public would be well understood by politicians. Somewhere along the way, a brave decision (in the 'Yes Minister' sense) would be required.

12   *Public health: some economic perspectives*

Spending on public health in Australia makes up only a small proportion of health services expenditure. Less than 5 per cent of total spending is attributed to 'community and public health', and much of this goes on community-based health care such as domiciliary nursing (Richardson et al. 1995). The importance of public health, however, is far greater than is implied by this accounting convention, and not merely because the costs of many public health activities, such as immunisation, appear under other budgetary headings.

With its focus on populations, the benefits of public health are experienced by more than just those who come into contact with formal health services. The high levels of health currently enjoyed by most Australians are, in part, a result of past investment in public health. Public health measures could also do much to improve the health of those, such as Aboriginal and Torres Strait Islander people, who have not shared the health gains of their fellow citizens (Lawson & Close 1991). It is fitting, therefore, that room has been found in this book to discuss the economics of public health policy.[1]

Our task is a daunting one, as the scope of public health is both broad and ill-defined (Detels & Breslow 1991; Holman 1992; Beaglehole & Bonita 1997). One of the most widely cited definitions of public health is that of the *Report of the Millbank Memorial Fund Commission* on higher education in public health in the USA (known as Last's definition). This states that (Higher Education for Public Health 1976):

> Public health is one of the efforts organised by society to protect, promote, and restore the people's health. It is the combination of sciences, skills, and beliefs that is directed to the maintenance and improvement of the health of all the people through collective or social actions. The programs, services and institutions involved emphasise the prevention of disease and the health needs of the population as a whole.
>
> Public health activities change with changing technology and social values, but the goals remain the same: to reduce the amount of disease, premature death, and disease-produced discomfort and disability in the population. Public health is thus a social institution, a discipline, and a practice.

Like most definitions of public health, this one readily accommodates interventions in the form of publicly financed health care to people who are ill. Every chapter in this book is therefore about some aspect of public health policy. Without seeking to resolve the issue of 'What is public health?', the definition does stress two aspects that serve to delineate the scope of this chapter.

The first of these is its social organisation. The allocation of resources both to and within public health is not left solely to private markets but is organised collectively. This defines public health as a political activity, albeit one without clear accountability. Unlike clinical medicine, public health is often delivered to groups of people without their individual consent (Seedhouse 1996). This raises such questions as what is it about public health that requires its collective or public provision, and what limits the extent of the public sector's 'interference' in private lives? The answers lie partly in the economic characteristics of public health strategies and partly in the philosophy of public health that defines its values. These values are not always consistent with the values that economists typically bring to the analysis of public health policy, which can lead to disagreement, even conflict, when assessing the merits of different actions.

Second, the primary interest of public health is in influencing and controlling the determinants of health (including personal, behavioural, social, economic and environmental factors). In addition to health care, therefore, health promotion is an important public health intervention (Green & Kreuter 1990). This is particularly important when we come to discuss aspects of economic evaluation and financing, where we argue that the characteristics of some health promotion interventions require changes to be made to the economic techniques that are usually brought to bear on such issues.

Social organisation of public health

Values in public health and health economics

Two distinct approaches can be distinguished in economics. The first of these suggests that only individual utilities, or levels of personal satisfaction, matter when judging the 'worth' or value of different social states. This view, known as *welfarism*, is reflected in orthodox (i.e. neoclassical or 'welfare') economics. The second view suggests that non-utility characteristics of people, such as their general health and the degree of freedom they enjoy, are also important elements of wellbeing. This view, which has been labelled *'extra-welfarist'*, is inclusive of, but goes beyond, individual utility (Sen 1979). It has had much influence in health economics thinking (Culyer 1989).

Welfarism is one of the cornerstones of utilitarianism (Sen 1979), and is based on the liberal philosophy that individual autonomy is paramount, even if people then act in ways that harm their health. It is assumed that individuals are usually the best judges of their own wellbeing (the 'consumer sovereignty' assumption)—a view which, with a few added conditions, gives substance to the neoclassical economist's faith in free markets. Markets work best when fully informed 'consumers' willingly meet the full costs and enjoy the full benefits of their actions. In such cases, people can be expected to organise their lives in ways that suit them best, weighing up the opportunities open to them within their budget constraints and making choices to maximise the utility they get from the goods and services that they consume.

In choosing how to live their lives, individuals are also expected to assess the risks and benefits to their health and act accordingly. In this view, health has instrumental value only. It is a means to an end (a resource, even), and is important only for the contribution that healthy time makes to one's utility. People who value health more highly will, other things being equal, be more responsive to health promotion messages. Others, for whom health is less important, will be more willing to risk their health in pursuit of other sources of satisfaction. No moral judgement is made about how each individual lives his or her life, providing that no harm is done to others in the process. Health, then, has no superior status or value.

According to this view there is little to be gained by public provision, as the best allocation of resources is achievable through markets. A government's only obligation in such circumstances is to maintain the conditions needed for competitive markets and to intervene if markets 'fail' in specific ways. Markets will fail to achieve a socially optimal outcome if consumers are ill-informed; if they are unable to choose freely; if they do not face the full costs of their actions; or if the benefits of their actions are also enjoyed by others. In such cases there is scope for government involvement.[2] The collective provision of public health is warranted only under these specific conditions. Any attempt to influence individual behaviour in circumstances other than these is dismissed as paternalistic (Littlechild & Wiseman 1984).

Extra-welfarism, on the other hand, rejects the notion that individual utility should be the ultimate arbiter of social value. It leaves unanswered the question of what should replace it. It is not clear, therefore, what the objectives of the public health system ought to be or whose values should be used to judge its success. Culyer (1989) has suggested that in health economics 'the extra-welfarist approach has taken "health" as the proximate maximand', and this explains why quality-adjusted life-years (or QALYs) have been suggested as the main, if not the only, measure of the outcome of health interventions. The desirability of this practice and its consistency with extra-welfarist principles in respect both to health services (Mooney 1994) and health promotion (Shiell & Hawe 1995; Jan & Mooney 1997), have been criticised, however. Culyer (1989) has also suggested that extra-welfarism is more tolerant of paternalism, though he does not specify the limits to this tolerance or the circumstances in which it is appropriate to override an individual's values, except when health is being maximised.

Statements of the value basis of public health are hard to find, though in the context of health promotion Downie and colleagues (1990) provide a notable exception to this. In their view, health is a positive value, of intrinsic and not just instrumental importance. Individuals and governments alike have a moral duty to do all that they can to promote health. As a result 'health promotion is strongly normative; it endeavours to persuade people to adopt certain lifestyles, and is committed to furthering certain values' (Downie et al. 1990: 156). The authors acknowledge that health is not a supreme value, and accept that in some circumstances it may make sense to weigh better health against other values, but the scope for such trade-offs is defined in strictly moral terms. Thus, it is appropriate to sacrifice one's health in the pursuit of scholarship, but not 'gratuitously' in the pursuit of hedonistic pleasure.

The criticism that this view is paternalistic is rejected by Downie et al. who claim support for their assertion that health has moral value in communitarian philosophy (Beauchamp 1985). This places greater emphasis on the social connectedness of individuals and, in one view, regards an injury to one member of the community as an injury to all (Forster 1982).[3] Public health provision is intrinsically good because collective action is seen as an expression of the community's concern for others.

Mooney (1996) agrees that communitarian philosophy may fill the void in economics caused by extra-welfarism's shift from individuals and their utilities. He disagrees with the view that health *necessarily* has superior value. What is needed, he suggests, is some mechanism whereby communitarian values, expressed by individuals acting as community members and ultimately as citizens, may be used to specify the objectives of the public health system.

Implications for public health policy

Though cloaked in a veil of civic duty and humanitarianism, the growth of organised public health in the Victorian era could be seen as a response to 'market failure' (Ringen 1979). Infectious diseases threatened everybody, not just those whose personal actions made them more prone to disease (i.e. they involved what economists refer to as 'externalities'). Government action was warranted to protect the interests of those who did take steps to promote their own health from those who did not. The actions taken, such as refuse collection and the regulation of water and environmental quality, are typical examples of 'public goods': that is, they have characteristics that make it difficult to leave their production and distribution to free markets. For example, it is costly to prevent people who have not contributed to the costs of clean air from enjoying its benefits (non-excludability). Furthermore, one person's enjoyment of clean air does not unduly prevent someone else from enjoying it (non-rivalry). Non-excludability makes it difficult for the market to work, while non-rivalry makes it unnecessary.

Much of what constitutes public health practice today falls within the realm of market failure. Health protection strategies usually have 'public good' characteristics which warrant their public provision. The external benefits associated with the control of infectious disease through vaccination continue to justify the social organisation of immunisation strategies (Fine & Clarkson 1986), while the external costs associated with environmental tobacco smoke (i.e. passive smoking) may justify control of tobacco use in public places. Some forms of health education can also be explained as a response to the market's 'failure' to provide adequate information about health risks and benefits.

According to the market failure argument, it is difficult to justify restrictions on the behaviour of individuals in order to prevent disease if they freely and knowingly bear the full costs of their actions and if the only people they affect in the process are themselves. Public health action taken in such circumstances has the characteristics of a 'merit good': that is, one that others believe is good for you even if you do not agree. The paternalism inherent in this view is apparent if one considers the results of Hilary Graham's study of tobacco use among single mothers (Graham 1994). The young mothers in this study knew of the risks of tobacco use to their own health, but continued to smoke because it was a cheap source of respite that allowed them to fulfil their child-rearing duties. Public health efforts that succeeded in persuading these mothers not to smoke might have improved their health but not necessarily their quality of life.

It is equally difficult to justify by the market failure argument aspects of health education, such as community development, which seek to empower individuals and communities in pursuit of social change. As the social structure is itself an outcome of market inter-actions, it must, (if you believe in market forces) reflect the best that can be achieved. Community development can be justified on communitarian grounds and is consistent with extra-welfarism (Shiell & Hawe 1996), but it draws stronger support from more radical schools of political economy (Minkler et al. 1994/5). What is missing from the 'market failure' critique of community development is any recognition of the differences in power that exist between social groups. Yet powerlessness is an important 'risk condition' for ill-health (Israel et al. 1994)—hence the importance given to empowerment as a health promoting strategy (WHO 1986, 1997).

In practice, it is doubtful whether the existence of market failure has been the central issue around which debates on public health policy in Australia have revolved. Certainly, the main reasons for government intervention in the health system more broadly have been 'extra-welfarist', in the sense that the objectives appear to have more to do with equity (fairness) and effectiveness (better health outcomes) than the efficient satisfaction of consumers' wants.

Arguments about the proper objectives of the public health system more generally, and not just public health per se, are value-laden, but debate about the principles that ought to underpin it has to take place. It is impossible to plan for an efficient health system without agreement on its rightful objectives. For example, in Australia, as elsewhere, there are different views about how comprehensively and by what means the principle of 'equity' should be given effect in the health sector. There is general agreement that the reduction of barriers to access is an important aspect of equity. But do public health services that promote 'wellness' (encouragement to exercise, stress-relief classes etc.) or provide services for apparently healthy people (screening, immunisation) rate as 'medical necessities' that warrant the same degree of access as mainstream care/cure services provided through Medicare?

From the perspective of maximising social welfare, the question arises whether it is appropriate to accept individual preferences for health care vis-à-vis other commodities, or should social policy be based on the assumption that the goal of public health policy is to maximise health or some other social goal? The question illustrates a fundamental difference in values between defining the benefits of public health in terms of their contribution to overall utility (the welfarist perspective) or defining benefits in terms of their contri-bution to other social ends (an extra-welfarist perspective). The implications of the two definitions of benefits are also likely to be very different.

Practical applications of health economics

Moving away from philosophical issues, extra-welfarism has given rise to a school of thought on what constitutes the theoretical foundations and role of economic analysis—called the 'decision-making approach' (Sugden & Williams 1979; Gold et al. 1996). Rather than look only at maximising individual utility, this approach focuses on the objectives of the decision-maker, which are likely to include such other objectives as equity, effectiveness, cost containment or empowerment. The perspective is 'societal' in that economics is used to aid decisions that affect society as a whole. The decision-maker is assumed to be entrusted with the task (usually via the political process) of making choices on behalf of the general public, and this trust implies the formation of objectives on their behalf.

In this respect, an important challenge for public health posed in the National Health Policy Review (National Health Strategy 1990) was to improve the health of Australians to a level comparable with that of any country in the world, within the constraints of available resources, while ensuring an equitable distribution of benefits. The extent of preventable illness and premature mortality among the population suggests that Australia is still well short of its potential to improve the health status of the community (Armstrong 1989). Better public health measures could also lead to reductions in the costs of health care in the order of $2.4 billion per annum (Carter 1993). The availability of such potential benefits raises three important questions connected with their realisation:

- How should priorities in public health be set?
- What evaluation should be carried out of individual programs? and
- What financing and institutional arrangements are required to ensure that services are provided efficiently and equitably?

Priority-setting and planning

There are a number of common approaches to planning public health services that may be thought to offer a framework for priority-setting, including historically based decision rules, best practice guidelines, needs assessment, and goals and targets. The last two of these are currently the most popular, with needs assessment entrenched in public health thinking at the regional and local level, and goals and targets dominant at the nation and state level. Internationally, the

World Bank and the World Health Organization have been advocating the use of disability-adjusted life-years (or DALYs) as a method of establishing health priorities (Murray & Lopez 1996).

In Australia cancer, heart disease, injury and mental health have been identified as health priorities on the basis that each of these represents a sizeable public health problem (i.e. the burden of disease is large); that effective interventions exist; and that good data are available to monitor progress towards specified targets. Priorities have also been identified in much the same way in the USA, the UK and New Zealand (Nutbeam & Wise 1996). Needs assessment methods utilise similar criteria, and may also survey the local community to assess its perceptions on local health needs.

For states and their regions involved with contracting on the purchaser/provider model, needs assessment has intuitive appeal as a source of information on what types of health care should be provided and to what extent. There is a certain appeal in the idea that the bigger the problem (as measured by epidemiological data, 'cost of illness', or community concern), the higher should be the priority. A more sophisticated approach to needs assessment involves equating need with capacity to benefit, rather than simply with illness or concern per se (Mooney et al. 1993). This is an important step for priority-setting for interventions (as opposed to research programs), as some diseases may not readily be addressed by available interventions, or are more or less amenable to prevention and control. More informed advocates of needs assessment see it as a three-step process, where needs are first described, then analysed, and then assigned priorities (Batterham 1997).

Economic criticisms of current methods of priority-setting

Both needs-based and targets-based approaches to priority-setting rank problems in order of importance and, despite the intuitive appeal of this approach, neither offers any guidance on how resources ought to be allocated across the priorities. For example, the National Health Goals and Targets for Cancer Implementation Working Group (1994) identified cancer of the breast, cervix, lung, colon and rectum along with melanoma as priority cancers. But what does this mean in terms of the allocation of resources? Should all resources be allocated to achieving the targets set for the cancer with the highest priority before anything is spent on preventing the next most important cancer? Or should resources be allocated across all seven priority areas pro rata, according to the relative burden of disease? In this case, how many, if any, resources should be allocated to preventing cancers not identified as priorities?

The problem arises because inadequate attention is paid to the relative cost-effectiveness of public health measures (Mooney et al. 1993). Economic approaches to priority-setting begin with the notion that the community's resources are scarce relative to its needs. Choices must be made about which needs ought to be met first, and should be based on the notion of 'opportunity costs' (i.e. benefit gained relative to benefit forgone). Economic theory provides a framework for the prioritisation of public health services to maximise health gain from limited resources (defined as allocative efficiency). The necessary condition for allocative efficiency is that *at the margin* health outcome per unit cost is equal for all interventions. If this condition is not satisfied, then as a matter of logic it is possible to increase the public's health, by redirecting resources to where the ratio of marginal benefit to marginal cost is highest.

If priorities are set on the basis of public health significance alone, there is no link made between the size of the problem and what can be done about it. Consideration of amenability to change and existence of an effective intervention is necessary in establishing priorities but not sufficient. It is important to know how effective the intervention is *at the margin*. As priorities are being set in order to allocate resources across competing programs, it is necessary also to know the resource costs of the interventions so that their *opportunity cost* can be established.

Finally, by focusing initially on big-ticket items where the burden of disease is large, potentially cost-effective solutions to small problems may be ignored. The rewording of vaccination reminder cards provides an excellent example (Hawe 1997). This low-cost intervention succeeded in increasing measles vaccination rates, and would therefore appear to be extremely cost-effective. It would be overlooked, however, by current methods of priority-setting, as the burden of disease caused by measles in Australia is low. Similarly, there may be important pockets of unmet need in areas of low total need. Total need may be unrelated to marginal (unmet need), and marginal need may or may not be a good proxy for marginal benefit.

Economic approaches to priority-setting

While the theoretical prerequisites for allocative efficiency are clear and logically compelling, implementation is difficult. The challenge is to develop a theoretically sound framework that is broad-based, which encompasses all pertinent interventions but which is feasible in terms of research effort required and the possibility for a staged analysis. Economic responses to priority-setting in public health are the Macro Economic Evaluation Model, or MEEM (Carter 1994), the disease-based framework (DBF) of Segal and Richardson (1994), and program budgeting and marginal analysis, or PBMA (Mooney et al. 1993).

The MEEM approach was developed in response to practical difficulties being experienced by the NHMRC in trying to rank a large number of projects (in the field of periodic health checks), in a way that included their economic merit. It incorporates economic principles, but is more in the decision-making school than the strict welfare economics school. In some respects it is similar to the methods of establishing public health priorities described above, in that its starting point is public health significance and preventability of disease. As such it provides another way of ranking diseases according to their relative burden and potential to benefit. The MEEM approach extends these methods, however, as a project appraisal component is built onto the estimates of burden of disease and potential to benefit.[4] This provides a link between what can be done about a problem and the average cost-effectiveness of relevant interventions.[5] It also enables a range of 'what if' questions to be analysed, and encourages 'opportunity cost' analysis as a way of thinking in policy development.

The advantage of the MEEM technique is its integration of economic and non-economic approaches to priority-setting, showing the impact of different ranking criteria (size, level of concern, potential to benefit, incremental cost-effectiveness ratio). Its focus on providing an information framework of best available data makes broad-based assessment more tractable.

In contrast to the total burden and/or the needs-based approach of the methods outlined above, PBMA and the DBF share a marginal approach. In both cases the aim is to increase the outcomes of service delivery by identifying the scope to reallocate resources at the margin, away from services yielding a poorer return per dollar to those yielding a higher return per dollar. Important differences between the two approaches are in the level at which they can be applied and their approach to making the appraisal task more manageable. The DBF is designed to cut across institutional boundaries and cover the whole health sector, with disease groupings as the context for analysis. This enables priorities to be set for each stage in the management of a disease (i.e. prevention, care, cure, rehabilitation, palliation) and across the whole spectrum of health services. In PBMA no restriction is placed on the definition of programs. Instead, it is left to local decision-makers to determine the configuration that best fits their needs. This could be disease groups or it could be client group, geographic location or population-based. This allows the technique to be applied at all levels, although the focus to date has been within organisational settings (e.g. hospitals, community health centres, area health services).

Key characteristics of the PBMA approach to appraisal are its user-friendliness and practical approach to benefit estimation (utilising provider judgement and option appraisal, where more rigorous data are not available). The DBF, on the other hand, tries to make the appraisal task more manageable by adopting a two-stage process: first, a crude ranking of interventions based on best available cost-effectiveness data is established; then a comprehensive appraisal of the cost-effectiveness of the 'best' and the 'worst' (i.e. the marginal) interventions is performed in an iterative fashion.

The economic principles underpinning both approaches are not new, but the practical application of these techniques to health planning is not widespread. The DBF has been applied to non-insulin-dependent diabetes mellitus, colorectal cancer and hypertension, while the PBMA approach has been trialled in three area health services in NSW, and in South Australia, and has been used extensively in the UK (Donaldson 1995). There has been little use of the PBMA approach within public health (Mooney et al. 1997), although one of the South Australian pilots involves community health (Peacock et al. 1997). The strengths and weaknesses of each approach thus have yet to be fully tested.

PBMA, like MEEM, is essentially a management tool with a societal theoretical basis (i.e. in the decision-making school). Its key strength—its ability to empower decision-makers and use best available information—is also its key potential weakness. If judgements about marginal benefits are based on limited or anecdotal experience of service providers, and insufficiently supported by research evidence, the resulting priorities must be viewed cautiously until the research base is developed (Posnett & Street 1996). Experience to date with PBMA has also demonstrated issues associated with the match between available cost data and the program structure, game playing/domination of group processes, and generation of the decrement list.

The focus on marginal analysis in the DBF is constrained by the availability of information (both epidemiological and economic data) and the breadth of the appraisal task. Experience to date has demonstrated a trade-off between the comprehensive perspective provided by the broad-based approach and the relevance to specific problems. The DBF in application, for example, has had to focus increasingly on population and clinical subgroups to make its marginal analysis meaningful and relevent.

These economic approaches need not be seen as mutually exclusive. They could be regarded as complementary and interlinking approaches that focus on different problems, with different strengths and weaknesses in guiding priority-setting in public health. There is no reason why the innovative features of each approach (e.g. benefit estimation in PBMA; two-stage appraisal in DBF; status quo description in MEEM) could not be used in combination where the research question warranted such an approach.

Public health investment portfolio approach

The push towards greater rationality in public health planning through the use of such techniques is a welcome one, though care needs to be taken to ensure that growing accountability pressure does not encourage public health decision-makers to opt *only* for 'tried and tested' interventions (Hawe & Shiell 1995). This will promote the adoption of best practice techniques as they are *currently* defined, but it may have a number of less desirable consequences. It may, for example, stifle practice-led innovation. It may be inequitable, as the public health programs on which we have the best evidence tend not to be those which serve 'hard to reach' populations. It may also encourage public health managers to retain control of safe and effective programs at a time when good public health practice suggests that they should be seeking to institutionalise successful programs by transferring their control to hospital and other community-based agencies. As a result, progress towards health gain will be unacceptably slow and inequitable (Hawe & Shiell 1995).

The pervasive lack of information about the size of the benefits of actual and potential public health programs implies that funding systems should promote a form of 'dynamic efficiency' (Richardson et al. 1995)—that is, a system that encourages controlled experimentation and progressive improvement in program efficiency. The portfolio approach to public health planning seeks to do this by drawing on investment economics to argue that the best returns (i.e. the highest health gains) will be achieved from the public health dollar if resources are invested wisely across a range of programs (Hawe & Shiell 1995). The resultant portfolio might include 'blue-chip' investments, such as patient education and GP smoking cessation advice, as well as higher risk, but potentially higher health gain per dollar investments in community development and intersectoral action. The theory underpinning strategies such as community development and intersectoral action points to their potential, but the quality of this evidence does not match that in other areas of public health. The portfolio approach would allow for prudent investment in these areas, but brings with it an obligation to evaluate the cost-effectiveness of the interventions in question.

Economic evaluation

The uptake of economic evaluation methods in public health, while not as widespread as it could be, is another mark of the progress of economics. A recent review of economic evaluations carried out in Australia found that almost one-half of the studies were in the areas of health promotion or illness prevention (Salkeld et al. 1995). Economic evaluation has also informed public health policy at the national level, as seen in the evaluation of the organised approaches to screening for breast and cervical cancer (AHMAC 1990, 1991).

Economic evaluation in the context of health care is discussed elsewhere in this book. The characteristics of public health (in this context, health promotion) interventions pose additional technical and methodological problems (Tolley 1993; Richardson 1995). The long time-frames involved make it more difficult to measure final effects, and the complex links between intervention and outcome make it harder to attribute one to the other. The relative timing of costs and outcomes makes the choice of discount rate critical (Cohen 1994). The range and nature of outcomes can be extensive, making it difficult to capture the full benefits of public health measures (Rosen & Lindholm 1992; Shiell & Hawe 1996). The evaluation of intersectoral action brings with it additional problems. With fewer bureaucratic limits on the range of alternatives that might be considered, it is difficult to contain the scope of the evaluation. The outcomes also become more diverse, making it difficult to rank the effectiveness of programs unambiguously. Road safety interventions, for example, may affect exhaust emissions and travel time, as well as morbidity and mortality, and it is difficult to compare programs when each of these outcomes is moving in different directions or at different rates (Drummond & Stoddart 1995).

Such technical difficulties make the task of the evaluator harder, but the problems they pose are not insurmountable. A variety of methods can be employed to overcome such problems, if only partially. Simulation techniques have been used to estimate the range of values that possible outcomes might take, providing upper and lower bounds on estimates of effectiveness (Gunning-Schepers 1989; Haycox 1994). Sensitivity analysis has been employed to the same end, and is particularly useful in drawing out the implications of different discount rates (Cohen 1994). More difficult problems emerge when the methods of economic evaluation are inconsistent with the interventions being appraised. This occurs particularly when one considers such activities as health advocacy and organisational and community development.

The concept of economic evaluation is based on the notion of a simple production function in which inputs are transformed smoothly into health outcomes. As inputs increase, so do health outcomes, though not necessarily pro rata. While this model is appropriate for some interventions, for activities such as political lobbying and advocacy, there is more likely to be a discrete relationship between inputs and outputs characterised by a threshold below which there will appear to be no relationship, even though important changes are taking place. If evaluation is carried out before the level of inputs reaches the critical level, the program may appear to be ineffective. Australia's experience with gun control illustrates the problem (Peters & Chapman 1995). Before the tragic events at Port Arthur there would have been little tangible outcome to show for the efforts invested in arguing for gun control, and any evaluation at this stage might have concluded that such efforts were ineffective. Yet this activity undoubtedly helped to create the climate which persuaded the government to act when it did.

In other activities, such as organisational and community development, the health promoter's aim is not to improve health directly but to increase the capacity of others to deal with health issues. The immediate goals of community development are community empowerment, enhanced sense of community and increased community competence, not health gain. These programs have the community, not individuals, as the basis of program theory and as the unit of analysis. The notion of community is more sophisticated than that typically employed in economic analysis (Hawe 1994). In community development programs, community is seen ecologically. In economics, it amounts to nothing more than an aggregate of individuals. Sense of community and community competence are therefore properties of the community, and it is questionable whether the full benefits of community action can be adequately captured by aggregating the effects on individuals (Shiell & Hawe 1996).

Financing and reimbursement

As so few public health activities are explicitly identified as such in health sector accounts, it is difficult to be precise about the sources of funds. Of readily identified sources, the most important are block grants from state health departments, as in NSW, and project funding through health promotion foundations, as in Victoria and Western Australia (Richardson et al. 1995). Apart from providing resources, financing mechanisms complement the priority-setting process by providing the necessary incentives to maximise the likelihood that agreed public health priorities will be implemented. The issue of incentives is an unavoidable one, as all methods of financing services generate incentives of one sort or another. The challenge is to tailor the system of finance such that services better meet the social goals of equity and efficiency.

A variety of 'actors' may be identified in the provision of public health: namely, 'providers', who supply services (e.g. health promotion units, community health centres, solo practitioners); 'purchasers' of public health activities (e.g. government regional health authorities or private sector) buying for defined populations or individual clients; 'funders' (government or private) that provide resources to purchasers; and 'regulatory authorities' that police the system. In addition, health promotion officers are increasingly seeing their role as one of 'agents of change': that is, not as direct providers of services but as initiators of service development and provision by other organisational and community entities (Hawe et al. 1997).

While the functions of each of these groups of actors are conceptually distinct, their relationship with each other varies according to the institutional structures and type of public health activity in which each is engaged. Thus, it is questionable whether any single model of funding would be suitable across the board. Instead, a set of general principles is required to determine the relationship that will increase the likelihood of achieving objectives. Richardson and colleagues (1995) have suggested the following principles:

- the need for information about expected program benefits, to facilitate discriminating purchasing and utilisation of public health services (by government and private individuals);
- the need for an institutional means for promoting and financing experimentation and the assessment of experimentation;
- the need for diversity of supply and responsive purchasers;
- the need for a financing mechanism that will translate program information into policy;
- the need for an independent process for the determination of the principles of social justice, which should be incorporated in the evaluation of public health programs; and
- the need for purchasers and regulators to have clear and transparent roles and responsibilities.

Richardson et al. (1995) argue that, in the case of dedicated personal or population-focused programs, the likelihood of achieving the principles outlined above will be maximised, as in the competitive model, by the adoption of an approach in which the purchasing and provision of services are separated. The introduction of limited and managed competition among the providers of health services should encourage greater technical efficiency, while allocative efficiency should be achieved by selective purchasing of services according to the priority-setting models described earlier. A small number of countries have moved towards such a health funding system (including the UK and New Zealand), and the possible relevance to Australia is a matter of current debate (see Chapter 11), but the merits of the model still need to be evaluated empirically in the public health context.

It is also questionable whether a competitive mechanism would be as useful in other areas of public health practice, such as in capacity building and health advocacy. Dedicated personal services, such as disease prevention programs, tend to be 'operational' in nature, and involve relatively structured and routine tasks that are easy to systematise and monitor. Capacity building and health advocacy are more 'facilitative', and involve creating the appropriate conditions for the execution of operational effort. This requires network building with partner organisations to ensure coordination and consensus and minimise goal conflict.

The two sorts of activity, facilitative and operational, do not necessarily respond to financial incentives in the same way (Nilakant & Rao 1994). It is more difficult to specify contracts that link payment to effort or outcome for facilitative effort, and as the outcomes of facilitation are more dependent on the actions of others it is less likely to be responsive to effort-based incentives.

This is not to argue that direct financial incentives have no role to play in such activities. The reorientation of mainstream health services, for example, has potential for improving health. Promoting the necessary change in attitudes and practice is problematical, but the effectiveness of facilitative effort directed to this end might be enhanced by appropriately targeted incentives. This might include payment to GPs for achieving immunisation targets or the modification of case-mix funding systems for hospitals so as not to discourage their continued involvement in public health.

Finally, many of the programs that contribute to public health involve activities outside the formal health sector, especially when the health-related activities of private individuals and workplaces are considered. While private sector resources should be included in planning public health policy, there is an important distinction in the way in which this can occur. First, public funds can be used to encourage individuals to demand, and employers to provide, health-promoting activities; that is, the funds are not used directly to subsidise the activities, but to change attitudes towards them. Second, public funds could be used to subsidise or tax particular activities to make them more accessible or (in the case of tobacco and alcohol) inaccessible. In principle, a series of taxes and subsidies could emerge to promote health-related activities. In practice, such a system would be administratively complex and controversial, and would almost certainly become arbitrary and have adverse economic consequences.

Conclusions

No discussion of the economics of public health policy can avoid raising the question of values. Economic analysis aims to improve the allocation of resources and therefore we must agree about what makes one allocation better than another. The notion of equity is obviously value-laden, and we have made reference to the need to debate what it means and how important it is in the context of public health. Even the supposedly technical concept of allocative efficiency involves a value judgement, as its achievement depends on what one defines as an important outcome. At the heart of this issue are questions relating to the value of health. Debate is needed about the rightful objectives of public health and what limits we should set around it.

Having clarified what it is that we wish to achieve, economic techniques can help to steer public health towards its goals. Economic evaluation, priority-setting and financing ought to act in concert; identifying where the best health gains are to be made, facilitating the achievement of such gains, and finally assessing the success of different polices. But it should be apparent, given the highly politicised and value-laden nature of public health, that economic methods cannot provide comprehensive answers to questions about resource allocation. The best they can do is to provide the framework in which complex questions can be considered; in which most, if not all, the important effects, including any incentive effects, of policy options can be identified; and in which at least some of these effects can be quantified.

We have suggested that public health has yet to fulfil its potential contribution to improving the health status of Australians. We close this chapter by suggesting that this is also true of health economics.

Gavin Mooney, Stephen Jan and Virginia Wiseman

13   *Economic issues in Aboriginal health care*

To write as non-indigenous economists about the health and health care of Aboriginal and Torres Strait Islander people (hereafter referred to as Aboriginal or indigenous people) is potentially dangerous, especially when we three have worked for such a short space of time (two years) on economic issues in Aboriginal health. Moving between cultures and attempting to make sense of different value systems is always difficult, yet it is enormously challenging. Relatively few economists have looked at concerns for efficiency and equity in resource allocation in Aboriginal health. We have been given the opportunity to do so and to work closely with Aboriginal people and with other non-Aboriginal people in tackling some of the economic problems here. Consequently, we feel not so much that we have a right to pontificate on these issues—rather that we have a responsibility to try to interpret what we have seen and what we and others have done.

While it is now a well-worked cliché, it is clear immediately that there are no quick fixes in Aboriginal health. What at times makes us despair, however, is that there are too few attempts being made by way of even slow fixes.

It is possible to argue with considerable justification that the 'solution' to Aboriginal health problems does not lie in simply spending more money. At the same time, any solution or substantial amelioration must include spending more money, at least in the short run, and in this context the short run is at least the next decade. There is also an important debate needed about where existing and any additional resources are best spent, especially whether these should go to health services or to environmental health, housing or water.

Much can be done for current generations of Aboriginal people, but the devastation that has been wreaked on these peoples and their health is such that truly radical improvement can only be looked for across generations. This time span is the main reason why we advocate the need to take Aboriginal health out of the maximum three-year time frame of contemporary Australian governmental policy-making. Short-term political expediency may have a virtue in other areas of policy—it has none in Aboriginal health.

No-one with any knowledge of the magnitude and complexities of the issues involved would argue that the current and indeed anticipated future levels of Aboriginal health are acceptable in any country, and certainly not alongside the high levels of health experienced by others in this rich and otherwise civilised country. Appropriate debate is not about the need for action—it is about the nature of that action.

In this chapter we largely bypass the debate about the optimal mix of investment in health services versus investment in housing, water, etc. The focus of the book and of this chapter is health services. We are nonetheless confident that the answer to the optimal investment mix is that the majority of any additional resources for Aboriginal health should go to non-formal health service influences. The evaluation of the National Aboriginal Health Strategy (1994), for example, suggested that the shortfall on these services was of the order of $2.5 billion; no estimate of the shortfall in health services expenditure was given. While clearly more information than this is needed to determine the optimal balance of any investment, the likely outcome is clear. The wider implications of this are left for another occasion.

Background

The state of Aboriginal health

In examining the state of Aboriginal health we draw attention to two issues. First, there has been a recent and comprehensive statistical overview by the Aboriginal and Torres Strait Islander Health and Welfare Information Unit of the Australian Bureau of Statistics (McLennan & Madden 1997). Second, this work has filled a serious void in indigenous health statistics, particularly at the national level, but the available data remain limited by incomplete identification of indigenous people in national administrative and hospital data collections.

In 1991 Aboriginal people comprised about 1.6 per cent of the Australian population. Between 1992 and 1994 indigenous people experienced higher death rates than non-indigenous people at every age, with the largest gap occurring among adults aged 25–54 years, where they were about 6–8 times higher.

In the period 1992–94, life-expectancy at birth among non-indigenous people was 74.9 years for men and 80.6 years for women. Life-expectancy at birth among Aboriginal people living in Western Australia, South Australia and the Northern Territory was 16–18 years lower for men and 16–20 years lower for women (Anderson & Sanders 1996).

Three of every four deaths among Aboriginal people are due to circulatory diseases, injury, respiratory diseases, cancer, endocrine and metabolic diseases such as diabetes. Higher rates occur for all these diseases than for non-indigenous people. For most categories of disease, indigenous people are about 2–3 times more likely to be hospitalised than would be expected if they had the same hospital-isation rates as Australians overall.

With respect to self-reported health status, the most recent source of information is the National Aboriginal and Torres Strait Islander Survey (NATSIS) (ABS 1994). About 40 per cent of men and 42 per cent of women reported that they had experienced an illness, injury or disability in the two weeks before being interviewed. Of those who said they had experienced a recent illness, 34 per cent reported that they had been affected by respiratory disease, making it the most commonly reported illness overall and for all age groups up to 45 years of age, after which diseases of the circulatory system were more often mentioned. The most commonly reported long-term conditions were asthma (13 per cent) and ear or hearing problems (9 per cent). Diabetes was reported by 4 per cent of the indigenous population overall, more commonly by women than men. Over the age of 45, about one in five people said that they suffered from diabetes.

Policy in Aboriginal health care

As indicated in detail in Chapter 2, current health policy in Australia is characterised by shared responsibilities between state and Commonwealth governments. Broadly speaking, the Commonwealth is responsible for financing health services, the states for service delivery (Palmer & Short 1994). This split reflects largely the respec-tive constitutional roles, revenue collection powers being vested mainly in the Commonwealth and the provision of health services with the states. In addition to mainstream services, primary health care is available to Aboriginal people through community controlled health services.

In spite of the substantial differences in health status between Aboriginal people and other Australians, there are generally few policy provisions specifically for Aboriginality in the funding and delivery of mainstream health services. Poor identification of Abori-ginality and consequent underreporting of utilisation make any measures aimed at indigenous people difficult to implement effec-tively. Two such policy areas where there does seem to be some recognition of the need for special provisions have been in the allocation of resources from Commonwealth to states and from the state government level to areas and districts. We have previously provided a review of the way Aboriginality has been dealt with within these funding guidelines, and concluded that in general the equity criterion they seemed to be using was fairly weak. The Commonwealth Grants Commission allocates resources across states on the basis of relative cost, while state-level resource allocation formulae generally employ a limited notion of relative 'need' (Mooney & Jan 1997). Neither of these adequately tackle the vertical equity concerns we raise below.

To gain a good understanding of the economic environment in which Aboriginal health and health services exist today, one should have an awareness of some of the relevant aspects of history. Thus Bartlett and Legge (1994) have argued that the federalist system involving separate responsibilities between states and the Commonwealth has served as a barrier to the improvement of the health of indigenous people. The problem stems mainly from a lack of certainty as to who should take ultimate responsibility for the funding of services. The possibilities for cost-shifting created by this system have meant, for instance, that states and territories have often held back on spending on Aboriginal health in the expectation that the Commonwealth will make up the shortfall: 'The consequence of this stand-off with respect to "primary" responsibility has been no responsibility'. (We return to this issue in more detail below.)

The development of community-controlled health services can be seen largely as a response to the failure of mainstream services to cater appropriately for the health needs of the Aboriginal population. Being community owned and controlled they supply the 'means . . . Aboriginal people have in countering the systems imposed on them by non-Aboriginal people' (National Aboriginal Health Strategy Working Party 1989). They are generally more holistic than mainstream services, providing, for instance, transportation for patients and dealing with wider community issues that may have an impact on health (Fagan 1991).

The most common funding arrangement is for these services to receive base funding from Medicare through the reimbursement of bulk-billed services. Such monies are then usually supplemented by funds from various other sources (Saggers & Gray 1991). Bartlett and Legge (1994) have argued that very little of the funding to this community-controlled sector has been available for 'system support' (i.e. functions such as regional planning, continuing professional development, evaluation).

The history of health policy in relation to indigenous populations needs to be seen within the broader context of relations between various levels of government and Aboriginal people. In general, this can be categorised in three historical phases: segregation, assimilation and, more recently, self-determination (Saggers & Gray 1991; Hunter 1993; Palmer & Short 1994). This history is one of colonial legacy in which such issues as dispossession, forced removals and neglect in custody have loomed large. These have had a lasting effect on indigenous people and their health today (National Aboriginal Health Strategy Working Party 1989; Bartlett & Legge 1994).

Saggers and Gray (1991) provide an account of how the early colonial expansion of European settlements, fuelled by the ever-growing economic benefits of wool production, resulted in a decimation of the Aboriginal populations through disease and violence. For much of the 19th century, following the findings of a committee of the British House of Commons and a report by Bruxton in 1837 expressing concern about the diminishing indigenous populations in NSW and Tasmania, a policy of 'protecting' indigenous populations through segregation was implemented.

Hunter (1993) suggests that, in Western Australia, government involvement in the health issues of Aborigines could be seen to be motivated by concern about infection spreading to the white population (citing the example of measures to contain leprosy and venereal disease). One result of this segregation policy was the confinement of large sections of the Aboriginal population to reserves. As noted by Saggers and Gray (1991: 385):

> One of the lasting effects of the reserves has been the dependence of Aboriginal people on the wider Australian society for the most basic of human needs. Diet, movement, employment, marriage, child-rearing arrangements, and the exercise of religious belief were all subject to the wishes of the mission or settlement custodians.

The period of assimilation that followed segregation probably began around the 1930s, and involved large-scale revocation of Aboriginal reserves without compensation (Saggers & Gray 1991). Within public hospitals and other medical services, exclusion of Aborigines was still commonplace—either through overt discrimination or through financial barriers. In the pre-Medibank era, most GPs required up-front payment, with the result that many sick Aborigines were forced into local hospitals and faced there with the trauma of racist treatment. According to Saggers and Gray (1991) not much changed immediately after the referendum of 1967, and it was only in 1972, with the election of the Whitlam government, that a new direction was taken in Aboriginal health.

Among the platforms on which the Whitlam government was elected was community control over health services, as one part of broader strategies for community development. Yet, as noted by Saggers and Gray (1991), the first Aboriginal Medical Service (AMS) (in Redfern, Sydney) predated any government initiative in that area. According to Fagan (1991) this represented a clear example of 'self-determination in action'. In 1992 there were 92 organisations throughout Australia receiving some funding from the Aboriginal and Torres Strait Islander Commission (ATSIC) for the running of health care programs (ATSIC 1992).

At an administrative level, in the early 1990s, ATSIC replaced the Commonwealth Department of Aboriginal Affairs. The aim was to create an administrative body more representative of the Aboriginal community. To this end, it had on its board elected representatives from Aboriginal and Torres Strait Islander communities, and until recently had responsibility for the administration of indigenous health care programs. This involved reallocation of funds to Aboriginal health services and various specific health programs in such areas as trachoma and eye health, communicable disease and substance abuse (ATSIC 1992). Ultimately ATSIC was unsuccessful in the task of managing effectively the competing demands of various groups (Bartlett & Legge 1994; Anderson & Sanders 1996). This responsibility for health services has since been transferred to the Office of Aboriginal and Torres Strait Islander Health in the Commonwealth Department of Health and Family Services.

While there seems to be recognition currently at a government level that community control is an important direction for policy in indigenous health, it has been suggested that inadequate support has impeded this development (Bartlett & Legge 1994). Some of the problems encountered by ATSIC in the administration of Aboriginal health highlight that successful self-determination requires appropriate levels of government support and funding, and is more than simply the transfer of responsibilities. Perhaps this is best summed up by Anderson and Sanders (1996: 24):

> Aboriginal self-determination in health, as in other spheres, should not be read as an opportunity for governmental disengagement. Aboriginal people's efforts need to be supported by appropriate resources and expertise, which perhaps only governments can provide. This support must, however, be provided in ways which respect Aboriginal people and organisations as full partners in the process. Aboriginal participation and priorities need to be seriously and concertedly addressed.

Possible future for policy on Aboriginal health services

Determining the optimal level of funding

Equivalent services

Looking at the level of health status in Aboriginal communities and the nature of the health problems—what might be termed the health care needs—one can try to translate these into levels of service provision or utilisation that would accompany such health problems if they were to be found in non-indigenous Australia. For example, in the case of diabetics, what levels of service are provided in Melbourne or Sydney and what levels of utilisation obtain? These levels of services could then be costed out—for Aboriginal communities—which would provide one estimate of the level of funding required.

Certainly such an approach has considerable merit. There are some potential difficulties with it, such as the fact that some health problems are unique to Aboriginal communities and do not exist in non-indigenous Australia. That is unlikely to be a major issue, however. Somewhat more problematical is that such an approach assumes that the appropriate treatment for non-indigenous Australians is also appropriate for indigenous Australians, which will not always be so. But such an approach might give an estimate of 'appropriate' funding levels, even if the monies were then used differently in some instances. What is perhaps more problematical is that this approach is based on the premise that the optimal amount of funding is set at that level where the needs of the indigenous population are to be met at the same rate of intensity as (or equal to) those of the non-indigenous population. In other words, there is no assumption about the greater desirability of reducing the needs of the indigenous population vis-à-vis those of the non-indigenous population. It is thus built on a weak principle of equity.

This criticism does not mean that such an approach ought not to be pursued. What view of equity will prevail in any debate about justice in health care for Aboriginal people is not something about which we feel able or competent to form a judgement. We feel it is best to put forward various approaches, accompanied by our view on each, to help to inform any debate about the future of funding of Aboriginal health care policy.

Basic primary health care

A second suggestion (Scrimgeour 1997) is that the 'core business' of health care delivery for Aboriginal communities ought to be identified and funded. This is in essence a 'rights-based' approach, arguing that in a country like Australia everyone ought to have the right of access to some basic level of primary health care services, at least in terms of its ready availability.

Again, it would be difficult to put up any strong opposition to such a proposal, but we look askance at it on two grounds—one in principle (or perhaps political), the other more practical. If such a basic level is determined it might become a goal in itself, and anything above that level will be seen politically as a sort of 'bonus'. It would lend itself to the political rhetoric of the kind which says that many Aboriginal communities are operating with health services well above what has been set (and agreed with the Aboriginal communities, even?) as basic (and with the implication being 'and aren't we doing well?' or, more likely still, 'and aren't they doing well?'). Thus a level of basic primary health care, which clearly no-one could argue any community should fall below, may turn out to be not just a floor but also a ceiling. It is also the case that the idea of a basic level is not otherwise a part of the philosophy of health care delivery in Australia. Indeed, Medicare has been thankfully free of such thinking. It would be ironic if this, to our mind, minimalist thinking were to gain an important foothold in Australian health care policy through the door of indigenous health.

At a more practical or pragmatic level there are difficulties in determining what in fact such a basic level would constitute. There is scope for considerable debate on this issue, and it is not one that we are aware has been resolved in other settings where the notion of a basic minimum has been discussed or flirted with, such as in Oregon (e.g. Brannigan 1993) or New Zealand (Core Health Services Committee 1993). Indeed, one of the messages that seems to emerge from Oregon is that what constitutes 'basic' ends up by being determined at least in part by the extent of the willingness to fund. This in turn can quickly be converted to a decision about what amount of care some politically acceptable size of budget will buy, which is then decreed to be the basic minimum. While perhaps understandable from the perspective of a government's fiscal stance (where budget constraints determine so much of the thinking), determining the appropriate level of funding by starting with the budget is not the intent of the exercise!

Having put forward these arguments against the notion of a core as advocated by Scrimgeour (1997), there may nonetheless be a case for developing such an approach—and costing it out—at least as a short-term, interim way of improving the current situation. As Scrimgeour indicates, the approach does at least recognise the fact that 'in many communities the current level of funding is inadequate and that the main concern of Aboriginal people is to have this remedied' (1997: 106).

Equity[1]

The best way to determine what the level of spending on Aboriginal health services should be is to argue from a basis of equity: that is, about what a fair share of total health care resources might be. This fits with a major strand of work of health economists in policy in the past two decades in examining resource allocation formulae, especially on a geographical basis. Such an equity-based objective drives many health services, not only in Australia (e.g. in NSW in the previous resource allocation formula, or RAF, and more recently as proposed in the resource distribution formula, or RDF) but also in other countries (e.g. with RAWP 1976 in the UK). Beyond that there is scope for considerable debate as to what the principles of equity should be that will then underlie such a policy.

Our preferred approach to Aboriginal health funding (and one which corresponds with the thinking of the NAHS 1989) is based on the principle of equal access for equal need, with both access and need defined in a particular way. When considering issues of access across different cultural groupings, it is not enough to use a definition of access based on opportunity cost. We would want to endorse a concept of fairness that also embraces different cultural values, essentially a welfare loss definition of access. Such a definition (as we have indicated previously: Mooney & Jan 1997) amounts to having access such that two individuals perceive the heights of the barriers that they face as being equal. Issues of cultural barriers, for example, might then be taken into account as well as the more conventional resource cost and distance barriers.

Need is perhaps one of the most confused and most confusing terms in the health policy lexicon. Here is not the place to debate that at any length. There are from an economics standpoint two key definitions, each of which assumes that some third party is exercising the value judgements involved in its construct. First, need is based on the extent of health problems such that, in any 'needs assessment' where relative needs are being ranked, the greater the health problems the greater the needs. Additionally, if the health problems in, say, cardiovascular disease were to be estimated at twice the health problems in cancer, the needs of the former might also be said to be twice those of the latter. Second, need can be seen as 'capacity to benefit' (Culyer 1995). Here account is taken of the ability of health services to resolve or ameliorate the health problems involved. It follows that need defined in this second way will certainly be no greater than when defined in the first way; what this will mean for relative needs (as in cardiovascular disease versus cancer) is less clear, and only resolvable empirically.

There remains beyond this the question of whether capacity to benefit ought also to take into account the relative efficiency with which different health-influencing activities do affect health and in turn need (e.g. health services versus housing which, as indicated above, is clearly important in Aboriginal health but not dealt with in this chapter). In other words, the concept of capacity to benefit might be made more relevant still by arguing that it is not enough that health services can influence health positively at all (i.e. they have a capacity to benefit) but that such services do so more efficiently than any alternative use of society's resources.

We believe that the concept of capacity to benefit is to be preferred in any context of resource allocation in health care, but given the differential that exists in health status between Aboriginal people and other Australians it is even more desirable to adopt this construct of need. The fact that the best mix is between health care resources and housing, water, etc. remains to be debated only adds to the advantages of a 'capacity to benefit' approach.

We would go further in elaborating on the standard view of equal access for equal need. In resource allocation formulae it is often assumed that all health gains have the same weight, so that the distribution of health gains does not affect the overall social valuation of any given amount of health gains. We would argue that such valuation is not independent of the existing level of health status of the groups affected (and have some preliminary evidence from health service decision-makers to support this hypothesis). Therefore, in evaluating across programs it might be deemed that the potential health gains to one population (e.g. where the health status is relatively low) be given greater weight than those to another. In essence, this is about weighting needs differentially to account for vertical equity (i.e. the unequal but equitable treatment of unequals).

In an earlier opportunistic survey of health care decision-makers carried out by us, respondents were asked how they would weight the same health gain to individuals of different gender, age, current health status and socioeconomic status (SES) (Mooney et al. 1995). Respondents generally were prepared to express a greater preference for a health gain in one context over the same health gain in another. A majority of respondents attached differences in weight (expressed ordinally) to health gains to individuals of different ages (with more favouring the young) and current health status (with more favouring those in poorer current health state). For the distribution of health gains across gender and SES, a majority of respondents were not prepared to weight health gains to one group differently from health gains to another. Perhaps unsurprisingly, but nevertheless importantly, an overwhelming number of the respondents who did express a preference for distribution across SES weighted health gains to those in lower SES higher than health gains to those in higher SES.

The potential application of the weights to a policy context was shown in another study, where distributive weights in relation to Aboriginality were applied to the NSW RAF (see Mooney et al. 1995; Mooney & Jan 1997). This type of weighting for Aboriginality has since been incorporated into the proposed RDF, which will supersede RAF (NSW Health Department 1996).

We have more recently attempted to obtain cardinal weights for health gains for different groups in the community, including indigenous peoples. We have conducted two surveys of groups of health service decision-makers (but not yet with community groups). While little emphasis should be placed on the results of these preliminary studies, the weights on health gains to Aboriginal people emerged as around 1.5–2. The alternative way forward, which would avoid the problems of differing conceptions of health gain, would be to focus community surveys on eliciting preferences over procedures rather than outcomes. In the context of procedural justice, what is important is that the mechanisms by which health care resources are distributed be seen as fair.

There is an even bigger and blacker hole with respect to relevant weights when it comes to combining procedural justice and vertical equity. This is an important economic aspect of policy on resource allocation. One key contender here is Broome's concept of 'claims' (Broome 1989):

> To take account of fairness we must start by dividing the reasons why a person should get a good into two classes: 'claims' and other reasons. By a claim to the good I mean a duty owed to the candidate herself that she should have it . . . Claims . . . are the object of fairness.

There are clear parallels between claims and rights; indeed, according to some definitions, claims are viewed as one form of rights (the others relating to powers, liberties and immunities; e.g. Almond 1991: 262). The points we would want to make with respect to our use of claims that may distinguish it from rights or at least make claims a more specific subset of rights are:

- There are no absolute claims; claims are relative.
- The bearer of the duty with respect to claims is society or the community.
- Claims exist whether or not the persons who are the claim-holders acknowledge them or not.
- Claims arise and gain strength from a more communitarian view

of individuals than is the case with the individualism often associated with rights.

This concept of claims is thus dependent on there being a society within which there is arbitration over claims. Such claims are not absolute. The community has to decide the strengths of different claims, as not all claims will be equal—nor, given scarcity of resources, will all claims be able to be met. It is here that we see the most promise for future work on vertical equity, particularly as it relates to Aboriginal health.

It is possible to cut through the complexities and come up with some actual numbers, as for example McDermott and Beaver (1996) have done. They show that while an allocation of health care expenditure based on equal expenditure per capita gives a figure of $700, if adjustments are made in various ways to move to, for example, equal use for equal need, spending in Aboriginal communities in central Australia would be over $3000 per capita. They do not, however, get into the weighting of health gains for the purposes of vertical equity. Had they done so, the latter number would have been yet higher for allocations to indigenous people. A weight to indigenous health gains of 2 would have the same impact on their dollar numbers: that is, increasing the $3000 figure to $6000.

There is certainly an argument that we as economists do want to advance for debating what principles of equity and what weights to use in examining equity of resource allocation in this context. Too much of the debate to date has centred on assessment of need, responsibilities and adequacy of resources. This needs to be put in a more economic framework by establishing more clearly that the key issue here is one of equity. That needs to be said loud and clear. Responsibilities for paying are secondary, well behind the question of the collective responsibility of this nation to pay equitably for indigenous health services. Resources for indigenous health just as resources for non-indigenous health will never be 'adequate', so questions of adequacy are red herrings.

Determining how to fund[2]

Turning to the question of how to fund Aboriginal health care, Tsey and Scrimgeour (1996) emphasise that 'there is a potential conflict of interests associated with the dual roles of the States/Territories as both funders as well as providers to Aboriginal people'. They further stress the problems created by the fact that 'neither the Commonwealth government, nor the State and Territory governments, accepts ultimate responsibility for Aboriginal health care'. This has prompted us to argue for a funding agency that would be above the hubbub of Commonwealth/states bickering, which would be permanent and would consequently have a greater ability to deal with problems that cannot be satisfactorily resolved in any time period short of a generation.

It is not always appreciated that the concept of a budget embraces the idea of a financial plan. Multiple budgets almost certainly mean multiple plans and multiple plans, almost certainly mean multiple opportunities for problems. In Aboriginal health care such budgetary problems are inevitably greater than in the case of mainstream services alone. Tsey and Scrimgeour (1996) call for a single funder, which we believe is ideal. Yet in the unfortunately highly charged political atmosphere that surrounds Aboriginal health care it is difficult to believe that such single funding will happen, at least for some time. Tsey and Scrimgeour suggest that the Commonwealth would be the party responsible for all funding under their model which, if it were to be achieved, 'would require the cooperation of the states and Territories'. These authors are right to suggest thereafter that there would be resistance from the states and territories, under the banner of 'states' rights', to this loss of power. While one can only agree that 'the Aboriginal health situation should be of sufficient concern that such considerations could ... be overridden', history would seem to suggest that, such are the tensions between Commonwealth and states/territories, this sense is unlikely to prevail.

There does not, however, seem to be a requirement to have a single funder and if the certain battles that would occur on that front can be avoided then they should be avoided. What is wanted, perhaps as an interim measure (but once in place that interim period might be a long time), is that whatever monies are available from whatever sources and from whatever funders are able to be used without concern for cost-shifting, and that they are all pooled in a single bucket even if the sources of funds are many. Pooling together can result in pulling together.

Left at that, there would be a risk with multiple funders that more money from A would result in B taking the opportunity to pull money out. A, next time around, would be wary of adding funds because A would then believe that the extra monies would not get to Aboriginal health care per se but would represent a transfer to B. (This is an issue identified by Bartlett & Legge 1994.) The stage would be set for yet another round of accusations, states' rights fights and, perhaps worst of all, that added perception of the Australian people that the 'problems' of Aboriginal health care are 'intractable'. In the meantime, the amount of money 'in the bucket' would not grow. What we suggest is that this might best be solved through a formula directly relating the various responsibilities and the extent of them to dollars. We need an agency in indigenous health care that would, together with the Commonwealth and states, first set out what proportion of any funding for Aboriginal health care is the responsibility of the Commonwealth and what proportion the responsibility of the state(s) (which could conceivably vary from state or territory to state or territory).

The second task of such an agency, which would be independent of the political parties in power in Canberra or in the states, would be to decide on the relevant level of expenditure to be spent on indigenous health. Such a body would have the power to determine both the total spending and the proportional split between the Commonwealth and the states. As the former might well change over time (and perhaps the latter would need to be reviewed from time to time), such a body would need to be permanent. It might also take on the role of monitoring both the inputs to this process and the outcomes. Almost inevitably it would at the same time perform the desirable role of informing the Australian public about Aboriginal health and about the funding and organisation of Aboriginal health care.

It is clear that such an agency would need all-party support to get established in the first place: indigenous health is too important to be left to the political expediencies that arise with governments having a maximum of three years' tenure. Tackling the issues of Aboriginal health in anything like a satisfactory way will take at least a generation. The policies here need much greater continuity, longevity, constancy and commitment than the standard electoral cycle allows. Through such an agency and in these ways the key problems in Aboriginal health care funding—the amount to be spent and the split between the different levels of government—would be overcome.

Other policy issues

There are clearly many other issues in the economics of Aboriginal health care policy that merit examination. Here we briefly touch on just a few.

Currently Aboriginal people can access both AMSs and mainstream services if these are available to them. Access to Medicare mainstream services is the right of all Australians, yet there are clearly difficulties with respect to access for many Aboriginal people. These stem in part from the fact that to exercise the right one must have a Medicare card, and that right can normally only be exercised to a medical practitioner.

It is ironic that many of these access problems stem from a

desire—justifiable, of course, in its own terms—to allow only eligible persons to use Medicare services. This means that potential users normally must carry a Medicare card. Medicare numbers are commonly held only by medical practitioners rather than by organisations such as AMSs. If the organisation could hold the information necessary for the patients to get access, many of the difficulties for Aboriginal people would disappear.

There is growing (if largely anecdotal) evidence that, with respect to the efficient use of resources for Aboriginal health services, community control is the way to go. It seems self-evident that if services are driven by the preferences of the Aboriginal community and Aboriginal people can exercise control over how they are run, they are more likely to be designed in such a way that they will be used. As in any community, whether indigenous or non-indigenous, the question thereafter of efficient use of services is one that will require a major input from epidemiologists and others. Respect for community control and community preferences does not mean leaving Aboriginal communities to make perhaps ill-informed choices. As indicated previously in the quote from Anderson and Sanders (1996: 240), 'Aboriginal people's efforts need to be supported by appropriate resources and expertise'. What is needed is yet more documented evidence to support the position of community control (backed by adequate expertise), as the 'self-evident' nature of this seems not to be carrying the weight with policy-makers that in our view it ought to carry.

Within the confines of formal health services (i.e. not getting into activities such as water and housing), the role of public health measures in Aboriginal health merits particularly detailed consideration, and this for two reasons: first, the health problems of indigenous people seem more effectively addressed through public health, lifestyle interventions; second, respecting the preferences of indigenous communities in devising public health interventions may involve more culturally delicate value questions than in more individually orientated health measures. As Mann (1997: 11) has remarked in a wider context: 'The language of biomedicine is cumbersome and ultimately perhaps of little usefulness in exploring the impacts of violations of dignity on physical, mental and social wellbeing'. In intervening with public health measures there is a need to ensure that they do not add to the dignity-impugning environment in which so many indigenous people live. These are matters that merit much more comprehensive review and expertise well beyond economics than can be incorporated in this chapter.

There are good and bad health care practices in Aboriginal communities. There are efficient and inefficient ways of organising services, just as there are in *any* communities. The good practices in Aboriginal communities need to be documented better and such information disseminated across different communities. Aboriginal communities and Aboriginal people are remarkably heterogeneous, but without expecting a single, common, uniquely best way of delivering services to Aboriginal people, there is scope for more sharing of experiences. There have been initiatives from the National Health and Medical Research Council (NHMRC) in recent years to try to foster good practice in indigenous health and to disseminate knowledge of such good practices to Aboriginal communities more widely. This type of program has been woefully underfunded.

More generally there is the question of how best to mount new research in Aboriginal health and health care. One can sympathise greatly with indigenous people who claim that they are the most researched people in Australia but who, when they then look at the state of the health of their people, wonder just what good has emerged from all of that research effort. It seems plain that the research on Aboriginal health needs to have two important components to it which have been played down or have even been missing in the past: it must reflect the preferences of Aboriginal people; and it must be more oriented to service delivery than previously. We do not need much more information on the epidemiology of indigenous health—it is not that enough is enough. It is that more information of this nature carries too high an opportunity cost in terms of forgone research opportunities and hence benefits on other aspects of indigenous health. We need some well-thought-out and well-worked-out policies for delivering services efficiently to Aboriginal people that are culturally appropriate. The paucity of investment of funding organisations such as NHMRC on health services research and in particular economic evaluation studies in Aboriginal health amounts to a dereliction of duty on the part of these organisations, if their intention through their funded activities (and one assumes that it must be) is to assist in maximising the health of the population.

Conclusions

There are signs of some hope, we believe, that Aboriginal health care policy is on a better footing than it has been before. There is today a greater recognition of the need to have such policy driven by Aboriginal preferences, and this is reflected in the greater acceptance of community-controlled health services. The movement of all health care matters at a Commonwealth level relating to indigenous health to the Department of Health and Family Services has, as Anderson and Sanders (1996) state, 'allowed long standing tensions in the institutional arrangements of Aboriginal health to be temporarily relieved'.

There is scope for much further movement. There remain very considerable problems in funding, with respect to both the level of funding and the arrangements for funding between the Commonwealth and the states and territories.

There is a need for better and more research, but of a different type. The focus now must be on what to do and not on what the problem is. Research, like policy, needs to be driven by indigenous people. Where are they in national research councils? (It is striking that the very first time an Aborigine addressed the Council of the NHMRC was in 1995.) Where is the Aboriginal Health Research Fund?

In the end, however, the problems that beset Aboriginal and Torres Strait Islander peoples' health stem not directly from economics or lack of funding or inefficient use of resources. Much of indigenous health and health care policy cannot be understood without an understanding of Australian history and relations between black and white. Many of the health problems that indigenous people face today stem from that historical legacy—a legacy that includes the stolen generation and the stealing of land from the Aborigines. There have been recent opportunities to set these issues to rights and with that to make major advances in removing some of the elements underlying the ill-health of generations of Aborigines. They have not been taken and, at the time of going to press (1998), there are few signs that they will be taken.

We have here discussed mainly issues related to health care and not covered other factors affecting indigenous health. As economists we do not feel fully competent to do so. As economists, however, we can still note that there is a strong relationship between health status and self-respect. It is not just a matter of Aborigines having access to more and better health care or more and better housing and water. That certainly is necessary, and is theirs by rights in any case. Economics can contribute to that process. Beyond that, recognition is needed of the collective responsibility of Australians to acknowledge the legitimate claims of indigenous peoples to self-respect.

Acknowledgements

We are grateful to Robyn McDermott for various contributions to the thinking underlying some aspects of this chapter and to Charles Kerr, Steve Leeder and David Scrimgeour for helpful comments on an earlier draft. We would also acknowledge with gratitude financial support for our work on Aboriginal health from OATSIHS and the NSW Health Department. Any remaining errors are the responsibility of the authors alone.

Notes

Chapter 2   The Australian health care system

1. For a comprehensive account of the Australian health care system, see Gardner (1997); AIHW (1996); and Palmer & Short (1994). For a detailed analysis of the history and politics of the Australian health system, see Gardner (1995); Scotton & MacDonald (1993); Gillespie (1991); and Sax (1984).
2. For a separation of publicly financed health care systems into generalised models, see OECD (1992).
3. The Department of Health and Family Services has estimated that cost-shifting has added several hundred million dollars to Commonwealth outlays in recent years (NCoA 1996).
4. For an overview of the coordinated care trials, see Healthcover (1995).
5. The main reasons for declining membership are first, rising premiums, and second, growing gaps in coverage as patients find themselves meeting rising out-of-pocket costs when they receive hospital treatment. As the majority of those who drop out are the young and healthy, the risk profile of existing members rises, which in turn causes premiums to rise. Rising premiums then perpetuate the 'vicious circle' of more people dropping out, which raises the risk profile. The consequences of *adverse selection* could reach a critical level, triggering an avalanche of people dropping out and joining the free public system, thereby undermining the entire private sector provision. For an extensive canvassing of the factors behind declining membership and rising premiums, see Industry Commission (1997).

Chapter 3   Health expenditure

1. Some statistics are beginning to emerge on time spent on hospital waiting lists in Australia. In 1995 it was found that the clearance time (the time required to remove all patients from waiting lists if clearance rates remained constant and patients could be treated at any hospital) for category 1 patients (those for whom admission is desirable within 30 days) was 0.6 months, with 27 per cent of patients waiting over 30 days as at the census date; for category 2 patients (no desirable time set for admission) the clearance time was 3.5 months, with 11 per cent of patients waiting over 12 months as at the census date (AIHW 1996: 160–2). However, these data have emerged only recently, and it will be some time before any trends in hospital waiting times can be discerned.

2. Total expenditure encompasses both public and private expenditures and includes capital expenditure.

3. An exception to this is a recent study by Blomqvist and Carter (1997), which found an income elasticity of demand slightly less than unity, and a time trend in the growth of per-capita health expenditure of roughly 2 per cent per annum, which was independent of income. This time trend may reflect technological change or other supply-side factors.

4. Studies using microlevel data (the individual, the family unit) have tended to find only weak associations between income and health care utilisation, suggesting that income is not an important determinant of health care expenditure (Grossman 1972; Newhouse & Phelps 1976; Wagstaff 1986). See Culyer (1988) for further discussion and a possible explanation of these apparently conflicting results.

5. Luxembourg was excluded from this analysis because the OECD has reported that recent revisions to the GDP estimates have resulted in a significant reduction in relative health expenditure.

6. In this simple bivariate model, the best fit was obtained using a log-linear formulation (heteroskedastic-consistent *t*-statistics as in White [1980] are shown in parentheses):

$$\text{Ln(TH/GDP)} = -4.5067 + 0.6764 \, \text{Ln(GDP per capita)}$$
$$(-5.32) \qquad (7.63)$$

   where TH is total health expenditure.

7. It is often useful to compute OECD averages excluding the USA because of the sheer size of the US economy within the OECD. In 1994 it had over one-quarter of the total population of the OECD countries, and accounted for nearly 38 per cent of total GDP and 52 per cent of total health expenditures in these countries.

8. Luxembourg actually recorded 98.8 per cent public financing, but due to recent revisions in statistics this figure may be subject to change (see note 3 above).

9. One of the more publicised attempts to prioritise the services to be included in a public insurance program was that by the US state of Oregon in relation to its Medicaid program (a program catering for the poor). For discussions of the Oregon approach, see Kaplan (1995) and Sloan and Conover (1995). An evaluation of the original Oregon proposal has been provided by the Office of Technology Assessment (1992). Some recent books dealing with methodological developments in the economic evaluation of health care include Sloan (1995) and Gold et al. (1996).

10. A similar result arises in an extension of the model reported earlier in this chapter. If the publicly financed share in total health expenditure is included in that model, a statistically significant negative relationship between the size of the health sector and the publicly financed share emerges (heteroskedastic-consistent t-statistics as in White [1980] are shown in parentheses):

$$\text{Ln(TH/GDP)} = -2.7454 + 0.75582\,\text{Ln(GDP per capita)} - 0.58837\,\text{Ln(PH/TH)}$$
$$(-3.66)\quad\quad(10.58)\quad\quad\quad\quad\quad\quad(-7.88)$$

where PH is publicly financed health expenditure (adjusted R-squared = 0.78).

To illustrate, if the Australian averages are used as the baseline in this model (per-capita GDP US$17 226.7 and ratio of publicly financed to total health expenditure 69.5 per cent), a 1.0 percentage point rise in the publicly financed share (to 70.5 per cent) reduces the predicted size of the health sector by 0.14 percentage points (from 8.54 per cent to 8.4 per cent of GDP). With this expanded model, the predicted size of the health sector in Australia is the same as its actual size (8.5 per cent of GDP), and the same is true of the USA (13.8 per cent). The actual size of the health sector in Japan (6.4 per cent) continues to be well below the predicted size (8.8 per cent).

11. A recent study (Cutler & Gruber 1996) considered the issue of crowding out in the context of Medicaid in the USA (a publicly funded health insurance program catering primarily for low-income persons). In the late 1980s and early 1990s eligibility requirements were relaxed, increasing the number of potential beneficiaries under the program. The authors found significant but less than complete crowding out, with 50 per cent of the increase in Medicaid coverage associated with a reduction in private insurance coverage.

12. In the OECD data, financial year data for Australia are labelled by the first year. For example, data for 1965/66 are reported as data for 1965 (see AIHW 1994, table 20).

13. A discussion of these intergovernmental aspects of health funding can be found in Butler (1991).

14. Not all 'public hospitals' are actually owned by the public sector in

Australia. For example, a number of large public hospitals are owned by the Catholic Church.

15. The Medicare Agreements are for a period of five years. The present Agreements expire at the end of June 1998.

16. A complete series on non-admitted patient services for every year from 1985/86 to 1993/94 is not available. The years included in Table 3.6 are the years for which data are available for both series. Note also that the data in Table 3.6 exclude medical services funded by the Department of Veterans' Affairs (DVA). In 1994/95 DVA funded 3.2 million non-specialist (GP) consultations, with expenditure on these consultations amounting to 3.4 per cent of total expenditure on Medicare-funded GP consultations in that year (Butler 1996, n.3, table 5.5).

17. & 18. Over the four years 1991/92–1994/95, the proportion of separations from private hospitals for which the patient was privately insured varied from 81.5 per cent to 82.9 per cent. Another factor contributing to the increasing separation rate from private hospitals has been a change in the composition of the insured population in favour of 'basic plus supplementary table' coverage and away from 'basic table only' coverage, with a consequent rise in demand by private patients for treatment in private hospitals rather than in public hospitals. The impact of these and other changes on private health insurance premiums has been analysed by the Industry Commission (1997, ch. 7).

Chapter 4   The doctor business

1. The history of Australian medical care organisation up to the 1980s has been comprehensively described (Pensabene 1980; Sax 1984; Gillespie 1991; Scotton & Macdonald 1993), but there is no single source for the diverse policy directions since the introduction of Medicare in 1984.

2. An Australian model incorporating arrangements of this kind is described in Chapter 12.

Chapter 8   Evaluation of health services

1. There are some problems with the criterion, in particular that it is not always decisive if the program alters the distribution of income. For a review of welfare criteria, see Mishan (1971).

2. The 'market failure' rationale for government intervention in the health sector is discussed more fully in Chapter 12.

3. For a fuller discussion of this issue in the context of public health and health promotion, see Chapter 12.

4. The difficulty of applying the marginal cost = marginal benefit rule

places greater emphasis on the identification of comparators (both current practice and project options). In practice, most health care organisations face rigidities in the free movement of resources (land, labour, capital etc.) and relatively fixed budgets. Under these circumstances opportunity costs are not measured by market prices for inputs, but by the value of the alternative health services or interventions that the organisation could produce (Richardson 1993). Prices that reflect opportunity cost are called 'shadow prices'. For a technical explanation of the concept of shadow prices, see Drèze and Stern in Layard and Glaister (1994). The use of shadow prices, reflecting opportunity costs, is what distinguishes economic appraisal from financial appraisal. For a fuller discussion of financial appraisal, its similarities and differences with economic appraisal in general, and cost–benefit analysis in particular, see Sugden and Williams (1978).

5. CBA provides an appropriate valuation of costs and benefits where market prices are distorted, do not reflect true individual valuations, or do not exist.

6. Refer to Chapter 12 for further information on PBMA and macroeconomic techniques developed for the planning and priority-setting context.

7. For further discussion of the PBAC process, see Chapter 6.

Chapter 9   Health insurance

1. In Australia there is an emphasis on all three types of pooling, whereas in countries with national health programs the emphasis is on the second and third. In the USA, the prime focus is on the first through private health insurance and the third through its Medicare and Medicaid programs.

2. This section draws heavily on the report of the Industry Commission inquiry into private health insurance (IC 1997), which I jointly directed as Commissioner.

3. 'Free' in the sense of not involving any additional payments (on top of tax and Medicare levy) for hospital care in the form of insurance contribution or out-of-pocket costs.

4. Note that this problem does not apply to universal national health insurance programs, in which the insured population is, by definition, the total population.

Chapter 10   The health care financing debate

1. The name 'Medicare' is used here broadly to include the entire health system and not simply the medical, hospital and funding arrangements introduced in 1994.

2. Chapters 2 and 3.
3. This presumes that, as in every Western country, there is no explicit or widespread private monopoly of key health services and that the best policy to offset concentrated provider power is to create a countervailing power on the demand side.

Chapter 11   Managed competition

1. These exceptions would continue basic features of present coverage arrangements.
2. Notably the Dutch 'basic package' and New Zealand 'core services', which were discussed in some detail in the Netherlands (1992: 80–95) and New Zealand (1991: 74–86).

Chapter 12   Public health

1. See Chapman and Leeder (1991) for an excellent description of the development of public health policy in Australia.
2. By this efficiency argument (as opposed to equity reasons for government involvement), market failure is a necessary condition for public provision, but not a sufficient one. It remains to be shown that the reality of public provision is better than the reality of a controlled market (i.e. whether 'government failure' is better than 'market failure').
3. This could be regarded as an extension of the economic concept of the caring externality and therefore incorporated within the market failure argument, as it suggests that one person's well-being is a function of another's health state (Labelle and Hurley 1991). To do so, would however, understate the importance of social connectedness in communitarian philosophy.
4. A macro cost-effectiveness index is calculated that incorporates the cost of interventions (less any cost offsets in current health expenditure) and reductions in disease burden.
5. While MEEM focuses on change in the burden of illness (rather than simply its size) and is in that sense a form of incremental analysis, the nature of the data sets and tasks for which it was designed (i.e. ranking large numbers of programs) makes any detailed marginal analysis difficult.

Chapter 13   Economic issues in Aboriginal health care

1. Part of this section is based on Mooney and Jan (1997).
2. This section is based on Mooney (1996).

References

Chapter 1   Health economics and health policy

Arrow, K.J. (1963) 'Uncertainty and the welfare economics of medical care', *American Economic Review* 53: 941–73.

Donaldson, C. & Gerard, K. (1993) *The Economics of Health Care Financing: The Visible Hand*, Macmillan, London.

Evans, R.G. (1981) 'Structure of the health care industry', in van der Gaag, J. and Perlman, M. (eds) *Health, Economics and Health Economics*, North Holland, Amsterdam.

Gaynor, M. & Vogt, W.B. (1997) 'What does economics have to say about health policy anyway? A comment and correction on Evans and Rice', *Journal of Health Politics, Policy and Law* 22, 2: 475–96.

Gillon, R. (1988) 'Ethics, economics and general practice', in Mooney, G. and McGuire, A. (eds) *Medical Ethics and Economics in Health Care*, Oxford University Press, Oxford.

Journal of Health Politics, Policy and Law (1977) Assessing markets; model and practice, 22, 2: 383–508. (This issue is devoted entirely to articles by proponents and opponents of the neoclassical model of health care markets.)

Nutbeam, D., Wiseman, M., Bauman, A., Harris, E. et al. (1993) *Goals and Targets for Australia's Health in the Year 2000 and Beyond*, AGPS, Canberra.

Pauly, M.V. (1986) 'Taxation, health insurance and the market failure in the medical economy', *Journal of Economic Literature* 24: 629–75.

Shiell, A. (1977) 'Health outcomes are about choices and values: an economic perspective on the health outcome movement', *Health Policy* 39, 1: 5–16.

Varian, H.R. (1984) *Microeconomic Analysis*, Norton, New York.

Weisbrod, B.A. (1978) 'Comment on M.V. Pauly', in Greenberg, W. (ed.) *Competition in the Health Care Sector*, Proceedings of a conference, Bureau of Economics, Federal Trade Commission, Aspen Systems, Germanstown.

Chapter 2   The Australian health care system

Armitage, M. (1994) *Proposed Structure for the Management of the State Health System*, Minister's Statement, South Australian Parliament, Adelaide.

Australian Institute of Health and Welfare (AIHW) (1996) *Australia's Health 1996*, AIHW, Canberra.

——(1997) *Health Expenditure Bulletin no. 13*, AIHW, Canberra.

Commonwealth Department of Health and Family Services (CDHFS) (1996a) *Annual Report 1995–96*, AGPS, Canberra.

——(1996b) *Hospital Admission Trends*, unpublished departmental paper.

Commonwealth of Australia (1997) *Report on Government Service Provision*, Steering Committee for the Review of Commonwealth/State Service Provision, Melbourne.

Council of Australian Governments (COAG) (1995) *Meeting (11 April 1995): Communiqué*, COAG Taskforce on Health and Community Services, Commonwealth Department of Health and Community Services, Canberra.

——(1996) *Meeting, (14 June 1996): Communiqué*, COAG Taskforce on Health and Community Services, CDHCS, Canberra.

Deeble, J.S. (1982) 'Unscrambling the omelette: public and private health care financing Australia', in McLachlan, G. & Maynard, A. (eds) *The Public/Private Mix for Health*, Nuffield Provincial Hospital Trust, London.

Gardner, H. (ed.) (1995) *The Politics of Health: The Australian Experience*, 2nd edn, Churchill Livingstone, Melbourne.

Gardner, H. (ed.) (1997) *Health Policy in Australia*, Oxford University Press, Melbourne.

Gillespie, J.A. (1991) *The Price of Health: Australian Governments and Medical Politics 1910–1960*, Cambridge University Press, Cambridge.

Healthcover (1995) Editorial, *Healthcover*, 5, 3: 10–12.

——(1997) Editorial, *Healthcover*, 7, 4: 1–2.

Health Insurance Commission (HIC) (1995) *Annual Report 1994–95*, HIC, Canberra.

——(1996) *Annual Report 1995–96*, HIC, Canberra.

——(1997) *Mediguide: Understanding Medicare*, 5th edn, HIC, Canberra.

Industry Commission (1997) *Private Health Insurance*, AGPS, Canberra.

National Commission of Audit (NCoA) (1996) *National Commission of*

Audit—June 1996: Report to the Commonwealth Government, AGPS, Canberra.

National Health Strategy (NHS) (1991) *The Australian Health Jigsaw: Integration of Health Care Delivery*, Issue Paper no. 1, National Health Strategy, AGPS, Canberra.

——(1992) *Enough to Make You Sick: How Income and Environment Affect Health*, Research Paper no. 1, National Health Strategy, AGPS, Canberra.

OECD (1992) *The Reform of Health Care: A Comparative Analysis of Seven OECD Countries*, OECD, Paris.

——(1995) *New Directions in Health Care Policy*, OECD, Paris.

——(1997) *OECD Health Data 97: Software for the Comparative Analysis of 29 Health Systems*, OECD, Paris.

Palmer, G.R. & Short, S.D. (1994) *Health Care and Public Policy: An Australian Analysis*, 2nd edn, Macmillan, Melbourne.

Paterson, J. (1996) *National Healthcare Reform: The Last Picture Show*, Department of Human Services, Government of Victoria, Melbourne.

Private Health Insurance Administration Council (PHIAC) (1993) *Annual Report 1992–93*, AGPS, Canberra.

——(1998) *Coverage and Basic Hospital Insurance Tables—Statistics (December 1997)*, PHIAC, Canberra.

Rowland, D., Lyons, B., Salganicoff, A. & Long, P. (1994) 'A profile of the uninsured of America', *Health Affairs* 13, 2: 283–7.

Saltman, R.B. and Otter, C.V. (1992) *Planned Markets and Public Competition: Strategic Reform in Northern European Health Systems*, Oxford University Press, London.

Sax, S. (1984) *A Strife of Interests: Politics and Policies in Australian Health Services*, Allen & Unwin, Sydney.

Scotton, R.B. & MacDonald, C.R. (1993) *The Making of Medibank*, Australian Studies in Health Administration no. 76, School of Health Services Management, University of New South Wales, Sydney.

Senate Select Committee on Health Legislation and Health Insurance (1990) *What Price Care? Hospital Costs and Health Insurance*, Parliament of the Commonwealth of Australia, Canberra.

South Australian Health Commission (SAHC) (1994) *Contestability in South Australian Health Commission Funded Hospitals and Health Services*, SAHC, Adelaide.

van de Ven, W.P.M.M. (1996) 'Market-orientated health care reforms: trends and future options', *Social, Science and Medicine*, 43, 5: 655–66.

Western Australia Department of Health (WADH) (1995) *Improving Health: Directions for Health Care in Western Australia*, WADH, Perth.

Chapter 3   Health expenditure

Australian Institute of Health (AIH) (1988) *Australian Health Expenditure 1970–71 to 1984–85*, AGPS, Canberra.

Australian Institute of Health and Welfare (AIHW) (1992) *Health Expenditure Bulletin no. 7*, July, AIHW, Canberra.

——(1993) *Health Expenditure Bulletin no. 8*, April, AIHW, Canberra.

——(1994) *Health Expenditure Bulletin no. 10*, December, AIHW, Canberra.

——(1995) *Health Expenditure Bulletin no. 11*, October, AIHW, Canberra.

——(1996) *Australia's Health 1996*, AIHW, Canberra.

——(1997a) *Health Expenditure Bulletin no. 13*, July, AIHW, Canberra.

——(1997b) *Australian Hospital Statistics 1995–96*, Health Services Series no. 10, AIHW, Canberra.

Baumol, W.J. (1967) 'Macroeconomics of unbalanced growth', *American Economic Review*, 57: 415–26.

Baumol, W.J. & Blinder, A.S. (1985) *Economics: Principles and Policy*, 3rd edn, Harcourt Brace Jovanovich, New York.

Blomqvist, G. & Carter, R.A.L. (1997) 'Is health care really a luxury?', *Journal of Health Economics* 16: 207–29.

Butler, J.R.G. (1991) 'Health care', in B. Galligan, O. Hughes & C. Walsh (eds) *Intergovernmental Relations and Public Policy*, Allen & Unwin, Sydney, pp 163–87.

——(1996) 'The financing of general practice', in Commonwealth Department of Health and Family Services, *General Practice in Australia: 1996*, General Practice Branch, CDHFS, Canberra, pp 135–68.

Butler, J.R.G. & Smith, J. (1992) 'Tax expenditures on health in Australia: 1960–61 to 1988–89', *Australian Economic Review* 3rd quarter: 43–58.

Commonwealth Department of Health (1981) *Australian Health Expenditure 1974–75 to 1978–79: An Analysis*, Commonwealth Department of Health, Canberra.

Commonwealth Department of Health and Family Services (CDHFS) (1997) *Medicare Statistics: 1984/85 to June Quarter 1997*, Medicare Benefits Branch, CDHFS, Canberra.

Commonwealth of Australia (1997) *Federal Financial Relations 1997–98*, Budget Paper no. 3, AGPS, Canberra.

Culyer, A.J. (1988) *Health Expenditures in Canada: Myth and Reality; Past and Future*, Canadian Tax Paper no. 82, Canadian Tax Foundation, Toronto.

Cutler, D.M. & Gruber, J. (1996) 'Does public insurance crowd out private insurance?', *Quarterly Journal of Economics* 111(2): 391–430.

Deeble, J.S. (1970) *Health Expenditures in Australia 1960–61 to 1966–67*, unpublished PhD thesis, University of Melbourne.

Fuchs, V. (1968) *The Service Economy*, Columbia University Press, New York.

Gerdtham, U.G., Søgaard, J., Jönsson, B. & Andersson, F. (1991) 'A pooled cross-section analysis of the health care expenditure of the OECD countries', in H.E. Frech III & P. Zweifel (eds) *Health Economics Worldwide*, Kluwer, Dordrecht, pp 287–310.

Gerdtham, U.G., Søgaard, J., Andersson, F. & Jönsson, B. (1992) 'An econometric analysis of health care expenditure: a cross-section study of OECD countries', *Journal of Health Economics* 11: 63–84.

Gold, M.R., Siegel, J.E., Russell, L.B. & Weinstein, M.C. (eds) (1996) *Cost-Effectiveness in Health and Medicine*, Oxford University Press, New York.

Grossman, M. (1972) *The Demand for Health: A Theoretical and Empirical Investigation*, NBER, New York.

Haig, B.D. (1975) 'An analysis of changes in the distribution of employment between the manufacturing and service industries 1960–1970', *Review of Economics and Statistics*, 57: 34–42.

Industry Commission (1997) *Private Health Insurance*, Report no. 57, Industry Commission, Canberra.

Kaplan, R.M. (1995) 'Utility assessment for estimating quality-adjusted life years', in F.A. Sloan (ed.) *Valuing Health Care: Costs, Benefits and Effectiveness of Pharmaceuticals and Other Medical Technologies*, Cambridge University Press, Cambridge, pp 31–60.

Leu, R.E. (1986) 'The public-private mix and international health care costs', in A.J. Culyer & B. Jønsson (eds) *Public and Private Health Services*, Blackwell, Oxford, pp 41–63.

Newhouse, J.P. (1977) 'Medical care expenditure: a cross-national survey', *Journal of Human Resources* 12: 115–25.

——(1987) 'Cross national differences in health spending: what do they mean?', *Journal of Health Economics*, 6: 159–62.

Newhouse, J.P. & Phelps, C.E. (1976) 'New estimates of price and income elasticities for medical care services', in R. Rosett (ed.) *The Role of Health Insurance in the Health Services Sector*, Neal Watson, New York.

Office of Technology Assessment (1992) Evaluation of the Medicaid Proposal, OTA-H-531, US Congress, Washington DC.

Organisation for Economic Cooperation and Development (OECD) (1987) *Financing and Delivering Health Care: A Comparative Analysis of OECD Countries*, OECD Social Policy Studies no. 4, OECD, Paris.

——(1996) *OECD Health Data 1996*, OECD/CREDES, Paris.

Private Health Insurance Administration Council (PHIAC) (1996) *Operations of the Registered Health Benefits Organisations, Annual Report 1995–96*, PHIAC, Canberra.

——(1997) *Quarterly Statistics, June 1997*, PHIAC, Canberra.

Sloan, F.A. (ed.) (1995) *Valuing Health Care: Costs, Benefits and Effectiveness of Pharmaceuticals and Other Medical Technologies*, Cambridge University Press, Cambridge.

Sloan, F.A. & Conover, C.J. (1995) 'The use of cost-effectiveness/

cost-benefit analysis in actual decision-making: current status and prospects', in F.A. Sloan (ed.) *Valuing Health Care: Costs, Benefits and Effectiveness of Pharmaceuticals and Other Medical Technologies*, Cambridge University Press, Cambridge, pp 207–32.

Wagstaff, A. (1986) 'The demand for health: some new empirical evidence', *Journal of Health Economics* 5: 195–233.

Weisbrod, B.A. (1991) 'The health care quadrilemma: an essay on technological change, insurance, quality of care, and cost containment', *Journal of Economic Literature* 29(2): 523–52.

White, H. (1980) 'A heteroskedasticity-consistent covariance matrix estimator and a direct test for heteroskedasticity', *Econometrica* 48: 817–38.

Wyke, A. (1997) *21st-Century Miracle Medicine: RoboSurgery, Wonder Cures, and the Quest for Immortality*, Plenum Press, New York.

Chapter 4   The doctor business

Arrow, K.J. (1963) 'Uncertainty and the welfare economics of medical care', *American Economic Review*, 53: 941–73.

Australian Bureau of Statistics (ABS) (1997) *Private Medical Practice Industry: Australia, 1994-95*, Catalogue no. 8685.0, ABS, Canberra.

Australian Institute of Health and Welfare (AIHW) (1991) *Health Workforce Information Bulletin no. 28: Immigration of Health Professionals to Australia, 1984–85 to 1989–90*, AGPS, Canberra.

——(1992) *Australia's Health 1992*, AGPS, Canberra.

——(1996) *Australia's Health 1996*, AGPS, Canberra.

——(1997a) *Health Expenditure Bulletin*, no. 13, July, AGPS, Canberra.

——(1997b) *Medical Labour Force 1995*, National Health Labour Series, no. 10, Canberra Force, AGPS, Canberra.

Australian Medical Workforce Advisory Committee (AMWAC)/Australian Institute of Health (1996a) *Australian Medical Workforce Benchmarks*, Report no. 1996.1, prepared for the Committee by the Australian Institute of Health and Welfare, Canberra.

——(1996b) *Female Participation in the Australian Medical Workforce*, AMWAC Report no. 1996.7, Canberra.

Barer, M., Nicoll, M., Diesendorf, M. & Harvey, R. (1990) *Australian Private Medical Care, Costs and Use, 1976 to 1986*, AGPS for Australian Institute of Health, Canberra.

Beck, R.G. & Horne, J.M. (1980) 'Utilization of publicly insured health services in Saskatchewan before, during and after co-payment', *Medical Care* 18: 787–806.

Birrell, B. (1995) 'Immigration and the surplus of doctors in Australia', *People and Place* 3, 3: 23–32.

——(1996) 'Medical manpower: the continuing crisis', *People and Place* 4, 3: 37–46.

——(1997) 'Implications of control on access to Medicare billing for GPs', *People and Place* 5, 1: 67–77.

Committee on Medical Schools (Chair, P. Karmel) (1973) *Expansion of Medical Education*, Report of the Committee on Medical Schools to the Australian Universities Commission, AGPS, Canberra.

Commonwealth Department of Health and Family Services (CDHFS) (1996) *General Practice in Australia: 1996*, General Practice Branch, Canberra.

——(1997a) *Medicare Statistics: 1984/85 to June Quarter 1997*, Canberra.

——(1997b) *Facts Sheet: Budget 96–97*, Canberra.

Deeble, J. (1978) *Health Expenditure in Australia 1960–61 to 1975–76*, Australian National University, Health Research Project, Research Project no. 1, Canberra.

——(1991) *Medical Services through Medicare*, National Health Strategy, Background Paper no. 2.

Douglas, R.M., Dickinson, J., Rosenman, S. & Milne, H. (1991) *Too Many or Too Few?* Medical Workforce and General Practice in Australia, NCEPH Discussion Paper no. 5, Australian National University, Canberra.

Evans, R.G. (1984) *Strained Mercy: The Economics of Canadian Health Care*, Butterworths, Toronto.

Feldman, R. & Morrisey, M.A. (1990) 'Health economics: a report on the field', *Journal of Health Politics, Policy and Law* 15, 3: 627–46.

Feldstein, M. (1973) 'The welfare loss of excess health insurance', *Journal of Political Economy* 81: 251–80.

General Practice Consultative Committee (1992) *The Future of General Practice: A Strategy for the Nineties and Beyond*, mimeo, AMA/DHHCS/RACGP.

Gillespie, J.A. (1991) *The Price of Health: Australian Governments and Medical Politics 1910–1960*, Cambridge University Press, Cambridge.

Henke, K-D., Murray, M.A. & Ade, C. (1994) 'Global budgeting in Germany: lessons for the United States', *Health Affairs* 13, 4: 7–21.

Hurst, J.W. (1991) 'Reforming health care in seven European countries', *Health Affairs* 10, 3: 7–21.

Lewis, D.E. (1992) 'Rectifying imbalances in the geographical distribution of doctors', in C. Selby Smith (ed.) *Economics and Health 1991*, Proceedings of the 13th Australian Conference of Health Economists, Monash University, Melbourne.

National Health Strategy (1992) *The Future of General Practice*, Issues Paper no. 3, Canberra.

Newhouse, J.P. & Health Insurance Experiment Group (1993) *Free For All?*

Lessons from the Rand Health Insurance Experiment, Harvard University Press, Cambridge, MA.

Palmer, G.R. & Short, S.D. (1994) *Health Care and Public Policy: An Australian Analysis*, 2nd edn, Macmillan, Melbourne.

Paterson, J. (1995) 'A new look at medical workforce strategy', *Australian Health Review* 17: 5–42.

Pensabene, T.S. (1980) *The Rise of the Medical Practitioner in Victoria*, Health Research Project, Research Monograph 2, Australian National University, Canberra.

Phelps, C.E. (1992) *Health Economics*, Harper Collins, New York.

Reinhardt, U.E. (1991) 'Health manpower forecasting: the case of physician supply', in E. Ginzberg (ed.) *Health Services Research: Key to Health Policy*, Harvard University Press, Cambridge, MA.

Richardson, J. (1991) *The Effects of Consumer Co-payments on Medical Care*, National Health Strategy, Background Paper no. 5.

Sax, S. (1984) *A Strife of Interests: Politics and Policies in Australian Health Services*, Allen & Unwin, Sydney.

Scotton, R.B. (1974) *Medical Care in Australia: An Economic Diagnosis*, Sun Books, Melbourne.

——(1980) 'Medical manpower: some policy issues', in M. Tatchell (ed.) *Economics and Health*, Proceedings, First Australian Conference of Health Economists, Health Research Project, Australian National University, Canberra.

——(1984) 'Medical Manpower', in M. Tatchell (ed.) *Perspectives on Health Policy*, Public Affairs Committee and Health Economics Research Unit, Australian National University, Canberra.

Scotton, R.B. & Macdonald, C.R. (1993) *The Making of Medibank*, Australian Studies in Health Service Administration, no. 76, School of Health Services Management, University of New South Wales, Sydney.

Street, A. & Jackson, T. (1993) 'Relating fees for medical services to their costs of production', in C. Selby Smith (ed.) *Economics and Health 1992*, Proceedings, 14th Australian Conference of Health Economists, Monash University, Melbourne.

Van de Ven, W.P.M.M., Schut, F.T. & Rutten, F.F.H. (1994) 'Forming and reforming the market for third-party purchasing of health care' (Editorial), *Social Science and Medicine* 39, 10: 1405–12.

Chapter 5   Economics of hospital care

Australian Institute of Health & Welfare (1997) 'Australian health services expenditure to 1995–96', *Health Expenditure Bulletin (AIHW)*, 13: 1–15.

Brooker, J. (1996) *An Evaluation of Casemix Funding in South Australia 1994–95*, Commonwealth Department of Health and Family Services, Casemix Development Program, Canberra.

Butler, J.R.G. (1993) *Economics and Health: 1993 Proceedings of the Fifteenth Australian Conference of Health Economists* in Selby-Smith, C. (ed.), Faculty of Business and Economics and National Centre for Health Program Evaluation, Canberra, 256–77.

Chandler, I.R., Fetter, R.B., et al. (1991) 'Cost accounting and budgeting', in R.B. Fetter (ed.). *DRGs: Their Design and Development*, Health Administration Press, Ann Arbor, MI: 91–120.

Commonwealth Department of Health and Human Services (1995) *Report on the development of AN-DRG (Version 3) cost weights*, AGPS, Canberra.

Duckett, S.J. (1988) 'Hospital financing reform: the first steps', *Australian Quarterly* 60, 4: 435–47.

——(1995) 'Hospital payment arrangements to encourage efficiency: the case of Victoria, Australia', *Health Policy* 34: 113–34.

——(1996) 'The new market in health care: prospects for managed care in Australia', *Australian Health Review* 19, 2: 7–21.

Duckett, S.J. & Jackson, T. (1993) 'Casemix classification for outpatient services based on episodes of case', *Medical Journal of Australia* 158: 489–92.

Evans, R.G. (1990) 'The dog in the night-time: medical practice variations and health policy', in T.F. Andersen & G. Mooney (eds) *The Challenges of Medical Practice Variations*, Macmillan, London: 117–52.

Fetter, R.B. (1991) 'Diagnosis related groups: Understanding hospital performance', *Interfaces*, 21: 6–26.

Health Solutions International (1997) *Victorian Acute Health Cost Weights Study 1996/97*. Final Report to Department of Human Services, Victoria, Health Solutions International, Melbourne.

Jackson, T. & Sevil, P. (1997) 'Problems in counting and paying for multi-disciplinary outpatient clinics', *Australian Health Review* 20, 3: 38–54.

Kewley, T.H. (1973) *Social Security in Australia: 1900–1972*, Sydney University Press, Sydney.

Lin, V. & Duckett, S.J. (1997) 'Structural interests and organisational dimensions of health system reform', in H. Gardner (ed.) *Health Policy in Australia*, Oxford University Press, Melbourne: 64–80.

MacIntyre C.R., Brooke, C.W. et al. (1997) 'Changes in bed resources and admission patterns in acute public hospitals in Victoria, 1987–1995', *Medical Journal of Australia* 167, 4: 186–9.

McGuire, T.E., Bender, J.A. et al. (1995) *Casemix episodic payment for private health insurance*, AGPS, Canberra.

Palmer, G., Aisbett, C. et al. (1986) *The Validity of Diagnosis Related Groups for Use in Victorian Public Hospitals*. Report to the Departments of Health and of Management and Budget, Victoria, School of Health Administration, University of New South Wales, Sydney.

Pearse, J. (1994) 'The Outcomes of the 1993 Medicare Agreements' in A. Harris (ed.) *Proceedings of the Sixteenth Australian Conference of Health Economists: Economics and Health*, vol. 78, Australian Studies in Health Service Administration, Canberra, 63–99.

Reid, B. (1992) *Measuring the Impact of Output-Based Payment of Hospitals on the Quality of Care*, Centre for Hospital Management and Information Systems, Sydney.

Renwick, M. & Sadkowsky, K. (1991) *Variations in Surgery Rates*, Australian Institute of Health: Health Services Series no. 2, AGPS, Canberra.

Robinson, R. (1996) 'The impact of the NHS reforms 1991–1995: A review of research evidence', *Journal of Public Health Medicine*, 18: 337–42.

Saltman, R.B. & Young, D.W. (1981) 'The hospital power equilibrium: an alternative view of the cost containment dilemma', *Journal of Health Politics Policy and Law* 6, 3: 391–418.

Scotton, R.B. & Macdonald, C.R. (1993) *The Making of Medibank*, School of Health Services Management, University of NSW, Sydney.

Scotton, R.B. & Owens, H.J. (1990) *Case Payment in Australian Hospitals: Issues and Options*, Public Sector Management Institute, Monash University, Melbourne.

Stoelwinder, J.U. & Abernethy, M.A. (1989) 'The design and implementation of a management information system for Australian public hospitals', *Health Services Management Research* 2, 3: 176–90.

Wilson, R., Runciman, W. et al. (1995) 'The quality in Australian health care study', *Medical Journal of Australia* 163, 6 Nov: 458–71.

Young, D.W. & Saltman, R.B. (1985) *The Hospital Power Equilibrium: Physician Behaviour and Cost Control*, John Hopkins University Press, Baltimore.

Chapter 6   Pharmaceuticals

Aristides, M. & Mitchell, A.S. (1994) 'Applying the Australian *Guidelines* for the reimbursement of pharmaceuticals', *PharmacoEconomics* 6: 196–201.

Australian Bureau of Statistics (ABS) (1996) *National Health Survey, 1995: First Results*. Catalogue no. 4392.0, ABS, Canberra.

Bureau of Industry Economics (BIE) (1991) *The Pharmaceutical Industry: Impediments and Opportunities*, Bureau of Industry Economics Program Evaluation Report 11, 1991.

Canadian Coordinating Office for Health Technology Assessment (1994)

Guidelines for Economic Evaluation of Pharmaceuticals. CCOHTA, Ottawa.

Carmine, B. (1996) 'Update and evaluation of Australian *Guidelines*: industry perspective', *Med Care* 34, 12(supp): DS226–32.

Chalanson, G. (1997) 'An industry's perspective on the French system of taking into account of a pharmacoeconomic dossier for setting prices of pharmaceuticals', 2nd Conference on the Scientific Basis of Health Services, Abstract S15.03. Amsterdam, October.

Commonwealth of Australia (1987) *Hansard.* National Health Amendment Bill (no. 2). Second Reading Speech, Canberra.

——(1990) *Draft Guidelines for the pharmaceutical industry on preparation of submissions to the Pharmaceutical Benefits Advisory Committee: including submissions involving economic analyses.* AGPS, Canberra.

——(1992) *Guidelines for the pharmaceutical industry on preparation of submissions to the Pharmaceutical Benefits Advisory Committee: including submissions involving economic analyses.* AGPS, Canberra.

——(1995) *Guidelines for the pharmaceutical industry on preparation of submissions to the Pharmaceutical Benefits Advisory Committee: including submissions involving economic analyses.* AGPS, Canberra.

——(1996a) *Pharmaceutical Benefits Pricing Authority Annual Report for the year ended 30 June 1996.* AGPS, Canberra.

——(1996b) *The pharmaceutical industry: Industry Commission Report, Vol. 2.* AGPS, Canberra.

——(1997a) *Expenditure and prescriptions twelve months to 30 June 1997.* CDHFS, Pharmaceutical Benefits Branch, Canberra.

——(1997b) *The Australian Pharmaceutical Benefits Scheme.* CDHFS, Canberra.

Davis, G., Wanna, J., Warhurst, J. & Weller, P. (1993) *Public Policy in Australia, 2nd edn.* Allen & Unwin, Sydney.

Drummond, M.F. (1994) *Value for Money Assessments in Australia and Beyond,* Spectrum Health Care Delivery and Economics, Decisions Resource, Ma.

Duckett, S. (1997) 'The policy change process', in H. Gardner (ed.) *Health Policy in Australia,* Oxford University Press, Melbourne.

Elgar, E. (1992) 'Policies and issues', in R. Ballance, J. Pogany & H. Forstner (eds) *The World's Pharmaceutical Industries: An International Perspective on Innovation, Competition and Policy,* United Nations Industrial Development Organisation, Geneva.

Food and Drug Administration (FDA) (1995) *Principles for the Review of Pharmacoeconomic Promotion: Draft Guidelines,* US Food and Drug Administration, Rockville, MD.

Freund, D.A. (1996) 'Initial development of the Australian *Guidelines*', *Med Care* 34, 12(supp): DS211–15.

Garattini, L., Grilli, R., Scopelliti, D. & Mantovani, L. (1995) 'A proposal for Italian guidelines in pharmacoeconomics', *PharmacoEconomics* 7: 1–6.

Genduso, L.A. & Kotsanos, K.G. (1996) 'Review of health economic *Guidelines* in the form of regulations, principles, policies, and positions', *Drug Information Journal* 30: 1003–16.

George, B., Harris, A. & Mitchell, A. (in press) 'Reimbursement decisions and the implied value of life: cost effectiveness analysis and decisions to reimburse pharmaceuticals in Australia 1993–1996', in Harris, A. (ed.) *Proceedings of the Nineteenth Australian Conference of Health Economists*, Australian Studies in Health Service Administration, University of New South Wales, Sydney.

Glasziou, P.P. & Mitchell, A.S. (1996) 'Use of pharmacoeconomic data by regulatory authorities', in B. Spilker (ed.) *Quality of Life and Pharmacoeconomic in Clinical Trials, 2nd edn*, Lippincott-Raven, Philadelphia, PA.

Gold, M.R., Siegel, J.E., Russell, L.B. et al. (1996) *Cost-Effectiveness in Health and Medicine: Report of the Panel on Cost-effectiveness in Health and Medicine*, Oxford University Press, New York.

Gorham, P. (1995) 'Cost-effectiveness *Guidelines*: the experience of Australian manufacturers', *PharmacoEconomics* 8: 369–73.

Grant, C. & Lapsley, H.M. (1996) *The Australian Health Care System, 1995*, Australian Studies in Health Service Administration, UNSW, Sydney.

Grobler, M.P., Macarounas, K., Pearce, G.S. & Stafford, M. (1996) 'Industry comment on the 1995 revised Australian pharmacoeconomic *Guidelines*', *PharmacoEconomics* 9: 353–6.

Grund, J. (1996) 'The societal value of pharmaceuticals: balancing industrial and health care policy', *PharmacoEconomics* 10: 14–22.

Hall, R. (1989) 'Drug regulation in Australia', *Med J Aust* 151: 338–40.

Harvey, K. & Murray, M. (1995) 'Medicinal drug policy', in H. Gardner (ed.) *The Politics of Health: The Australian Experience, 2nd edn*, Churchill Livingstone, Melbourne.

Henry, D. (1992) 'Economic analysis as an aid to subsidisation decisions', *PharmacoEconomics* 1: 54–67.

——(1997) 'Prescribing costs: whose responsibility?', *Australian Prescriber* 20: 26–7.

Hill, S., Henry, D. & Smith, A. (1997) 'Rising prescription drug costs: whose responsibility?', *Med J Aust* 167: 6–7.

Langley, P.C. (1996) 'The November 1995 revised Australian *Guidelines* for the economic evaluation of pharmaceuticals', *PharmacoEconomics* 9: 341–52.

Langley, P.C. & Sullivan, S.D. (1996) 'Pharmacoeconomic evaluations: *Guidelines* for drug purchasers', *J Managed Care Pharm* 2: 671–7.

Lomas, J. (1996) *The Sound of One Hand Clapping*, Department of Public Health and Community Medicine, University of Sydney, Sydney.

Marley, J. (1996) 'Cost-effectiveness: the need to know', *Australian Prescriber* 19: 58–9.

Milio, N. (1988) *Making Policy: A Mosaic of Australian Community Health Policy Development*, Commonwealth Department of Community Services and Health, Canberra.

Mitchell, A.S. (1996a) 'Current experience in Australia', *Drug Information Journal* 30: 495–502.

——(1996b) 'Update and evaluation of Australian *Guidelines*: government perspective', *Med Care* 34, 12(supp): DS216–25.

Mitchell, A.S. & Menon, D. (1996) '*Guidelines* for pharmacoeconomics: state of the art', in A. Szczepura & J. Kankaanpaa (eds) *Assessment of Health Care Technologies: Case Studies, Key Concepts and Strategic Issues*, John Wiley & Sons, New York.

Neumann, P.J. & Johannesson, M. (1994) 'Commentary. From principle to public policy: using cost-effectiveness analysis', *Health Affairs* Summer: 206–14.

Neumann, P.J., Zinner, D.E. & Paltiel, D. (1996) 'The FDA and regulation of cost-effectiveness claims', *Health Affairs* 15: 54–71.

Ontario Ministry of Health (1994) *Ontario Guidelines for Economic Analysis of Pharmaceutical Products*, Queen's Printer for Ontario, Toronto.

Agence du Médicament (1995) *Acceptabilité des Études Médico-Économiques: Contenu et Presentation*, Agence du Médicament, Saint-Denis.

Salkeld, G., Davey, P.D. & Arnolda, G. (1995) 'A critical review of health-related economic evaluations in Australia: implications for health policy', *Health Policy* 31: 111–25.

Shiell, A. & Salkeld, G. (1997) 'The economic aspects of interferon', in R. Stuart-Harris & R. Penny (eds) *Clinical Applications of the Interferons*, Chapman & Hall Medical, London.

Chapter 7 The economics of aged care

Aged Care Australia (1994) *Inter-Hostel Financial Comparison Survey*, Aged Care Australia, Canberra.

Australian Institute of Health and Welfare (AIHW) (1995) *Australia's Welfare 1995: Services and Assistance*, AGPS, Canberra.

——(1997) *Australia's Welfare 1997: Services and Assistance*, AGPS, Canberra.

Barer, M.L., Evans, R.G., Hertzman, C. & Lomas, J. (1987) 'Aging and health care utilisation: new evidence on old fallacies', *Soc Sci Med* 24: 851–962.

Braithwaite, J., Makkai, T., Braithwaite, V. & Gibson, D. (1993) 'Raising the standard: resident centred nursing home regulation in Australia', *Aged and Community Care Service Development and Evaluation Reports*, no. 10. AGPS, Canberra.

Commonwealth of Australia (1996) *Portfolio Budget Statements: Health and Family Services Portfolio. Budget Related Paper No. 1.8*, The Treasury, Canberra. pp. 44, 214–17, 239–40.

Dargavel, R. & Kendig, H. (1986) 'Political rhetoric and program drift: House and Senate debates on the Aged and Disabled Persons' Homes Act', *Australian Journal on Ageing* 5: 23–31.

Department of Community Services and Health (1987) 'Variations in nursing home funding and moves towards standardisation', *Australian Health Review* 10: 264–73.

Department of Health and Family Services (1997) *Aged and Community Care Fact Sheets*, DHFS, Canberra.

Department of Health, Housing and Community Services (DHHCS) (1991) *Aged Care Reform Strategy Mid Term Review 1990–91 Report*, AGPS, Canberra.

——(1993) *Aged Care Reform Strategy Mid Term Review Stage 2 Report*, AGPS, Canberra.

Duckett, S., Gray, L. & Howe, A.L. (1995) 'Designing a funding system for rehabilitation services. Part 1: Rationales and recent developments', *Australian Health Review*, 18(3), pp. 30–45.

Getzen, T.E. (1992) 'Population aging and the growth of health expenditures', *Gerontology: Social Services* 47: S98–104.

Goss, J., Mathers, S., Eckermann, S. et al. (1997) *The Impact of Population Ageing on Health Expenditures in Australia in the 21st Century*, AIHW, Canberra.

Gregory, R.G. (1993a) 'Review of the structure of nursing home funding arrangements, stage 1', *Aged and Community Care Service Development and Evaluation Reports*, no. 11, AGPS, Canberra.

——(1993b) 'Some dynamics of Australian aged care policies', in C.E. Baird & R.G. Gregory (eds) *Health Policy: International Comparison and Special Issues*, Centre for Economic Policy Research, Australian National University, Canberra.

——(1994) 'Review of the structure of nursing home funding arrangements, stage 2', *Aged and Community Care Service Development and Evaluation Reports*, no. 12, AGPS, Canberra.

Holmes, A. (Chair) (1977) *Report of the Committee on Care of the Aged and Infirm*, AGPS, Canberra.

Howe, A.L. (1986) 'Finance of health care of the aged', in R. Mendelsohn (ed.) *Finance of Old Age*, ANUTech, Canberra.

——(1990) 'Nursing home care policy in Australia—from laissez faire to restructuring', in H. Kendig & J. McCallum (eds) *Grey Policy: Australian Policies for an Ageing Society*, Allen & Unwin, Sydney.

——(1996) 'Changing the balance of care: Australia and New Zealand', in OECD, *Caring for Frail Elderly People: Policies in Evolution*, Social Policy Studies, no. 19, OECD, Paris.

——(1997a) 'Health care costs of an aging population: the case of Australia', *Reviews in Clinical Gerontology* 7: 359–65.

——(1997b) 'The Aged Care Reform Strategy: a decade of changing momentum and margins for reform', in A. Borowski, S. Encel & E. Ozanne (eds) *Ageing and Social Policy in Australia*, Longman Cheshire, Sydney.

Howe, A.L. & Sharwood, P. (1989) 'Present and potential roles of hostels in the Australian aged care system', *Lincoln Papers in Gerontology*, no. 2. La Trobe University, Melbourne.

Johnson, P. (1996) 'Grey horizons: Who pays for old age in the 21st century?' *Economic Record*, 72: 261–71.

Kewley, T.H. (1973) *Social Security in Australia 1900–1972*, Sydney University Press, Sydney.

Martin, G. (1997) 'Windfall profits for nursing home operators', *Australian Health and Aged Care Journal* February: 93.

McLeay, L.B. (Chair) (1982) *In a Home or at Home: Home Care and Accommodation for the Aged*, Report of the House of Representatives Standing Committee on Expenditure inquiry into home care and accommodation for the aged, AGPS, Canberra.

National Commission of Audit (1996) *Report to the Commonwealth Government*, AGPS, Canberra.

Rhys Hearn, C. (1997) *Development of a Single Instrument for the Classification of Nursing Home and Hostel Residents*, Report, vol. 1. Aged Care Research and Evaluation Unit, University of Western Australia, Perth.

Senate Community Affairs Reference Committee (1997) *Report on Funding of Aged Care Institutions*, Senate Publishing Unit, Parliament House, Canberra.

Taylor, R. & Salkeld, G. (1996) 'Health care expenditure and life expectancy in Australia: how well do we perform?', *ANZ J Public Health* 20: 233–40.

Walsh, J. & De Ravin, J.W. (1995) *Long Term Care, Disability and Ageing*, Institute of Actuaries, Sydney.

Chapter 8   Evaluation of health services

Abel-Smith, B. (1985) 'Global perspective on health service financing', *Social Science and Medicine* 21, 9: 95–163.

Arrow, K.J. (1963) 'Uncertainty and the welfare economics of medical care', *American Economic Review*, vol. 53: 941–73.

Arrow, K., Solow, R., Portney, P.R., Leamer, E.E., Radner, R. & Schuman, H. (1993) 'Report of the NOAA panel on contingent valuation', *Federal Register* 58: 4601–14.

Australian Institute of Health and Welfare (AIHW) (1990) *Breast Cancer Screening in Australia: Future Directions*, Prevention program evaluation series no. 1, AGPS, Canberra.

——(1991) *Cervical Cancer Screening in Australia: Options for Change*, Prevention Program Evaluation Series no. 2, AGPS, Canberra.

Berwick, D.M. and Weinstein, M.C. (1985) 'What do patients value? Willingness to pay for ultrasound in normal pregnancy', *Medical Care* 23: 881–93.

Birch, S. & Gafni, A. (1991) *Cost Effectiveness/Utility Analysis: Do Current Decision Rules Lead Us to Where We Want to Be?*, Working Paper Series no. 9–6, McMaster University, Montreal.

Bureau of Transport Economics (BTCE) (1984) *Social Audit and Australian Transport Evaluation*, AGPS, Canberra.

Bush, J.W., Chen, M. & Patrick, D.L. (1973) 'Cost-effectiveness using a health status index: analysis of the New York State PKU screening programme', in R. Berg (ed.) *Health States Indexes*, Hospital Research and Education Trust, Chicago.

Butler, J. (1992), 'Welfare economics and cost-utility analysis', P. Zwerfel & A.E. French III (eds) *Health Economics Worldwide*, Kluver Academic Publishers, Amsterdam, pp.143–57.

Chestnut, L.G., Keller, L.R., Lambert, W.E. & Rowe R.D. (1996) 'Measuring heart patients' willingness to pay for changes in angina symptoms', *Med Decision Making* 16: 65–77.

Commonwealth Department of Health and Family Services (CDHFS) (1997) *Budget 1997/8 Fact Sheet 7*, Commonwealth of Australia Budget Papers, Canberra.

Commonwealth of Australia (1995) *Guidelines* for the Pharmaceutical Industry on Preparation of Submissions to the Pharmaceutical Benefits Advisory Committee: including major submissions involving economic analysis, CDHFS, Canberra.

Culyer, A.J. (1991) *The Economics of Health, vols 1 and 2*, Edward Elgar, London.

Cummings, R.G., Brookshire, D.S. & Schulze, W.D. (1986) *Valuing Environmental Goods: An Assessment of the Contingent Valuation Method*, Rowman & Allenheld, New Jersey.

Diamond, P. & Hausman, J. (1994) 'Contingent valuation: is some number better than no number?', *Journal of Economic Perspectives* 8, 1: 45–64.

Donaldson, C., Atkinson, J., Bond, J. & Wright, K. (1988) 'Should QALYs be programme-specific?', *Journal of Health Economics* 7: 239–57.

Donaldson, C., Shackley, P., Abdalla, M. & Miedzybrodzka, Z. (1995) 'Willingness to pay for antenatal carrier screening for cystic fibrosis', *Health Economics* 4: 439–52.

Drummond, M.F. (1981) *Studies in Economic Appraisal in Health Care*, Oxford University Press, Oxford.

——(1983) 'Economic appraisal and health service decision making', *Effective Health Care* 1, 1: 25–32.

——(1987) 'Economic evaluation and the national diffusion and use of health technology', *Health Policy* 7: 309–24.

——(1990) 'Economic evaluation and health services decision making in the United Kingdom: a status report', paper prepared for REMQUAS Association, Paris.

Drummond, M.F. & Davies L. (1991) 'Economic analysis alongside clinical trials: revisiting the methodological issues,' *International Journal of Technology Assessment in Health Care* 7, 4: 561–73.

Drummond, M.F., Lawson, K.V., Ludbrook, A. & Steele, R. (1986) *Studies in Economic Appraisal in Health Care vol. 2*, Oxford University Press, Oxford.

Drummond, M.F., Stoddart, G. & Torrance, G. (1987) *Methods for the Economic Evaluation of Healthcare Programs*, Oxford University Press, Oxford.

Drummond, M.F., Hailey, D. & Selby Smith, C. (1991) 'Maximising the impact of health technology assessment', in C. Selby-Smith (ed.) *Economics and Health*, Proceedings of the Thirteenth Australian Conference of Health Economics, Monash University, Melbourne, pp. 234–73.

Drummond, M.F., Brandt, A., Luce, B. & Rovira, J. (1993) 'Standardising economic evaluation methodologies in health care: practice, problems and potential', *International Journal of Technology Assessment in Health Care* 9, 1: 26–36.

Elliot, S.L. & Harris, A.H. (1997) 'The methodology of cost effectiveness analysis: avoiding common pitfalls', *Medical Journal of Australia* 166, 12: 636–49.

Gaber, A.M. & Phelps, C.E. (1995) *Economic Foundations of Cost-Effectiveness Analysis*, National Bureau of Economic Research, New York.

George, B., Harris, A.H. & Mitchell, A. (1997) 'Reimbursement decisions and the implied value of life: cost effectiveness analysis and decisions to reimburse pharmaceuticals in Australia 1993–1996', Conference of Australian Health Economics, Melbourne.

Gerard, K. (1992) 'Cost-utility in practice: a policy maker's guide to the state of the art', *Health Policy* 21: 249–79.

Gold, M.R., Siegel, J.E., Russell, L.B., & Weinstein, M.C. (eds) (1996) *Cost-Effectiveness in Health and Medicine*, Oxford University Press, Oxford.

Hall, J. & Mooney, G. (1990a) 'What every doctor should know about economics, part 1: the benefits of costing', *The Medical Journal of Australia* 152: 29–31.

——(1990b), 'What every doctor should know about economics, part 2: the benefits of economic appraisal', *The Medical Journal of Australia* 152: 80–2.

Hall, J. (1993) 'From research to action: does economic evaluation affect health policy or practice?,' in C. Selby-Smith (ed.) *Economics and Health: Proceedings of the Fifteenth Australian Conference of Health Economics*, Monash University, Melbourne, pp 244–52.

Hanemann, W.M. (1994) 'Valuing the environment through contingent valuation', *Journal of Economic Perspectives* 8: 19–43.

Harris, J. (1987) 'QALYfing the value of life', *Journal of Medical Ethics* 13: 117-23.

Harvey, R. (1991) *Making it Better: Strategies for Improving the Effectiveness and Quality of Health Services in Australia*, National Health Strategy Background, Treble Press, Commonwealth Department of Human Services & Health, Canberra.

Hausman, J.A. (ed.) (1993) *Contingent Valuation: A Critical Assessment*, North-Holland, Amsterdam.

Hawthorne, G., Richardson, J., Osborne, R. & McNeil, H. (1997) 'The Australian quality of life (AQoL) instrument: initial validation', Working Paper 66, Centre for Health Program Evaluation, Monash University, Melbourne.

Hodgson, T.A. & Meiners, M.R. (1982) 'Cost-of-illness methodology: a guide to current practices and procedures', *Milbank Memorial Fund Quarterly* 60, 3: 429–62.

Johannesson, M. (1996) *Theory and Methods of Economic Evaluation in Health Care*, Kluwer Academic Publishers, Amsterdam.

Johannesson, M., Jonsson, B. & Borgquist, L. (1991) 'Willingness to pay for antihypertensive therapy—results of a Swedish pilot survey', *Journal of Health Economics* 10: 461–74.

Johannesson, M., Johansson, P.O. & Jonsson, B. (1992), 'Economic evaluation of drug therapy: a review of the contingent valuation method', *PharmacoEconomics* 1: 325–37.

Johannesson, M., Jonsson, B. & Borgquist, L. (1993), 'Willingness to pay for antihypertensive therapy: further results', *Journal of Health Economics* 12: 95–108.

Johnsson, B. & Weinstein, M.C. (1997) 'Economic evaluation alongside multinational clinical trials', *International Journal of Technology Assessment in Health Care*, 13(1), pp. 49–58.

Jones-Lee, M.W. (1989) *The Economics of Safety and Physical Risk*, Oxford University Press, Oxford.

Keeler, E. (1995) 'Decision trees and Markov models in cost-effectiveness research', in F.A. Sloan (ed.) *Valuing Health Care: Cost, Benefits, and*

Effectiveness of Pharmaceuticals and Other Medical Technologies, Cambridge University Press, New York, pp 185–205.

Klarman, H.E., Francis, J.O.S. & Rosenthal, G. (1968) 'Cost-effectiveness analysis applied to the treatment of chronic renal disease', *Medical Care* 6: 48–54.

Koopmanschap, M.A. & Rutten, F.F.H. (1993) 'Indirect costs in economic studies: confronting the confusion', *PharmacoEconomics* 4: 446–54.

Laska E.M., Meisner, M. & Siegel, J.E. (1997) 'Statistical inference for cost effectiveness ratios', *Health Economics* 6, 3: 229–42.

Layard, R. & Glaister, S. (eds) (1994) *Cost-Benefit Analysis*, 2nd edn, Cambridge University Press, Cambridge.

Lindholm, L., Rosen, M. & Hellsten, G. (1994) 'Are people willing to pay for a community-based preventive program?', *International Journal Technology Assess Health Care* 10: 317–24.

Loomes, G. & McKenzie, L. (1989) 'Use of QALYs in health care decision making', *Social Science and Medicine*, 28(4), pp. 299–308.

Ludbrook, A. & Mooney, G.L. (1984) *Economic Appraisal in the NHS: Problems and Challenges*, Northern Health Economics, Health Economics Research, University of Aberdeen, Aberdeen.

Mishan, E.J. (1971) *Cost Benefit Analysis*, Unwin University Books, London.

Mitchell, A. (1996) 'Update and evaluation of Australian Guidelines: government perspective', *Medical Care* 34, 12: DS216–25.

Mooney, G. (1988) 'Health economics and economic evaluation: an introduction', in Australian Institute of Health (1991) Health Economics Series, no. 1. Economic evaluation of health services: report from an April 1986 workshop, AGPS, Canberra.

——(1993) *Economics, Medicine and Health Care*, 2nd edn, Harvester Wheatsheaf, Hampstead, UK.

——(1996) The Consequences of Process Utility for Consequentialism in Health Economics, Paper presented at the 18th Annual Conference of the Australian Health Economists' Society, Coffs Harbour.

Mooney, G., Gerard, K., Donaldson, C. & Farrar, S. (1992) 'Priority setting in purchasing: some practical guidelines', NAHAT Research Paper no. 6, Health Economics Research Unit, University of Aberdeen, Aberdeen.

National Health and Medical Research Council (NHMRC) (1995) *Guidelines for the Development and Implementation of Clinical Practice Guidelines*, AGPS, Canberra.

Neuhauser, D. & Lewicki, A.M. (1975) 'What do we gain from the sixth stool guaiac?', *New England Journal of Medicine* 293: 255–58.

Nord, E. (1992) 'An alternative to QALYs: the saved young life equivalent', *British Medical Journal* 305: 875–7.

O'Brien, B.J. (1996) 'Economic evaluation of pharmaceuticals: Frankenstein's monster or vampire of trials?', *Medical Care* 34, 12: DS99–119.

O'Brien, B.J., Drummond, M.F. & Labelle, R.J. (1994) 'In search of power and significance: issues in the design and analysis of stochastic cost-effectiveness studies in health care', *Medical Care* 32, 2: 150–63.

O'Brien, B.J. et al. (1995) 'Assessing the economic value of a new antidepressant: a willingness-to-pay approach', *PharmacoEconomics* 8: 34–45.

Olsen, J.A. (1993) 'Some methodological issues in economic evaluation in health care', PhD Thesis, Department of Economics, University of Tromso.

Olsen, J.A. & Donaldson, C. (1998) 'Helicopters, hearts and hips: using willingness to pay to set priorities for public sector programmes', *Social Science and Medicine*, vol. 56, no. 1, pp. 1–12.

Peacock, S., Richardson, J. & Carter, R. (1997) 'Setting priorities in South Australian Community Health II: marginal analysis of mental health services', Research Report 14, Centre for Health Program Evaluation, Monash University, Melbourne.

Polsky, D., Glick, H.A. & Willke, R. et al. (1997) 'Confidence intervals for cost effectiveness ratios: a comparison of four methods', *Health Economics* 6, 3: 243–52.

Richardson, J. (1991) 'Economic assessment of health care: theory and practice', *The Australian Economic Review* 1st quarter: 1–21.

——(1993) 'Commentary', in C. Selby-Smith (ed.) *Economics and Health 1993: Proceedings of the 15th Australian Conference of Health Economists*, National Centre for Health Program Evaluation, Monash University, Melbourne.

——(1994) 'Cost utility analysis: what should be measured?', *Social Science and Medicine* 39, 1: 7–21.

——(1995) 'Economic evaluation of health promotion: friend or foe?', Working Paper 50, Centre for Health Program Evaluation, Monash University, Melbourne.

Richardson, J., Hall, J. & Salkeld, G. (1990) 'Cost utility analysis: the compatibility of measurement techniques and the measurement of utility through time', in C. Selby-Smith (ed.) *Economics and Health 1990: Proceedings of the 11th Annual Conference of Australian Health Economics*, Public Sector Management Institute, Monash University, Melbourne.

Ross, J. (1995) 'The use of economic evaluation in health care: Australian decision makers' perceptions', *Health Policy* 31: 103–10.

Salkeld, G. (1997) 'Do process attributes enter the maximand for preventive goods?', in A.H. Harris (ed.) *Economics and Health 1996: Proceedings of the 18th Australian Conference of Health Economists*, Australian Studies in Health Service Administration no. 81, School of Health Services Management, University of New South Wales.

Salkeld, G., Davey, P. & Arnold, G. (1995) 'A critical review of health-related economic evaluations in Australia: implications for health policy?', *Health Policy* 31: 111–25.

Shiell, A. & Hawe, P. (1996) 'Health promotion community development and the tyranny of individualism', *Health Economics* 5: 241–7.

Sugden, R. & Williams, A.H. (1978) *The Principles of Practical Cost-Benefit Analysis*, Oxford University Press, Oxford.

Tolley, G.S., Kenkol, D. & Fabian R. (1994) *Valuing Health for Policy: An Economic Approach*, University of Chicago Press, Chicago.

Torrance, G.W. (1986) 'Measurement of health-state utilities for economic appraisal: a review', *Journal of Health Economics* 5: 30.

Viscusi, W.K. (1978) 'Labor market valuations of life and limb: empirical evidence and policy implications', *Public Policy* 26, 3, 359–86.

——(1993) 'The value of risks to life and health', *Journal of Economic Literature* 1, 4: 1912–46.

Wagstaff, A. (1991) 'QALYs and the equity-efficiency trade-off', *Journal of Health Economics* 10, 1: 21–42.

Weisbrod, B. (1961) *Economics of Public Health: Measuring the Impact of Diseases*, University of Pennsylvania, Philadelphia.

Williams, A.H. (1987) 'Response: QALYfying the value of life', *Journal of Medical Ethics* 13: 123.

——(1993) 'Cost-benefit analysis: applied welfare economics or general decision aid', in A. Williams & E. Giardina (eds) *Efficiency in the Public Sector*, Edward Elgar, London.

Zarnke, K. et al. (1997) 'Cost benefit analysis in the health care literature: don't judge a study by its label', *Journal of Clinical Epidemiology* 50: 813–22.

Chapter 9 Health insurance

Arrow, K. (1963) 'Uncertainty and the economics of medical care', *American Economic Review* 53: 941–73.

Australian Institute of Health and Welfare (AIHW) (1997) *Health Expenditure Bulletin no. 13*, AGPS, Canberra.

Industry Commission (IC) (1997) *Private Health Insurance*, Report no. 57, AGPS, Canberra.

Prices Surveillance Authority (PSA) (1993) *The Cost of Private Health Insurance*, Discussion Paper no. 2, Melbourne.

Private Health Insurance Administration Council (PHIAC) (1996) *Annual Report 1995–96*, AGPS, Canberra.

——(1997) *Quarterly Statistics*, September, AGPS, Canberra.

Richardson, J. (1995) 'Medicare: radical reform or incrementalism?', *Australian Health Review*, 18, 1: 2–8.

Schofield, D. (1997) 'The distribution and determinants of private health insurance in Australia in the 1990s', in A.H. Harris (ed.) *Economics and Health 1996*, Proceedings of the 18th Australian Conference of Health Economists, School of Health Services Management, University of New South Wales, Sydney.

Scotton, R.B. (1997) 'Health insurance policy', in Jay M. Shafritz (ed.) *International Encyclopedia of Public Administration and Policy*, Westview Press, Boulder, CO.

Scotton, R.B. & Macdonald, C.R. (1993) *The Making of Medibank*, Australian Studies in Health Service Administration, no. 76, University of NSW, Sydney.

Wilcox, S. (1991) *A Healthy Risk? Use of Private Health Insurance*, National Health Strategy, Background Paper no. 4, AGPS, Canberra.

Chapter 10   The health care financing debate

Australian Bureau of Statistics (ABS) (1995) *Private Hospitals*. Catalogue 4390.0.

Australian Institute of Health and Welfare (AIHW) (1996) *Australia's Health*, AGPS, Canberra.

Crichton, A. (1990) *Slowly Taking Control? Australian Governments and Health Care Provision 1788–1988*, Allen & Unwin, Sydney.

Evans, R.G. & Law, M.N. (1995) 'The Canadian health care system: where are we and how did we get here?', in D. Dunlop & J. Martens (eds) *An International Assessment of Health Care Financing: Lessons for Developing Countries*, Economic Development Institute of the World Bank, EDI Seminar Series, The World Bank, Washington, DC.

Feldman, R. & Morrisey, A. (1990) 'Health economics: A report on the field', *Journal of Health Politics Policy and Law*, 15: 627–46.

Gerdtham, U., Johnsson, B. et al. (1994) 'Factors affecting health spending: a cross country econometric analysis', in H. Oxley & M. MacFarlane (eds) *Health Care Reform*, Economic Department, Working Papers 1, 49, OECD, Paris.

Hayes, B. & Vanden Heuvel, A. (1995) 'Public attitude towards government spending on health care', *Australian Journal of Social Issues* 30, 3: 275–90.

Industry Commission (1996) The Pharmaceutical Industry Report No. 51, Australian Government Publishing Service, Canberra.

——(1997) Private Health Insurance Report No. 57, Commonwealth of Australia, Canberra.

Kirkman-Liff, B. (1997) 'The United States' in C. Ham (ed.) *Health Care*

Reform: Lessons from International Experience, Open University Press, Philadelphia, PA.

Leape, L., Park, R., Solomon, D., Chassin, M., Kosecoff, J. & Brook, R. (1990) 'Does inappropriate use explain small area variations in the use of health care services', *Journal of the American Medical Association* 265, 5: 669–72.

Lohr, K. (1986) 'Use of medical care in the Rand health insurance experiment: diagnosis and specific service analysis in a random controlled trial', *Medical Care* 24(supp): 1–87.

Lomas, J. (1990) 'Finding audiences, changed beliefs: The structure of research use in Canadian health policy', *Journal of Health Politics Policy and Law*, 15, 3: 525, 542.

McClelland, A. (1991) 'In fair health? Equity and the health system', National Health Strategy Background Paper No. 3, Commonwealth Department of Health & Family Services, Canberra.

McPherson, K. (1990) 'International differences in medical care practice', in *Health Care Systems in Transition: The Search for Efficiency*, OECD, Paris.

Miller, R. & Luft, H. (1997) 'Does managed care lead to better or worse quality of care?', *Health Affairs*, 16.5, Sept/Oct, 7–21.

Newhouse, J. (1993) *Free For All: Lessons from the Rand Health Insurance Experiment*, Harvard University Press, Cambridge, MA.

Palmer, G. & Short, S. (1994) *Healthcare and Public Policy: An Australian Analysis*, Macmillan Education, Melbourne.

Patterson, J. (1996) *National Health Care Reform: The Last Picture Show*, Department of Human Services, Government of Victoria, Melbourne.

Reinhardt, U.E. (1996) 'A social contract for 21st century health care: three tier health care with bounty hunting', *Health Economics*, 5, 6: 479–500.

Renwick, M. & Sadkowsky, K. (1991) 'Variations in surgery rates', Australian Institute of Health Services, Series 2, Australian Institute of Health, Canberra.

Richardson, J. & Wallace, R. (1983) 'Health economics', in F. Gruen, (ed.) *Surveys of Australian Economics, vol. 3*, George Allen & Unwin, Sydney.

Richardson, J. (1987a) *Privatisation: An Australian Perspective*, Australian Professional Publications, Sydney. Reprinted in J Butler and D Doessel (eds) (1989) *Health Economics: Australian Readings*, Australian Professional Publications, Sydney.

——(1987b), 'Financial incentives and entrepreneurial medicine: problems and solutions', Australian Studies in Health Service Administration no. 61, School of Health Administration, University of NSW, Sydney.

——(1989) 'Ownership and regulation in the health care sector', in Butler J. & Doessel, D. *Health Economics, Australian Readings*, Australian Professional Publications, Sydney.

——(1991) 'The effects of consumer copayments in medical care', National

Health Strategy Background Paper no. 5, Treble Press, Commonwealth Department of Human Services & Health, Canberra.

Rosenman, S. (1996) 'What is managed care', *Health Cover*, 6, 2: 31–4.

Sackett, D.I. & Rosenberg, W.M.C. (1995) 'On the need for evidence based medicine', *Health Economics*, 4: 249–54.

Saltman, R. & von Otter, C. (eds) (1995) *Implementing Planned Markets In Health Care: Balancing Social And Economic Responsibility*, Open University Press, Buckingham, UK.

Scott, M.A. (1997) 'Equity and the distribution of health care in Australia', in A. Harris (ed.) *Economics and Health: 1996*, Proceedings of the 18th Australian Conference of Health Economists, Australian Studies in Health Service Administration, School of Health Service Management, University of NSW, Sydney.

Walker, B. (1990) 'Health financing options in the 21st century: a paper for the Office of Health Policy', New South Wales Department of Health, Sydney.

Wennberg, J. (1988) 'Improving the decision making process', *Health Affairs*, Spring, 99–106.

Wilton, P. & Smith, R. (1997) 'GP budget holding for Australia: panacea or poison', Working Paper 75, Centre for Health Program Evaluation, Melbourne.

Withers, G. Throsby, D. & Johnston, K. (1994) *Public Expenditure in Australia*, Commission Paper 3, Economic Planning Advisory Commission, AGPS, Canberra.

Chapter 11   Managed competition

Chernichovsky, D. (1995) 'Health system reforms in industrialized democracies: an emerging paradigm', *The Milbank Quarterly*, 73: 339–72.

Ellwood, P.M., Enthoven, A.C. & Etheredge, L. (1992) 'The Jackson Hole initiatives for a twenty-first century American health care system', *Health Economics* 1, 3: 149–68.

Employer Benefit Research Institute (EBRI) (1994) *The Effectiveness of Health Care Cost Management Strategies: A Review of the Evidence*, EBRI Issue Brief no. 154, Washington, DC.

Enthoven, A.C. (1978) 'Consumer-choice health plan', *New England Journal of Medicine* 28: 650–8, 709–20.

Industry Commission (1997) *Private Health Insurance*, Report no. 57, AGPS, Canberra.

Jensen, G.A., Morrisey, A., Gaffney, S. & Liston, D.K. (1997) 'The new dominance of managed care: insurance trends in the 1990s', *Health Affairs* 16, 1: 125–36.

National Health Strategy (1991) *The Australian Health Jigsaw: Integrated Health Service Delivery*, Issues Paper no.1, July, AGPS, Canberra.

Netherlands (1992) *Choices in Health Care*, Report by the Government Committee on Choices in Health Care, Rijswijk.

Newhouse, J.P. (1996) 'Reimbursing health plans and providers: efficiency in production versus selection', *Journal of Economic Literature* 34: 1236–63.

Newhouse, J.P., Manning, W.G., Keeler, E.B. & Sloss, E.M. (1989) 'Adjusting capitation rates using objective health measures and prior utilization', *Health Care Financing Review*, 10, 3: 41–54.

New Zealand (1991) *Your Health and the Public Health*, Statement of Government health policy by the Hon. Simon Upton, Minister of Health.

OECD (1995) *New Directions in Health Care Policy*, Health Policy Studies no. 7, Paris.

Paterson, J. (1996) *National Healthcare Reform: The Last Picture Show*, Department of Human Services, Government of Victoria, Melbourne.

Peacock, S. (1998) Program budgeting and marginal analysis (PBMA), Forum proceedings from 'Options for Health Sector Reform', Centre for Health Program Evaluation, 16 April, Melbourne.

Reinhardt, U.E. (1994) 'Lineage of managed competition' (note), *Health Affairs*, 13, 2 (spring II): 290.

Robinson, J.C. & Casalino, L.P. (1996) 'Vertical integration and organizational networks in health care', *Health Affairs* 15, 1 (spring): 7–22.

Scotton, R.B. (1995) 'Managed competition: issues for Australia', *Australian Health Review* 18, 1: 82–104.

Somers, H.R. & Somers, A.R. (1972) 'Major issues in national health insurance', *Milbank Memorial Fund Quarterly* 50, 2, April: 177–210.

Trauner, J.B. & Chesnutt, J.S. (1996) 'Medical groups in California: managing care under capitation', *Health Affairs* 15, 1 (spring): 159–69.

Van de Ven, W.P.P.M. (1996) 'Market-oriented health care reforms: trends and future options', *Social Science and Medicine*, 43, 5: 655–66.

Van de Ven, W.P.M.M. & Rutten, F.F.H. (1995) 'Managed competition in the Netherlands: lessons from five years of health care reform', *Australian Health Review* 18, 1: 9–27.

Van de Ven, W.P.M.M. & Schut, F.T. (1994) 'Should catastrophic risks be included in a regulated competitive health insurance market?', *Social Science and Medicine* 39, 10: 1459–72.

Van de Ven, W.P.M.M., Schut, F.T. & Rutten, F.F.H. (1994) 'Forming and reforming the market for third-party purchasing of health care', *Social Science and Medicine* 39, 10, November: 1405–12.

White, J. (1995) *Competing Solutions: American Health Care Proposals and International Experience*, The Brookings Institution, Washington, DC.

WHO (1996) *European Health Care Reforms*, World Health Organization, Regional Office for Europe, Copenhagen.

Chapter 12   Public health

Armstrong, B. (1989) 'Morbidity and mortality in Australia: how much is preventable?', Paper presented to the Western Australian Health Education Professional Association Annual General Meeting, Perth.

Australian Health Ministers Advisory Council (AHMAC) (1990) *Breast Cancer Screening in Australia: Future Directions*, Australian Institute of Health and Welfare, Prevention Program Evaluation Series no. 1. AGPS, Canberra.

——(1991) *Cervical Cancer Screening in Australia: Options for Change*, Australian Institute of Health and Welfare, Prevention Program Evaluation Series no. 2. AGPS, Canberra.

Batterham, R. (1997) 'Current accepted practice in the assessment of community health needs: a guide to divisions of general practice', Support and Evaluation Resource Unit (SERU) in Access, Centre for Health Program Evaluation, University of Melbourne.

Beaglehole, R., Bonita, R. (1997) *Public Health at the Crossroads: Achievements and Prospects*, Cambridge University Press, Cambridge.

Beauchamp, D.E. (1985) 'Community: the neglected tradition of public health', *Hastings Center Report* December: 28–36.

Carter, R. (1993) Chapters 13–15 in *Pathways to Better Health*, National Health Strategy Issues Paper no. 7, AGPS, Canberra.

——(1994)'A macro approach to economic appraisal in the health sector', *Australian Economic Review* 2nd quarter: 105–12.

Chapman, S., Leeder, S.R. (1991) 'Public health services in Australia', in W.W. Holland, R. Detels & G. Knox (eds) *Oxford Textbook of Public Health*, Oxford Medical Publications, Oxford.

Cohen, D.R. (1994) 'Health promotion and cost-effectiveness', *Health Promotion International* 9: 281–7.

Culyer, A.J. (1989) 'The normative economics of health care finance and provision', *Oxford Review of Economic Policy* 5: 34–58.

Detels, R., Breslow, L. (1991) 'Current scope and concerns in public health', in W.W. Holland, R. Detels & G. Knox (eds) *Oxford Textbook of Public Health*, Oxford Medical Publications, Oxford.

Donaldson, C. (1995) 'Economics, public health and health care purchasing: reinventing the wheel', *Health Policy* 33: 79–90.

Downie, R.S., Fyfe, C. & Tannahill, A. (1990) *Health Promotion: Models and Values*, Oxford Medical Publications, Oxford.

Drummond, M., Stoddart, G. (1995) 'Assessment of health producing measures across different sectors', *Health Policy* 33: 219–31.

Fine, P.E.M., Clarkson, J.A. (1986) 'Individual versus public priorities in the determination of optimal vaccination policies', *American Journal of Epidemiology* 124: 1012–20.

Forster, J.L. (1982) 'A communtarian ethical model for public health interventions: an alternative to individual behavior change strategies', *Journal of Public Health Policy* 3: 150–63.

Gold, M.R., Siegel, J.E., Russell, L.B. & Weinstein, M.C. (eds) (1996) *Cost-Effectiveness in Health and Medicine*, Oxford University Press, Oxford.

Graham, H. (1994) 'Gender and class as dimensions of smoking behaviour in Britain: insights from a survey of mothers', *Social Science and Medicine* 38: 691–8.

Green, L.W. & Kreuter, M.W. (1990) 'Health promotion as a public health strategy for the 1990s', *Annual Review of Public Health* 11: 319–34.

Gunning-Schepers, L. (1989) 'The health benefits of prevention—a simulation approach', *Health Policy* 12: 1–255.

Hawe, P. (1994) 'Capturing the meaning of "community" in community intervention evaluation: some contributions from community psychology', *Health Promotion International* 9: 199–210.

——(1997) *The Challenge of Measles Control in the Under Five Age Group*, Unpublished PhD Thesis, Department of Public Health and Community Medicine, University of Melbourne, Melbourne.

Hawe, P. & Shiell, A. (1995) 'Preserving innovation under increasing accountability pressures: the health promotion investment portfolio approach', *Health Promotion Journal of Australia* 5: 4–9.

Hawe, P., Noort, M., King, L. & Jordens, C. (1997) 'Multiplying health gains: the critical role of capacity building in health promotion programs', *Health Policy* 39: 29–42.

Haycox, A. (1994) 'A methodology for estimating the costs and benefits of health promotion', *Health Promotion International* 9: 5–11.

Higher Education for Public Health (1976) *A Report of the Millbank Fund Commission*, New York.

Holman, C.D.J. (1992) 'Something old, something new: perspectives on five "new" public health movements', *Health Promotion Journal of Australia* 2: 4–11.

Israel, B.A., Checkoway, B., Shultz, A. & Zimmerman, M. (1994) 'Health education and community empowerment: conceptualizing and measuring perceptions of individual, organizational and community control', *Health Education Quarterly* 21: 149–70.

Jan, S. & Mooney, G., (1997) 'The outcomes of health promotion: are QALYs enough?', *Health Promotion Journal of Australia* 7: 91–99.

Lawson, J.S. & Close, G. (1991) *Public Health Approach to Aboriginal Health*, Report to the New South Wales Department of Health, Sydney.

299

Littlechild, S.C. & Wiseman, J. (1984) 'Principles of public policy relevant to smoking', *Policy Studies* 4: 54–67.

Minkler, M., Wallace, S.P. & McDonald, M. (1994/5) 'The political economy of health: a useful theoretical tool for health education practice', *International Quarterly of Community Health Education* 15: 111–25.

Mooney, G. (1994) 'What else do we want from our health services?', *Social Science and Medicine* 39: 151–4.

——(1996) 'A communitarian critique of health (care) economics', Paper presented to the 1st International Health Economics Association Conference, Vancouver, May.

Mooney, G., Gerard, K., Donaldson, C. & Farrar, S. (1993) *Priority Setting in Purchasing*, Research Paper no. 6, National Association of Health Authorities and Trusts and Health Economics Research Unit, University of Aberdeen, Aberdeen.

Mooney, G., Haas, M., Viney, R. & Cooper, L. (1997) *Linking Health Outcomes to Priority Setting, Planning and Resource Allocation*, Report to the NSW Health Department on the application of program budgeting and marginal analysis in NSW, CHERE, University of Sydney, Sydney.

Murray, C.J.L. & Lopez, A. (eds) (1996) *The Global Burden of Disease: A Comprehensive Assessment of Mortality and Disability from Diseases, Injuries, and Risk Factors in 1990 and Projected to 2020*, Harvard University Press, Cambridge, MA.

National Health Goals and Targets for Cancer Implementation Working Group (1994) *Draft Report*, Department of Human Services and Health, Canberra.

National Health Strategy (1990) *Setting the Agenda for Change*, Background Paper no. 1, National Health Strategies Unit, Canberra.

Nilakant, V. & Rao, H. (1994) 'Agency theory and uncertainty in organizations: an evaluation', *Organization Studies* 15: 649–72.

Nutbeam, D. & Wise, M. (1996) 'Planning for health for all: international experience in setting goals and targets', *Health Promotion International* 11: 219–26.

Peacock, S. et al. (1997) *Program Budgeting and Marginal Analysis (PBMA)*, Paper presented at the Centre for Health Program Evaluation Open Day Forum, Monash University, Melbourne, April 6.

Peters, R. & Chapman, S. (1995) Cars, boats, dogs . . . why not guns? The case for national gun registration in Australia', *Australian Journal of Public Health* 19: 213–5.

Posnett, J. & Street, A. (1996) 'Programme budgeting and marginal analysis: an approach to priority setting in need of refinement', *Journal of Health Services Research and Policy* 1: 147–53.

Richardson, J. (1995) *Economic Evaluation and Health Promotion: Friend or Foe?* Working Paper 50, Health Economics Unit, Centre for Health Program Evaluation, Monash University, Melbourne.

Richardson, J., Segal, L., Carter, R., Catford, J., Galbally, R. & Johnson, S. (1995) *Prioritising and Financing Health Promotion in Australia*, CHPE Research Report no. 4. Centre for Health Program Evaluation, Monash University, Melbourne.

Ringen, K. (1979) 'Chadwick, the market ideology and sanitary reform: on the nature of the 19th century public health movement', *International Journal of Health Services* 9: 107–20.

Rosen, M. & Lindholm, L. (1992) 'The neglected effects of lifestyle interventions in cost-effectiveness analysis', *Health Promotion International* 7: 163–69.

Salkeld, G., Davies, P. & Arnolda, G. (1995) 'A critical review of health-related economic evaluations in Australia: implications for health policy', *Health Policy* 31: 111–25.

Seedhouse, D. (1996) *Health Promotion: Philosophy, Prejudice and Practice*, John Wiley, Chichester.

Segal, L. & Richardson, J. (1994) 'Economic framework for allocative efficiency in the health sector', *Australian Economic Review* 2nd quarter: 89–98.

Sen, A. (1979) 'Personal utilities and public judgements: or what is wrong with welfare economics?', *Economic Journal* 589: 537–58.

Shiell, A. & Hawe, P. (1996) 'Community development, health promotion and the tyranny of individualism', *Health Economics* 5: 241–7.

Sugden, R. & Williams, A. (1979) *The Principles of Practical Cost–Benefit Analysis*, Oxford University Press, Oxford.

Tolley, K. (1993) *Health Promotion: How to Measure Cost-Effectiveness*, Health Education Authority, London.

World Health Organization (WHO) (1986) *Ottawa Charter for Health Promotion*, WHO Euro, Copenhagen.

——(1997) *The Jakarta Declaration on Health Promotion in the 21st Century*, WHO Euro, Geneva, HPR/HEP/41CHP/BR/97.4.

Chapter 13   Economic issues in Aboriginal health care

Almond, B. (1991) 'Rights', in P. Singer (ed.) *A Companion to Ethics*, Blackwell, Oxford.

Aboriginal and Torres Strait Islander Commission (1992) *ATSIC Annual Report 1991/92*, AGPS, Canberra.

Anderson, I. & Sanders, W. (1996) *Aboriginal Health and Institutional Reform Within Australian Federalism*, Centre for Aboriginal Economic Policy

Research Discussion Paper 1 17/1996, Australian National University, Canberra.

Australian Bureau of Statistics (ABS) (1994) *National Aboriginal and Torres Strait Islander Survey 1994: Detailed Findings*, Catalogue no. 4190.0, ABS, Canberra.

Bartlett, B. & Legge, D. (1994) *Beyond the Maze: Proposals for More Effective Administration of Aboriginal Health Programs*, NCEPH Working paper no. 34, National Centre for Epidemiology and Population Health, ANU, Canberra.

Brannigan, M. (1993) 'Oregon's experiment', *Health Care Analysis* 1: 15–32.

Broome, J. (1989) 'What's the good of equality?', in J.D. Hey (ed.) *Current Issues in Microeconomics*, Macmillan, London.

Core Health Services Committee (1993) *The Best of Health NZ*, Core Health Services Committee, Wellington.

Culyer, A.J. (1995) 'Need: the idea won't do—but still we need it', *Social Science and Medicine* 40, 6: 727–30.

Fagan, P. (1991) 'Self-determination in action', in J. Reid & P. Trompf (eds) *The Health of Aboriginal Australia*, Harcourt Brace Jovanovich, Sydney, pp 400–401.

Hunter, E. (1993) *Aboriginal Health and History: Power and Prejudice in Remote Australia*, Cambridge University Press, Cambridge.

Mann, J.M. (1997) 'Medicine and public health, ethics and human rights', *Hastings Center Report* May–June: 6–13.

McDermott, R. & Beaver, C. (1996) 'Horizontal equity in resource allocation in Aboriginal health', *Australian and New Zealand Journal of Public Health* 20, 1: 13–15.

McLennan, W. & Madden, R. (1997) The Health and Welfare of Australia's Aboriginal and Torres Strait Islander Peoples—ABS Catalogue no. 4704.01, ABS, Canberra.

Mooney, G. (1996) 'Funding Aboriginal health care', *Australian and New Zealand Journal of Public Health* 6, 20: 564–65.

Mooney, G. & Jan, S. (1997) 'Vertical equity: weighting outcomes? or establishing procedures?', *Health Policy* 39, 1: 79–88.

Mooney, G., Jan, S. & Wiseman, V. (1995) 'Examining preferences for allocating health gains', *Health Care Analysis* 138: 231–4.

National Aboriginal Health Strategy Evaluation Committee (1994) *The National Aboriginal Health Strategy: An Evaluation*, AGPS, Canberra.

National Aboriginal Health Strategy Working Party (1989) *Report*, AGPS, Canberra.

NSW Health Department (1996) *Implementation of the Economic Statement for Health*, NSW Health Department, Sydney.

Palmer, G. & Short, S. (1994) *Health Care and Public Policy: An Australian Analysis*, Macmillan Education, Melbourne.

Resource Allocation Working Party RAWP (1976) *Report, Sharing Resources for Health*, HMSO, London.

Saggers, S. & Gray, D. (1991) 'Policy and practice in Aboriginal health', J. Reid & P. Trompf (eds), in *The Health of Aboriginal Australia*, Harcourt Brace Jovanovich, Sydney, pp 381–420.

Scrimgeour, D. (1997) *Community Control of Aboriginal Health Services in the Northern Territory*, Menzies Occasional Papers 2/97, Menzies School of Health Research, Darwin and Alice Springs.

Tsey, K. & Scrimgeour, D. (1996) 'The funder-purchaser-provider model and Aboriginal health care provision', *Australian and New Zealand Journal of Public Health* 6, 20: 661–4.

Index

For Product Safety Concerns and Information please contact our EU
representative GPSR@taylorandfrancis.com
Taylor & Francis Verlag GmbH, Kaufingerstraße 24, 80331 München, Germany

www.ingramcontent.com/pod-product-compliance
Lightning Source LLC
Chambersburg PA
CBHW060145280326
41932CB00012B/1640